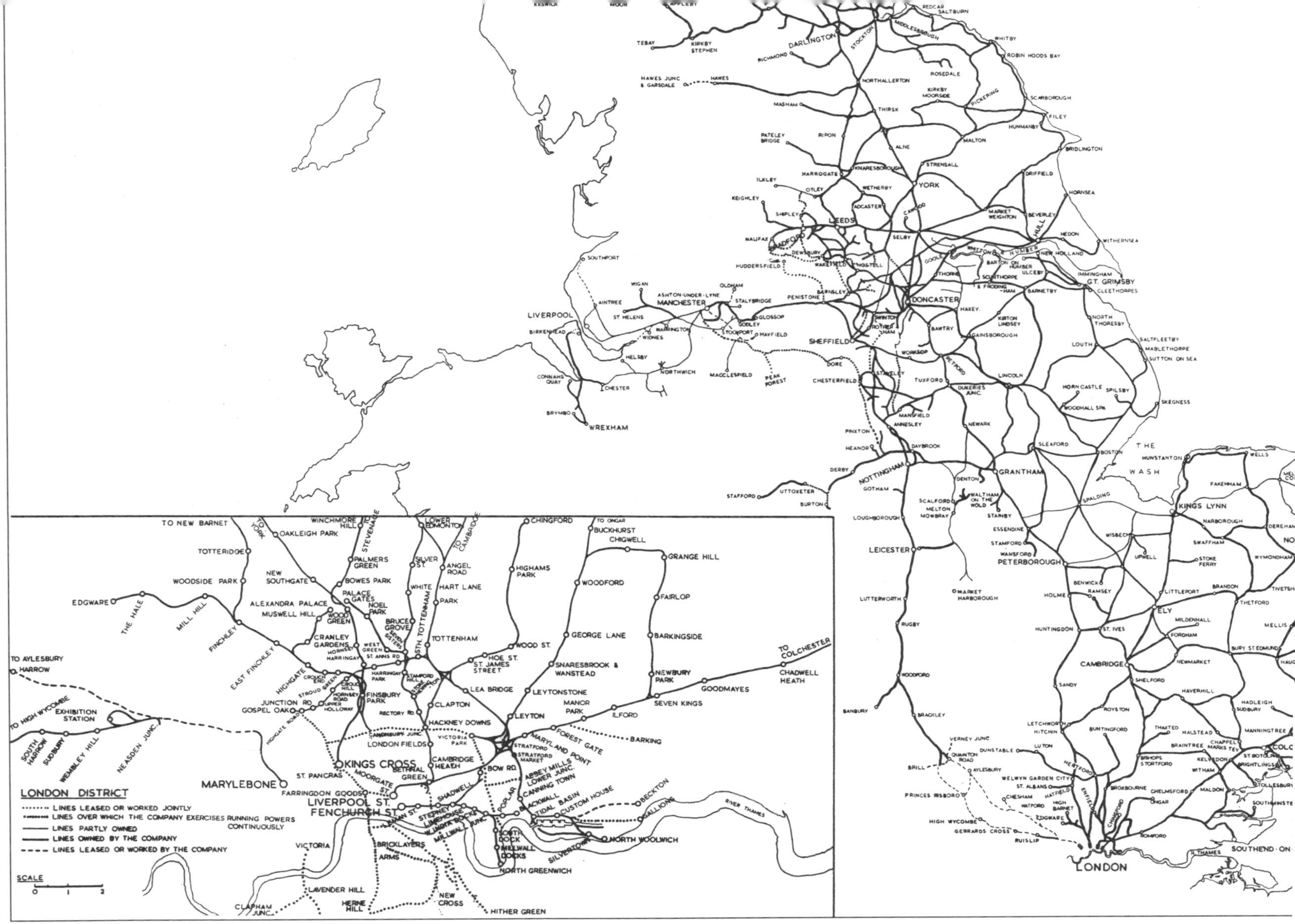

LONDON DISTRICT
LINES LEASED OR WORKED JOINTLY
LINES OVER WHICH THE COMPANY EXERCISES RUNNING POWERS CONTINUOUSLY
LINES PARTLY OWNED
LINES OWNED BY THE COMPANY
LINES LEASED OR WORKED BY THE COMPANY
SCALE
0
1
2
DARLINGTON
YORK
LEEDS
HULL
DONCASTER
GT. GRIMSBY
MANCHESTER
LIVERPOOL
SHEFFIELD
WREXHAM
NOTTINGHAM
GRANTHAM
LINCOLN
LEICESTER
PETERBOROUGH
KINGS LYNN
NORWICH
GREAT YARMOUTH
ELY
CAMBRIDGE
IPSWICH
LONDON
THE WASH
SOUTHEND-ON-
MARYLEBONE
KINGS CROSS
LIVERPOOL ST.
FENCHURCH ST.
ST. PANCRAS
FARRINGDON GOODS
CHINGFORD
TO COLCHESTER
RIVER THAMES
NORTH WOOLWICH

LNER

HANDBOOK

1923–1947

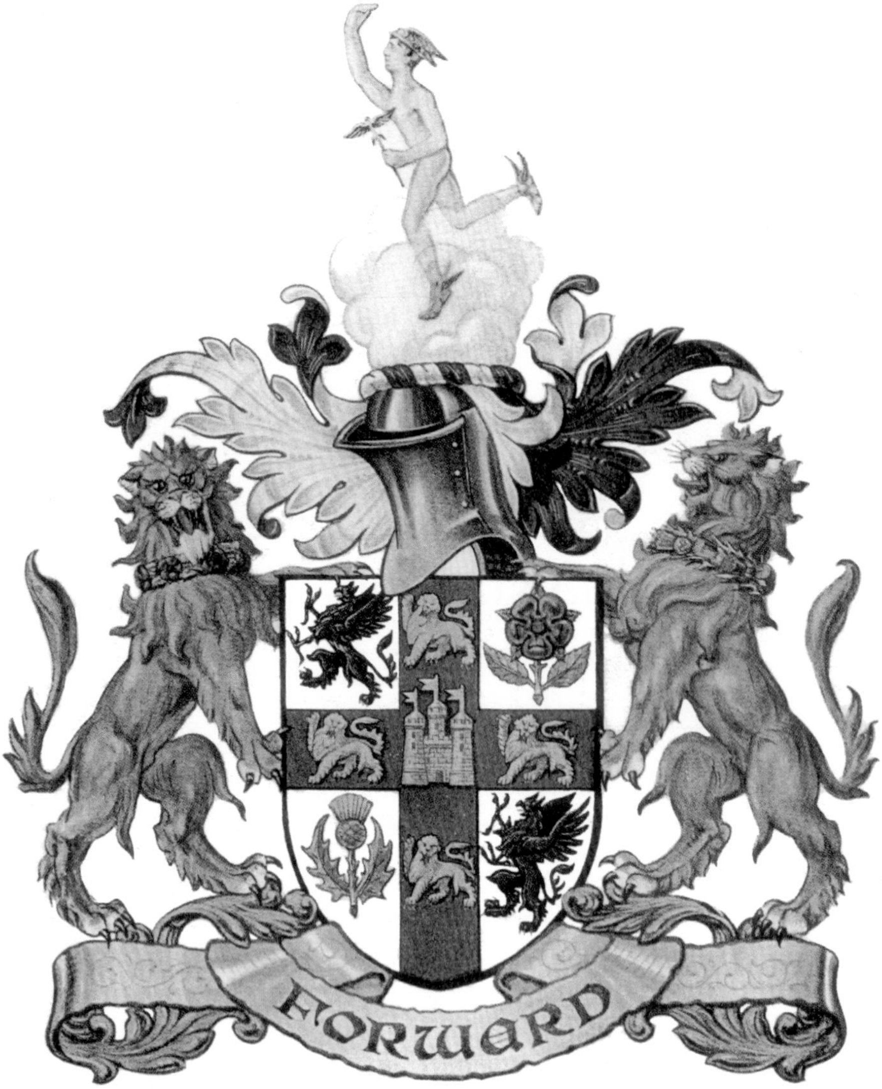
FORWARD

LNER HANDBOOK

THE LONDON & NORTH EASTERN RAILWAY 1923–1947

DAVID WRAGG

Haynes

First published in April 2011

A catalogue record for this book is available from the British Library

ISBN 978 1 84425 827 7

Published by Haynes Publishing,
Sparkford, Yeovil, Somerset BA22 7JJ, UK
Tel: 01963 442030 Fax: 01963 440001
Int. tel: +44 1963 442030 Int. fax: +44 1963 440001
E-mail: sales@haynes.co.uk
Website: www.haynes.co.uk

Haynes North America Inc.,
861 Lawrence Drive, Newbury Park, California 91320, USA

Designed and typeset by Donald Sommerville, Montacute, Somerset

Printed in the USA by Odcombe Press LP, 1299 Bridgestone Parkway, LaVergne, TN 37086

Endpapers: The LNER in 1930, showing the long line from London to Aberdeen and beyond, with a dense network running into East Anglia. *(Map by courtesy of the Railway Correspondence & Travel Society)*

Page 2: The Coat of Arms of the London & North Eastern Railway, with the former Great Central Railway motto, 'Forward'.

Contents

Acknowledgements 6
Preface 7
Introduction 9

Chapter 1 The Ancestors and the Neighbours 11
Chapter 2 The London Termini 33
Chapter 3 LNER Destinations 45
Chapter 4 Building a New Railway Company 60
Chapter 5 The Managers 65
Chapter 6 Steam Locomotives at the Grouping 69
Chapter 7 Atlantic to Pacific 74
Chapter 8 The Streamliners 82
Chapter 9 Electrics and Diesels 90
Chapter 10 The Named Expresses 99
Chapter 11 Carrying the Goods 123
Chapter 12 The Passenger Business 132
Chapter 13 Publicity 145
Chapter 14 The Record Setters 153
Chapter 15 Shipping 156
Chapter 16 Road Transport 162
Chapter 17 Accidents 164
Chapter 18 The Infrastructure 168
Chapter 19 Railways at War 177
Chapter 20 Under Attack 195
Chapter 21 Peace and Nationalisation 201
Chapter 22 What Might Have Been 206

Appendices
1 LNER Locomotive Numbering 209
2 LNER Locomotives as at 31 December 1947 211
3 Named LNER Locomotives 219
4 Named Locomotives Inherited by the LNER 227
5 Locomotives Absorbed at Grouping and Later Acquisitions 232

Bibliography 250
Index 252

Acknowledgements

I should like to thank both John Hancock of the Historical Model Railway Society (HMRS) and Paul Chancellor of Colour-Rail for their help in providing copies from their vast stock of excellent images, and the staff of the Search Engine at the National Railway Museum in York for their help, and in particular, making available so many LNER publications. Thanks are also due to The Railway Correspondence & Travel Society for the provision of the LNER system map.

David Wragg
Edinburgh

Preface

Of all the great railway companies, the London & North Eastern Railway was that the one evaded me in my youth. I was in any case born too late to have known the actual company, but my experiences of the Eastern, North Eastern and Scottish Regions of what had become British Railways, were held back until I was a young adult. Strange to think that today, I am more likely to be travelling on the East Coast Main Line than any other. As it was, my experiences were at first limited to joining the family on holiday in Norfolk, travelling from Liverpool Street, and later visiting Edinburgh and Aberdeen, initially, while writing for *The Scotsman* and later, while working for P&O, although my Aberdeen trips were mainly by air except when a strike at British Airways forced me to use the overnight sleeper. I enjoy travelling by train, but to this day I hate sleepers, even first class.

Nevertheless, every young boy of my generation 'knew of the LNER', the company that owned *Mallard*, the steam locomotive that remains today unchallenged as holding the world speed record for steam.

Then, for those of us who remained interested in railways, there was Gerald Fiennes excellent book, *I Tried to Run a Railway*, in which he aptly described the LNER as 'poor, but honest'. This was a memorable comment, and one cannot challenge the reflection of a man who knew the company so well. Others, outside the company, strongly supported young men embarking on a career with the LNER recommending it as a 'company run by gentlemen'.

Many of the LNER's predecessor companies were anything but poor, although ambition and especially the ambition to reach London, brought poverty on the Great Central. Ruin came with the way in which the state ran the railways during the Great War, with costs spiralling out of control so that once peacetime normality returned the managements of the various companies found themselves in an impossible situation. If this was not bad enough, the succession of strikes by miners, culminating in the Miners' Strike and General Strike of 1926 brought misery and poverty on the country, with many markets for British coal lost for good, and then came the Great Depression, so much the worse for the industrial trauma that had gone before.

There is no doubt that the LNER missed the potential that electrification of the London suburban lines would have brought, but with a large and straggling railway, although not quite as large or as straggling as the LMS on the other side of the Pennines, choosing such a way forward was more difficult than we might think today. Of all the 'Big Four' grouped railway companies, the LNER was the most dependent upon freight traffic, and this could not be ignored. Perhaps the preoccupation with freight meant that the chance of realising the full potential of the suburban and outer suburban passenger business was overlooked. Certainly, the LNER had the least comfortable and most cramped suburban rolling stock, although Gresley tried to improve the ride of the inherited six-wheel carriages by forming them into four-carriage articulated units, the famous, or infamous, quad-arts.

The company was also slow to realise the potential of the diesel, although there were experiments with diesel shunters and railcars or rail-buses, but the LNER seems to have put more effort into Sentinel steam railmotors, which did not seem to be very reliable or durable.

Nevertheless, this was the first British railway to really believe in high speed railway travel and to find that the travelling public appreciated speed. Its six-hour schedule between Edinburgh and London was Britain's best, and passenger comfort was not neglected, at least in first class. The LNER did much to make long-distance railway travel fashionable, and it was to take the advent of the High Speed Train in the 1970s to repeat the process. In retrospect it seems a shame that the company did not emulate the Southern in running through sleeper trains into Europe. The Southern only linked London and Paris with its 'Night Ferry', but while the LNER could have linked London and Amsterdam, it could also have gone further, although the long run from Amsterdam to Berlin would probably have still required a change of train.

Note: 'Up' and 'Down'

Anyone with an interest in Britain's railways will know that 'up' has traditionally meant the line leading to London or the train heading for the Capital, while 'down' means exactly the opposite. In considering the railways that cross the border into Scotland, however, the situation is more complicated. North of the border, 'up' means Edinburgh-bound and 'down' means the train heading from Edinburgh or the line leading away from the Capital.

In short, a train from London to Aberdeen via Edinburgh heads down to the Scottish border, then up to Edinburgh and then down to Aberdeen. There were one or two exceptions to these rules. The Midland Railway, as the only company not to abandon its provincial roots when it finally reached London, always had trains running 'up' to Derby and 'down' from the Capital, while the Taff Vale Railway ran 'down' to the coast.

Introduction

Renowned for its crack express locomotive *Mallard*, which set a world speed record that endures to this day of 126mph for steam locomotives, the London & North Eastern Railway was the second largest of the 'Big Four' railway companies created during the Grouping of more than a hundred smaller companies. The LNER was a mixture, with the crack expresses from King's Cross, balanced by an intensive suburban and commuter service from Liverpool Street. Its passenger operations were in effect much less significant than its goods.

The London & North Eastern Railway's constituent and subsidiary companies are listed early in Chapter One. The difference between a constituent and a subsidiary was that the former appointed at least one director to the board of the LNER and were closely involved in the frantic year of preparation for the merger, 1922. Many of the smaller companies survived as separate entities almost by accident as they were often leased and operated by the larger companies.

Roughly two-thirds of the LNER's revenues came from goods traffic and a third from passenger traffic, making it the most heavily dependent on freight traffic of any of the railway companies. From the outset, the LNER's markets in the industrial areas of the North and Scotland were in decline. Much has been written about the Miners' Strike of 1926 and the accompanying General Strike, and indeed, this had a massive impact on coal traffic as export markets for British coal were lost for good, but from shortly after the end of the First World War, industrial unrest was a recurring feature of the British economy. Added to this, the chairman, William Whitelaw, was from the North British Railway (NBR), a railway that was notorious for its economy. The net result was that the LNER board and management were cautious, and the company gained a reputation for being 'poor but honest'. Many non-preference shareholders saw little for their investment in the company, and it paid its management less than did the other companies, even though productivity did improve with employee numbers falling from 207,500 in 1924 to 175,800 in 1937.

The LNER board overruled Wedgwood's proposed departmental organisation in favour of strong decentralisation with three areas, London, York and Edinburgh, each of which had its own divisional general manager and area board. There remained a small cadre of 'all-line' officers, including the chief mechanical engineer, Nigel Gresley, formerly of the Great Northern Railway (GNR).

Despite some electrification in the north of England, the LNER was primarily a steam railway. A series of attractive high-speed locomotives were built for the main services, including the non-stop London–Edinburgh 'Flying Scotsman' as well as others such as the 'Silver Jubilee', 'Coronation' and 'West Riding Limited'. The LNER was famous for the use of articulation, with adjoining carriages sharing a bogie, on both its expresses and on the suburban services, cutting weight and improving the ride. The company served the suburbs of north and east London, which became renowned for trains that were overcrowded and slow, as well as dirty, but nevertheless, the LNER achieved much in operating such a high-intensity service worked entirely by steam, especially with the congested approaches to Liverpool Street.

The Arms of the constituent companies, with the Great Northern at the bottom centre and the Great Central at top centre.

Chapter 1

The Ancestors and the Neighbours

The London & North Eastern Railway was the second largest of the 'Big Four' (after the LMS), these being the railway companies that emerged as a result of the Railways Act 1921. This combined more than a hundred railway companies into just four companies, the LNER, LMS, GWR and Southern Railway. This was no foregone conclusion, however, as the original proposals for Grouping the railways envisaged seven companies rather than four, and a clue that the LNER might not have been a single railway lies in the fact that after Nationalisation it was split into three regions of the new British Railways (Eastern, North Eastern and Scottish). The original Railways Bill envisaged Scotland having a separate railway company while the other six companies would cover England and Wales. It was only after strong objections from Scotland that a Scottish railway company would have to raise fares and goods charges more than Anglo-Scottish companies, that the decision was taken to form what would eventually be the LNER and its West Coast counterpart, the London Midland & Scottish Railway (LMS). The government's original plans would have seen a 'North-Eastern' company rather than a London & North Eastern and Scottish business. In many ways, the original plan for the railways was what was foisted on them on Nationalisation when once again, a separate Scottish Region was introduced.

The story becomes even more complicated when one takes into account that at one time, a merger between the Great Northern and Great Central was mooted, but did not go ahead leaving the latter company to overstretch its resources building its own route to London, and also creating Marylebone, the last of the London termini to be built. Early in the 20th century, in 1909, Parliament refused to approve a merger in the east of England, involving the Great Northern, Great Eastern and Great Central companies, but after the First World War, it pressed ahead and insisted on an even more extensive merger to create what became the LNER. The 1909 merger of the three companies was actually intended to be a measure to eliminate wasteful competition and amalgamate receipts, leaving the individual companies to manage their own railways. This is perhaps why Parliament rejected the idea, as the railway companies were seen as strong regional monopolies with competition only at the fringes.

It is also worth speculating on whether the first stage would have led to a merged management of the three companies along the lines of the South Eastern & Chatham Management Committee. The point is, of course, that Parliament rejected a limited step towards a merger in 1909, but in 1921 forced through an even bigger merger of the railway companies.

To some extent, Grouping was a policy adopted in lieu of nationalisation, which had become a matter of debate before the First World War. It was also meant to rationalise the railways and curb competition while also exerting greater control over them, but it allowed the London Tilbury & Southend Railway to pass to the LMS, perpetuating competition on the busy lines between London and Southend. This was one of the drawbacks of the Railways Act 1921: it did not allow for reallocation of routes or territory, and in failing to do so, made the job of efficient management more difficult. There were former North British lines in the Western Highlands of

Scotland that could have been better as LMS territory, or Great Central lines around Wrexham that could have gone to the Great Western or, if as some believe, the former Cambrian Railway should have been passed to the LMS, then so too should these routes, even though it would have made an overlarge and unwieldy railway even more so.

The London & North Eastern Railway's constituent companies were:

Great Central Railway
Great Eastern Railway
Great North of Scotland Railway
Great Northern Railway
Hull & Barnsley Railway
North British Railway
North Eastern Railway

The subsidiaries included:

Brackenhill Light Railway
Colne Valley & Halstead Railway
(not taken over until 1 July 1923)
East & West Yorkshire Union Railway
(not taken over until 1 July 1923)
East Lincolnshire Railway
Edinburgh & Bathgate Railway
Forcett Railway
Forth & Clyde Junction Railway
Gifford & Garvald Railway
Great North of England Railway
Clarence & Hartlepool Junction Railway
Horncastle Railway
Humber Commercial Railway & Dock
Kilsyth & Bonnybridge Railway
Lauder Light Railway
London & Blackwall Railway
Mansfield Railway
Mid-Suffolk Light Railway
Newburgh & North Fife Railway
North Lindsey Light Railway
Nottingham & Grantham Railway
Nottingham Joint Station Committee
Nottingham Suburban Railway
Seaforth & Sefton Junction Railway
Stamford & Essendine Railway
West Riding Railway Committee

Under Grouping, the plan was simply to create a 'North Eastern, Eastern and East Scotland' railway company and it took all of 1922 for appointments and structures to be agreed. As with the other grouped companies, the companies absorbed were defined either as constituent companies, which meant that they had a director on the board of the new company, or as subsidiary companies.

The Constituent Companies

Great Central Railway

The last mainline railway to reach London, the Great Central Railway, was the new name coined for the Manchester Sheffield & Lincolnshire Railway to celebrate its transition from a trans-Pennine railway, when it opened its new line to London in 1899 with a new terminus at Marylebone. The company had its origins in the Sheffield Ashton-under-Lyne & Manchester Railway, opened in 1845, and which had required construction of the Woodhead Tunnel, three miles long through the Pennines and at the time, the longest in the UK. The SAMR acquired three railway companies and the Grimsby Docks Company in 1847, to form the Manchester Sheffield & Lincolnshire Railway. The company continued to prosper, and in 1863 it entered the South Yorkshire coalfield through the acquisition of the South Yorkshire Railway. Expansion westward lay in the creation of the Cheshire Lines Committee with the Great Northern Railway and the Midland Railway. This gave the MSLR access to North Wales and to the port of Liverpool. Earlier alliances involved the London & North Western, Lancashire & Yorkshire and East Lancashire, as well as the Midland, in what was known as the Euston Square Confederacy, but this was

Former Great Central inspection saloon No. 1234 at Dukinfield yard in 1924, before it was painted in LNER livery. (*HMRS ABZ 112*)

dissolved in 1857 and replaced with a 50-year agreement with the Great Northern Railway, hitherto viewed as a rival.

In 1864, a new chairman, Sir Edward Watkin, was appointed. This was just one of his railway chairmanships and he was an early advocate of a Channel Tunnel. His other ambitions included taking the MSLR to London, and the company embarked on a period of expansion at the cost of its profitability, with no ordinary dividends paid after 1889. The London Extension was widely regarded as wasteful, with centres such as Nottingham, Leicester and Rugby already having good links to London, and was achieved by building a new line from Annesley in Nottinghamshire to Quainton in Buckinghamshire, and then running over a joint line with another Watkin company, the Metropolitan Railway, and from that a short line to the new terminus at Marylebone, to which the headquarters was moved from Manchester in 1905. Perhaps not surprisingly, the nickname for the MSL became 'Money Sunk and Lost', but the Great Central was little better, for all of its ambitions, as it was known as 'Gone Completely'.

During this period, expansion was also helped by the acquisition of the Lancashire Derbyshire & East Coast Railway in 1907.

A new chairman in 1899, Alexander Henderson (later Lord Faringdon), appointed Sir Sam Fay as general manager in 1902, and he was joined that year by John G. Robinson, who had trained at Swindon. Robinson started to equip the GCR with powerful new locomotives, built at the company's Gorton Works, Manchester, as well as comfortable new carriages. It was amongst the first railways to use bogie goods vehicles, and in 1907, one of the first hump marshalling yards at Wath in the South Yorkshire coalfield proved capable of sorting 5,000 goods wagons in 24 hours. A new port was built at Immingham, which allowed expansion of the company's Humber shipping services, and when opened by King George V in 1912, Fay was publicly knighted. The port included an innovation when the Grimsby District Light Railway, which was opened in 1912 by the GCR to serve the new port, was electrified, but this was effectively a 4½-mile tramway with 16 single-deck tramcars drawing 500V dc power from overhead wires, and not connected to the rest of the GCR.

Elsewhere, power signalling was also introduced. Under Fay, the company expanded its through passenger services. There were also trials of steam and petrol-electric railcars, while a second route to London via High Wycombe was built jointly with the GWR. Nevertheless, despite the work on passenger services, 67 per cent of its turnover came from goods traffic and just 22 per cent from passengers.

The First World War ended expansion, and while three ships were seized in Continental ports by the Germans, the rest were requisitioned for the Royal Navy. Robinson saw his 2-8-0 heavy goods locomotive adopted as the standard for War Office use overseas, while Fay became director of movements at the War Office from 1916 until the end of the war.

Great Eastern Railway

The Great Eastern Railway was formed in 1862 on the long overdue amalgamation with three railways which were being worked by the Eastern Counties Railway, the East Anglian, Eastern Union; East Suffolk & Norfolk railways. The new GER gave East Anglia a single unified railway network east of Cambridge, but even so, relations between the companies were such that it took four years before the finances could be rationalised, and by that time, 1866, during the banking and railway finance crisis, the new company was forced briefly into liquidation. Nevertheless, the company had already purchased land in the City of London for a new terminus to replace the inconveniently sited Bishopsgate.

An unusual feature of the ex-GER Y5 class 0-4-0ST was that the coal was carried on top of the saddle tank. This view at Stratford carriage works in 1947 shows No. 8081. (*HMRS ABT 114*)

Lord Cranbourne, who later became Marquess of Salisbury, became chairman in 1868, and the GER began to move forward. The new Liverpool Street station opened during 1874–75, the last terminus to open in the City, and only permitted because it was approached in tunnel. By this time the GER also had a dense network of suburban lines in north-eastern London.

The GER inherited a broad spread of business, with extensive commuter traffic, albeit working class and less prosperous than that of the lines to the south; goods and passenger traffic to five ports (Felixstowe, Harwich, King's Lynn, Lowestoft and Yarmouth), with the last two providing heavy fish traffic for London and the Midlands; holiday traffic, especially to Clacton, Lowestoft, Southend and Yarmouth; race traffic to and from Newmarket, and agricultural traffic, although this declined during the 1870s and 1880s with a crisis in Britain's arable farming. Later, it developed coal traffic from Yorkshire to East Anglia when a line was opened in 1882 jointly with the Great Northern from south of Doncaster through Lincoln and Spalding to March. Although mishandled at first, from 1883 onwards, the GER also operated steam packet services, mainly to the Netherlands.

Despite the race and Continental traffic, the company suffered from a mass of low-fare business, and because of this, in 1872 it followed the Midland Railway by providing third-class accommodation on all passenger trains. In 1891, it was the first to provide restaurant car accommodation for third-class passengers. The company gained a reputation for punctuality and efficiency, although it struggled to cope with its peak period commuter traffic. The pressure on peak traffic declined sharply from 1901 after electric trams appeared in the East End of London, and the cost of electrification meant that it was rejected, even though the GER obtained Parliamentary powers as early as 1903.

For goods traffic, in 1899, its goods yard at Spitalfields, London, was the first in the UK to have electro-pneumatic power operation. Main line services were recast in 1914 by a new general manager, the American Henry Thornton, and after the First World War he did the same for the suburban services. The company was amongst the first to use distinctive stripes on its carriages to identify classes, with first having yellow lines and second blue, which earned them the title of the 'Jazz Trains'.

In the meantime, a number of independent branch lines had been built in GER territory, while west of King's Lynn several lines had been built with the support of the Great Northern and the Midland, which then continued across Norfolk to Cromer, Norwich and Yarmouth before being merged to form the Midland & Great Northern Joint Railway in 1893. Competition ensued for the goods traffic, especially fish, from the Norfolk ports to the Midlands, and for holiday traffic from the Midlands. Nevertheless, the Continental traffic grew unabated and in 1883 a massive extension to Harwich was opened at Parkeston Quay, named after the then chairman. A complementary development at the Hook of Holland that opened in 1903 encouraged further growth in traffic across the North Sea. During the First World War, Harwich became an important naval base.

The GER's locomotives from 1878 onwards were mainly built at its works in Stratford, East London. While a number of its locomotive engineers were with the company for a short time, others lasted far longer, notably James Holden, who was amongst the first to experiment with oil-fired steam locomotives, which the GER introduced in 1897 with considerable success. The 'oil' was tar that was a by-product of gas oil production and which was largely regarded as waste, so it was very cheap initially, but became very expensive once its value for industrial use began to be appreciated and so the GER reverted to coal.

The company's early problems meant that the dividend was low before 1882, but by the turn of the century, it was an attractive 6 per cent, before the marked decline in its London suburban traffic depressed revenue so that by 1913, an otherwise good year for many of Britain's railways, it was just 2 per cent.

Great North of Scotland Railway

Sometimes described as 'neither Great nor North of Scotland', this opened in stages between Aberdeen and Keith between 1853 and 1856, along the alignment of the Aberdeenshire Canal as far as Inverurie. The GNSR was built to link with the Inverness & Aberdeen Junction Railway, completed two years later, as well as extend services that reached Aberdeen over the Aberdeen Railway, forerunner of the Caledonian Railway. There were disagreements with the IAJR, including payment for a bridge over the River Spey, and these continued even after the IAJR changed its name to the Highland Railway in 1865, when it tried to block running powers to Inverness, while the GNSR was refused approval for a rival line to Inverness. Relationships between the two companies improved considerably during the last two decades of the 19th century, with the pooling of receipts and through running, while in 1905, an amalgamation was proposed. An alternative, amalgamation with the Caledonian was rejected.

Despite the logic of through connections with the Caledonian at Aberdeen, the GNSR maintained its own station and did little to ensure connections for passengers arriving from the south. It even delayed becoming a member of the Railway Clearing House. Nevertheless, a new joint station opened in Aberdeen in 1867, considerably easing connections, notably for those on lengthy journeys. The main line was doubled between 1861 and 1900 and lines to Elgin via Dufftown and a new coast route opened, all incorporating lines started as local projects. Significant branches were opened to Peterhead in 1862, Fraserburgh in 1865, Ballater, for Balmoral in 1866, Macduff in 1872, Boddam in 1897, and St Combs in 1903, as well as a number of minor branches.

A suburban line was developed between Aberdeen and Dyce in 1887, and extended to Culter in 1894. Much of the goods traffic was provided by the fishing ports which thrived following the arrival of the railway, as did the distilleries on Speyside, while another major traffic was cattle. Resorts on the Moray Firth were promoted as the Scottish Riviera. A hotel was built at Cruden Bay, with an electric tramway to the local railway station.

Most of the company's locomotives were built by independent builders and only two were built at the main locomotive depot at Kittybrewster, Aberdeen, but there was some further locomotive building after the works moved to Inverurie in 1903. Despite its small size, the

EASTERN GROUP OF RAILWAYS.
EAST COAST ROUTE.
ENGLAND & SCOTLAND
Via Forth and Tay Bridges.
FOR TRAIN SERVICE, SEE PAGES 332, 728, 734, 776, and 782:
THE ONLY ACTUAL "COAST" ROUTE.
Quickest Route
LONDON & EDINBURGH
(KING'S CROSS)
(WAVERLEY)
IN 8½ HOURS.
RESTAURANT CARS attached to Day Trains,
SLEEPING CARS attached to Night Trains
between
LONDON (King's Cross) and...
EDINBURGH,
GLASGOW,
FORT WILLIAM,
DUNDEE,
ABERDEEN,
PERTH,
INVERNESS.

With Britain's railways comprising more than a hundred companies prior to 1923, this did not prevent long-distance through services from operating. Three of the LNER's constituent companies, the Great Northern, North Eastern and North British, collaborated as the Eastern Group of Railways. (*Bradshaw*)

GNSR experimented with single-line tablet exchange, equipment for dropping and collecting mail bags while the train was moving, and also was amongst the first to provide electric lighting at its stations.

Great Northern Railway

Originating as the London & York Railway, authorised in 1846 in the face of heavy opposition, the GNR title was adopted by the following year. The first services used a leased section of line between Louth and Grimsby from 1848, but the main line opened between a temporary station at Maiden Lane, London, and Peterborough, and between Doncaster and York, in 1850, by which time it was also able to serve all the important centres in the West Riding. It was in 1852 that the through line between London and Doncaster was completed along with King's Cross station, along with the main works at Doncaster in 1853. Other smaller companies were acquired or running powers obtained so that the GNR served Bradford, Cambridge, Halifax, Leeds and Nottingham, and with an agreement with the Manchester Sheffield & Lincolnshire Railway (see Great Central), express services from London to Manchester started in 1857. The following year, the Midland Railway ran over the GNR line south of Hitchin to London, helping to undermine the 'Euston Square Confederacy' sponsored by the London & North Western Railway.

The revenue from the Yorkshire coal traffic attracted the jealous attention of the Great Eastern and the Lancashire & Yorkshire, who twice attempted unsuccessfully to promote a bill through Parliament for a trunk line from Doncaster through Lincolnshire. In the meantime, the GNR improved its position by joining the MSLR in buying the West Riding & Grimsby Railway, linking Doncaster with Wakefield. In 1865, with the MSLR, both companies promoted a Manchester–Liverpool line, and expanded into Lancashire and Cheshire with the Midland through the Cheshire Lines Committee. In 1879, it joined the GER in the Great Northern & Great Eastern Joint lines between Huntingdon and Doncaster, a route that required some new construction.

GNR main line services were reliable and punctual, especially after Henry Oakley became general manager in 1870. It was soon running more expresses than either the LNWR or MR, including some of the world's fastest, hauled by Patrick Stirling's famous single driving-wheel locomotives. The intensity of service required block signalling and interlocking, while stations and goods sidings had to be enlarged and working improved. By 1873, it had reached a peak of profitability, but for the rest of the decade, investment grew more quickly than revenue and especially in the extension of the Cheshire Lines network, the company risked over-extending itself. In the East Midlands, it constructed new lines jointly with the LNWR, to some extent spurred by an earlier rates war with the Midland, but, in 1889, with the MR, it acquired the Eastern & Midlands Railway, creating the Midland & Great Northern Joint Railway.

Earlier, the creation of through services on the East Coast Main Line was helped in 1860 when the East Coast Joint Stock, a common pool of passenger vehicles, was created by the GNR, North Eastern and North British. In 1862, the first through services from King's Cross to Edinburgh Waverley started, with the 10 am departure in each direction being named the 'Flying Scotsman' from the 1870s, by which time the company was also able to reach Glasgow over the North British Railway. The first regular restaurant cars appeared in 1879 and continuous vacuum braking was introduced from 1881. The company later introduced the first fully-fitted goods trains. As traffic and the weight of trains increased, the entire route had to be relaid with heavier rails from the mid-1890s, with widening at the southern end of the route, while heavier trains were worked by H.A. Ivatt's new locomotives, and from 1905, Nigel Gresley designed new carriages, including some using articulation to improve the ride and reduce weight.

The company also expanded its London suburban traffic, not just from King's Cross but also using Broad Street as a convenient City terminus in conjunction with the North London Railway.

Hull & Barnsley Railway

The smallest of the constituent companies, with just 106½ route miles, the full title of this railway was the Hull Barnsley & West Riding Junction Railway & Dock Company. It was authorised in 1880 as a deliberate attempt to break the monopoly held by the North Eastern Railway and the Hull Dock Company, and enjoyed the backing of Hull Corporation. The 53-mile long line opened in 1885 at the same time as the associated Alexandra Dock, having overcome both engineering and financial difficulties, running from Hull's Cannon Street station to join the Midland Railway at Cudworth, two miles from Barnsley. In an attempt to avoid level crossings, it ran on embankment near Hull and used 34 bridges, while further west, there were severe gradients as it crossed the Yorkshire Wold, with 1 in 100 westbound and 1 in 150 eastbound, compared with the easier gradients of the NER along the Humber.

The excellent facilities of the Alexandra Dock enabled the line to make a significant impact, and after initial competition on freight rates, the situation eased so that during the 1890s, the relationship with the NER became close and the two companies jointly built the King George V Dock, which opened in 1914. The two companies merged in 1922, and the NER then passed into the London & North Eastern Railway the following year.

North British Railway

The North British Railway was authorised in 1844 after the York & North Midland Railway was persuaded by George Hudson to provide £50,000 to complete an East Coast line between Edinburgh and London. Hudson's intervention was necessary after Scottish investors had failed to provide sufficient capital. The line opened over the 57 miles to Berwick-on-Tweed in 1846, but had been poorly constructed and within three months, floods swept away many weak bridges and undermined embankments. Despite this, the NBR built branches to Duns, North Berwick and Hawick, with the last providing a link via Carlisle, the 'Waverley' route, with the West Coast line when it opened in 1862. In return for allowing the North Eastern Railway to run over its line between Berwick and Edinburgh, the NBR was allowed running powers between Newcastle and Hexham.

After an extremely shaky start, with poor punctuality and scant dividends, Richard Hodgson became chairman in 1855 and began to rebuild the company's operations. It acquired the Edinburgh Perth & Dundee Railway in 1862, and in 1864, the Edinburgh & Glasgow Railway in the face of fierce competition from its stronger rival, the Caledonian. Hodgson's reign ended in 1866 when it was discovered that he was falsifying the accounts in order to pay an improved dividend, and his departure nearly led to a merger with the Caledonian, but for a shareholders' revolt. It was not until the completion of the Settle & Carlisle line by the Midland Railway in 1876, allowing through trains from St Pancras to reach Edinburgh over the Waverley route, that the company's circumstances improved. Dugald Drummond, the NBR's locomotive superintendent, designed a new 4-4-0 express locomotive to handle the Anglo-Scottish expresses, before being poached by the Caledonian in 1882.

Competition with the Caledonian continued and proved ruinous. Both companies wanted the lucrative Fife coal market and both wanted to be the best route to Aberdeen, while the NBR wanted its share of the growing Glasgow commuter traffic. The two companies built large and prestigious hotels, with the NBR's flagship being that at Waverley station, now known as the New Balmoral. Still more ambitious was the effort made to create a port and a resort at Silloth in Cumberland, which also included building much of the town, as well as a hotel and golf course. The port attracted ferry services to Ireland and the Isle of Man, but the resort failed. Rather more success was enjoyed in developing the resort of North Berwick. The company later bought the port of Methil in Fife to handle shipments of coal from the local coalfields. The NBR even attempted to compete with the CR on the Clyde, initially putting two ferries into service

Grouping meant that many locomotives strayed far from their home territory, including this ex-North British Railway D32 class 4-4-0 No. 9887, seen at Darlington in 1939. (*HMRS ACW 502*)

in 1866, but soon had to withdraw them, and a second attempt, based on Dunoon, saw heavy losses. A later attempt in conjunction with the Glasgow & South Western saw steamer services from Greenock, while steamers were also operated on Loch Lomond after the NBR purchased a local company.

The heavily indented coastline of Eastern Scotland meant that the North British had substantial ferry operations of its own across both the Forth and the Tay, until bridges could be built across these two wide estuaries. The first attempt at building the Tay Bridge resulted in disaster, with the structure collapsing in a storm while a train was crossing, on 28 December 1879, with the loss of all 72 people aboard. A new bridge was built and this was followed by the imposing Forth Bridge, completed in 1890. These two bridges meant that the NBR was the fastest and most direct route to Dundee and Aberdeen. Nevertheless, the company failed to get the NER to allow it to handle expresses from London on the stretch of line between Berwick-on-Tweed and Edinburgh.

Traffic boomed, however, with heavy congestion at Waverley that required the station to be rebuilt and the tracks to Haymarket, with the intervening tunnels, quadrupled. The result was that when the rebuilt station opened with its suburban platforms in 1898, it was claimed to be second only to Waterloo in London in size. Freight traffic also grew, and shipments of coal through the port of Methil rose from 400,000 tons in 1888 to 2.8 million tons twenty years later.

While most of the railway network had been completed by 1880, the NBR had two of the last major railway projects in the country prior to the Channel Tunnel Rail Link. The first of these was the West Highland Line, which ran from Craigendoran, west of Glasgow, to Fort William, and opened in 1894, and then the extension to Mallaig, completed in 1901. This had taken Robert McAlpine four years for just forty miles and almost uniquely in Great Britain, had needed a subsidy of £260,000 (about £17.5 million today) of taxpayers' money. These were followed by a line from Dunfermline to Kincardine and a small number of light railways, essentially infilling gaps in the system.

With the major naval base of Rosyth, opened in 1916 although its railway station opened the previous year, on the coast of Fife, plus the anchorages in the Cromarty Firth and at Scapa Flow in Orkney, the NBR was heavily involved in the First World War. This included handling the famous 'Jellicoe Specials', of which there were two kinds, one carrying coal from Pontypool Road on the GWR to Grangemouth, and the other carrying naval personnel, which ran from London to Thurso, and put a heavy strain on a largely single-track route north of the Forth. Rosyth alone received 1.25 million tons of coal from Wales in 1918. As with the other railways, the shortage of skilled men and the demands placed on the system combined to ensure that there were serious arrears of maintenance as the war ended. Nevertheless, the NBR was one of the more successful in obtaining compensation from the government, receiving just under £10 million.

The NBR was the largest Scottish railway company, contributing 1,300 track miles, 1,100 locomotives, 3,500 carriages and 57,000 wagons to the new London & North Eastern Railway on 1 January 1923.

This powerful A8 class 4-6-2T, No. 2153, was rebuilt from a Raven H1 class 4-4-4T during the early 1930s. It is seen at Darlington in 1936. *(HMRS AAB 112)*

North Eastern Railway

The North Eastern Railway was the largest and most profitable of the companies brought together to form the LNER, with 1,757 route miles. The NER was formed in 1854 when four railway companies merged their operations, the York Newcastle & Berwick, the York & North Midland, the Leeds Northern, and the tiny Malton & Driffield Junction, although the three larger companies did not amalgamate their shareholdings until 1870. The NER came into being with 700 route miles, but was not a complete rationalisation of railway operations in the North East as four other companies in the area remained independent for the best part of ten years.

One of the independent companies, the Stockton & Darlington, which had supported the construction of the South Durham & Lancashire Union line, allied with the London & North Western Railway, but after the SDR and SDLUR merged, they were taken over by the NER in 1863. Similar action was taken by the West Hartlepool Railway, which served a port that was a strong competitor to Hull and Middlesbrough, and sought an alliance with the LNWR, planning to compete with the NER, and it was not until 1865 that it agreed to be taken over, and that year the Newcastle & Carlisle was also absorbed. This left just the Blyth & Tyne as an independent company within the NER area, and this was not absorbed until 1874. The acquisition of these companies was often difficult, and once in NER ownership, integration proved to be slow and problematic.

The NER was a vital link in the line from London to Edinburgh, linking the Great Northern in the south with the North British Railway at Berwick-on-Tweed, which formed what is now the East Coast Main Line. Between 1868 and 1871, it built cut-offs amounting to 26 miles, with the two main ones being between Durham and Gateshead, and between Doncaster and York. Nevertheless, the NER was slow to introduce the block system of signalling and interlocking of points and signals, and these as well as management failings contributed to the four accidents suffered in late 1870.

William O'Brien, the general manager was sacked and Henry Tennant succeeded him, making the necessary reforms both to the structure of the company and to its operating practices, despite which the newly integrated company managed to pay a dividend of more than 8 per cent during the 1870s. It also mounted the 'Jubilee of the Railway System' at Darlington on the SDR's 50th anniversary in 1875. The stubborn and independent streak shown by the railway meant that it was the last of the trunk railways to abandon iron rails in favour of steel, although it could be argued that this was possibly to appease the powerful iron masters. Nevertheless, it also refused to send a delegate to the Railway Clearing House to discuss standardising railway telegraph codes as it would not consider any revision of its own codes!

The NER's monopoly in the North East soon came under threat. Hull Corporation was angered by the NER entering into a traffic-pooling agreement for freight receipts for all of the ports between the Tyne and the Humber. The Corporation backed plans for a new dock to ease congestion on the Humber, and a new independent railway to bring coal from South and West Yorkshire. Originating as the Hull Barnsley & West Riding Junction Railway & Dock Company, but later becoming the Hull & Barnsley Railway, the new 66-mile line was authorised in 1880. The railway and the new docks were both completed in 1885. A rate war ensued, which forced

Only a small number of Q7 class 0-8-0 three-cylinder locomotives were built by the NER as limitations on the length of goods trains meant that they could rarely be used to their full advantage. This is No. 628 in LNER black livery. (*HMRS AAB118*)

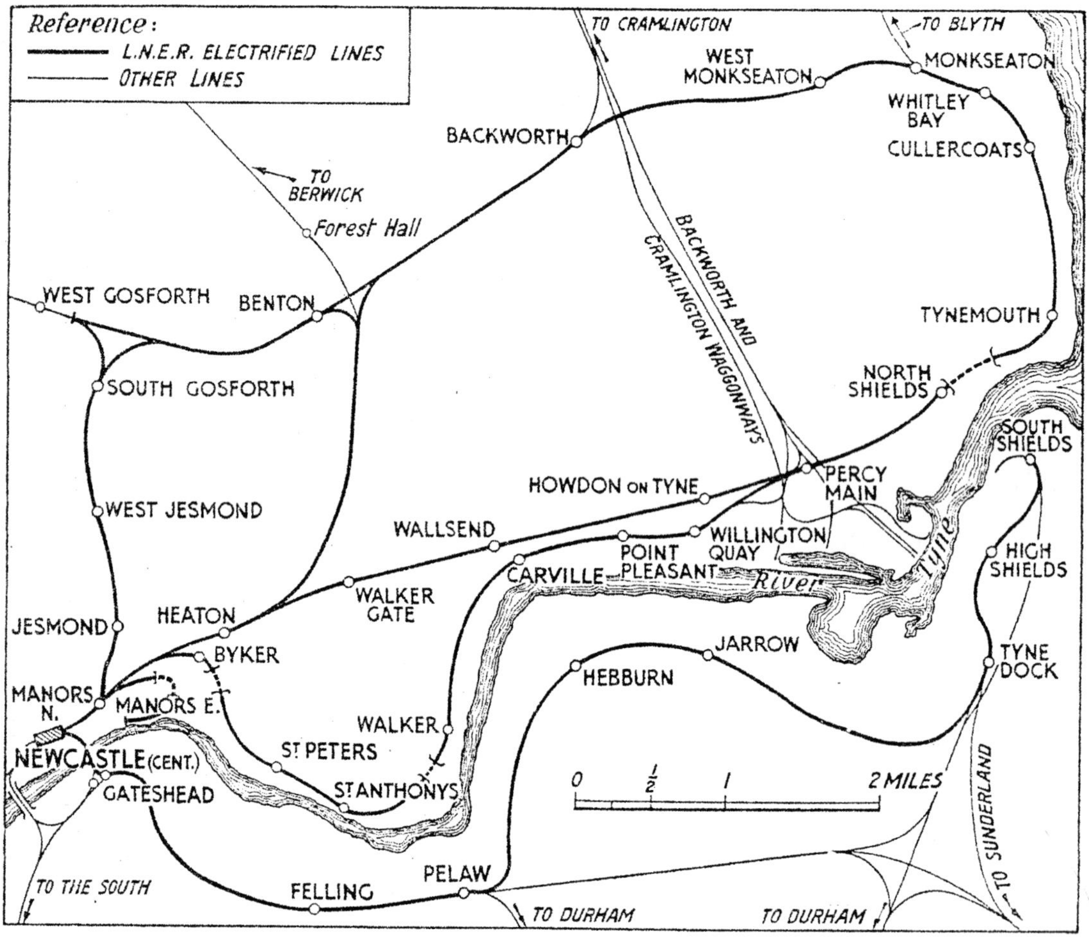

The Tyneside electrification, which was expanded under the LNER having originated with the NER.

the Hull & Barnsley into receivership during 1887–89, but an agreement was reached, and while the NER was never able to acquire the HBR, the two companies shared construction of the large new deep water dock, the King George V, which opened in 1914.

The 1870s were not a period of easy growth for the railways, and the financial performance of the NER is all the more creditable for this. Faced with a recession in mineral traffic, the company began to encourage third-class travel.

The NER gained momentum and prominence when Tennant was superseded by G.S. Gibb in 1891. Gibb believed in building a management team with diverse experience rather than continuing the NER's own introspective policies, and recruited R.L. Wedgwood, Frank Pick and E.C. Geddes, all of whom rose to prominence in the industry. Gibb changed the NER's working statistics, using ton-mileage rather than train-mileage to assess performance. At first other companies were dubious about the changes when introduced in 1899, but in due course these became the industry standard.

Forward thinking was also evident when the NER became the first railway to negotiate with trade unions on hours and wages. Gibb himself moved on in 1906, becoming managing director of London's Underground Group of Companies. Wedgwood became the first chief general manager of the LNER. Geddes moved into politics, became first Minister of Transport and was largely responsible for forcing through the Grouping of the railways, before moving into manufacturing industry.

Meanwhile, a succession of chief mechanical engineers, starting with Wilson, and then Thomas Worsdell and Vincent Raven, took the company into electrification. It started with the

Quayside freight line at Newcastle in 1902, and then the suburban system north of the city in 1904, and by 1915 the company had also electrified the longer-distance line from Shildon to Middlesbrough. The company even planned for electrification of the ECML between York and Newcastle, but in the end, this was shelved through Grouping and Nationalisation and did not take place until 1991.

Nevertheless, the NER passed on to the LNER 58 route miles of electrified line, albeit in three separate schemes, and a total of 126 multiple unit motor coaches and trailers, and 13 electric engines in three separate classes. Had Raven's ideas been supported by the LNER, electrification could have come earlier, but it would have required a chief general manager with a determination to electrify along the lines of the Southern Railway's Sir Hebert Walker for this to have happened.

The HBR was finally absorbed by the NER in 1922.

Subsidiary Companies

Brackenhill Light Railway

Although authorised as early as 1901, the standard gauge line did not open until 1914, linking Brackenhill Junction on the line between York and Sheffield to Hemsworth Colliery, while a short spur was built to Ackworth Moor. It was a freight line, although there were occasional holiday special excursions over its tracks. From the outset, it was worked by the North Eastern Railway and followed the NER into the LNER on Grouping.

Colne Valley & Halstead Railway

Opened between 1860 and 1863, the Colne Valley & Halstead Railway linked Chappel & Wakes Colne to Halstead and Haverhill, becoming part of the London & North Eastern Railway on 1 July 1923. It had just four steam locomotives, one of which was unserviceable. A short section at Castle Hedingham is now preserved as the Colne Valley Railway.

Clarence & Hartlepool Junction Railway

Named after the Duke of Clarence, later King William IV, as a compliment, the Clarence Railway was the first new railway promoted specifically to compete with an existing railway, the Stockton & Darlington, which was being extended to Middlesbrough. Authorised in 1828, it was intended to serve a new port on the north bank and branched out of the S&D at Simpasture. The line opened in 1833–34, three years after the S&D's extension, and from the start undercut the earlier railway's freight charges, which enabled it to attract its share of the rapidly growing coal traffic, but also meant that it struggled to pay its way, and was nearly closed in 1842. It managed to survive until 1844, when it was leased and in 1853 the lessees merged with the Hartlepool West Harbour & Dock Company, purchasing the railway outright and changing its name. It was acquired by the North Eastern Railway in 1865.

East & West Yorkshire Union Railway

Opened between Stourton Junction, Leeds, and the Lofthouse and Newmarket Collieries in 1891, it operated a nine-mile long line serving collieries and remained independent until absorbed by the London & North Eastern Railway in 1923.

East Lincolnshire Railway

Connecting Grimsby to Louth and Boston, the East Lincolnshire was incorporated in 1846, but even before it opened throughout in 1848, it was leased by the Great Northern, and on Grouping passed to the London & North Eastern Railway.

Edinburgh & Bathgate Railway

Opened in 1849 and sponsored by the Edinburgh & Glasgow Railway as the start of a second route between Scotland's two largest cities, the through line was finally opened in 1871. The route suffered many sharp curves and steep gradients so it was never a rival for through running on the main line, but along the line lay rich mineral fields that provided valuable goods traffic. The line passed into North British ownership, but the company retained its separate legal entity until Grouping.

Forcett Railway

Authorised in 1865 and opened in 1866, the line was never completely independent and from opening it was worked by the North Eastern Railway.

Forth & Clyde Junction Railway

The concept of the Forth & Clyde Junction Railway was first raised in Stirling in 1845 and was intended to run through the countryside north of the Campsie Fells to connect with the Caledonian & Dunbartonshire Railway. The project was dropped in the aftermath of the Railway Mania, but revived in 1851, largely with goods traffic in mind. The 30-mile long line opened in May 1856. The line never met the expectations of its promoters and was operated initially by the Scottish Central Railway, but the line arranged its own rolling stock after 1860, although the company still struggled to pay its way and in 1870 it was leased to the North British, which took full control of all operations and provided rolling stock, although the company itself survived until Grouping.

Gifford & Garvald Light Railway

Sponsored by the North British as a spur from its line at Ormiston, it opened as far as Gifford in 1901, but never reached Garvald and survived only to 1933 when it was closed.

Great North of England Railway

An ambitious plan to provide a link from York and Leeds to Newcastle and create a trunk route from London, the line as completed only ran for the 43 miles between York and Darlington, with the former terminus shared with the York & North Midland Railway. It was almost level throughout with just one short and gentle incline. The original engineer, Thomas Storey, was replaced by Robert Stephenson after difficulty with a number of smaller structures, while the two main viaducts were designed by other engineers.

The GNER was leased by George Hudson in 1845 and some of its statutory authority was transferred to the Newcastle & Darlington Junction Railway, authorised in 1842. The plan was to use these railways and the YNMR for a line from London to Edinburgh via Rugby and Derby and spoil plans for a direct line from London to York. In 1846, the NDJR acquired the GNER, and the combined company became the York & Newcastle, before changing again in 1847 to the York Newcastle & Berwick, while the lease passed to the North Eastern Railway in 1854.

Horncastle Railway

Opened in 1855 between Horncastle and Kirkstead Junction, the line was worked by the Great Northern Railway and under Grouping was incorporated into the London & North Eastern Railway.

Humber Commercial Railway & Dock

Opened between Ulceby and Immingham Docks in 1910 and leased by the Great Central Railway, it was opened throughout in 1912, when it also acquired the Barton & Immingham Light Railway, also leased to the GCR. The entire operation passed to the London & North Eastern Railway in 1923.

Kilsyth & Bonnybridge Railway

An extension of the Kelvin Valley Railway, which opened in 1879, the Kilsyth & Bonnybridge opened in 1888. While the KVR was operated by the North British Railway, the KBR was operated jointly by both the North British and the Caledonian Railway, and although it passed to the London & North Eastern Railway in 1923, as with other pre-Grouping joint railways, joint working of the Kilsyth & Bonnybridge Railway with the London Midland & Scottish Railway continued until Nationalisation in 1948.

Lauder Light Railway

Known to the locals as 'Auld La'der Licht', it was authorised by a Light Railway Order in 1898, the Lauder Light Railway opening between Fountainhall and Lauder in 1901. It was worked by the North British Railway, with through trains from Edinburgh Waverley, and became part of the London & North Eastern Railway in 1923. It closed to passengers in 1932.

London & Blackwall Railway

Originally authorised in 1836 as the Commercial Railway, the 5ft gauge line linked the Minories, to the east of the City of London with Blackwall, with the first 2½ miles of the 3½-mile route being on a viaduct 18ft above street level. An extension to Fenchurch Street was authorised in 1839, the company adopting the London & Blackwall title, and the line opened the following year. The line was worked by cable powered by stationary steam engines to reduce the risk of fire to shipping and cargo in the docks. Each carriage had a brakeman and carriages were slipped and picked up at intermediate stations. It was the first to adopt an even headway service with a train every 15 minutes. In 1849, the line was converted to standard gauge and steam traction adopted, while the company connected with the Blackwall Extension Railway, which ran from Stepney Junction to Bow, then the Eastern Counties Railway, and in 1856, the line was linked with the London Tilbury & Southend Railway at Gas Factory Junction.

The Great Eastern Railway leased the London & Blackwall in 1866 for 999 years.

Mansfield Railway

Opened in stages between 1913 and 1917, the Mansfield Railway linked the Great Central at Kirkby, via Mansfield, with the same company's Chesterfield–Lincoln line (originally built as the Lancashire, Derbyshire & East Coast Railway) at Clipstone. The line was worked by the GCR and passed to the London & North Eastern Railway on Grouping.

Mid-Suffolk Light Railway

Authorised by a light railway order in 1901, the Mid-Suffolk opened to goods in stages between 1904 and 1906, and to passengers in 1908. Running between Haughley, Laxfield and Cratfield, some sections were closed in 1912 and in 1915. It was in receivership before being acquired by the London & North Eastern Railway in 1924, when it had just three locomotives, but one was immediately scrapped. The line was closed completely in 1952, four years after Nationalisation.

Newburgh & North Fife Railway

This was a short branch line serving the small port of Newburgh in Fife, which was largely by-passed when the railway bridge over the River Tay was opened.

North Lindsey Light Railway

Opened in 1906 between Scunthorpe and Winterton and Thealby, the NLLR was extended to Winteringham in 1907, and Whitton in 1910. It was worked from the start by the Great Central Railway, before passing to the London & North Eastern Railway in 1923.

Nottingham & Grantham Railway

Opened in 1850 with a terminus at London Road, Nottingham, the N&GR was taken over by the Great Northern Railway, but was also used by the London & North Western Railway running from Market Harborough.

Nottingham Joint Station Committee

Nottingham was served by a number of companies and to ease the management of Nottingham Victoria station, used mainly by the Great Northern and the Great Central, a committee was formed by the participating railways.

Nottingham Suburban Railway

This was a railway linking Trent Lane Junction with St Ann's Well, Sherwood and Daybrook; opened in 1889 and closed in 1951.

Seaforth & Sefton Junction Railway

This was a short line enabling other companies to reach the docks at Seaforth, near Bootle, operated by the Great Central Railway.

Stamford & Essendine Railway

Little is known about this small branch line, almost certainly worked by other railways.

West Riding Railway Committee

This was a coordinating committee, given the intense competition between the Lancashire & Yorkshire, Great Northern and London & North Western railways.

Joint Ventures

Manchester South Junction & Altrincham Railway

The MSJR was formed in 1845 to provide a link between its owners, the Liverpool & Manchester Railway and the Sheffield Ashton & Manchester, a predecessor of the Great Central, and ran for 1½ miles on a brick viaduct on the south side of the city, but with an eight-mile branch from Castlefield to Altrincham, which soon became far busier than the connecting line as it encouraged the development of suburbs. Both shareholding companies provided frequent suburban trains to Altrincham, initially from Oxford Road and then, in 1879, from London Road, by which time they had developed into the London & North Western and Manchester Sheffield & Lincolnshire railways.

Despite having come together to build the MSJAR, the two proprietors had an increasingly unhappy relationship, to the extent that a further Act in 1858 ensured that an arbitrator should attend their meetings. The MSJAR had its own carriages and wagons, but most locomotives came from the MSLR. In 1931, by which time the owners had become the London Midland & Scottish and London & North Eastern railways, the line was electrified using a 1,500V dc overhead system. Conversion in 1971 to 25kV ac system, as used for electrification of the main line services to London enabled through services to be run onto other lines. In 1993, the Castlefield to Altrincham line was rebuilt to become part of the Manchester Metrolink tramway system, but from there remains in use for trains to Chester.

Midland & Great Northern Joint Railway

The longest of the several joint railways in the British Isles, at 183 route miles, the line was an attempt by the Midland and Great Northern railways to penetrate East Anglia, bringing Midland and Yorkshire coal to Norfolk and fish and agricultural products to the industrial centres of the Midlands and the North. Initially, the line used four short contractors' lines, promoted by Waring Brothers, to get from Peterborough to Bourne, Spalding and King's Lynn, which were opened between 1858 and 1866, and worked by the MR and GNR. Later, other lines were opened beyond King's Lynn with the Lynn & Fakenham, opened in 1882 and a line between Yarmouth and North Walsham, opened throughout in 1888, which combined to form the Eastern & Midlands Company, running across Norfolk. Later, a branch to Norwich was added, followed by one to Cromer in 1887.

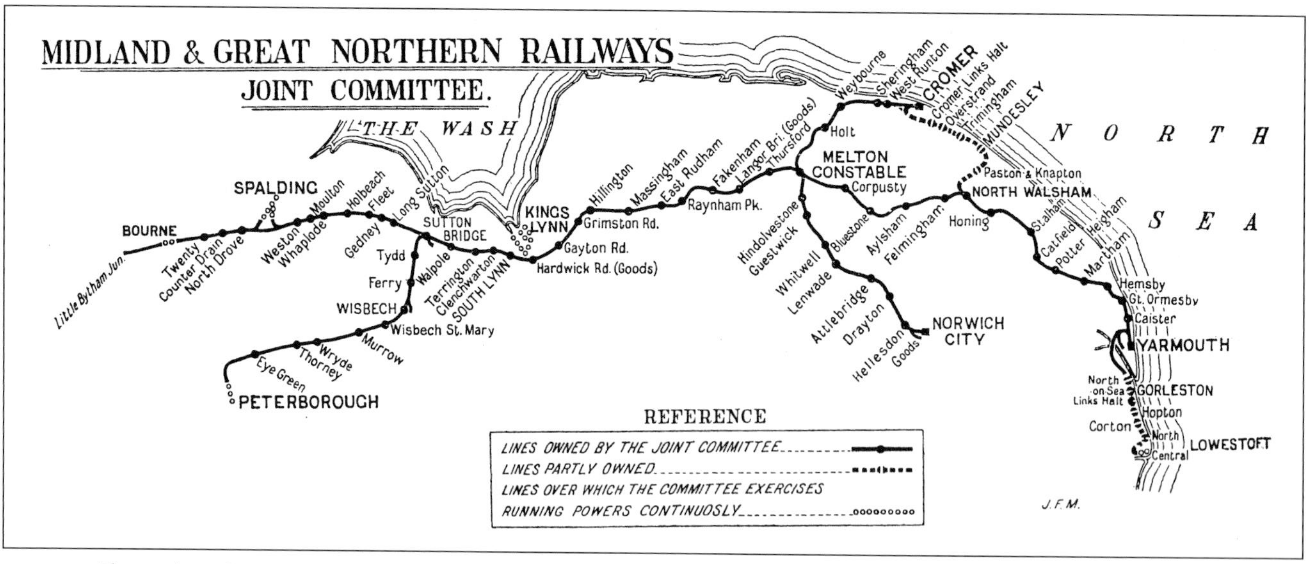

The need to take East Anglia's agricultural produce and fish to the Midlands and the North of England, and to transport coal into East Anglia from the Midlands and Yorkshire, resulted in the creation of the Midland & Great Northern Railways Joint Committee.

Nevertheless, the EMR passed into receivership in 1890, when the MR and GNR purchased it and added the earlier sections to it to form the Midland & Great Northern Joint Railway in 1893. The following year, a branch was opened westwards from Bourne to meet the MR at Saxby, adding through services to Nottingham, Leicester and Birmingham. The new owners also doubled some of the line, but even so, 77 per cent remained single track, but operations were much improved after new tablet-exchange equipment was introduced in 1906. While the two owners had operating rights, the line also pursued an independent existence with its own locomotive works at Melton Constable. With the wide range of destinations served by this time, cattle and fish traffic alone required five trains daily during the summer, while the line also brought holidaymakers to Cromer

A distant view of a Midland & Great Northern 4-4-0 locomotive with a train described as being of 'tourist stock', at South Lynn in 1933. This was before the line was taken over completely by the LNER, which had to scrap many of its locomotives as they were in poor condition. (*HMRS ABJ 534*)

and Yarmouth. The GNR even ran through trains between London and Cromer, but this was a lengthy route at 174 miles, 35 more than on the Great Eastern.

Rivalry with the GER was left behind in 1896, when the three companies agreed to develop the Norfolk & Suffolk Joint Railway, but only two sections were completed, between Cromer and North Walsham in 1898, and Yarmouth and Lowestoft in 1903. Nevertheless, this meant that the M&GNJR and its owners could reach Lowestoft. On Grouping, the line remained jointly operated, passing to both the London Midland Scottish and London & North Eastern railways, but in October 1936 administration and control was taken over completely by the LNER, through whose home territory the line ran. The line duplicated much of the LNER's existing network and no doubt economies were hoped for, through having complete possession of the M&GNJR. The railway had used locomotives that were generally of Midland design, but little had been done to keep the fleet up-to-date.

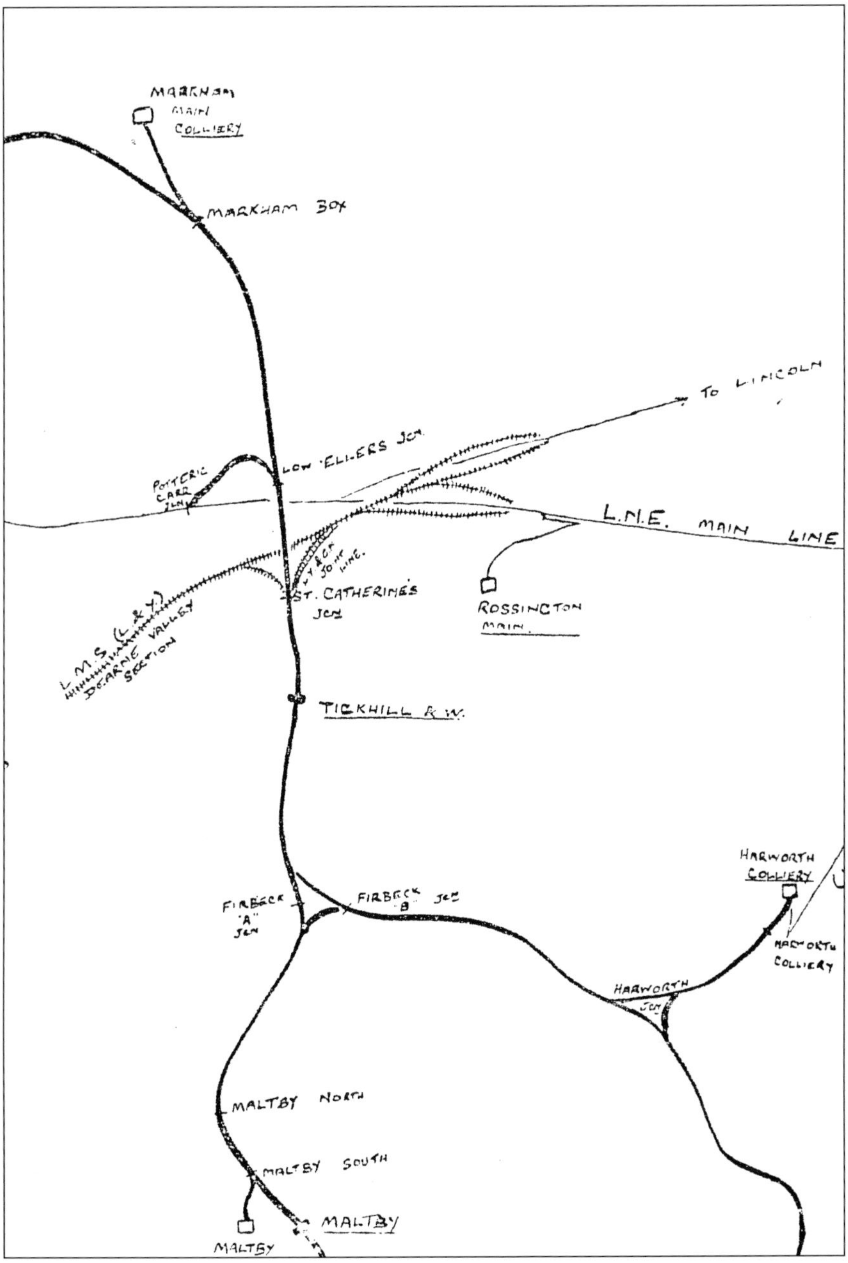

No fewer than five of the pre-Grouping companies were involved with the South Yorkshire Joint Lines, which remained a joint operation after Grouping with the LMS and LNER working together.

The mainstay of the M&GNJR's locomotive stud was a fleet of 45 4-4-0s spread across four classes, while there were also another 40 0-6-0s and 0-6-0Ts, all of which were bought for a total of £50,879, but 25 of these were so dilapidated that they were withdrawn and did not join the LNER's stock. Of those that did, many were withdrawn over the next few years, and even during the Second World War, with locomotives at a premium, some were seen as more use to the country as scrap than remaining in service! Only the shunting tanks lasted a worthwhile period.

South Yorkshire Joint Line Committee

The importance of the vast South Yorkshire coalfield was such that all the railway companies bordering on the area wished and needed to become involved. In 1903, an Act of Parliament authorised the South Yorkshire Joint Line Committee, the members of which included the Great Central, Great Northern and North Eastern railways, all of which became constituent companies of the London & North Eastern, and the Midland Railway and the Lancashire & Yorkshire Railway, which passed into the London Midland & Scottish.

The core of the SYJLC was the line from Kirk Sandal Junction on the old Great Central line between Doncaster and Barnby Dun, which led to an end-on junction with the GCR and Midland Joint Line, which in turn led to the GCR's Retford to Sheffield main line at Brancliffe Junction. Each company worked its own traffic over the SYJLC, although the trading title for the network was the 'South Yorkshire'. Excluding sidings, the system had a total route mileage of just over 38 miles.

The line opened for mineral traffic on 1 January 1909, but it was almost two years before passenger traffic started on 1 December 1910, with four trains daily between Doncaster and Shireoaks. This started as a joint venture between the GNR and GCR, but the Great Northern withdrew after a year. Passenger trains were suspended except on Saturdays during the First World War, and again during the General Strike and Miners' Strike of 1926, and not reinstated afterwards.

Under Grouping, the line became a joint LMS and LNER venture.

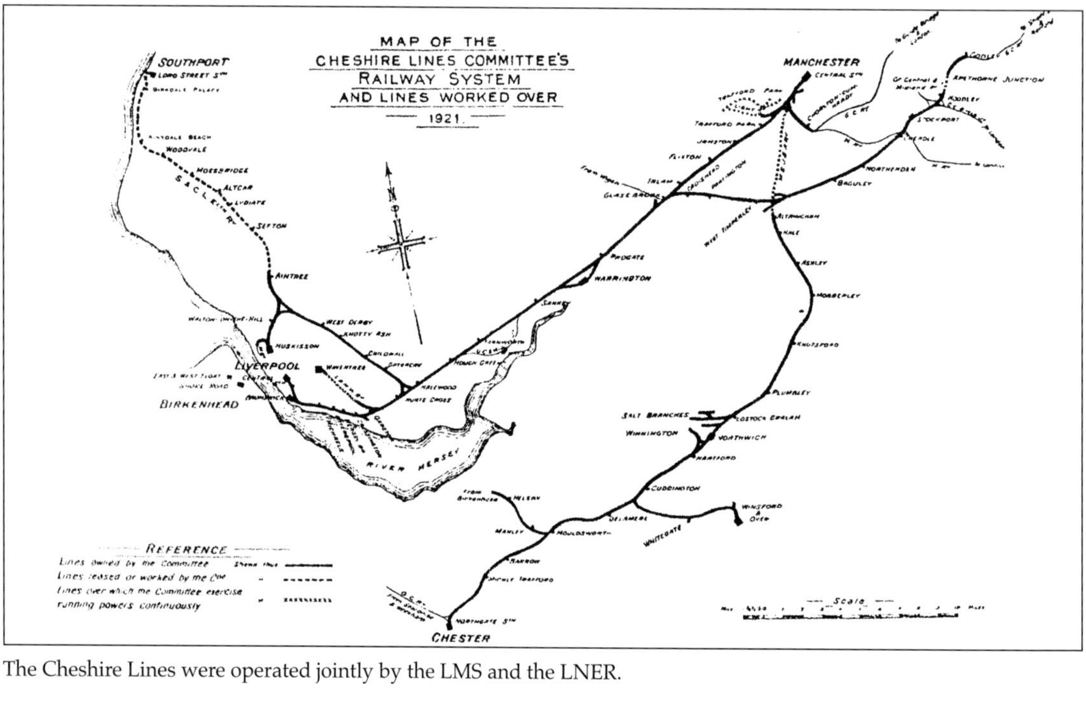

The Cheshire Lines were operated jointly by the LMS and the LNER.

The Neighbours

Cheshire Lines Committee

Despite the name, most of the 143 route miles of this railway were in Lancashire, as well as the largest of its 70 stations, including Liverpool Central and Manchester Central, connected by punctual expresses taking just 40 minutes, while most of its revenue came from the same county. In 1865–66, the Manchester Sheffield & Lincolnshire Railway (see Great Central), the Great Northern and the Midland railways formed a committee with the intention of breaking the London & North Western Railway's monopoly in Manchester. Companies were formed to build lines in the Manchester and Stockport areas that linked to the MSLR, while the company also gained access to Liverpool docks, and reached Birkenhead docks over the Wirral Railway. A line was built to Chester Northgate to connect with the GCR lines to Bidston and North Wales. Highly profitable, it was estimated that at one time the CLC took almost a fifth of the trade of the port of Liverpool. Locomotives were provided by the member companies, and after Grouping in 1923 mainly by the LNER, but the CLC had its own rolling stock, including four Sentinel railcars.

Derwent Valley Light Railway

A 16-mile long privately owned railway, the Derwent Valley ran from Layerthorpe on the outskirts of York to Cliffe Common, near Selby and the southern end between Wheldrake and Cliffe Common opened in 1912, with the remainder opened in 1913. Intended as a freight line, passenger trains were operated from 1913 and during the First World War the North Eastern Railway used the line as a relief route. It was not included in the Grouping. Passenger services ended in 1926, but it remained as a freight line and evaded Nationalisation in 1948.

London Tilbury & Southend Railway

Authorised in 1852 as a joint scheme by the Eastern Counties and London & Blackwall Railways, the LTSR ran from Forest Gate Junction on the ECR to Tilbury and Southend, ending rivalry between the two companies to expand into the area. In many ways, this was a contractors' line as the impetus had come from G.P. Bidder, as engineer, and the contractor Samuel Morton Peto, who was joined by two others, Thomas Brassey and E.L. Betts, who built the line, which opened in stages between 1854 and 1856. It was then worked under lease until 1875, although rolling stock was supplied by the ECR. The sponsors' ambitions were to attract the excursion traffic from Tilbury to Gravesend, and only later did the holiday market for Southend become important.

At first, trains were divided at Stratford with portions for Bishopsgate and Fenchurch Street. A branch was opened to Thames Haven in 1855 by the Thames Haven Dock & Railway Company, and this was taken over by the LTSR on opening. Traffic grew quickly, and an avoiding line had to be built to avoid Stratford, opening in 1858, which then became the main line while all trains ran to and from Fenchurch Street only. The LTSR became independent in 1862, although the main shareholders remained the LBR and the newly created Great Eastern. The LTSR started operating the line in 1875, after which the line was modernised and received its own 4-4-2T locomotives and carriages, with the LTSR running its own trains from 1880.

Full independence followed in 1882, with the other two railways no longer appointing directors. In 1884, an extension from Southend to Shoeburyness, long delayed by War Office objections, was opened, with a shorter line from Barking to Pitsea via Upminster opened between 1885 and 1888, and in 1893, a branch opened from Grays to Romford. Meanwhile, the opening of new docks at Tilbury in 1886 provided goods traffic and called for boat trains when liners called, while the line served the new housing developments in the east of London as well as a growing commuter market at Southend.

Although acquisition of this thriving line by the GER was widely expected, in 1912 the LTSR was acquired by the Midland Railway, and under Grouping passed to the London Midland & Scottish, a self-contained and isolated line away from the company's main area of operations.

Metropolitan Railway

Eventually to be of importance to the Great Central Railway in its thrust towards London, the Metropolitan Railway's first section opened on 10 January 1863, between Paddington and Farringdon Street. It was the world's first passenger underground railway and was constructed using the cut-and-cover system running for the most part beneath streets. At the outset, it was sponsored by the Great Western Railway and laid as 7ft broad gauge to enable the GWR's passengers to reach the City of London. Nevertheless, the relationship between the two railways was unhappy and it was finally severed in 1867, when the line changed to standard gauge.

A programme of expansion followed, reaching Hammersmith in 1864, Harrow-on-the-Hill between 1868 and 1880, and, using the East London Railway, New Cross in 1884. By this time the intention was one of creating a railway circle around central London with the Metropolitan District Railway that would link the major termini north of the Thames. Known as the 'City Widened Lines', the original Metropolitan was also intended to provide access to the City of London for the Midland Railway, Great Northern Railway and London Chatham & Dover Railway.

Further expansion saw the railway extending out into the countryside, reaching Aylesbury from Harrow in 1892. With connections to the Great Central Railway, which gained its original access to London over the Metropolitan in 1899, the two companies ran the line north of Harrow jointly after 1906. Uxbridge was reached in 1904, Watford in 1925 and Stanmore in 1932, while it acquired the Great Northern & City tube line in 1913, but the two lines were never linked. More than any other railway in London, the Metropolitan was popularly associated with the expansion of the suburbs, and even had a country estates subsidiary while its catchment area became known as 'Metroland'. Uniquely amongst the London underground railways, the Met. provided three classes for its passengers, and even operated two Pullman cars. Second class was abandoned in 1905 and first class disappeared under the wartime restrictions on suburban railways in 1941. Goods and parcels traffic was also handled. Electrification of the underground section was introduced in 1905, initially with trains switching to or from steam haulage at Harrow, but electrification was later extended to Rickmansworth.

Growing competition from motor buses after 1910 meant that the outer suburban services became increasingly important, and indeed the Bakerloo Line was eventually developed to relieve the inner sections of the Metropolitan. The company used its country routes to argue unsuccessfully, against its incorporation into the new London Passenger Transport Board in 1933. Under London Transport and later Transport for London, the Met. increasingly lost some of its distinctiveness, with the Hammersmith & City Line separated, although continuing to use the Widened Lines along with the Circle Line.

In 1937, the LNER took over the London Transport line between Rickmansworth and Aylesbury, and replaced the line's H2 class 4-4-4Ts with A5 class Pacific tank locomotives.

Chapter 2

The London Termini

The LNER inherited three London termini, of which two, King's Cross and Liverpool Street, were significant, while Marylebone never reached more than half the size originally envisaged by the Great Central Railway. Many other London termini proved to be too small as originally envisaged and had to be enlarged, sometimes more than once. Only the Great Western had fewer London termini, with just the single terminus at Paddington, and how many post-Grouping railway directors and senior managers must have envied the GWR.

There were considerable differences between the businesses of the three termini. King's Cross was mainly used by long-distance services and had relatively little suburban traffic until well into the 20th century. Liverpool Street was overwhelmingly a suburban station, despite its Continental boat trains to Harwich for the packet service to Hook of Holland, and its services into rural Suffolk and Norfolk. Marylebone was the arriviste, the newcomer, with much suburban potential, just providing that it did not offend the relationship with the Metropolitan. It struggled to prove that it could run competitive trunk services to Manchester, Sheffield, Nottingham and Derby, despite its routes often being considerably longer than those of the other railways.

An atmospheric view of two locomotives at the end of the platform at King's Cross in 1938, including an Ivatt Atlantic, with rising steam showing that a third locomotive is hidden behind the N2 class 0-6-2T. (*HMRS ABT 100*)

King's Cross

King's Cross was built for the Great Northern Railway to replace its temporary station, used since 1850 and located next to Maiden Lane, now renamed York Way. To reach King's Cross, the line had to be buried under the Regent's Canal and then through the 528-yard Gas Works Tunnel. The temporary facilities at Maiden Lane were named 'King's Cross' in the timetable, and consisted of two timber platforms, which had to cope with the Great Exhibition traffic of 1851, and were also used by Queen Victoria and Prince Albert for their trip to Scotland that August.

The present station, the 'real' King's Cross, was built on a ten-acre site which had been occupied by the smallpox and fever hospitals, while a number of houses were also demolished. It opened on 14 October 1852. Initially, the daily service consisted of twelve trains in each direction, with just three of them expresses, with departures starting at 7am and ending at 8pm, while the last arrival was at 10pm. Passengers were met by horse buses which for 6d (2½p) would convey them to London Bridge, Waterloo or Paddington.

Lewis Cubitt designed a simple, yet practical, station, with two 800ft long, 105-ft wide, train sheds which were joined at the southern end by a 216ft façade of London stock bricks with two arches, but with little ornament. The lack of pretension was spoiled somewhat by a central square clock tower, 112ft high, with an Italianate turret with a clock with three faces, as the north-facing one was blocked off as it could not be seen from the ground. The clock's chimes were silenced at the outbreak of the First World War and not reinstated until 1924, then silenced again in 1927.

The west side of the station had a departure platform, now No. 10, while on the east was an arrival platform, now No. 1, with 14 carriage roads in between them. A carriage road ran alongside the arrival platform, while between the departure platform and an external carriage road were refreshment rooms and first- and second-class waiting rooms and ladies' rooms, as well as the station offices. As was the custom at the time, a hotel was also built, opening in 1854, but the Great Northern Hotel was set apart from the station to the south-west.

Around three-quarters of the roof was glazed, supported by arches and laminated wood girders, which had to be replaced on the east side during 1869–70, and on the west, during 1886–87.

Carrying the mails was an important role for all of Britain's railways, and they did not have a choice as the Post Office had a statutory right to demand that they did so. This is an LNER travelling post office van in 1929, No. 2339; earlier versions had the corridor connection offset to match the interior layout of the vehicle. (*HMRS AAB024*)

Once finished, King's Cross was for the time the largest terminus in the British Isles, but the GNR was accused of extravagance, which was denied by the Board, who pointed out that they had obtained good value. In fact, the portico and Grand Hall at Euston had cost as much.

At the start, King's Cross was a main line station, with just four stations between London and Hatfield, 17¾ miles away, but intermediate stations were opened over the next decade or so. In February 1858, the GNR trains were joined by those of the Midland Railway, although these were later removed when St Pancras was opened in September 1868. Shortly after the Metropolitan Railway opened in 1863, a station was opened at King's Cross slightly to the east of the terminus, and in October of that year, all GNR suburban trains were diverted to Farringdon Street, with up suburban trains having to back into the terminus, using the departure platform: up trains had to stop at a platform outside the terminus named York Road, before descending to the Metropolitan.

King's Cross was marred from the outset by the difficult approach. In 1860, an excursion train from Manchester mounted the buffers after the guard, who was drunk, had forgotten that he needed to provide additional assistance with his brake as the train descended into the station. No-one was killed, but the damage was considerable. On 2 November 1865, a coal train running through one of the tunnels broke in two, leaving one portion to run away down into King's Cross itself. The guard jumped clear, while the wagons hit the buffers and overturned, losing their loads. Frantically, rescue parties dug at the coal for fear of finding casualties, but no-one was hurt.

The Growing Station

In 1862, a further arrival platform was inserted, replacing some of the carriage roads, with one face, later No. 2, of full length, while the other presented a short bay, but long enough for a short train. Meanwhile, a connection between the Metropolitan and the London Chatham & Dover Railway in 1866 meant that the approaches to King's Cross carried a heavy goods traffic, mainly of coal trains, having run south on the GNR and then diverted on to the Metropolitan for Kent. Suburban services were introduced by the GNR with the opening of branches to Edgware and Finchley in 1867, which later became part of the Northern Line. Cross-London trains were introduced, initially by the GNR, running from Hatfield to Herne Hill in 1866, but diverted to Victoria in 1868.

In 1878, an Enfield to Muswell Hill service was introduced, but this passed to the South Eastern Railway in 1880. In the meantime, the City Widened Lines had been constructed alongside the Metropolitan, and new junctions had to be built outside King's Cross, which were opened in 1868. Further suburban branches opened during the early 1870s, to Enfield, High Barnet and Alexandra Palace. These branches and the traffic they generated as well as the coal and other trains resulted in heavy congestion, so that it could take 30 minutes in the rush hour to cover the 1½ miles between Holloway and King's Cross, during the mid-1870s.

Temporary relief came when the North London Railway took over much of the traffic running over GNR tracks and then to Broad Street. Nevertheless, it was essential to undertake substantial works to improve the approaches, with additional tunnels and a skew bridge to separate trains for the goods yard from passenger services, and much of this work was done between 1875 and 1877, but further works were needed and were completed in mid-1886. A third tunnel under the Regent's Canal was finished in 1892, allowing separate tunnels for up and down trains. The approaches were congested and confused, while the run down into the tunnels and then up again placed a strain on many a heavily loaded train, with runbacks a real danger, while the tunnels and the yard could flood in heavy rain. On 25 July 1901, traffic had to be suspended completely for 4½ hours after a flood.

The growing suburban traffic initially used the sole departure platform, which was also backed into by trains coming from the Metropolitan. In 1875, three short platforms and two tracks just outside the western wall were opened, with the clumsy title of 'King's Cross Main

The guard's van of a 'quad-art' set departing from King's Cross in 1928, clearly showing the connection with the next carriage in the unit and also second-class compartments. This class had disappeared from most railways by then, but remained on LNER London-area suburban services. (*HMRS ABZ 508*)

Line (Local) Station', with three platform faces. This replaced a carriage repair shop, but was used only for departures. In 1878, the Metropolitan connecting trains no longer had to back into the terminus, but instead used the new King's Cross (Suburban) platform, but it suffered from a steeply graded and curving platform that became an embarrassment for fully loaded trains, while the tunnel from the Metropolitan, known as Hotel Curve, was also steeply graded and curving, and shrouded in smoke that required repeater signals and hand-held lamps for safety.

Double-heading was not permitted as the pilot locomotive would smother the crew of that behind with smoke and fumes. In this dense and unwelcoming, not to say unhealthy, atmosphere, the GNR provided a man whose job it was to spread sand on the track after each train had passed. In July 1932, a train slipped so badly on the climb from the Metropolitan that the following train ran into it. The report on the accident noted that, in the darkness, enginemen could only judge if the train was moving forward by reaching out and touching the tunnel walls, while breathing was difficult and drivers had 'little or no chance of rectifying an error'. Lights were fitted in the tunnel to help them judge their speed.

Between 1867 and 1881, the number of season ticket holders using King's Cross rose from 2,500 to 14,400. The passenger business was growing overall, but as with most of the London termini, trains were stopped and tickets checked before the station was reached. For King's Cross, the checks were conducted at Holloway until this was abandoned in 1896. In the meantime, with no checks at King's Cross, 'The Cross' in railway jargon, or at York Road, many a youngster enjoyed a free ride between the two.

The two train sheds were separated by a central wall, which incorporated arches, and in 1893, new platforms, which eventually became Nos 5 and 6, were built on either side, with the westernmost becoming the long-awaited second departure platform. An iron girder footbridge came into use at the same time, located about halfway down the platforms and allowing easy access across the station. Next, in 1895, an additional track and a new island platform, 500ft long, were added to the local station. This required the locomotive yard, coaling stage and turntable to be moved westwards, while the curve to the Metropolitan was flattened to some extent and the

Like so many of the London termini, the approaches to King's Cross were congested and space was limited, with two tunnels close to the station. This is the view towards the bridge and the first tunnel, in 1936. (*HMRS ABJ 025*)

platform for the connection rebuilt, with a short bay also built. New milk and horse and carriage docks filled the remaining space between Cheney Street and the back of Culross Buildings.

To avoid confusion with the main line station, the local platforms were designated A to E from west to east, with A and B designated as suburban platforms to distinguish them from C to E, the local platforms. The arrival and departure platforms in the main station were confusingly numbered 1 and 2 departures, and 1 to 5 arrivals, until a more logical station-wide system was introduced in 1921. In addition, there was separate access from the terminus to the Metropolitan, and from 1906 this also gave access to the Piccadilly Line tube platforms, and access was provided to a separate booking hall for the City & South London tube, which reached King's Cross in 1907. The arrival of the underground trains and electric trams caused many of the suburban through workings across London to be reduced, and they were withdrawn finally in 1907.

Despite these changes, the station itself continued to develop piecemeal, and nowhere was this more evident than outside, where the empty space, left after the diversion of the St Pancras Old Road in the 1870s to run alongside St Pancras station, was occupied by sellers of garden furniture and sheds, hoping to interest the homeward-bound commuter. Later, shops appeared at the front of the station, with the hard-pressed LNER doubtless anxious for some rental income.

Major changes were made during 1922–24 to impose a more consistent approach to the station, while the off-peak through workings to the Metropolitan had ended in 1915 and were never reinstated. Changes were made to the approaches, including turning the up carriage road in the centre of the three Gas Works tunnels into an up relief running line. Other changes saw arrivals able to use all platforms other than 16 and 17, while up suburban trains used 11 and 13. The new Gresley Pacific locomotives were catered for by a 70ft turntable at King's Cross which reduced light engine working in the approaches and eased congestion.

The difficulty of operating the complicated track layout on the approaches, and the fact that not all of it was visible from either the East or West boxes, meant that a primitive form of track circuiting was in use on some of the lines in the tunnels from 1894. Full track circuiting was completed by 1923, while power-operated upper quadrant signals had started to appear the previous year. On 3 October 1932, colour light signalling replaced all the semaphore signals at King's Cross, and a new box, situated centrally at the ends of Platforms 5 and 6 superseded the separate East and West boxes.

Wartime and Beyond

For safety's sake, during the First World War, main line trains were drawn into the tunnels whenever enemy airships or bombers were overhead, but King's Cross remained unscathed. This was fortunate, as not only did the terminus and its immediate surrounding lines carry much coal and many passenger trains, explosives also passed through the station, often on passenger trains.

Post-war, by the time the railways were freed from state control, it was almost time for Grouping, with the GNR becoming part of the London & North Eastern Railway. While the GNR's management had encouraged people to buy houses in 'Bracing Barnet' and on the 'Northern Heights' before the war to stimulate suburban traffic, pre-war relief came when the Northern Line took over the High Barnet and Mill Hill branches in 1939. Before this, the northern extension of the Piccadilly Line also reduced suburban traffic into King's Cross. While the LNER imposed logic on platform numbering, it was not adverse to creating fresh mysteries of its own, as when Platform 4 was extended to full length, Platform 3 disappeared!

The Second World War once again saw King's Cross extremely busy. Trains often carried as many as 2,000 passengers, and to cope with the demands of wartime, could be as long as twenty or more carriages. Locomotives would pull one portion out of the platform, and then reverse on to the second portion. This imposed risks of its own. On 4 February 1945, the 6pm to Leeds stalled in the tunnel and then ran backwards into the front of the 7pm 'Aberdonian' standing in Platform 10. Despite the low speed, the moving carriages rose into the air and demolished the signal gantry, while two passengers were killed. It took two weeks before a new gantry could be installed, causing the termination of all up suburban services at Finsbury Park.

King's Cross did not escape the impact of enemy action in the Second World War. Two 1,000lb bombs, chained together, fell on the west side during the Blitz early on Sunday, 11 May 1941, destroying much of the general offices, the grill room and bar, and wrecking the booking hall, killing twelve men. Fortunately, the station was quiet at the time. Temporary booking and refreshment facilities were organised quickly, and no trains were cancelled. Elsewhere, bombing on the Metropolitan lines meant that services to Moorgate were suspended from 30 December 1940, and not reinstated until after the war.

Liverpool Street

Possibly the grandest of the LNER's London termini, and the largest terminus within the City of London, Liverpool Street was built to replace the Shoreditch terminus of the Eastern Counties Railway. When the ECR was absorbed into the Great Eastern Railway in 1862, the question arose again of a terminus in central London, coupled with the building of additional suburban lines and the conversion of Shoreditch to a goods station. A number of locations were considered, including Finsbury Circus, and for the track to continue from Bishopsgate on viaduct. Parliament approved the scheme in 1864, mainly because the line approached Liverpool Street in tunnel so that the demolition of London's housing stock would be kept to the minimum, but also because it was beside the terminus of the North London Railway then being built at Broad Street.

The plan was that the lines should leave the existing high level route at Tapp Street, just west of Bethnal Green, and fall to below street level, and then run in tunnel under Commercial Street and Shoreditch High Street, before turning to enter the terminus. This would be built on what had been the gardens of the Bethlehem Hospital. Some demolition was inevitable, including the City of London Theatre and the City of London Gasworks, and 450 tenement dwellings housing around 7,000 people. The GER was bound under the terms of the Act to run a 2d daily return train between Edmonton and Liverpool Street, and another between the terminus and Walthamstow. Later claims by the GER to pay between 30 and 50 shillings as compensation to displaced tenants can be discounted as the payments at the time would have been much lower.

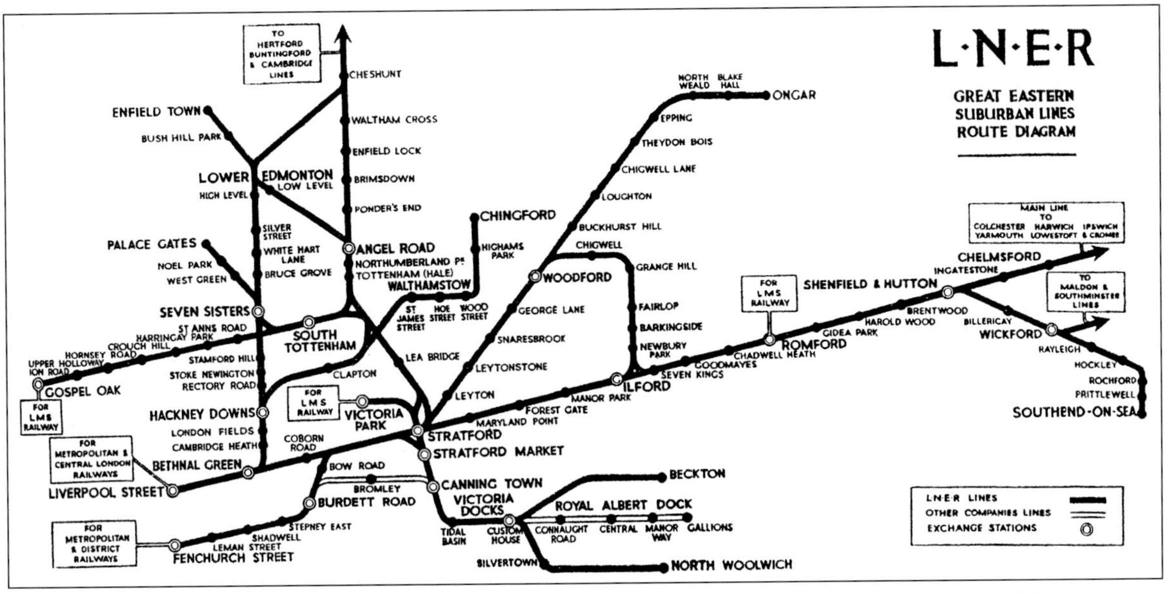

Part of the LNER's network in the London area served from the former Great Eastern terminus at Liverpool Street – the King's Cross suburban network was smaller.

The terminus was built below street level, much to the consternation of many of the directors, but Samuel Swarbrick, the GER's general manager, was concerned to cut costs, despite the fact that departing trains would be faced with a tunnel through which the track climbed steeply. The new station opened in stages, with the first being on 2 February 1874, handling just the suburban services to Enfield and Walthamstow, and the station was not fully open until 1 November 1875, when the old Bishopsgate terminus was handed over to be converted for goods traffic, reopening in 1881 and remaining in use until it was destroyed by fire in December 1964.

Liverpool Street occupied ten acres in the heart of the City and had ten platforms, numbered from west to east. Platforms 1 and 2 ran under the station building and the street to a junction with the Metropolitan Railway, to the west of its Liverpool Street underground station, known until 1909 as Bishopsgate. Until its own station was completed in July 1875, the Metropolitan trains used Platforms 1 and 2 of the terminus. In fact, debate over charges for through workings completely defeated the exercise, and the connecting tunnel was in the end used only for special workings, the last being a Met. working from Rickmansworth to Yarmouth in 1904, and the junction was removed in 1907. The main line arrival and departure platforms were Nos 9 and 10, and were 900ft long. The street front of the new station consisted of three blocks, with the main one 90ft high and running along Liverpool Street itself. The second ran from its western end into the third at its northern end, set at right angles to it, 67ft high. In the space left by the blocks were four roadways for pedestrians and vehicles. The roof was perhaps the best feature of the building, set high and with a delicate appearance, with four glazed spans. There was a clock tower on the outside of the building, on the roof of the north block. Inside, the train shed the roof later had two four-faced clocks suspended from it.

Behind the north block, was the suburban station with eight tracks and ten platform faces, while the main line platforms were to the east of the middle block. Later, the suburban platforms were numbered 1 to 8, with Platform 9 used by both suburban and long-distance services.

The cost of building a terminus in the heart of the City of London was high, and while compensation for the displaced tenants was poor, the landowners received far higher compensation, so that the total for Liverpool Street's construction eventually mounted to £2 million (£120 million by today's prices), and to allow for this, an Act of 1869 allowed the GER to charge the two-mile fare for the 1¼-mile extension.

The opening of Liverpool Street encouraged the GER to build a set of three suburban branch lines north of Bethnal Green, serving Hackney Downs and Tottenham, Edmonton, with a junction with the original Enfield branch, and from Hackney Downs through Clapton to a junction with the Cambridge line, and the still-new branch to Walthamstow. The latter was extended to Chingford in 1873, and the line to Tottenham and Edmonton was extended to Palace Gates at Wood Green in 1878. Some of these lines were open before Liverpool Street was ready, so a new station, Bishopsgate Low Level, was opened on the new extension to Liverpool Street in November 1872. The low level station was under the existing terminus, and with no room for smoke and steam to escape, the tank engines used were equipped with condensing apparatus, which was also seen as necessary for the projected through running on the Metropolitan. The low level station was eventually closed as a wartime economy measure in 1916.

Added to the GER's own branches were services running from the East London Railway, completed in April 1876. In July of that year, the London Brighton & South Coast Railway introduced a service from East Croydon, while the South Eastern Railway started a service from Addiscombe in April 1880, which lasted until March 1884. At the beginning of 1886, the GER took over the LBSCR services, although from 1911, they terminated at New Cross and were withdrawn when the ELR was electrified in 1913.

The Growing Station

The new suburban lines, the continued growth on the earlier lines, and a growing business to and from the holiday resorts and market towns of East Anglia, meant that by 1884 it was realised that the traffic at Liverpool Street itself would soon outgrow the station. Fortunately, the GER had been steadily acquiring land to the east of the station, and eventually owned land up to Bishopsgate 188ft wide and six acres in extent.

Clearance began and on 1890 work began on what was to become the East Side station. A sign of social change was that Parliament insisted that alternative accommodation be found for the tenants in the properties cleared away, and indeed, that they be rehoused at low rents. Accommodation could only be found for 137 tenants in existing property, so another 600 were housed in tenements built by the GER.

It was not enough simply to expand the station: the approach lines had to be expanded as well to avoid congestion. A third pair of approach tracks was built between Bethnal Green and Liverpool Street, enabling the westernmost set of tracks to be reserved entirely for the Enfield and Walthamstow services, so from 1891, these were known as the suburban lines, the middle set became the local lines and the easternmost, the through lines. The four tracks continued as far as Romford. Inside the terminus, Platforms 1 to 5 became West Side Suburban, handling suburban and local services, while No. 6 also handled Cambridge trains; Platforms 7 to 14 handled both local and through services, and 15 to 18 handled through services only. The services to and from the ELR used Platform 14, or if this was not available, No. 18.

The new Liverpool Street was the largest London terminus until Victoria opened, rebuilt, in 1908. By the number of passengers handled daily, it remained the busiest terminus even after 1908. In a typical day, it handled 851 passenger arrivals and departures, as well as 224 empty carriages trains, ten goods trains and five light engine movements.

The new East Side frontage was taken by the Great Eastern Hotel, completed in May 1884, and the largest hotel in the City. Designed by C.E. Barry, the hotel presented a far more impressive face to the world than the original station buildings. Beneath the hotel, an area known as the 'backs' included an extension of the tracks from Platforms 9 and 10. This was used by a nightly goods train that brought in coal for the hotel and the engine docks, as well as small consignments for the offices and the hotel, while taking away the hotel's refuse and ashes from the engine docks. The eastward extension also meant that these two platforms split the station in two, and so a footbridge was built right across the station, although on two levels and too

Cambridge in 1939, and a local train of four six-wheel carriages is hauled by E4 2-4-0 No. 7473. (*HMRS AEU 813*)

narrow to accommodate the numbers needing to use it at peak times. Relief came when the Central London Railway reached the terminus in 1912, with the tube station under the west side, but the subway to the booking office ran the full width of the station. It was not until after Nationalisation that the extension into the 'Backs' was ended and level access provided around the ends of Platforms 9 and 10.

Meanwhile, other suburban branch lines had been added to the GER network, although the first of these, the line to Southend, completed in 1889, would not have been regarded as even outer suburban at the time! It was joined by a line from Edmonton to Cheshunt, known as the Churchbury Loop, in 1891, and between Ilford and Woodford, known as the Hainault Loop, in 1903. The former closed in 1909 due to disappointing traffic, and that to Hainault was not much more successful, so it must have been a relief when an eastwards extension of the Central Line took it over some years later.

Despite these disappointments, overall traffic continued to grow, so that by 1912, Liverpool Street was handling a thousand trains daily. These included Britain's first all-night service, half-hourly between the terminus and Walthamstow, introduced in 1897. Walthamstow's population had grown from 11,092 in 1871 to 95,131 in 1901. This was not unusual and other suburbs saw similar growth.

Of all the London termini, Liverpool Street had the most difficult time during the First World War. Several bombs fell on the approach lines on the night of 8/9 September 1915, wrecking the suburban and through lines, while the local lines were flooded by a burst water main. Repairs were completed and normal services resumed by 11am on the morning of 9 September. Worse was to follow. A daylight raid on 13 June 1917 saw three bombs hit the outer end of the station, wrecking carriages on the noon train for Hunstanton, standing at Platform 9, as well as destroying two carriages in the dock between Platforms 8 and 9 which were being used for medical examinations. In all, 16 people were killed and another 36 wounded.

Competition from the expanding London Underground and the electric trams meant that electrification was considered as early as 1903. Nevertheless, the Underground seemed to have stopped expanding and while Parliamentary approval was obtained, nothing was done, even though daily passenger numbers rose from around 200,000 in 1912 to 229,073 in 1921, but just 14 trains had been added to the timetable. The cost would have been enormous, however, estimated in 1919 at £3.5 million (equivalent to more than £70 million today), with little prospect of achieving a worthwhile return. The alternative, a stop-gap measure, costing £80,000, was to change the layout of the approaches, the station arrangements and signalling, so that steam trains could continue to operate, but at maximum efficiency.

The new service was officially described as the 'Intensive Service', but was named the 'Jazz Service' by one evening newspaper, partly because jazz music was the rage at the time, and also because to speed loading, second-class carriages had a blue line painted above the windows, and first-class had yellow lines, while third remained unmarked. Sixteen-carriage trains of four-wheeled stock operated with 24 per hour at peak periods on just one line between Liverpool Street and Bethnal Green, still using manual signalling and 0-6-0 tank locomotives that had first appeared in 1886. Trains spent just four minutes in a platform, while platforms 1 to 4 had their own engine docks and layouts that enabled locomotives to be shunted without going beyond platform limits. At peak periods, trains started every two minutes in sequence from Platforms 4 to 1, followed by a four-minute gap for arrivals.

A miners' strike in 1921 meant that the intensive service had to be suspended to save coal, and again during the General Strike and the prolonged miners' strike of 1926. However, the pressure began to ease not just because of the additional trains but because commuters were moving further out into the country. Gresley improved the standard of the rolling stock by producing five-car articulated units with a much improved ride. Nevertheless, traffic continued to fall, with the daily number of passengers peaking at 244,000 in 1923, but dropping to 209,000 in 1938, and eventually to 171,000 in 1959.

Grouping and Beyond

The London & North Eastern Railway took over the GER and Liverpool Street on 1 January 1923. The company, impoverished by the collapse of its hitherto heavy coal traffic as a result of the 1926 strike, could do little to implement electrification and concentrated on its more glamorous expresses to Yorkshire and Scotland from King's Cross. The East Side booking office was modernised in 1935 and equipped with ticket issue and accounting machines, while during 1938 and 1939, an attempt was made to clean the station and improve its general appearance.

The Second World War was even harsher to Liverpool Street than the earlier conflict. When bombs fell on Platforms 1 and 4 during the Blitz, a train was wrecked and this took some days to remove. The East Side booking office was also damaged as was Platform 18, while a delayed action bomb exploded in the engine sidings beyond Platform 10 and killed two men, despite being surrounded by four trucks of ballast. A bomb that fell on Broad Street threw a wagon on to the roof of Liverpool Street. The station buildings also suffered heavy damage, with the clock tower burnt out, and it took British Railways until 1961 to replace the clock.

The war also disrupted plans for electrification once government-sponsored loans became available, and the extension of the Central Line to Loughton and Hainault did not take place until 1947, when services from Liverpool Street to these towns ended. The LNER plans for overhead electrification of the line to Shenfield were not completed until after Nationalisation, starting in late September 1949.

Marylebone

Marylebone was built for the London Extension of the Great Central Railway and to fulfil the ambitions of one man, the GCR's chairman, Sir Edward Watkin, whose interests in railways were wide and varied. He was chairman of the Metropolitan Railway from 1872. Earlier he had become chairman of the Manchester Sheffield & Lincolnshire Railway, a cross-country operation whose main line ran from Grimsby to Manchester. Without a London route of its own, it lost this growing traffic to the Great Northern Railway and, later, the Midland Railway. Opposition to Parliamentary approval was strong, especially from the cricketing fraternity as the line would run close to Lords. There was also opposition from the artists of St John's Wood. Eventually, the extension from near Nottingham to London was authorised in 1893.

The MSLR was not allowed to use the Metropolitan lines, which had a new chairman after Watkin stood down due to a stroke, but was able to use the same alignment. This was not just spite on the part of the new chairman, John Bell: the Metropolitan was already very busy with its own suburban traffic. Fresh powers had to be obtained so that new lines could be laid. It was also considered expedient to change the company's somewhat provincial title to the more impressive Great Central Railway, on 1 August 1897.

The GCR needed more than 50 acres for the terminus, coal and goods depots, and 4,448 persons were evicted during the slum clearance that followed. Many were moved to homes nearby, but 2,690 were moved to six five-storey blocks of flats, known as Wharncliffe Gardens after the new chairman of the GCR, built by the company. This was despite much of the approach being in tunnel or cut-and-cover construction passing under the streets of St John's Wood. The gradient was kept to 1 in 100. The engineers for the difficult two-mile approach were Sir Douglas and Francis Fox. To allow for possible future quadrupling, not one but two tunnels were excavated under Hampstead. Between the Hampstead tunnels and St John's Wood Tunnel, the line crossed the London & North Western Railway main line on a bridge. Three further parallel tunnels took the line under Lords.

Approaching Marylebone, the seven tracks expanded to 14 as the line passed over the Regent's Canal, which included a second span for the proposed and authorised, but never built, Regent's Canal, City & Docks Railway. Coal and goods depots were built on both sides of Lisson Grove. Finally, outside the terminus the lines became down slow, up slow, down main, and to the east of these, a siding road, carriage sheds, locomotive yard and a platform or wharf for fish and milk. Provision was made for 16 tracks over Rossmore Road, with a terminus of five double-faced platforms, but only part of this was built.

The feeble resources of the GCR were stretched almost to breaking point by its expansion southwards. In its best year, 1864, its predecessor, the MSLR had achieved a dividend of just 3.5 per cent. An architect for the station was beyond the company's resources, while the terminus was a modest affair, albeit conveniently at street level, and the Great Central Hotel was left to others to develop. The extension demanded extra locomotive and rolling stock, but these could only be afforded by creating a trust company which bought the necessary equipment, and then sold them to the GCR under a form of hire purchase. A three-storey office block was provided, with provision for additional floors when required, but most of the accommodation remained unused until the GCR moved its headquarters from Manchester in 1905.

The concourse, intended for a terminus twice the size, stretched beyond the nine tracks and four built at its eastern end. At the eastern wall were two tracks, then arrival Platforms 1 and 2, separated by a 30ft wide roadway. Two more tracks followed, with departure Platforms 3 and 4 beyond and then a single track. Even the Great Central Hotel, with its 700 bedrooms, was over-ambitious, and in 1916 it was requisitioned by the government as a convalescent home for wounded officers. Its one oddity was a cycle track on the roof! In the end, after being purchased as offices by the London & North Eastern Railway after the Second World War, it became 222 Marylebone Road, headquarters of the British Transport Commission, and when that was dissolved, the British Railways Board.

Goods traffic on the London Extension started in 1898 with coal trains. On 9 March 1899, a ceremonial opening was performed by the President of the Board of Trade, and public services started on 15 March. For the first month, only two platforms were used. By summer, there were eleven trains daily each way, of which seven were Manchester expresses, but while the track bedded in, running times were not fast, at five hours for the 212 mile journey. Where the GCR did score was in the comfort of its new carriages, all of which were corridor stock with electric lighting.

The problem was that the GCR route to Manchester was longer than that of the LNWR, and that to Sheffield longer than that of the Great Northern. The GCR was best for Leicester and Nottingham, neither of which matched the other cities for traffic. Even so, the Marylebone to Manchester journey time was down to 3hr 50min by 1904, and Sheffield was three hours.

Much of these improved timings were due to a new general manager, Sam (later Sir Sam) Fay, who understood the need for good publicity and high standards of service. Timings were reduced, through services introduced to Bradford and Huddersfield using the LCR, and to Stratford-upon-Avon using the Stratford-upon-Avon & Midland Junction Railway. Buses were laid on to carry arriving passengers to the West End, for which Marylebone was well placed, and to the City, for which it was not.

Before Fay joined the GCR, the MR had completed quadrupling its lines as far as Harrow, and later, in 1906, the MR lines to Chesham, Brill and Verney Junction were leased to a new joint operating company of the GCR and Metropolitan, with the companies taking turns every five years to manage and staff the line. The agreement was that the GCR should not take local traffic between Marylebone and Harrow, but it was allowed to develop suburban traffic on the joint lines. The GCR soon took advantage of this, introducing local trains to Chesham and Aylesbury from March 1906. A year later, the opening of the Bakerloo tube line meant that Marylebone had good quick connections throughout the West End and to Waterloo and Charing Cross.

Despite the new found alliance between the GCR and the Metropolitan, the former still wanted a new route of its own. The Met. line was more steeply graded than the GCR wanted for its planned express network, and also the curves were too severe for high-speed running, especially at Aylesbury, which had a severe reverse curve. The answer lay in using the Great Western's new line from Paddington to Birmingham, with a connecting line from near Quinton Road to Ashendon, and then from Neasden to Northolt. The shared section of the main line was managed jointly by a committee of the GCR and GWR. In return for its generosity, the GWR had the GCR abandon its own plans for a route to Birmingham. The new route also offered new local and suburban possibilities, and brought welcome new traffic to Marylebone.

There was one serious accident at Marylebone. During the afternoon of 28 March 1913, a train arriving from Leicester was crossing to Platform 4 as a train left Platform 3 for High Wycombe. The fireman on the High Wycombe train could not see the starter signal which was obscured by smoke from the Leicester train, but the driver could see that the intermediate starter was off and believed that his foreman could see the starter signal. Too late, the driver realised his mistake and braked, but his locomotive collided with the last carriage of the up train, killing one passenger and injuring 23, while five passengers on his train suffered slight injuries.

The terminus was largely unaffected by the First World War, and by retaining restaurant cars and not reducing train speeds by too much, it actually increased its share of the market.

Grouping

The GCR passed into the London & North Eastern Railway under Grouping, giving the company three termini in London. The LNER reduced the use of the joint line with the GWR, but suburban traffic continued to grow. When Wembley Stadium opened in 1923, sporting events ensured that Marylebone became busy, while the British Empire Exhibition at Wembley Park in 1924 and 1925, prompted modernisation of the signalling. During the first year of the exhibition, a ten-minute frequency non-stop service was provided that was superior to the Metropolitan alternative.

The LNER was, if anything, even shorter of funds for investment than the GCR had been. The recession and the strikes of 1926 saw much of its coal traffic lost, and as the member of the 'Big Four' most dependent upon goods traffic, the years of the Depression had the worst effect.

In 1937, the LNER took over the London Transport line between Rickmansworth and Aylesbury, which it served from Marylebone.

Marylebone itself escaped unscathed during the Second World War, with a few incendiary bombs soon extinguished, but the tunnel approach through St John's Wood was badly damaged, forcing Marylebone to close between 5 October and 26 November 1940, with single-line working until August 1942. The goods depot was destroyed by fire on 16 April 1941. Finally, towards the end of the war, the signalbox was hit by a flying bomb, killing two men.

Chapter 3

LNER Destinations

The London & North Eastern Railway served a wide variety of destinations with little in common. They included industrial Glasgow and Manchester, but the industries in these two cities differed considerably as did Doncaster and Sheffield; there was Edinburgh, a major financial centre and port; Aberdeen and Hull had the fishing industry in common, but Norwich was a market town. There was shipbuilding at Newcastle. The fact was that the services from Liverpool Street and from King's Cross had very little in common, and could have been separate railways, indeed some would have wished they had remained so. The services from Marylebone reflected the folie de grandeur of the Great Central Railway, and while doubtless useful for a small proportion of its passengers and merchants, the vast majority of its destinations and traffic were already served by other railways.

As with the London Midland & Scottish, the LNER had a core, or even a spine, to its network. The former was the logical successor to the West Coast Group of Companies and the latter the logical successor to the East Coast Group of Companies. Nevertheless, both had extensive additional operations that made management difficult and made finding a common theme to the operations or the destinations impossible.

Developed from the C7 4-4-2 was the Raven Pacific, the LNER's first A2 class of 4-6-2s. This is No. 2403 *City of Durham* at Edinburgh Haymarket in 1927. These large locomotives worked the Anglo-Scottish expresses, but still needed a banker for some of the gradients on the line north to Aberdeen. (*HMRS AAB 203*)

Aberdeen

Prior to the advent of the railway, Aberdeen was isolated and the most reliable means of transport was by sea. Such was the enthusiasm for the new mode of transport that the Harbour Board made a site available close to the centre of the city for a terminus. While a prospectus was issued for the Aberdeen Railway as early as 1844, proposing a link with the Northern Junction Railway at Forfar, difficulties in construction, with a viaduct collapsing and a bridge being swept away in a flood, as well as the financial crisis of 1848, meant that the line did not open until 1850.

Meanwhile, the Great North of Scotland Railway approached the city from the north, using much of the route of the Aberdeen Canal which was abruptly drained for the purpose. The GNSR did not share the Guild Street terminus of the AR but instead stopped at Waterloo Quay, 1½ miles away. It was not until 1867 that a connecting line through the Denburn Valley was completed and a joint station opened. This was replaced in 1915 by the present station, completed in sandstone.

The opening of the railway benefited both the fishing industry and agriculture, with Aberdeenshire farmers specialising in cattle fattening. Instead of sending live cattle by sea, butchered meat could be sent south by rail. Initially the city was reached from the south by the West Coast route, but after the completion of the bridges over the Forth and Tay, overnight fish and meat trains could reach the London markets at Billingsgate and Smithfield. A small network of commuter services was also established around Aberdeen, with workmen's trains to the Stoneywood paperworks by 1870, and later a suburban service linking the city with Dyce, so that by the turn of a century, 2 million passengers a year were being carried. Nevertheless, these were short distance passengers and stations were close together, with eight in the six miles to Dyce, so the service was vulnerable when motorbus competition appeared after the First World War, and the suburban service ended in 1937.

Doncaster

Even before the advent of the railway, Doncaster was an important coaching town on the long journey from London to the North of England and Scotland, but it was not until 1849 that the Great Northern Railway reached the town and made a connection four miles to the north with the Lancashire & Yorkshire Railway. Nevertheless, Doncaster soon became one of the greatest British railway towns, with the GNR opening its works in 1853, adding 3,000 to the local population within a very short time, for which the company built two schools and its shareholders subscribed to the building of a church. Within half-a-century, the works was employing 4,500 men and had 60 miles of sidings, which were largely cleared every September to allow space for stabling the passenger rolling stock for race specials arriving for the St Leger race meeting, which was transformed into a popular event in the racing calendar.

Doncaster became an important junction with direct lines to both Sheffield and Hull, while it was also the main centre for marshalling the coal trains from the South Yorkshire collieries, brought by the South Yorkshire Railway which also connected the town with the steelworks at Scunthorpe. Grouping led to the town becoming the main works for the London & North Eastern Railway.

Edinburgh

Scotland's capital was already a tightly built up area by the time the railways arrived, while the topography included high ridges running from east to west. There was substantial passenger traffic to be had from the affluent areas around the city centre, but goods traffic depended on being able to reach the port and industrial area of Leith to the north, and the coal mining areas

The large signal box at Edinburgh Waverley West, with the National Gallery of Scotland and the Castle Hill rising in the background. (*HMRS AAM 315*)

to the south. The first railway was the horse-drawn Edinburgh & Dalkeith, which was extended to the docks at Leith, but which was effectively a tramroad.

When the first steam railway, the Edinburgh & Glasgow, reached the city, it stopped in the West End, then under construction, at Haymarket, with strong local opposition to any further advance eastwards. It was not until the North British Railway arrived in 1846 that a short connecting line was built under the shadow of the castle to a new joint station at Waverley, situated out of sight in a valley that divided the medieval Old Town from the Georgian New Town. The Edinburgh Leith & Granton Railway, next to be built, had its platforms at right angles to those of the NBR at Waverley and ran in tunnel under the New Town.

Clearly heading south to the Forth Bridge and Edinburgh is this N2/3 0-6-2T, No. 894 steaming out of the tunnel at North Queensferry. (*HMRS ADG404*)

History repeated itself in 1848 when the Caledonian Railway reached Edinburgh, having to stop at the bottom of Lothian Road, close to the western end of Princes Street, which it took as its name. Nevertheless, by 1850, the NBR provided a link to the north of England and eventually this became the East Coast Main Line, and the opening of a branch to Hawick later led the way through the Border Union Railway to Carlisle, giving the NBR a second route over the border and Edinburgh a second route to Carlisle, and south via the Midland Railway. The last major link in the network of railways in and around Edinburgh followed in 1890 with the completion of the Forth Bridge, which meant that the city sat astride the most direct route between Aberdeen and London.

Included in the Edinburgh network were a number of suburban and country branches, with lines opened to Polton and North Berwick in 1850, Peebles in 1855, Dolphinton in 1864, Penicuik in 1876, and Gullane in 1898. There was also a link line to Galashiels, while a light railway was opened to Gifford in 1901. Eventually, a number of routes of varying degrees of directness linked Edinburgh and Glasgow. In 1884, the NBR opened the Edinburgh & District Suburban Railway. The inner suburban railways soon suffered from competition from electric trams, and this was especially so of the EDSR, which was laid out as an oval and so often did not provide the most direct route between two points.

Most of these lines terminated at Waverley, which became very congested and needed rebuilding in 1890, and has been rebuilt again in 2007. A new station at Leith was opened to ease the pressure on Waverley, but Leith Central was not convenient for most of the passenger traffic, and especially not for the first-class traveller looking for an express. Both the NBR and the Caledonian built branches into the docks at Leith.

The NBR had two locomotive sheds in Edinburgh, at Haymarket and St Margaret's, but after merging with the Edinburgh & Glasgow, it transferred most of its heavy work to Cowlairs at Glasgow.

Not all of the big locomotive sheds were in London or the major cities of the north of England, as this is a scene at Glasgow Eastfield in 1935. The coaling tower is visible in the background. (*HMRS AEP 007*)

Linlithgow station, looking east, on the main line between Edinburgh Waverley and Glasgow Queen Street, the most direct route between Scotland's two largest cities. (*HMRS AAM 316*)

Glasgow

Once known as the 'Workshop of the British Empire', Glasgow, the largest city in Scotland with twice Edinburgh's population, was one of the world's leading industrial cities during the 19th century, with a substantial proportion of the world's merchant shipping built on the Clyde. This was not a one-industry city, however, and its engineering activities included several major railway locomotive works, some of which were independent, and later commercial vehicles were also built, while lighter engineering included the Singer sewing machine factory and there were also cotton mills and breweries. These industries and the surrounding coal mines were served by a rudimentary network of tramroads developed during the 18th century.

Glasgow's first railway was the Glasgow & Garnkirk, opened in 1831, which soon built an extension to a temporary wooden terminus at Buchanan Street, which was taken over by the Caledonian Railway, initially for services to Aberdeen, but it later also became the terminus for services to London Euston. The city soon became a focal point for a growing number of railways, with the next being the Glasgow Paisley Kilmarnock & Ayr, which shared a terminus at Bridge Street, south of the Clyde, with the Glasgow Paisley & Greenock. North of the river was the Edinburgh & Glasgow's Queen Street station, initially reached by a cable-working from Cowlairs.

Initially, the Clyde proved to be a major barrier with the north and the south of the city kept separate, partly because of Admiralty objections to a fixed bridge. The river was not bridged until 1876 when the Glasgow & South Western sent its line into St Enoch, also the terminus for Midland Railway services from London St Pancras. In 1879, the CR opened Glasgow Central station. The North British Railway was able to use land vacated by the university as it sought more suitable premises, and also had the support of the city council in demolishing some particularly bad slums, in building its sidings and sheds, while it used Queen Street, acquired with the EGR. Between 1885 and 1910, the rival companies each built their own competing lines into the docks and many industrial areas. Suburban and even urban routes proliferated, and included the Glasgow Subway, a separate 4ft gauge circular route initially worked by cable.

Glasgow was the only city outside London to have a Royal Commission on its railways, but unlike that in London, which imposed an inner limit on construction of new surface lines and termini, that in Glasgow had no effect. The city's industry contributed much, and the CR in particular was predominantly a freight railway, but even so, passenger numbers at Central station rose from 4.75 million in 1880 to reach 15.75 million in 1897. The termini included hotels, such as the St Enoch, which when opened, was the largest hotel in Scotland. Suburban lines developed on a scale second only to London, including the famous 'Cathcart Circle', albeit never a true circle, which operated out of Glasgow Central. The expansion of Central between 1901 and 1905 took it over Argyll Street, which famously, became a meeting place for exiled Highlanders, known as the Highlandman's Umbrella, or, colloquially, Hielanman's Umbrella.

As with other major cities, passenger numbers began to fall as the urban and inner suburban networks soon proved vulnerable to competition, first from the electric tram, and then after the First World War, from the motor bus. Cathcart Circle or not, traffic at Central began to decline from 1905 onwards. Glasgow also began to lose its competitive edge, with heavy industry beginning a slow decline, while the 1926 Miners' Strike hit demand for coal particularly hard. To counter this, new stations were opened close to new residential or industrial developments. The Glasgow Subway was taken over by the city and electrified between the wars.

Grouping had little impact on the pattern of railways services. There was some rationalisation of the networks to the south-west, mainly favouring the former G&SWR lines than those of the rival CR, but plans to rationalise the four termini (Buchanan Street, which would have been enlarged, Central, Queen Street and St Enoch), into two failed, for regardless of the economies that could have been achieved and the greater convenience of passengers, the money was simply not available. Another plan never implemented was to expand the Glasgow Subway.

Hull

Unlike Southampton, which owes its importance as a port to the railways, Hull was already an important port attracting traffic from a large area to the east of the Pennines. By the late 18th century, the port was already inadequate and three further docks were built between 1778 and 1829. The railway first reached Hull in 1840, when the Hull & Selby (see Leeds & Selby) ran along the banks of the Humber to its terminus at Manor House, close to the docks. Further lines were sent into the town, with the next being the York & North Midland Railway's line to Bridlington in 1846, which leased the Hull & Selby before itself becoming part of the North Eastern Railway. Paragon station opened in 1848, closer to the city centre, while Manor House became a goods station. The docks were further extended in 1850, with a railway connection into the new Victoria Dock.

By this time, Hull also had a railway connection from the south, but by ferry, when the Manchester Sheffield & Lincolnshire Railway, predecessor of the Great Central, provided a service across the Humber from New Holland. As with the London & South Western at Southampton, the NER's monopoly made it unpopular in Hull, but a rival emerged in 1885 in the form of the Hull & Barnsley Railway, but before long both companies collaborated in the building of the King George V Dock, and amalgamated almost on the eve of Grouping in 1922.

Leeds

A centre both of industry and, from the days of the canals, transport, Leeds had its first railway as early as 1758, when the first Parliamentary authority for a railway was obtained by Charles Brandling, for a double-track 4ft 1in gauge wooden wagonway from his colliery at Middleton to Leeds Bridge. Worked by horses, the line opened that year and for a while gave Brandling a monopoly over the coal supply to industry in Leeds. The Middleton Railway later became the first on which a steam locomotive ran commercially on rails, but this was in 1812.

The railway age can truly be said to have reached Leeds as early as 1834 when the Leeds & Selby Railway opened, linking the city from its station at Marsh Lane with the rivers Ouse and Humber, where passengers could catch a steam packet to Hull. The LSR was soon followed by two more significant railways, the North Midland Railway linking the city with Derby to the south, opened in 1840, and the following year it provided access to Leeds for the Manchester & Leeds Railway, giving a strategic link through the Pennines. None of these railways managed to get closer than a mile from the town centre, until, in 1846, the Leeds & Bradford Railway ran into the Central station. This was originally intended to be an imposing structure that could be used by all of the city's railways, but in the end, the only other users were the Great Northern and the Lancashire & Yorkshire. Meanwhile, the NMR had become part of the Midland Railway and its Wellington terminus was becoming congested as it was also used by the London & North Western and North Eastern railways. The solution was to build the New Station, a collection of dark arches that straddled the River Aire and the canal, but unlike many city centre stations, lacked a frontage. All three railways used New Station, and the NER built a connection through the LSR's terminus at Marsh Lane providing a through route from Leeds to York and Hull.

The improved communications provided by this network of railways benefited industry in Leeds, which rapidly became the major centre of the textile trade, while several steam locomotive builders, amongst whom were Fowler; Hudswell, Clarke; Hunslet; Kitson and Manning Wardle, also based themselves in the city. It was not until 1938 that the scheme for a single station was realised, when Wellington and New were connected to provide Leeds City, but even this was a makeshift solution and it was not until 1967 that a new Leeds City was completed and Central station could close.

Manchester

The opening of the Liverpool & Manchester Railway in 1830 was a reflection of the city's importance as a centre for the cotton industry in particular, for which it needed access to the docks at Liverpool both for the import of raw materials and the export of finished goods. Nevertheless, that not all was well in relations between the two cities was demonstrated by the opening of the Manchester Ship Canal in 1894 to avoid the high harbour dues at Liverpool. The Manchester Ship Canal Company became a major railway operator in its own right and one that escaped Grouping by running entirely through the dock system. The history of Manchester's

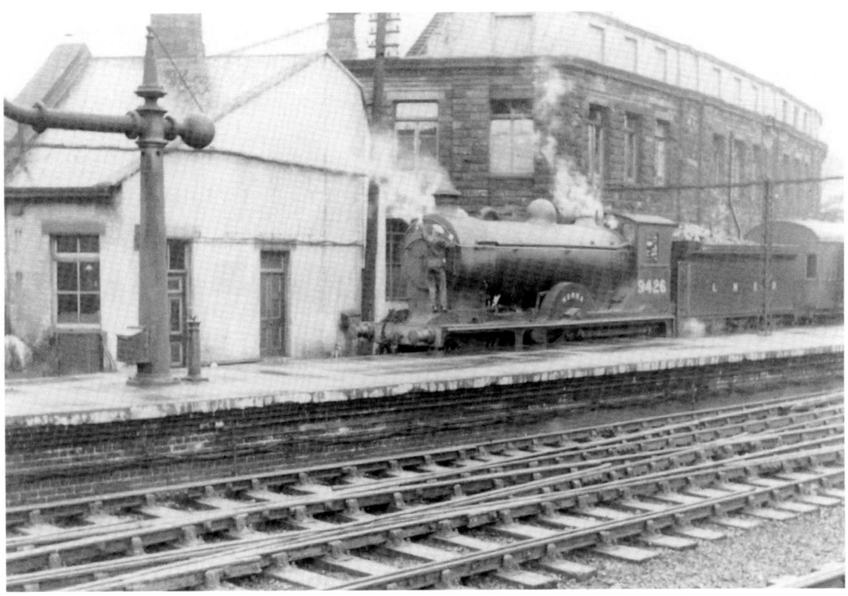

Just a small part of the large station at Newcastle Central in 1939, with a local train headed by D30 class 4-4-0 No. 9426 *Norna*. (*HMRS ACW 501*)

railway network is bound up with that of four companies, the London & North Western, the Midland and the Lancashire & Yorkshire, all of which were merged into the LMS, and the Great Central, which became a constituent company of the LNER.

Newcastle

Horse-worked wagon ways or tramways existed on both sides of the River Tyne from early in the 18th century, while the Newcastle & Carlisle Railway reached Gateshead in 1837, leaving passengers to be ferried across the river. The Tyne was bridged by the NCR in 1839, which also extended its line into the centre of Gateshead. In 1844 the Great North of England and the Newcastle & Darlington Junction railways provided a through line to York and London from Gateshead, but could not bridge the Tyne because of the depth of the gorge. It was not until George Hudson agreed in 1844 to provide a double-deck structure carrying trains on the upper level and wagons below, that a bridge could be built by Robert Stephenson. Completed in 1849, at the then astronomical cost of £500,000, Newcastle Central was opened the following year.

For a while, the NER had a monopoly of railway services in and around Tyneside, but this was broken in 1864 when the Blyth & Tyne Railway entered the city with its terminus at Picton House. However, the port of Blyth did not fulfil its promise and in 1874, the BTR was purchased by the NER. It was not until the opening of the King Edward VII Bridge, west of Stephenson's high level bridge, in 1906, that trains running through, to and from Scotland, were spared the time-consuming reversal at Central.

Newcastle was the first city in the British Isles to have its surface suburban railways electrified when the NER introduced the third-rail system with multiple unit operation on its North Tyneside network, starting in 1904. This was followed in 1905 by a short overhead system on the steep line to the quayside, with electric power obviously being attractive given the steep gradient. The NER also considered electrification of the East Coast Main Line between Newcastle and York, but strangely not northwards, possibly because the line soon passed into North British territory.

Not quite what it seems, this is No. 2870, *City of London*, one of the two B17 4-6-0s rebuilt with A4-style streamlining for publicity purposes to promote the East Anglian services. Here, it heads an express to Norwich in 1940. (*HMRS AEU 105*)

Two C1 class 4-4-2s, with No. 3272 leading, head a train at Cambridge in 1939. Is that another photographer on the left? (*HMRS AEU 815*)

Grouping had little impact on railway services in the area, except that the LNER electrified the South Tyneside suburban network using the same third-rail system as in the north to ensure interoperability, but post-Nationalisation, a number of branch lines were closed.

Norwich

Incredible as it might seem today, in 1831, Norwich was the eighth most populous city in England and Wales, as an important market town with other industries such as textile manufacture and brewing, as well as being a cathedral city and the county town. Despite this, and the largely level countryside for many miles around Norwich, the railways did not reach the city until 1845, with a line from Cambridge meeting up with another from Great Yarmouth. The Norfolk Railway was formed from a merger of the Norwich & Brandon, which linked into the Eastern Countries Railway coming from Cambridge at Brandon, and the locally funded Yarmouth & Norwich Railway.

Although a direct line by the Eastern Counties was authorised as early as 1836, it did not open until 1849, and even then an inter-company disagreement at Colchester meant that through trains could not run until 1854. Peace did not really come until the Great Eastern Railway was formed in 1862 when the main railways in East Anglia merged.

The result of the piecemeal development of the railways around the city meant that it had two stations. The station at Thorpe handled trains from Cambridge and Yarmouth, while Victoria was used for trains from Ipswich. It was not until 1886 after enlargement that Thorpe became the main station, although Victoria was used by some passenger trains until 1916 and the economies forced upon the railways by the First World War.

Norwich eventually became a hub for the branch lines to the north of the county, but this also took longer than one would have expected given the importance of agriculture and fishing. The line to Cromer did not open until 1877, and eventually no fewer than eight railways converged on the city. A third station, Norwich City, had to be opened when the Lynn & Fakenham Railway, later part of the Midland & Great Northern Railway, reached the city in 1882. Many believe that the railways into and around Norwich would have been better coordinated had the council moved the central cattle market to Trowse, a suburb on the railway. This is one city that did not grow with the railways; by 1951, it had slipped from the eighth most populous city to the 30th!

Sheffield

An old centre for the iron industry, the coming of the railways enabled the industry and the new steel industry to grow rapidly and the city became famous for its cutlery, the population tripling between 1843 and 1893. The railways performed the double act of not only improving transport for raw materials and fuel, and for the finished articles, but also of being a major market for steel plate and rails.

Strong competition developed between the Midland Railway and the equally ambitious Manchester, Sheffield & Lincolnshire Railway, which later renamed itself as the Great Central ready for its advance on London. Yet, at the outset, George Stephenson planned the North Midland Railway in such a way that the city was by-passed and was served by a branch line. A direct rail link to Manchester was delayed by the massive engineering feat needed to take the railway through the Pennines, with the need for a three-mile-long tunnel under the watershed at Woodhead, and despite being authorised in 1837, this and the inevitable funding difficulties for such a costly route, meant that the 35-mile long line was not completed until 1845.

The city's early railway termini were shabby and cheaply built, with that for Manchester having to make do with a temporary wooden structure at Brighouses.

When the Sheffield, Ashton-under-Lyme & Manchester Railway was absorbed into the Manchester, Sheffield & Lincolnshire Railway in 1847, matters started to improve and an extension opened to Gainsborough and Grimsby in 1849. The MSLR opened a new terminus worthy of the city at Victoria in 1851, with a glass roof.

By 1864, Sheffield was producing 96 per cent of Britain's cast steel, and moves were made to construct a north–south railway line, largely underground, but nothing came of this, and it was not until 1870 when the Midland built a line from Chesterfield to a new station at Pond Street that the city eventually found itself on a main line. This came at a cost, with the demolition of a thousand homes, a significant proportion for a city with a population of 200,000. The Midland developed its services with a new line through to Manchester, which required a tunnel of more than 3½ miles at Totley, while Pond Street was rebuilt and enlarged in 1906.

The LNER tried to gain an advantage over what had become the LMS route to Manchester by starting electrification of the Woodhead route on a 1,500V dc overhead system in 1936, but wartime delays meant that this was not completed until 1954, well after Nationalisation.

LONDON, SHENFIELD, WICKFORD, and SOUTHEND-ON-SEA.—Great Eastern.

Miles from Shenfield	Down.	Week Days.																					
		1&3 mrn	1&3 mrn	1&3 mrn	1&3 mrn	mrn	1&3 mrn	mrn	1&3 mrn	1&3 mrn	1&3 noon	aft	S aft	S aft	S aft		S aft	E aft	S aft	S aft	E 1&3	E aft	S aft
	Liverpool Street...dep.	5 10	5 26	6 54	7 48	....	9 1	9 6	10 3	1030	11 56	....	1248	....	1 20	...	1 50	....	....	....	2 0	....	2 [illegible]
	276 Colchester 301 dep.	....	....	....	7 34	7 41	8 21	....	9 34	....	11 5	....	....	....	....	...	1253	....	....	1 17	1 17	....	....
—	Shenfield & Hutton dep.	5 55	6 29	8 0	8 37	9 2	9 50	....	1042	1123	12 38	1242	1 21	....	....	...	2 22	....	2 27	2 40	2 43	2 47	....
4¼	Billericay	....	6 38	8 8	....	9 10	9 59	1020	1051	1131	....	1250	1 29	....	....	...	....	....	2 35	2 47	....	2 55	....
8¾	Wickford arr.	....	6 45	8 15	....	9 17	10 5	1027	1058	1137	....	1257	1 35	....	....	...	....	....	2 42	2 53	....	3 2	[illegible]
	Wickford dep.	....	6 49	8 17	8 54	9 25	10 8	1029	11 1	1139	....	1 0	1 36	1 41	....	...	....	....	2 43	2 54	....	3 4	[illegible]
12¾	Rayleigh	....	6 58	8 26	8 56	9 34	....	1038	....	1148	....	1 9	....	1 50	2 10	...	....	2 40	2 52	3 3	....	3 13	....
15¾	Hockley	....	7 4	8 32	....	9 40	....	1044	....	1154	....	1 15	....	1 56	2 17	...	....	2 46	2 58	3 9	....	3 19	....
18½	Rochford	6 19	7 10	8 38	....	9 46	....	1050	1114	12 0	1 2	1 21	....	2 2	2 23	...	....	2 52	3 4	3 15	....	3 25	....
20½	Prittlewell 653	6 23	7 14	8 42	....	9 50	....	1054	1118	12 4	1 6	1 25	1 51	2 6	2 27	...	2 49	2 56	3 8	3 19	3 9	3 29	[illegible]
21¼	Southend-on-Sea arr.	6 27	7 18	8 46	9 16	9 54	1025	1058	1122	12 8	1 10	1 29	1 55	2 10	2 31	...	2 53	3 0	3 12	3 23	3 13	3 33	[illegible]

Down.	Week Days—*Continued.*																						
	S aft	E aft	S aft	S aft	1&3 aft	b aft	1&3 aft	E a	S aft	E aft	aft	E aft	E aft	E 1&3		E aft	S 1&3	E aft	S aft	E aft	E 1&3	S 1&3	E aft
Liverpool Street...dep.	....	2 20	2 58	....	3 26	4 15	4 18	4 48	....	5 23	5 39	6 5	....	6 26	....	....	6 26	7 10	....	7 16	8 2	8 2	....
276 Colchester 301 dep.	....	1 17	....	....	2 14	....	....	....	....	....	4 9	5 22	....	5 22	....	....	5 22	....	....	....	7 8	7 8	....
Shenfield & Hutton dep.	....	3 17	3 31	3 35	4 18	....	4 59	5 19	....	....	6 12	6 38	6 43	7 3	....	7 7	7 12	....	....	7 54	8 39	8 40	8 43
Billericay	....	3 27	3 39	3 43	4 25	....	5 7	5 27	....	....	6 20	....	6 50	....	....	7 15	7 20	....	....	8 2	....	8 48	8 51
Wickford arr.	....	3 33	....	3 49	4 32	4 54	5 14	5 34	....	....	6 27	....	6 56	....	....	7 22	7 27	....	....	8 9	....	8 54	8 57
Wickford dep.	3 16	3 37	....	3 52	4 35	4 55	5 16	5 35	....	....	6 29	....	6 57	....	....	7 24	7 29	....	7 55	8 10	....	8 56	8 59
Rayleigh	3 25	3 47	3 51	4 1	4 44	....	5 25	5 43	5 56	....	6 38	....	7 5	7 21	....	7 33	7 38	7 57	8 4	8 19	....	9 5	[illegible]
Hockley	3 31	3 53	....	4 7	4 50	....	5 31	5 50	6 2	....	6 44	....	7 11	....	....	7 39	7 44	....	8 10	8 25	....	9 11	9 14
Rochford	3 37	3 59	....	4 13	4 56	5 8	5 37	5 56	6 8	....	6 50	....	7 17	....	....	7 45	7 50	...	8 16	8 31	....	9 17	9 20
Prittlewell 653	3 41	4 3	4 2	4 17	5 0	5 12	5 41	6 0	6 12	6 20	6 54	7 3	7 21	7 34	....	7 49	7 54	8 7	8 20	8 35	9 4	9 21	9 24
Southend-on-Sea arr.	3 45	4 7	4 6	4 21	5 4	5 16	5 45	6 4	6 16	6 24	6 58	7 8	7 25	7 38	....	7 55	7 58	8 11	8 24	8 39	9 8	9 25	9 28

Down.	Week Days—*Continued.*								Sundays.														
	aft	E 1&3	S 1&3	E aft	1&3 aft	1&3 ngt.	ngt.		mrn	mrn	mrn	mrn	mrn	mrn	1&3 mrn	aft	aft	aft	1&3 aft	1&3 aft	aft	aft	1&3 aft
Liverpool Street...dep.	8 45	9 45	9 45	....	11 0	12 0	....	....	....	8 30	8 45	9 30	1030	1045	1130	....	2 30	....	6 0	6 42	8 46	....	[illegible]
276 Colchester 301 dep.	....	8 43	8 43	....	9B30	....	....	....	....	....	....	....	....	1024	....	....	....	....	5 47	....	7 9	....	....
Shenfield & Hutton dep.	9 22	1019	1019	1026	1149	1236	....	....	....	9 20	9 52	1024	1120	1145	1220	....	3 37	....	6 50	7 35	9 44	....	11 [illegible]
Billericay	9 29	....	1026	1034	1157	1243	....	....	....	....	10 0	1034	....	1155	....	....	3 46	....	....	7 45	9 52	....	[illegible]
Wickford arr.	9 35	....	1032	1041	12 3	1249	....	....	....	....	10 7	1041	....	12 2	....	....	3 53	....	....	7 52	9 59	....	[illegible]
Wickford dep.	9 36	....	1033	1042	12 4	1250	1257	....	8 20	....	10 9	1045	....	12 5	....	2 40	3 55	5 50	....	7 56	10 0	1020	1117
Rayleigh	9 45	....	1042	1051	1212	....	1 6	....	8 29	9 38	1018	1054	....	1214	....	2 49	4 4	5 59	7 8	8 5	10 9	1029	1126
Hockley	9 51	....	1048	1057	1218	....	1 12	....	8 35	9 44	1024	11 0	....	1220	....	2 55	4 10	6 5	7 14	8 11	1015	1035	1132
Rochford	9 57	....	1054	11 3	1224	....	1 18	....	8 43	9 50	1030	11 6	1147	1226	1247	3 1	4 16	6 11	7 20	8 17	1021	1041	1138
Prittlewell 653	10 1	1043	1058	11 7	1228	1 5	1 22	....	8 47	9 54	1034	1110	1151	1230	1251	3 5	4 20	6 15	7 24	8 21	1025	1045	1142
Southend-on-Sea arr.	10 5	1047	11 2	1111	1232	1 9	1 26	....	8 51	9 58	1038	1114	1155	1234	1255	3 9	4 24	6 19	7 28	8 25	1029	1049	1146

a 3rd class Pullman Car, London to Southend-on-Sea. *b* 3rd class Pullman Car, London to Southend-on-Sea on Saturdays only. **B** Via Brentwood. **E** Except Saturdays. **S** Saturdays only.

Services between London Liverpool Street and Southend improved considerably between 1922 and 1938, with the LNER service (*overleaf*) being much more frequent, and also a little faster than the GER service (*above*), despite the line not being electrified. (*Bradshaw*)

Southend

This was the main resort served by the LNER. Railways reached Southend in 1856 after delays caused by rivalry between the London & Blackwall Railway and the Eastern Counties Railway. The problem was resolved by an act of 1852 which authorised a joint line from Forest Gate via Tilbury, but the driving force was the contractor Samuel Peto, who not only built the line

LONDON, SHENFIELD, WICKFORD, and SOUTHEND-ON-SEA

Down — Week Days

Down	mn	mn	mn	mn	mn	mn	mn	mn	mrn	mrn	mrn	mrn S	mrn S	mrn Y	mrn	mrn S	mrn S	mrn	non	aft E	aft S	aft S	aft S	aft E	aft	aft S	aft E	aft S
London (L S) dp.	510	538	..	655	747	..	832	845	9 1	9 6	9 26	..	9 45	10 7	1030	1046	1121	10 49	12N0	..	1213	1246	..	1219	1 20	1 13	..	151
Brentwood & W. "	548	627	..	742	830	..	913	928	9 43	10 6	10 20	..	..	1043	1116	1129	..	11 45	12N38	..	..	..	..	1 16	..	2 1	158	..
Shenfield & H. "	555	633	..	755	836	..	919	938	9 49	1012	10 30	1035	1043	1049	1125	1142	..	11X53	12K45	1249	..	1 18	..	1 26	1E56	2 7	225	224
Billericay "	6 3	640	..	8 3	844	..	926	944	9 57	1019	10E36	1041	1050	1056	1132	1148	..	11X59	12S46	1256	1256	1 25	..	1 32	..	213	231	..
Wickford arr	610	646	..	8 9	850	..	932	949	10 3	1025	10E43	1047	1056	11 2	1138	1154	12 1	12X4	12N57	1 2	..	1 31	..	1 37	2E8	219	236	..
Wickford dep	611	648	721	811	852	859	934	950	10 5	1027	10E44	1048	1057	11 3	1139	..	12 2	12X5	12N58	1 5	..	1 32	141	1 38	2E9	220	237	..
Rayleigh	620	656	727	820	..	9 5	943	956	..	1035	10E52	1055	11 5	..	1147	..	..	12X11	..	1 13	1 8	..	148	1 44	2 17	..	243	..
Hockley	626	7 2	733	826	..	911	949	102	..	1041	10E58	11 1	1111	..	1153	..	..	12X17	..	1 19	1 14	..	154	1 50	2S15	..	249	..
Rochford	632	7 7	737	831	..	915	954	106	1020	1046	11E3	11 5	1116	1117	1158	..	..	12X21	1N11	1 24	..	..	158	1 54	2S20	234	253	..
Prittlewell [674	636	711	741	836	..	919	958	109	..	1050	11E7	11 9	1120	1121	12 2	..	1217	12X25	1N15	1 28	1 21	1 47	2 2	1 58	2S28	238	257	248
Southend B ar.	639	714	744	839	912	922	10 1	104	1027	1053	11Y10	1112	1123	1124	12 5	..	1220	12X28	1N18	1 31	1 24	1 56	2 5	2 1	2 31	241	3 0	251

Down	aft S	aft E	aft S	aft E	aft S	aft S	aft S	aft E	aft S	aft S	aft E	aft S	aft	aft	aft	aft	aft E	aft S	aft E	aft S	aft E	aft	aft	aft E	aft S	aft E	aft S	aft E	aft E	aft S	aft E	aft
London (L S) dep.	..	2 0	..	..	230	..	223	2 30	257	..	250	..	332	415	..	418	448	..	..	..	522	5 0	539	6 1	..	6 5	6 8	626	..	626	646	7E10
Brentwood & W. "	..	234	229	..	..	..	3 7	3 12	325	..	341	350	411	..	4S26	448	..	457	..	..	..	540	..	..	..	634	647	656	..	7 4	..	..
Shenfield & H "	229	240	240	244	..	..	313	3 18	331	340	356	4 0	422	..	4 48	459	520	520	524	..	..	556	610	635	..	640	656	7 2	7 7	710	718	..
Billericay	236	..	247	250	..	..	320	3 25	339	346	4 2	4 6	428	..	4 55	5 5	..	526	530	..	..	6 3	617	..	..	646	7 2	7 9	713	718	724	..
Wickford arr.	242	..	253	255	3 9	..	326	3 31	..	352	4 7	412	434	454	5Z3	511	..	532	536	..	..	6 8	623	..	..	652	7 8	..	718	724	731	..
Wickford dep.	243	..	254	256	310	314	327	3 33	..	353	4 8	413	435	455	5Z4	512	..	533	537	549	..	6 9	625	..	..	663	7 9	..	719	726	732	..
Rayleigh	252	..	3 2	3 3	..	321	335	3 41	351	4 0	414	420	442	..	5 8	519	..	540	544	557	6 7	616	633	..	655	7 1	716	721	726	734	741	7K56
Hockley	257	..	3 8	3 8	..	327	341	3 47	..	4 6	420	426	448	..	5 14	525	..	546	550	6 3	..	622	638	..	7 1	7 7	722	..	731	740	746	7S57
Rochford	3 2	3 1	313	313	..	331	346	3V52	..	410	424	430	452	5 8	5 19	529	..	550	554	6 8	..	627	643	..	7 5	712	726	..	736	745	751	8S1
Prittlewell [674	3 6	3 5	317	316	325	335	350	3V56	4 2	414	428	434	456	512	5 23	533	542	554	558	612	618	631	647	657	7 9	716	730	731	739	749	755	8 5
Southend B arr.	3 9	3 8	320	319	328	338	353	3V59	4 5	417	431	437	459	515	5 26	536	545	557	6 1	615	621	634	650	7 0	712	719	733	734	742	752	758	8 8

Down — Week Days—*Continued*; Sundays

Down	aft E	aft S	aft E	aft S	aft E	aft	aft	aft E	aft	aft	aft	aft S	aft S	aft	aft	night	night	Sun. mn	mn	mn	mn	mn	mn	mn	mrn	mrn	mrn	mrn	mrn
London (L.S) dp	..	713	713	..	753	7S53	848	..	9 5	9 45	..	1028	..	11 0	..	12 0	..	..	8 5	..	820	827	835	850	8 57	9 20	9 27	..	..
Brentw'd & W. "	..	..	..	745	825	8S25	..	..	9 43	1012	..	1056	..	1141	..	1232	..	..	..	846	..	913	..	930	9 43	..	1013	..	1036
Shenf'ld & H. "	..	752	752	756	832	8N36	921	..	9 57	1019	1023	11 3	11 7	1152	1156	1239	..	..	..	852	..	919	..	936	9 49	..	1020	1024	1042
Billericay	..	..	8 0	8 3	838	8Z42	928	..	10 3	..	1030	..	1113	..	12 3	1246	..	..	..	..	..	927	..	..	..	..	..	1032	..
Wickford ar.	..	..	8 6	8 9	843	8 45	934	..	10 8	..	1036	..	1119	..	12 9	1252	..	..	..	..	..	934	..	..	..	1012	..	1039	..
Wickford dp.	754	..	8 7	813	844	8 47	935	..	10 9	..	1037	..	1120	..	1210	1253	1 0	821	..	..	..	935	..	..	..	1013	..	1040	..
Rayleigh	8 2	..	816	822	..	8 54	943	10 5	1015	..	1045D	..	1127	12 7	1217	..	1 8	828	..	..	..	944	..	..	..	..	..	1049	..
Hockley	8 8	..	822	828	..	9 0	949	1010	1021	..	1051D	..	1133	..	1223	..	114	835	..	..	..	950	..	..	..	..	..	1055	..
Rochford	813	..	827	834	..	9 4	954	1015	1025	..	1056H	..	1137	..	1227	..	119	840	..	..	..	955	..	..	..	..	..	11 0	..
Prittlewell [674	817	814	831	838	858	9 8	958	1018	1029	1041	11H0	1125	1141	1216	1231	1 8	123	844	..	..	..	959	..	..	..	..	..	11 4	..
Southend B ar.	820	817	834	841	9 1	9 11	101	1021	1032	1044	11H3	1128	1144	1219	1234	1 11	126	847	917	926	938	102	947	109	1023	1032	1053	11 7	1115

Down — Sundays—*Continued.*

Down	mrn	mrn	mrn	mrn	mrn	mrn	mrn	aft	aft	aft	aft	aft	aft	aft	aft	aft	aft	aft	aft	aft	aft	aft	aft	aft	aft	aft	aft	aft
London (L.S) dp	9 57	1020	1027	..	1057	1127	1157	..	1227	1 27	..	2 27	257	330	427	457	527	557	6 27	657	7 27	757	9 27	9 57	..	1038	..	1057
Brentw'd & W. "	1043	..	1113	..	1143	1213	1243	..	1 13	2 12	..	3 13	343	416	513	543	613	643	7 13	743	8 13	843	1013	1043	..	1120	..	1144
Shenf'ld & H. "	1049	..	1119	1123	1151	1219	1249	1253	1 19	2 19	230	3 23	349	422	519	553	619	649	7 19	749	8 19	849	1019	1049	1053	1127	1132	1152
Billericay	..	..	..	1131	1159	..	..	1 1	1 27	..	238	3 31	..	430	527	6 0	..	657	..	757	..	857	1027	..	11 0	..	1138	1158
Wickford ar.	..	..	..	1138	12 6	..	..	1 8	1 34	..	245	3 38	..	437	534	6 7	..	7 4	7 31	8 4	8 31	9 4	1034	..	11 7	..	1144	12 3
Wickford dp.	..	..	..	1139	12 7	..	..	1 9	1 40	..	246	3 39	..	438	535	6 8	..	7 5	7 32	8 5	8 32	9 5	1035	..	11 8	..	1145	12 4
Rayleigh	..	..	..	1148	1216	..	..	1 18	1 49	..	255	3 48	..	447	544	617	..	714	..	814	8 41	914	1044	..	1116	..	1152	1210
Hockley	..	..	..	1154	1222	..	..	1 24	1 55	..	3 1	3 54	..	453	550	623	..	720	..	820	8 47	920	1050	..	1122	..	1158	1216
Rochford	..	..	1143	12 0	1227	1243	1 13	1 30	2 0	2 43	3 6	3 59	..	458	555	628	..	725	..	825	..	925	1055	..	1127	..	12 2	1220
Prittlewell [676	..	..	1147	12 4	1231	1247	1 17	1 34	2 4	2 47	310	4 3	..	5 2	559	632	..	729	..	829	..	929	1059	..	1131	1149	12 6	1224
Southend B ar.	1123	1132	1151	12 7	1234	1250	1 20	1 37	2 7	2 50	313	4 6	423	5 5	6 2	635	653	732	7 53	832	8 58	932	11 2	1123	1134	1152	12 9	1227

Extra—Rochford to Southend-on-Sea, calling at Prittlewell: on Sats. at 2-48 aft. on Suns. at 2-56 aft.

Above: LNER Liverpool Street to Southend timetable of 1938.

Right: London to York timetable of 1922 (1938 is shown on page 58).

Left: A B12 class 4-6-0 takes a Southend train through Romford in 1938. (*HMRS AEQ 618*)

LONDON, PETERBRO', NOTTINGHAM, RETFORD, MANCHESTER, LIVERPOOL, DONCASTER, LEEDS, YORK, &c.—G.N.

Offices—King's Cross Station, N.1. Gen. Man., C. H. Dent. Sec., E. Burrows.

Week Days.

Miles	Down.	1	2	3	4	5	6	7	8	9	10	11	12	13	14	15	16	17	18	19	20	21	22	23	24	25	26	27	28	29
		mrn	mrn	mrn	mrn		mrn	mrn	mrn	mrn	mrn	mrn	non	mrn	mrn	mrn	mrn	mrn	mrn	aft	aft	aft	mrn	aft	mrn		aft	mrn	aft	aft
—	KING'S CROSS dep.				4 45			5 5		7 15				7 45	8 45		9 50	10 0	10 10				1025		11 20			11 30		
—	Broad Street "									London, Leeds, Harrogate, & Bradford Breakfast Car Exp.				7 38	8 34		East Coast Luncheon and Dining Car Express, London to Newcastle and Edinburgh	East Coast Luncheon and Dining Car Express, London to Glasgow, Perth, and Aberdeen.	London, Leeds, and Bradford Luncheon Car Express.				1011		Luncheon Cars, London to Scarboro'.			10 27		
2½	Finsbury Park "							5 19						7 53	8 52								1032					11 37		
17¾	Hatfield "							5 38						8 23	9 16								11 7					12 3		
—	350 Cambridge dep.													7 40	8 27								10 0					11 0		
32	Hitchin dep.							6 6	7 0					8 45	9 36								1138					12 25	1250	
36	Three Counties							6 13	7 7					8 52									1145						1258	
37	Arlesey and Shefford Road ‖							6 16	7 10					8 55									1149						1 1	
41	Biggleswade							6 25	7 19					9 4									1157					12 40	1 10	
44	Sandy 435							6 31	7 25					9 13	9 52								12 4					12 47	Saturdays only.	
47½	Tempsford							6 38	7 31					9 20									1222							
51¾	St. Neots							6 46	7 39					9 28									1230					12 59		
55¾	Offord and Buckden							6 53	7 46					9 35									1238							
58¾	Huntingdon 291, 656							6 59	7 55					9 43	1012								1246					1 10		
63½	Abbotts Ripton							7 8	8 4					9 53									1255							
69½	Holme 353 [663							7 18	8 14					10 4									1 6							
72½	Yaxley and Farcet [436, 437,							7 25	8 21					1011									1 13							
76¼	Peterbro' 289, 328, 358, arr.				6 12			7 31	8 27	8 42				1017	1034				11 37				1 19		1247			1 33		
160½	328 Cromer (Beach) arr.				10 10					1 22					2 45										4R33					
—	Peterbro' dep.				6 17			7 36		8 46	9 25				1039	1045			11 42						1252			1 39		1 45
84¾	Tallington **							7 50			9 41					1058														1 59
88¼	Essendine 335				6 35			7 59			9 52					11 7												1 58		2 8
92¼	Little Bytham ‡‡							8 7			10 2					1115														2 16
97	Corby							8 16			1013					1124														2 25
102	Great Ponton							8 27	Mondays only.		1026					1134														2 35
105½	Grantham 359, 360, 364 arr.				6 59			8 33		9 23	1035				1117	1140		12 8	12 19						1 30			2 24		2 41
130	359 Lincoln (High Street) arr.				8 5					10 26					1216													3 40		3 40
128½	364 Nottingham "				8 45			9 54							1230	1 7			1 7									3 34		3 34
	366 (Victoria) dep.				5 45			7 20		8 30					1035										1145					
—	Grantham dep.			6 25	7 4			8 38		9 25					1121			1213	12 21					1220	1 35			2 30		2 45
109¾	Barkston			6 32				8 45																1237						2 52
111½	Hougham			6 37				8 50																1242						2 57
115¼	Claypole [662			6 45				8 58																1250						3 5
120	Newark §§ 360, 364, 661 arr.			6 53	7 21			9 6							1139									1258	London, Harrogate, Scarborough, and Glasgow Express.			2 49		3 13
—	366 Nottingham (Vic.) dep.				6 20																							1 50		
—	Newark dep.			6 55	7 23			9 8							1141									1 0				2 51		3 15
126½	Carlton-on-Trent			7 5				9 19																1 10						3 25
127½	Crow Park, for Sutton-on-Trent			7 9				9 23																1 14						3 29
131½	Dukeries Junction 718							9 31																						Cc
132	Tuxford †			7 18				9 35																1 23						3 38
138½	Retford 703, 708 arr.			7 28	7 46			9 45		10 3					12 4									1 33				3 16		3 48
146	703 Worksop arr.			8 7	8 7	London, York, Leeds, and Bradford Express.		1022		10 22					1 33									3 8				4 31		4 31
161¼	708 Sheffield (Victoria) "			8 42	8 43			1045		10 45					2 10									3 44				4 57		4 57
237¾	709 Stockport (Tiviot Dale) "				11 14										3 53									5 54				8 58		8 58
203	709 Manchester (Lon. Rd) "			1010	10 10			1242		12 42					3 52									5 19				6 47		6 47
209	709 " (Central) "				11 4			1214		12 14														6e0				7e23		7e23
253¾	709 Southport (Lord St.) "							2 48		2 48					6 10									8 43				9 57		9 57
237¾	709 Liverpool (Central) "				12a15			1a15		1a15					5 0									6 33				8a15		8a15
—	Retford dep.				7 50		8 5			10 5		1015			12 6									1 35				3 19		
141¾	Barnby Moor and Sutton						8 11					1021												1 41						
144	Ranskill				7 58		8 16					1027												1 47				3 29		
145¾	Scrooby						8 20					1031												1 51						
147¾	Bawtry ††	5 35			8 5		8 25					1037			1219						1 40			1 57				3 37		
151¼	Rossington [709, 765	5 43					8 32					1045									1 48			2 5						
156	Doncaster 327, 337, 702, arr.	5 51			8 17		8 40			10 26		1053			1231		125V		1 17		1 56			2 15	2 32			3 51		
196¾	765 Hull (Paragon) arr.	8 15			10 20		1020			12 0		1232							2 40		3 42			3 50	3 50			5 31		
175¾	337 Wakefield (Westgte) arr.	8 13			9 0					10 56		12 4							1 47		3 9									
193½	368 Bradford (Exchange) "	9 42			9 52					11 45		1 12							2 30		4 22									
176½	374 Wakefield (Kirkgte) "	8 53			9 18					11 23									1 58		3 17									
201¾	370 Halifax 518 "				10 48					12 46		2 6							3 4		5 19									
190¾	518 Huddersfield "				12 J5					12 47									3 16		4 50									
185¼	337 Holbeck "	8 40			9 21					11 16		1231							2 6		3 39									
202¾	751 Harrogate arr.				10 44					12K5		1 48							3 18		5 10									
214¼	752 Ripon "				12 7					2 38		2 38							4 43		7 7									
201	518 Halifax (v. Holbeck) arr.	9e49			10 55							1 33							3e48		4e23									
195¼	372 Bradford (v. Holbeck) "	9 58			9 58					12 45		1 34							2 51		4 28									
185¾	337 Leeds (Central) "	8 44			9 25					11 20		1235							2 10		3 45									
—	Doncaster dep.		7 18		8 27					10 35			12 0		1236		1 3	Will not convey passengers from King's Cross to Newcastle.		1 40					2 38	2 44	3 35	3 57		
158	Arksey		7 23										12 5																	
163	Moss		7 32										1214													Via Church Fenton				
166	Balne ‡		7 38										1220																	
168½	Heck		7 42										1224																	
169¾	Temple Hirst		7 48										1230																	
174½	Selby 750, 768, 770 arr.		7 55		8 54					11 0			1237		1 1												4 8	4 22		
205¼	770 Hull (Paragon) arr.		9 26		9 55					12 41			1 33		3 9													6 28		
—	Selby dep.		8 1		8 59					11 5			1241		1 4							2 50					4 13	4 30		
178¾	Riccall		8 9										1249																	
181½	Escrick		8 15										1255																	
184	Naburn [763		8 21										1 1																	
188	York ¶ 728, 758, 761 to arr.		8 32		9 18					11 25			1 12		1 24			1 57		2 25		3 10			3 21		4 33	4 50		
208	763 Harrogate 728, 753 arr.		1034		11 20					1 42								4 18				4 18				3 45		5 33		
219½	752 Ripon 728, 753 "		10 5[illegible]		11 42					1 47								4 43				4 43				4 43	6 22	6 38		
230	758 Scarborough 761 "		10 5[illegible]		10 52					1 23								5 48		3 48		4 37			4 37			6 3		
268¼	728 Newcastle (Central) "				11 10					2 53					3 18		1 23	3 44		5 28					5 35		6 45			
335½	734 Berwick "				2 17													5 15							7 27					
393	776 Edinbro' (Waverley) "				1 45												6 20	6 30							8 45					
440½	790 Glasgow (Queen St.) "				3 10													7 45							10 0					
452¾	782 Dundee (Tay Bridge) "				3 45													8 24												
523½	782 Aberdeen § "				5 46													1026												
440¾	786 Perth (v. Forth Bridge) "				3 30													8 16							1046					
558¾	786 Inverness "				8 12													6A0												

For Notes, see pages 336 and 337; for Continuation of Trains, see pages 334 to 337.

LONDON, PETERBRO', GRANTHAM, RETFORD, MANCHESTER, LIVERPOOL, DONCASTER, LEEDS, YORK, &c.

Down. — **Week Days**—*Continued.*

Down.	1	2	3	4	5	6	7	8	9	10	11	12	13	14	15	16	17	18	19	20	21	22	23	24	25
	mrn	mrn	mrn	mrn	mrn	mrn	mrn	aft	mrn	aft	aft	mrn	aft	aft	mrn	mrn	mrn	mrn	mrn	mrn	mrn	mrn	mrn	mrn	mrn
			W				S															E			
LONDON (King's Cross) ..dep.	9 20	10 0	10 5	1010	1015	1015	1021	..	1028	..	..	1035	..	..	1050	11 0	1110	1120	..	1125	..	1040	1140	1150	
Finsbury Park .... "		..	..		..	..		..		..	..	1045	..	..	..	..	..		..	..	..	1048	..	..	
Hatfield .... "		..	..		..	..		..		..	..	11 2	..	..	..	..	..		..	..	..	1053	..	..	
866 CAMBRIDGE ......dep.		..	..		..	..		..		..	..	1020	..	..	..	..	..		..	..	..	1020	..	..	
Hitchin ......dep.		..	..		..	..		..		..	..	1142	..	..	..						..	1134	..		
Three Counties		..	..		..	..		..		..	..	1148	..	..	..						..	1142	..		
Arlesey and Henlow		..	..		..	..		..		..	..	1154	..	..	..						..	1145	..		
Biggleswade		..	..		..	..		..		..	..	12 2	..	..	..						..	1152	..		
Sandy 469		..	..		..	..		..		..	..	1215	..	..	..							1159	..		
Tempsford		..	..		..			..		..	..	1222	..	..	..							12 6	..		
St. Neots		..	..		..			..		..	..	1230	..	..	..							1215	..		
Offord and Buckden		..	..		..			..		..	..	1237	..	..	..							1222	..		
677 CAMBRIDGE M 879 ...dep.	..	..	..		..			..		..	..	..	..	..	..							1132			
Huntingdon (North) 677, 879.			..					..		..	..	1242	..	..								1229			
Abbots Ripton			..					..		..	..		..	..								1238			
Holme 882 ......[887, 1080			..			..		..		..	..		..	..								1248			
Yaxley and Farcet ..[691, 880,			..			..		..		..	..		..	..								1255			
Peterbro' (N.) 471, 472, ..arr.			..			1137	1144	..	1151	..	..		..	..								1 2			
887 BOSTON ......arr.						1042	1045	..	1045	..	..		..	..			..								
888 GRIMSBY TOWN ...... "						..	..	..	..	..	..		..	..			..								
1080 CROMER (Beach) ...... "						4F7	4 13	..	4 13	..	..		..	..			..								
877 NEWMARKET 880 ......dep.						8 20	8 20	..	..	..	..		..	..	..		..		9 40		9 40		..		..
879 CAMBRIDGE 880 ...... "						9 0	9 0	..	..	..	..		..	..	..		..		1020		1020		..		1020
880 HARWICH (Parkeston Qy) "						7f25	7 20	..	..	..	..		..	..	..		..		8 57		30		..		..
877 IPSWICH 880 ...... "						8 6	8 6	..	..	..	..		..	..	..		..		1015		8 25		..		..
862 YARMOUTH (V.) 880 .. 1081 "						7 5	7 5	..	..	..	..		..	..	..		..		9 25		8k38		..		1030
862 LOWESTOFT (C.) 880 .. "						6 25	6 25	..	..	..	..		..	..	..		..		8 55		8 [illegible]		..		1020
864a CROMER 880 ...... "						8k0	8k0	..	..	..	..		..	..	..		..		8 57		9k40		..		..
880 NORWICH (Thorpe) ...... "						8 17	8 17	..	..	..	..		..	..	..		..		1012		9k30		..		..
Peterbro' (North) ......dep.	..					1140	1147	..	1154	..	..	..	..		..	..	..		..		1253			..	
Tallington B	..					..	..	..	..	..	..	..	..		..	..	..		..		1 6			..	
Essendine 886	..					..	..	..	..	..	..	..	..		..	..	..		..		1 15	Stop		..	
Little Bytham	..					..	..	..	..	..	..	..	..		..	..	..		..		1 24	..		..	
Corby	..					..	..	..	..	..	..	..	..		..	..	..		..		1 34	..		..	
Great Ponton	..					..	..	..	..	..	..	..	..		..	..	..		..		1 52	..		..	
Grantham 894, 895, 896. arr.	..		1156	12c3	1211	1216	1223	..	1230	..	..	..	..		..	..	..		..		1 58	..		..	
896 NOTTINGHAM (Vic.) ......arr.	..		..	..	..	1 5	1 5	..	2 23	..	..	..			..	..	..		..		..	..		..	..
894 LINCOLN (L.N.E.) ...... "	..		..	..	..	1F3	1r53	..	1r53	..	..	..			..	..	..		1 53		3 42	..		..	2 6
Grantham ......dep.	..		1158	12 7	1215	1218	1225	..	1232	..	..	..	1222	1 17		..	..		..		Stop	..		..	..
Barkston	..				..			..	..	..	..	..	1229	1 24		..	..		..	..	..	..		..	..
Hougham	..				..			..	..	..	..	..	1234	1 29		..	..		..	..	..	..		..	..
Claypole	..				..			..	..	..	..	..	1252	1 37		..	..		..	..	..	..		..	..
Newark 700, 701, 896 .. arr.	..				..			..	..	..	..	..	1 0			..	..			..	..	..		..	..
Newark dep.	..				..			..	..	..	..	..	1 7			..	..			..	..	..		..	..
Carlton-on-Trent	..				..			..	..	..	..	..	1‡25			..	..			..	..	..		..	..
Crow Park, for Sutton-on-Trent	..				..			..	..	..	..	..	1 30			..	..			..	..	..		..	..
Dukeries Junction 903	..				..			..	..	..	..	..	..			..	..			..	..	..		..	..
Tuxford (North)	..				..			..	..	..	..	..	1 39			..	..			..	..	..		..	..
Retford 905, 910 ......arr.	..				..			..	..	..	..	..	1 49			..	..			..	..	..		..	..
905 LINCOLN (L.N.E.) ......arr.	..	..			..	..	..	..	..	..	..	..	2‡25		..		..		..	..	..	..	..	..	..
905 GRIMSBY TOWN ...... "	..	..			..	3F06	3 13	..	3 13	..	..	..	4 25		..		..		..	..	..	..	..	..	..
910 SHEFFIELD (Victoria) .. "	..	..			..	2e49	2V15	..	2V15	..	..	..	3 36		..		..		3V44	..	..	..	..	..	..
911 MANCHESTER (Lon. Rd.) "	..	..			..	5M3	4V34	..	5V3	..	..	..	5 3	Stop	..		..		5V3	..	..	..	..	..	..
911 " (Central) . "	..	..			..	4d10	4V14	..	4V14	..	..	..	..		..		..		..	..	..	..	..	..	..
911 LIVERPOOL (Central) ... "	..	..			A	5d15	5V15a	..	5/15a	..	..	..	6 47	..	..		..		6V35	..	..	..	..	..	..
	1	2	3	4	5	6	7	8	9	10	11	12	13	14	15	16	17	18	19	20	21	22	23	24	25

Column remarks (upper table):
- 1: Saturdays only. RC King's Cross to Glasgow.
- 2: The Flying Scotsman. Non-stop K. Cross to Edinburgh (Wav.). RC King's Cross to Edinburgh, and Edinburgh to Aberdeen.
- 3: RC King's Cross to Glasgow. RC King's Cross to Perth and Aberdeen.
- 4: Mondays & Saturdays; also on 22nd & 29th inst. RC King's Cross to Newcastle (except 16th, 23rd and 30th inst). RC King's Cross to Edinburgh on 16th, 23rd and 30th inst.
- 5: Saturdays F only (Except 9th inst.). RC King's Cross to Newcastle.
- 6: Except 16th, 23rd, and 30th inst. RC King's Cross to Leeds.
- 7: RC Kings Cross to Leeds (C.) except 9th, to Hull on 9th inst. Saturdays only.
- 9: On 16th, 23rd & 30th inst. RC King's Cross to Hull.
- 12: Saturdays only.
- 13: Except Saturdays.
- 14: Saturdays only. Arr. Doncaster at 3 34, see Col. 7, p. 812.
- 15: Saturdays only. RC King's Cross to Scarborough.
- 16: RC King's Cross to Scarborough. The Scarborough Flier. TC King's Cross to Newcastle, except Saturdays.
- 17: Saturdays only. (Except 9th inst.) RC King's Cross to Scarborough.
- 18: The Queen of Scots. Limited accommodation. Pullman Cars only (1st and 3rd class extra charge), King's Cross to Leeds, Harrogate, Darlington, Newcastle, Edinburgh (W.), and Glasgow (Queen St.).
- 19: Saturdays only. RC Ipswich to Leeds (C.). TC Yarmouth to Leeds (C.).
- 20: RC King's Cross to Whitby (arr. 4 39 aft), see page 942. Saturdays only.
- 21: Saturdays only.
- 22: Except Saturdays.
- 23: Saturdays only. TC King's Cross to Sunderland. TC King's Cross to Saltburn.
- 24: Saturdays only. RC King's Cross to Glasgow.
- 25: RC Yarmouth and Lowestoft to York, via March, Spalding, & Lincoln, page 8.. Saturdays only.

Down.	1	2	3	4	5	6	7	8	9	10	11	12	13	14	15	16	17	18	19	20	21	22	23	24	25
Retford ......dep.	..	..	W		..	..			..		..	..	1 55	..	..	..	..	..	..	..	..	..	..	..	..
Barnby Moor and Sutton	..	..	..		..	..			..		..	..	2 1	..	..	..	..	..	..	..	..	..	..	..	..
Ranskill	..	..	..		..	..			..		..	..	2 6	..	..	..	..	..	..	..	..	..	..	..	..
Bawtry G	..	..	..		..	..			..		..	..	2 14	..	..	..	..	..	..	..	..	..	..	..	..
Rossington ......(911, 932..	..	..	..		..	..		1 30	..	2 6	..	..	2 21	..	..	..	..	..	..	..	..	..	..	..	..
Doncaster (C.) 893, 904. arr.	..	..	..		..	1 11	1 18	1 37	1 25	2 15	..	..	2 29	..	..		..	..	2 48	..	..	..	..	..	3 4
9.. HULL (Paragon) ......arr.		..	..		..	2F20	2p20	3 36	2 30	Stop	..	..	3 51	aft	..		..	..	3 51	..	..	..	..	..	..
Doncaster (Central) ......dep.		..	..		..	1 15	1F22	1 43		..	..	..	..	2‡20	..		..		2 52	..	..	..	..	..	..
Carcroft & Adwick-le-Street..		..	..		..		..			..	..	..	..	2‡27	..		..		..	..	..	..	..		..
Hampole		..	..		..		..			..	..			2‡32	..		..		..	..	..	..	..		..
South Elmsall		..	..		..		..			..	..			2‡28	..		..		..	..	..	..	..		..
Hemsworth ¶		..	..		..		..			..	..			2‡45	..		..		..	..	..	..	..		..
Nostell		..	..		..		..			..	..			2‡53	..		..		..	..	..	..	..		..
Hare Park and Crofton		..	..		..		..			..	..			2‡57	..		..		..	..	..	..	..		..
Sandal		..	..		..		..			..	..			3‡2	..		..		..	..	..	..	..		..
Wakefield (Westgate) 928 arr.		..	..		..	1 40	1F47			..	..			3‡6	..		..		3 20	..	..	..	..		..
926 BRADFORD (Ex.) ......arr.		..	..		..	2 21	2F28	..		..	..			4 16	..		..		..		..	..	..		..
931 HALIFAX (Old) ...... "		..	..		..	2 59	2F59	..		..	..			5 18	..		..		..		..	..	..		..
Wakefield (K'gate) 554 ..arr.		..	..		..	1 53	1F53	2 49		..			..	3E13	..		..		..		..	..	..		..
554 HALIFAX ......arr.		..	..		..	3‡20	3F9	..		..			..	..	..		..		4o51		..	..			..
554 HUDDERSFIELD ...... "		..	..		..	3 11	3F11	3 32		..			5L25	4E49	..		..		4o49		..	..			..
Wakefield (Kirkgate) ....dep.	..		..		..	..	..	Stop		aft		aft	..	2 55	..		..		..		..	..		..	..
" (Westgate) ... "	..		..		..	1 43	1F50			2x20	..	2 48	..	3 13	..		..		3 24		..	..		..	
Lofthouse and Outwood	..		..		..	..	..			2‡29	2 44	2 54	..	3 20	..		..		..		..	..		..	
Ardsley	..		..		..	..	..			2j34	2 50	3 0	..	3 27	..		..		..		..	..		..	
Beeston	..		..		..	..	..		Stop	2 39	2 55	3 11	..	3 32	..		..		..		..	..		..	
Holbeck 927, 952	..		..		..	1 58	2F5	..		2j44	3 0	3 16	..	3 37	..		..		3 41		..	..		..	
927 BRADFORD (Ex.) ......arr.	..		..			..	..	..	..	4EB3	..	..	..	4 42	..	..	..	3B1	4 42		..	..	..	..	
554 HALIFAX ...... "	..		..			2F28	..	..	..	..	..	..	..	4‡30	..	..	..	4B7	4 35		..	..	..	..	
952 ILKLEY ...... "	..		..			3 40	3F40	..	..	3E40	..	..	..	4 56	..	..	..	3K40	4 56		..	..	..	..	
952 HARROGATE ...... "	..		..			2B44	2d50	..	aft	4K13	..	..	..	4B28	..	..	..	3B4	4B28		..	..	..	..	
954 RIPON ...... "	..		..			3B35	3d35	aft	E	4K34	..	..	..	5B9	..	..	..	3B35	5B9		..	..	..	..	
Leeds (Cen.) 706, 947 ...arr.	..		..			2 1	2F8	E	S	2j47	3 3	3 20	..	3 42	..	..	..	2 31	3 45		..	..	..	..	..
Doncaster (Central) ......dep	..		..					1 33	1 49		..		..	..	..	..					..		..	..	3 9
Arksey	..		..								..		..	..	..	..					..		..	..	..
Moss	..		..								..		..	..	..	..					..		..	..	..
Balne H	..		..								..		..	..	..	..					..		..	..	..
Heck	..		..								..		..	..	..	..					..		..	..	..
Temple Hirst	..		..								..		..	..	..	..					..		..	..	..
Selby 934, 935, 939 ......arr.	..		..					1 57	2 19		..		..	..	..	..					..		..	..	3 33
934 HULL (Paragon) ......arr.	..							3 12	..		..	..	..	..		..					aft	aft	..	..	5 8
Selby ......dep.	..		..					1 59	2 21		..	..	..	..		..			..		2‡50	3 17	..	..	3 35
Riccall	..		..					..	..		..	..	..	..		..			..		..	3 25	..	..	..
Escrick	..		..					..	..		..	..	..	..		..			..		..	3 31	..	..	..
Naburn ......[947	..		..					..	..		..	..	..	..		..			..		..	3 37	..	..	..
York 822, 937, 938, 942, arr.	1232		1t21	1e34	1 48			2 18	2 42		..	..	..	..		2E0			..		3‡10	3 45	3 0	..	3 54
947 HARROGATE 822, 955 ..arr.	1 30	..	..	..	3 0			4 13	4 20	..	..	..	..	..	..	4b13	..	..	..	..	4x13	5 3	4 20	..	5 3
954 RIPON 822, 955 ...... "	2 40	..	..	..	3 35			4 34	5 9	..	..	..	..	..	..	4b34	..	..	..	..	4‡34	5 30	5 9	..	5 30
942 SCARBOROUGH (C.) 939.. "	1 48	..	2t35	2E35	2 50			3 36	4 45	..	..	..	..	..	3 7	2t55	3 27	..	..	..	4§25	..	4 45	..	..
822 MIDDLESBROUGH ...... "	2 8	Q	2 56	3c27	3 27			4 27	..	..	..	..	..	..	..	3E56	..	4 27	..	..	4 57	..	4 22	..	..
822 SUNDERLAND ...... "	2 50	..	3t38	4f17	4 17			5 22	r	..	..	..	..	..	..	4E36	..	5 19	..	..	5 40	..	5 17	5 36	..
822 NEWCASTLE (Central) ... "	2 17	..	2t55	3c22	3 35			5r6	..	..	..	..	..	..	..	3E50	..	4 37	..	..	5 18	..	..	4 49	..
830 EDINBURGH (Wav.) ...... "	4 45	5 0	5t25	5P50	..			7k5	..	..	..	..	..	..	..	..	..	7 5	..	..	8 25	..	..	7 30	..
990 GLASGOW (Queen St.) .. "	6 3	6y40	6 45	7P22	..			8 13	k	..	..	..	..	..	..	..	..	8 13	..	..	9 57	a	..	8 43	..
1001 FORT WILLIAM ...... "	..	..	..	..	..			..	..	..	..	..	..	..	..	..	..	..	..	..	..	..	..	..	..
984 STIRLING ...... "	..	..	7 16	..	..			9 37	k	..	..	..	..	..	..	..	..	9 37	..	..	..	..	..	9 37	..
838 DUNDEE (Tay Bridge) .. "	..	6 37	7 11	..	..			8 58	k	..	..	..	..	..	..	..	..	8 58	..	..	..	..	..	1030	..
985 PERTH (via Forth Bdg.) "	..	..	7 13	..	..			..	..	..	..	..	..	..	..	..	..	..	..	..	..	..	..	..	..
838 ABERDEEN J ...... "	..	8 15	9 0	..	..			1045	k	..	..	..	..	..	..	..	..	1045	..	..	..	..	..	..	..
985 INVERNESS ...... "	..	..	..	..	..			..	..	..	..	..	..	..	..	..	..	..	..	..	..	..	..	..	..

Column remarks (lower table):
- 1: Saturdays only.
- 2: The Flying Scotsman. TC King's Cross to Aberdeen.
- 3: W
- 4: On 16th, 23rd and 30th inst, conveys Passengers for Berwick and beyond only. Mondays and Saturdays; also on 22nd and 29th inst.
- 5: Saturdays only. (Except 9th inst.)
- 6: TC to Harrogate. TC King's Cross to Hull, except Sats.
- 7: Sats. only. TC King's Cross to Harrogate except 9th inst. RC King's Cross to Hull on 9th inst only. Except 16th, 23rd and 30th inst.
- 8: Except Sats. Via Knottingley. Except Sats.
- 9: On 16th, 23rd and 30th inst. Sats. only.
- 10: Sats. only. Change at Lofthouse except Sats. Change at Ardsley on Sats.
- 11: Saturdays only.
- 12: Except Saturdays. Change at Tingley
- 13: Except Saturdays
- 15: Saturdays only.
- 16: TC King's Cross to Whitby except Sats. arr. 3 55 aft., see page 942.
- 17: Saturdays only. (Except 9th inst.)
- 18: Luncheon and other Refreshments can be obtained on the Cars. The Queen of Scots.
- 19: Saturdays only.
- 20: TC King's Cross to Bridlington, arr. 3 25 aft. Saturdays only.
- 22: Except Saturdays.
- 23: Saturdays only
- 24: Saturdays only.
- 25: Saturdays only.

NOTES

- **A** Passengers ross from London Road to Cen. at Manchester at own expense
- **a** Arr 9 41 aft Sats
- *a* Via Manchester (Cen)
- **B** Via Leeds (Central)
- *b* Except Sats. Arrive Harrogate 3 0 and Ripon 3 35 aft Weds
- **C** Via Grantham
- *c* Except 16th, 23rd and 30th inst
- *d* Except 9th inst. Via Leeds (Central)
- **E** or E Except Sats
- **F** Except 9th inst
- **f** Dep 7 20 mrn Mons, Fris and 9th inst
- *f* Except 16th, 23rd and 30th inst. Arr 3 53 aft on 9th inst
- **I** Cromer, via March
- **J** Arr 2 37 aft Fris
- *j* 10 mins later Sats
- **K** Via Leeds (Central and City) Stations
- **k** Pullman Car Express from Darlington, 1st and 3rd class, extra charge
- *k* Beach Station
- **L** Via Retford, Sheffield and Penistone
- *l* Arr 3 15 aft on Sats
- **M** Passengers change from Huntingdon (East) to Huntingdon (North)
- **M** Via Doncaster. Arr 4 10 aft on Mons and Fris
- *n* Mons and Fris. Via Doncaster
- *o* Via Wakefield (Westgate). Passengers must cross the town to Kirkgate at their own expense
- **P** On 16th, 23rd, and 30th inst
- *p* On 9th inst only
- **Q** Londesborough Road Station
- **q** Except Mons and Sats also 22nd & 29th inst
- **r** Passengers arr Sunderland 5 19 and Newcastle 4 37 aft by Pullman Car (1st and 3rd cl., extra charge) from Darlington
- *r* Via Sleaford
- **RC** Restaurant Car
- **S** or S Sats only
- **T** Arr 5 9 aft Sats
- *t* Except Mons: also 16th 22nd, 23rd, 29th, and 30th inst
- **TC** Through Carriages
- **U** Arr 3 9 aft on 9th inst
- *u* City Station
- **V** Via Doncaster
- *v* Except Sats. Via Doncaster
- **W** On Mons and 22nd and 29th inst. conveys passengers for Berwick and beyond only. On 16th, 23rd, and 30th inst. conveys passengers for stas beyond Edinburgh only
- *x* 8 mins later Sats
- *y* Fris. and Sats.
- *z* Except 16th, 23rd, and 30th inst
- † Arr 10 mins *earlier*
- ‡ 5 mins later Sats
- § 20 mins. later on Sats
- ¶ "Halt" at Fitzwilliam between Hemsworth and Nostell

For **Other Notes** and explanation of letter references in the Station Columns, see pages 815 and 815a.

but operated it from partial opening in 1854 until 1875. At first, the objective was to secure the lucrative excursion traffic to Gravesend, for which the Tilbury–Gravesend ferry was hired, and Southend was only a secondary objective, although this soon changed and the town became important both for holidaymakers and, increasingly, commuters.

The ECR was merged into the Great Eastern Railway in 1862, and the LTSR became an independent company that year, although still with directors appointed by the GER. The GER continued to run the line until 1876, when over the next four years the LTSR acquired its own rolling stock and trains ran from Fenchurch Street only. Even earlier, a loop had to be built to avoid congestion at Stratford, and this opened in 1858.

The GER opened its own branch to Southend with services from Liverpool Street in 1889, seven years after the LTSR had become completely independent. Southend was the end of the line until 1884, when the War Office dropped its objections to an extension to Shoeburyness, an artillery training area.

The dawn of the new century saw the line from Fenchurch Street to Southend as one of the most profitable in the country with a growing season ticket traffic as well as summer excursions and boat trains for liners calling at Tilbury. It was widely expected that the GER would acquire the LTSR and thus establish a monopoly between London and Southend, but in a surprise move the Midland Railway acquired the LTSR in 1912. With the extensive suburban development at the London end of the line, electrification was expected, promised and even planned, but not delivered until some time after Nationalisation.

York

Before the railway, York was already an important religious centre, market town and commercial centre with good water transport links via the River Ouse to the Humber and Hull. During the 1830s, York had first the York & North Midland Railway and then the Great North of England Railway, so that the city had lines to London, Leeds and Hull, while local lines followed, linking the city to Scarborough, Harrogate, Market Weighton and Beverley, and by 1850 there was a line north to Edinburgh. These lines were promoted by a single man, George Hudson, whose activities benefited York most of all, and made the city the most important railway junction between Newcastle and London. His influence was such that the railway was able to site its station actually inside the ancient and confined city, even to the extent of breaching the city walls.

By 1854, the North Eastern Railway had a monopoly, but another seven railway companies had running powers into York. New lines to the south were built twice to reduce mileage, while the station eventually had to be rebuilt outside the city walls to ensure that enough space was available for the growing demand and to avoid the need for trains to reverse. It eventually reached 16 platforms, but was built on a sharp curve.

More than a major junction, York also had railway workshops built from 1842 onwards, but in 1905, lack of space meant that locomotive building had to be moved to Darlington, but York continued to produce carriages and wagons. Grouping meant that York ceased to be the NER's headquarters, although it was considered briefly by the LNER before they decided that the head office should be in London, but York remained the centre of its North Eastern Division and under LNER management, the divisional general managers enjoyed much delegated authority.

In addition to the main line railways which placed York firmly on the East Coast Main Line, in 1913 a light railway, the Derwent Valley, was opened, mainly an agricultural line. This evaded Grouping and Nationalisation, but lost its passenger services in 1926 and closed in stages between 1965 and 1981.

The LNER opened a museum in York in 1928, and this has developed over the years to become today's National Railway Museum, opened in 1975 on a much larger site.

Left: London to York timetable of 1938 (1922 is shown on page 57.

Chapter 4

Building a New Railway Company

The task bestowed on the managements of the four grouped railway companies by Parliament was far from easy, especially for the two largest companies, the LNER and the even bigger LMS. The Great Western had the easiest of it, simply taking over the other companies and imposing its will on all of them. The Southern was able to shirk the task to some extent by keeping divisions that approximated to its three constituent companies, although in many matters, it was the London & South Western view that won.

One of the early decisions taken by the LNER was that it should omit the ampersand from the abbreviated title, but before this, a few locomotives did appear with 'L&NER'. This rare view shows K3 2-6-0 No. 1000N so lettered. (*HMRS ADF 615*)

For a start, there was the vexed question of a name for the new company. The 'Great North Railway' was one title that found favour for some time, although it could have raised objections from the LMS. 'North Eastern' was ruled out as it seemed to favour the largest constituent company, and in any case, much of the railway wasn't in the North East. Late in the Second World War, locomotive tenders did indeed start to appear with the shortened initials 'NE' on the side instead of LNER. Eventually, the compromise was reached as the 'London & North Eastern Railway', and the coat of arms included the old Great Central slogan, 'Forward'. At first, the abbreviation L&NER was used, but this was almost immediately simplified to LNER and only a few locomotive tenders have been recorded with 'L&NER' on the sides. No-one seems to have considered a 'London, North-Eastern & Scottish Railway', which would have been too long even though more accurate. Perhaps the difficulty in choosing a name was a reflection of the fact that the Grouping may have gone too far. As it was, this was a long sprawling railway, with its own lines from King's Cross to Lossiemouth, some miles to the north of Aberdeen, with other lines to Mallaig and Fort Augustus, and a network of lines radiating from Liverpool Street into East Anglia.

It was clear from the outset that despite not having a London terminus, the former North Eastern Railway, rather than the Great Northern, was to be the dominant company within the new LNER, and this may have been one reason for a regional divisional structure rather than an integrated company.

The core of the railway was the East Coast Main Line from King's Cross to Edinburgh, 392.8 miles long, although the line continued to Aberdeen, 523.3 miles from London. It then went beyond to Lossiemouth on the Moray Firth, although this was beyond what might be described in recent years as the inter-city network. There were important centres off the main line, however, such as Leeds, while there was a substantial spider's web network radiating out from Liverpool Street and into East Anglia. All in all, the LNER inherited 6,307 route miles – some 500 miles less than the total for the LMS – of which 62½ were electrified. The new railway also inherited 7,423 steam locomotives and 13,467 passenger carriages, plus 281,748 goods wagons of all kinds, 140 electric multiple unit carriages and trailers, six electric engines, and ten steam rail motor cars as well as a diesel-electric railcar operated by the Great Central. There were also six turbine steamers and 36 other steamers, as well as a number of river boats, and as in common with the other railway companies, the LNER also found itself to be a major ship owner and operator of ports. It was one of just two companies, the other being the Southern Railway, with a substantial Continental business.

More than any other company, the grouped company had difficulty in reconciling the various types of share issued by its predecessors. The table below shows the complicated and confusing arrangement that was finally used to resolve the problem.

Capital Formation of the LNER

Stock	*Nominal value*	*Opening price per £100*
3% debenture ranking	£66,352,793	£62
4% debenture 'parri passu'	£33,617,629	£82
4% first guaranteed	£29,838,251	£88
4% second guaranteed	£27,329,739	£79
4% first preference	£48,145,988	£78
4% second preference	£65,683,531	£74
5% preferred ordinary	£41,873,116	£77
Deferred ordinary	£35,514,228	£33 10s
	£348,355,275	

From the very outset, it is clear that the company was already marked down by the stock market. The shareholders in the pre-Grouped companies had no choice in the matter. An envelope came through the letterbox, and on being opened they would find that their shares had been transferred to one or the other of the categories above. There was no cash alternative. The deferred ordinary stocks were worth a few shillings more than a third of their nominal value. At the time, gilt-edged securities were paying 5 per cent per annum. Part of the problem was that the company was over-capitalised, not helped by the value of its stock being worth considerably more than the total of the grouped companies, but the prevailing mood was one of pessimism, and as events were to prove, the years that followed were not to be easy.

The over-capitalisation was due in part to the aggressive demands of the directors of some of the constituent companies, anxious to do their best for their shareholders, but in fact limiting the potential of their investment in the years ahead. Some of the pre-grouped companies had been very profitable, and no doubt the feeling within many of these was that they would be again. It was to be a forlorn hope.

Just rebuilt and still in workshop grey is this D16 'Claud Hamilton' 4-4-0 No. 1805, in 1923. (*HMRS ADF 721*)

Divisional Management

The LNER lay on the opposite side of the Pennines from the LMS, and its structure was the opposite as well. The LMS was strongly centralised, while the LNER was decentralised. It did not have to be this way, as the first Chief General Manager, Sir Ralph Wedgwood, favoured a strongly centralised structure, possibly having seen the short-comings of the NER's divisional structure, but he was overruled by the board of directors who favoured strong decentralisation. The rationale was partly that it was felt that many of those coming from other companies would not want to feel that they had been taken over by the NER. It was also felt that the divisional management would be closer to the company's customers. As there were to be many general managers, Wedgwood's title had strong emphasis on the 'chief'.

Despite having the whole of 1922 to prepare for the new LNER, and despite the desire to play down the NER involvement, the company's employee publication was initially still titled as the *North Eastern Railway Magazine*, simply expanding the circulation of an existing publication to embrace the wider area of the new company. The question over whether the NER would have run the railway is an interesting one.

It must not be forgotten that the railway was only a part of the business, albeit the most important part. In common with all of the 'Big Four', the LNER was a conglomerate in a day when such corporate structures were rare. All of the railways had extensive hotel and shipping interests, including ports, and the ships were not just ferries or packet vessels, but included cargo steamers as well. The only area in which the LNER did not become involved, unlike the other grouped companies, was air transport. Like the others, it became involved in road passenger transport as soon as it was allowed to move beyond services feeding into its stations and acquire bus companies, and the 'Big Four' moved into road haulage jointly.

Three divisions were agreed, London, York and Edinburgh, officially known as the Southern Area, the North Eastern Area and the Scottish Area, with the latter divided at first into the Southern Scottish Area and the Northern Scottish Area, based on Aberdeen. During the year allowed for completion of formalities and the appointment of the senior officers and directors, an organisation committee was formed with each of the constituent companies providing a member, although because of its size the NER was allowed to send two, and was chaired by Wedgwood. It is worth noting that the structure created by this group was similar to that adopted by British Railways post-Nationalisation, while the LMS was divided into two regions.

The meeting of the constituent company representatives was not without precedent as the railway companies even before Grouping had seldom worked in isolation. One of the best examples of inter-company liaison was when the Great Northern, North Eastern and North British railway companies had collaborated closely on the development of through express services along the East Coast Main Line, even having specially designed rolling stock built for both day and night passenger trains. Collaboration even pre-dated this as these three companies and the Midland Railway had supported the construction of the massive railway bridge across the Forth, opened in 1890. Few of the pre-Grouped railways had operated in isolation, and over and above it all was the Railway Clearing House which not only ensured that money was paid for tickets or freight that involved journeys over more than one company's metals, but also looked at standardisation of items such as headcodes.

Looking back, with the benefit of hindsight, the directors and senior officers of the 'Big Four' railway companies faced a terrible challenge. There was no precedent for what they were asked to do, and the railway companies dwarfed even the leading companies in other industries, at least until more government interference led to a reorganisation of the chemicals industry to create Imperial Chemical Industries (ICI), and the electrical industry to create Associated Electrical Industries (AEI). One director, or 'president' as he was known, of the LMS once said that he considered the company too big to be run efficiently or effectively, and while the LNER was smaller, it was still the second largest railway company and it is probable that it was also too big. By contrast, the GWR and Southern seemed to be the natural evolution of the railway in their areas.

The policy as laid down by Sir Ralph Wedgwood, the first LNER chief general manager, was put simply: 'We decide the policy and deal with the Board. You get on with operating the railway.' This sounded like a good, firm guideline, but in practice there was a lack of precision and the divisional general managers had considerable freedom of action and their powers were wide-ranging. The problem was that it was hard to define a consensus amongst the divisions on matters of policy, and long-term strategy was difficult to prepare. Some even maintain that at meetings of the Railway Companies Association, it was hard for the LNER representative to present a company view.

As it was, from the start the board members pressed for additional chief officers with company-wide responsibilities, including a chief mechanical engineer and a chief buying agent. Both of these made sense as each would have ensured increasing standardisation and enabled economies to be achieved, without interfering with the local relationship between the railway and its customers and indeed, without undue limitations on the powers of the divisional management. In fact, the purchasing and distribution of supplies was placed under the chief stores superintendent, whose title was later changed to chief purchasing officer. The first company-wide appointment was that of W.M. Teasdale as advertising manager, who moved from the NER.

Just as there was competition for the roles of chairman and chief general manager, so there was for chief mechanical engineer. The incumbents at the NER and GCR were both over sixty years of age. It was important that the holders of the key positions in the new organisation should have experience, but also be young enough to remain in post for a worthwhile number of years, giving the new organisation time to settle down and also ensuring continuity. The choice of CME eventually fell on Nigel Gresley, the locomotive engineer of the Great Northern, and their equivalent of CME, who was 46 years old and awarded the salary of £4,500. There was nothing actually wrong with any of the other candidates, but several of them, such as the Great Eastern's Hill, lacked stature and experience, while the others had produced successful designs, or at least capable locomotives, but none of them had the flair and originality of Gresley.

It seems odd, however, that the position was not given priority before Grouping and in fact it took seven weeks for the appointment to be made. The reason was that some board members had to be convinced that the appointment was necessary and there could have been a CME for each division, just as there were divisional track and signal engineers. The problem was that this could have meant three different designs of locomotives for each class.

A compromise was that in a break with the traditions of all the constituent companies in the CME having control of locomotive running, this was not given to Gresley, but instead handed to the area locomotive superintendent, who would report to the divisional general manager. This was a decision recommended by the former NER CME, Sir Vincent Raven, who had retired at the end of 1922, but was retained by the LNER as a technical adviser to the Board. It was the first of three reports he made to the LNER. He also produced a report on the railway workshops, another area in which standardisation and rationalisation could produce economies.

One of Raven's other tasks was to chair a committee to consider electrification of the Great Northern suburban lines. One would have thought the needs of the Great Eastern suburban lines to have been more pressing. Nevertheless, none of his colleagues, and especially none of the general managers, shared his devotion to electrification and certainly lacked the determination to see this through.

A number of other company-wide posts were allowed, at assistant general manager level. Amongst these were employment and Parliamentary matters.

The company decided that its head office would be in London, although York was given consideration because of its central position to the core King's Cross–Scotland route. This was undoubtedly wise with the former GCR and GER operations in mind, but despite decentralisation, none of the premises in London proved adequate for the head office staff. In the end, the chief general manager, chief mechanical engineer and chief accountant were housed at King's Cross, while the joint secretaries and the board room were at Marylebone, two miles away by the Underground. There was no attempt to build a new head office, as happened at the LMS.

An oddity of many of the pre-Grouping railway companies was that senior salaries had been paid after tax, but the LNER made it clear that its directors and senior officers would have to pay their own income tax.

Despite the desire for continuity, there were some poor choices that only became apparent under the stress of actually running the company. The most prominent of these was S.A. Parnell, from the GER who had been appointed Divisional General Manager, Southern Area. He was the most senior of the three divisional general managers, but also the one with the most difficult task as he had to pull together the very different and dispersed operations out of the three London termini. Perhaps there should have been three smaller southern divisions, and indeed, in 1927 the Southern Division was sub-divided into two, with one superintendent for the 'Eastern Section' covering the old GER services, and the other for the 'Western Section', covering the former GNR and GCR. Parnell had lacked the strength and force of character to cope with the task, and was pressed to resign, which he did in July 1924 at the age of just 39 years. He seems to have attracted the sympathy and affection of his colleagues, but not the directors. He returned to the firm of City surveyors for whom he had worked before joining the Great Eastern.

Nevertheless, the Board seemed incapable of tackling the problems that arose. After the Miners' Strike, the coal traffic that was so important slumped, not just because of the years of the Great Depression but because many markets for coal, and especially export markets, were lost for ever. This deprived the company of much revenue at a time when investment was needed.

There were serious delays on the Great Northern line with too many stretches without a relief line to ease congestion at peak periods, and with slow-moving freight trains hampering fast and semi-fast trains. The Great Eastern had lightweight track and lightweight trains incapable of standing up to the pressure put upon them and while pressure for electrification grew, the LNER seemed incapable of funding it. Only the Great Central, a much more modern railway with minimal suburban traffic and marginalised on its longer distance routes by competition from more direct services, proved relatively easy to run.

Chapter 5

The Managers

Choosing a management team for the new railway was not an easy task. Parliament had allowed the grouped railways a whole year in which to organise themselves, and this was none too long, especially for the LNER and its western counterpart, the LMS. Both railways included substantial constituent companies whose senior people could consider themselves candidates for the top posts in the new organisation.

One candidate, who was ruled out immediately by everyone, although he went to great pains to let everyone know that he was available, was Sir Eric Geddes, who as Minister of Transport, was responsible for the Grouping. Geddes had the experience having been deputy general manager of the North Eastern Railway with expectations of becoming GM had not war intervened with Geddes seconded to the government before he entered politics. The NER was clearly keen to be rid off him as it paid him £50,000 (equal to around £1 million today) to buy out his contract of service. This was a considerable sum for the time, especially since the golden handshakes of recent years were unknown until well after the Second World War. During the debates on the Railways Bill, Geddes was not allowed to forget that he had accepted this massive payment, and questions were asked whether it had come from the company's taxed income or from the compensation paid by the government, the taxpayer, for the use of the railways in wartime. Tables that show the changing value of money over a lengthy period are unreliable as different products have varying changes in inflation or even deflation, but for comparison, the head of the Civil Service earned less than £3,500 in 1922, and apart from Wedgwood and the LNER's chief legal adviser, none of its senior officers received more than £4,500.

Candidates for chief executive included Sir Sam Fay of the Great Central and Charles Dent of the Great Northern, as well as the North Eastern's Wedgwood and James Calder of the North British, though he made clear that he did not want to leave Scotland. Sir Henry Thornton of the Great Eastern was also in the running, and had experience of railway operation in the United States, but was regarded with suspicion as being much in the mould of Geddes, with strong ambitions. Fay was 66 years old and Dent 60, so the view was taken that, as the youngest of the three best candidates, Wedgwood would have the strength to undertake what was to prove a mammoth task, and would be in office long enough to make an impact. This was probably a wise choice, although Fay had wide experience and had seen considerable success, perhaps most notably during the 1890s when he restored viability to the Midland & South Western Junction Railway, and a contemporary credited him with making 'an empty sack sit upright'.

One problem with the LNER was that its policy of having a very small central management team with substantial delegation to the operating areas meant that there were relatively few names at the top and even fewer to have made their mark on railway history. The substantial degree of delegation was the result of a pragmatic decision by Wedgwood, who recognised that the rest of the organisation would resent being tied to what they would see as 'old North Eastern' practices, especially as Butterworth, the general manager of the NER had been very forceful in pressing the company's case during the pre-Grouping discussions.

The decentralised structure and small head office function of the LNER also means that one of the notable managers, John Miller, was an 'area' manager rather than a head office man.

Gresley, Herbert Nigel, later Sir 1876–1941

Initially apprenticed at Crewe on the London & North Western Railway, he moved to the Lancashire & Yorkshire Railway. In 1905, he became carriage and wagon superintendent on the Great Northern Railway, where he succeeded Henry Ivatt as chief mechanical engineer in 1922. On Grouping, he became CME of the London & North Eastern Railway. He was knighted in 1936, the same year that he was elected president of the Institute of Mechanical Engineers.

Gresley was initially best known for his introduction of elliptical-roofed carriages on the GNR, which was also adopted for the East Coast Joint Stock in 1905. He gave the GNR a modern 2-6-0 locomotive in 1912, and followed this with 2-8-0s, initially with two cylinders but later with three. His first A1 class Pacific was *Great Northern*, which appeared in 1922. His Pacific locomotives saw steady improvement from 1926, with long-lap valves and higher pressure boilers, and included the famous A3 *Flying Scotsman*. The peak of his locomotive design and performance was the streamlined A4 class, first introduced in 1935 and used for high-speed trains such as the 'Silver Jubilee' and 'Coronation'. One of the class, *Mallard*, set a speed record of 126mph in July 1938, which has never been beaten for steam locomotives. At the other end of the scale, his V2 2-6-2 mixed-traffic locomotives were in volume production from 1936 and many were taken up for use by the War Office during the Second World War.

The LNER paid its senior staff less than the other railway companies, and from the start made clear that, unlike many of its constituent companies, it would not pay their income tax. One perk, however, was that locomotives were often named after senior personnel. This is Sir Nigel Gresley with A4 Pacific No. 4498 *Sir Nigel Gresley*. (*NRM DON/313*)

Gresley designed teak-panelled carriages for the GNR, and these were adopted by the LNER. He was famous for his advocacy of articulation as a means of improving the riding of passenger rolling stock and also of increasing the number of seats within a given train length, as well as saving cost and weight. He applied the concept to improve the riding of six-wheel carriages inherited from the Great Eastern, but earlier, in 1921, he introduced the first articulated five-car dining set, also the first to use electric cooking, followed by an articulated sleeping twin-car set in 1922, and four and five-car suburban sets between 1923 and 1930. He applied pressure ventilation and even air conditioning to his prestige passenger carriages during the 1930s. He introduced welded underframes in 1934, and used aluminium and plywood for body panels.

At a time when many locomotive engineers were suspicious of anything to do with electricity or the internal combustion engine, he famously reminded members of the Institution of Locomotive

Engineers that they were not the Institution of Steam Locomotive Engineers. He was not alone in this as Maunsell and Bulleid on the Southern were also open-minded on the subject.

Gresley was a firm believer in a scientific approach to railway development. For many years he urged the railway companies, the independent locomotive builders and the government, to fund and build a locomotive testing station similar to that at Vitry sur Seine in France. In a period of extreme economic difficulty, his pleas fell largely on deaf ears, but eventually the LNER and its arch-rival the LMS agreed to set up a testing station together at Rugby, but the Second World War and then Nationalisation intervened, and the station did not open until 1948, by which time attention was turning to the potential of diesel and electric propulsion for the railways.

Gresley was approaching retirement age and so it seemed inevitable that his life's work was coming to an end. He was warned by his doctor in 1940 that he was in danger of a heart attack, and on 5 April 1941, he died just two months before he was due to retire.

Miller, John 1872–1942

An Ulsterman, Miller initially worked in London before going to the USA in 1909 to work on the Pennsylvania Railroad, from which he was recruited in 1916 by Sir Henry Thornton, the only American to run a major British main line railway, to work in the civil engineer's department of the Great Eastern Railway. He became the GER's chief civil engineer in 1919, and in 1925, after Grouping was appointed as chief civil engineer of the North Eastern Area.

His spell at York was noteworthy for his ability to maintain high standards on a tight budget, including such matters as improving the appearance of the lineside. Described as a born leader of men, he is credited with improving morale as well as performance, and despite a severe financial stringency he even managed to equip company sports grounds and build a gymnasium! He retired in 1937.

Thompson, Edward 1881–1954

After an early career in industry, he joined the railways and then became carriage and wagon superintendent for the Great Northern Railway in 1912. After Grouping he became an area workshops manager for the new LNER, later becoming mechanical engineer at Stratford Works in 1930. At Stratford he was responsible for the successful rebuilding of the former Great Eastern B12 class 4-6-0s and D16 class 4-4-0s. When Gresley died in 1941, he became chief mechanical engineer, a post he held until retirement in 1946. There has to be a suspicion that the appointment was made due to the lack of a serious rival and that Thompson, at the age of 60, was unlikely to be the next great locomotive designer. It is sometimes claimed that there was personal animosity between Thompson and Gresley, and certainly the austere Thompson, who frequently had difficulties with his staff, was the complete opposite of the more genial Gresley.

While his role as CME was limited by wartime restrictions on the types of locomotive that could be built, he also had to face the problems of maintaining the conjugated valve gear of Gresley's locomotives and the solution lay in extensive rebuilding. His B1 class 4-6-0s, built from 1942 onwards, were very successful, but the same could not be said for the L1 class 2-6-4Ts. In 1945, he started to build new, steel corridor carriages.

Wedgwood, Sir Ralph Lewis 1875–1956

After graduating from Cambridge, he became a traffic apprentice at the North Eastern Railway, after which he made rapid progress, becoming company secretary in 1905 and chief goods manager in 1911. He worked for the government during the First World War as director of ports, and on his return to the NER he became deputy general manager, and general manager in 1922, before becoming the first general manager of the new London & North Eastern Railway in 1923, the same year that he was knighted.

Under Wedgwood, the LNER operated a policy of decentralised management, leaving a small team to look after finance and policy matters. He also found time to be a member of the Weir Committee on main line electrification in 1931, and in 1936 visited India with a team investigating the state of the country's railways. On his return, he was one of the figures behind the 'Square Deal' campaign in which the railways pleaded unsuccessfully for the freedom to set their own freight rates. When he retired in 1939, he was appointed chairman of the Railway Executive Committee, which oversaw the running of the railways in wartime, before finally retiring in 1941.

Whitelaw, William 1868–1948

Although not from a railway background, but a landowner and bank director in Scotland, Whitelaw was appointed a director of the Highland Railway in 1899 and became its chairman during 1902–12, while he also became a director of the North British Railway and became its chairman in 1912, a position he held until Grouping. Some sources appear surprised that he was selected chairman of the LNER, but this may have been to overcome any rivalry between the larger constituent companies such as the Great Eastern, Great Northern and Great Central. The chairman of the Great Northern, Sir Frederick Banbury, was known to be an opponent of grouping. It does appear that Whitelaw managed to establish a good working relationship with the new company's management team.

William Whitelaw was the LNER's first chairman. Having come from the North British Railway, where he was well known to be thrifty, he applied the same disciplines to the new company.

He also had a fondness for riding on the footplate, where he found himself in a different environment from his two previous railway companies, which were small enough for the staff to know him.

Active in the Church of Scotland, he brought to his position caution and financial rectitude, but found himself running a company that was over-capitalised and suffering from the impact of the Miners' Strike and the Great Depression, which were especially serious for a company heavily dependent upon freight traffic.

From 1932, he insisted on dividend restraint, but in any case, the market value of the LNER's complicated issue of shares was far below par, even on Grouping. He broke ranks with the chairmen of the other three grouped railways in 1933 by declaring in public that nationalisation could be acceptable, although this was probably on the basis that the company could then have leased the business from the government and operated it as a contractor.

He retired in 1938, but remained a member of the board.

Chapter 6

Steam Locomotives at the Grouping

In common with all of the other grouped companies, the new LNER was obviously dependent at first on locomotives inherited from its predecessor companies. The trouble was that many of the locomotives were elderly, with even the North Eastern Railway having around 700 steam locomotives that were more than 30 years old, and that was no less than a third of the locomotives that it bequeathed to the LNER. The situation had been made worse by wartime restrictions on new building and as Grouping approached, the pace of new locomotive construction slackened as the pre-Grouping companies held on to their money. This in itself was not necessarily a bad thing as it left the way clear for the LNER to standardise its new construction programme, something that was much needed as the 7,423 locomotives it inherited were of 32 different types and 232 pre-Grouping classes.

Each constituent company, and many of the subsidiaries, had its own ideas about steam traction, often reflecting the type of operation or permanent way and other restrictions, but more often the inclinations of the chief mechanical engineer. Nevertheless, there were two oddities with the LNER. The first was that four of its predecessor companies had favoured outside cylindered 4-4-0 Atlantic locomotives for express passenger work, these being the Great Northern, North Eastern, North British and the Great Central. The second was that alone of the 'Big Four'; the LNER actually had a number of 4-6-2 Pacific locomotives from the North Eastern. The GWR had one Pacific, later converted to a 4-6-0; the LMS and the Southern had none.

The LNER inherited no fewer than 241 4-4-2 Atlantics and these proved capable of handling the heaviest expresses, including in one case, an Ivatt Atlantic hauling an express of more than 600 tons and yet losing just four minutes against its schedule. Many of these remained in service for long periods, especially after Gresley fitted them with larger superheaters, boosting their performance. Less successful was an experiment with a booster engine driving the trailing wheels, or pony truck, as the boiler could not provide enough steam for the booster to make an impact on performance.

Logic would have dictated a 'scrap-and-build' policy to ensure standardised rolling stock, but the money simply wasn't available. Standardisation would also have had its limits as some parts of the network, especially in Scotland, had tight curves that limited the size of locomotives, while the former Great Eastern lines had severe weight restrictions. A serious attempt at standardisation was made by Thompson when he took over from Gresley, but the country was at war and there were restrictions on the types of locomotive that could be built as well as shortages of materials and skilled manpower. At first, all that could be done was to establish a 'composite gauge', in effect a loading gauge, to which many of the inherited steam locomotives were adapted to ensure that there were no embarrassing incidents with lineside structures and bridges. Locomotive chimneys were often cut down, and on major overhauls, Robinson superheaters were installed in place of the many different types favoured by individual companies.

An ex-GER F3 class 2-4-2T condensing tank locomotive, No. 7244, waiting coaling, in 1930. (*HMRS ABX 102*)

Locomotive Trials

The new company did what any sensible organisation would do at first, setting out to compare the performance of the different classes of Atlantic, although the tests were not as comprehensive as they should have been. The original Atlantics had first appeared in 1898 on the Great Northern, designed by Henry Ivatt, the company's CME, and were followed in 1902 by a much improved version with a wide firebox feeding a massive boiler for the day. These locomotives were the stalwarts of the GNR fleet until Gresley introduced his Pacific just before Grouping.

The following year, 1903, the North Eastern introduced Atlantics designed by Worsdell, and in 1911 these were joined by a three-cylinder version designed by Vincent Raven, which handled the East Coast expresses over both the NER and the North British sections of the route to avoid an engine change at Berwick-on-Tweed. This practice was not popular with the NBR, but it did make sense, even though journey times on the Anglo-Scottish routes were more leisurely than they needed to be at the time because of the agreement between the rival railways not to resume racing.

The NBR did in fact have its own Atlantics, first introduced in 1906 by W.P. Reid, and used on the demanding route between Edinburgh and Aberdeen as well as on the Waverley route to Carlisle. They were not too popular with the directors as they were expensive machines and allegedly heavy on coal. They had large diameter boilers and Belpaire fireboxes.

Finally, the Great Central had Atlantics designed by J.G. Robinson and first introduced in 1903, and although similar in some ways to those of the NBR, were smaller and more elegant, being nicknamed 'Jersey Lilies' after the famous actress and mistress of King Edward VII. These were good performers and it is all the more surprising that they were the one set of locomotives not included in the trials. Also missed was the opportunity to test the Atlantics against the increasingly fashionable 4-6-0s, although this may have been because alone of the companies, only the GER had modern large-wheeled 4-6-0s capable of heavy express work.

The NER had introduced this wheel configuration to Britain as early as 1899, but the type had also been employed by the GCR.

On the other hand, borrowing a suitable locomotive from another railway would have been possible, and while the London & North Western and Lancashire & Yorkshire 4-6-0s had their limitations, those of the Great Western had been more successful, with the 'Star' class being regarded as the best at the time. Yet, here again, the preoccupation with the ECML may have been the overriding factor as the Great Eastern had not used Atlantics, but Holden's 4-6-0s were generally regarded as being the best in the country at the time.

Perhaps a straw in the wind was that plans laid in 1922 for new locomotives to enter service after the Grouping saw the NBR looking for five more Atlantics, but in the end the depots concerned received five of Gresley's new Pacifics.

The trials were conducted in 1923, probably as early as could have been managed, and were held on the East Coast Main Line between Newcastle and Edinburgh, possibly because this stretch was the quietest and also provided some gradients, unlike the line around York. The outcome was almost exactly the opposite of what might have been expected, with the NBR locomotive proving economical while that of the GNR not performing as well as expected.

Later in the year, trials were conducted between the NER and GNR Pacifics to see which could provide the basis for a new standard design. There was little between the two, with the former designed by Raven and the latter by Gresley, but it was the Gresley design that held most potential for future development, with a large boiler and wide firebox, three cylinders and Walschaerts valve gear. It had adopted features from the US Pennsylvania Railroad's K4 Pacifics. In short, it was powerful, fast and elegant, and many of its features were adopted by the LMS and Southern Railways. At this time of transition, an indication of the importance of the Gresley design was that the GNR ordered twelve for delivery during 1922/23, including the famous *Flying Scotsman*, and another 40 for 1924/25 with cut-down boiler mountings and cab roofs to allow their use on the former NBR lines.

Post-Grouping, most locomotives, including the Atlantics, remained in their original areas, which made sense as the enginemen and maintenance personnel at the depots were familiar with their old company's locomotives. Even so, ex-NER locomotives could be seen at King's Cross on occasion, especially when handling excursion trains, and seven ex-GNR Atlantics found their way onto former GCR lines while some of that company's Atlantics put in the occasional appearance at King's Cross. In fact, the ex-GER 4-6-0s were powerful and yet had a relatively light axle loading, essential for the company's network, but also giving them wide route availability, and during the 1930s several were moved to the Northern Scottish Area to replace 4-4-0s.

In 1924, with the express locomotive trials over, attention turned to the needs of shunting and short distance freight, for this was after all a railway that was heavily dependent on goods traffic. Several classes of 0-6-0T and 0-6-2T shunting locomotives were assessed, and the best was found to be the GNR's 0-6-0ST, which was adopted by Gresley as the basis for a new shunter, the J50, albeit with side tanks rather than a saddle tank.

The 'Directors' and Other Classes

All of the constituent companies had operated 4-4-0s, of which the best were undoubtedly the GCR 'Director' class, which were sufficiently powerful to remain on the Marylebone routes express trains until the mid-1930s. Another worthwhile 4-4-0 was the NER's powerful R class, while the GER's elegant, if slightly dated in appearance, D15 class 'Claud Hamilton' had led to a 'Super-Claud', with most of the originals rebuilt to this design. The design changed with an extended smokebox and superheater introduced from 1928, and then was rebuilt by Gresley from 1934 onwards. The NBR 4-4-0 'Scott' and 'Glen' classes were also successful.

On the other hand, many of the 4-4-0s were mundane. The GNR regarded its 4-4-0s as being only suitable for the secondary lines and lighter trains, while the Great North of Scotland had no fewer than 100 of its 122 locomotives as 4-4-0s, but these were generally very low-powered.

The small GER 2-4-0 locomotives were ideal for the East Anglian branch lines, and of the hundred or so inherited by the LNER at Grouping, 18 were still in service on Nationalisation. Earlier, some of these had been transferred to Darlington and Hull to replace ex-GNR 4-4-0s.

Yet, the most common configuration inherited by the LNER was the 0-6-0, with only the Great North of Scotland Railway having few of these. On Grouping, some were as old as fifty years, clearly obsolete, while others were capable locomotives, with the NER P3s remaining in service on coal trains into the 1960s. Perhaps the GER examples were the most powerful of these locomotives with the heavier versions as powerful as many eight-coupled locomotives, while there was also a lightweight class, dating from 1883. The NBR's final class of 0-6-0s was powerful and no fewer than 25 had spent the war years with the British Army in France, reflected in their being awarded French names on their return home. Of the 168 passed to the LNER, as many as 123 were handed on to British Railways. On the GNR, Ivatt's series of 0-6-0s was continued by Gresley. Even the relatively small Hull & Barnsley contributed 138 steam locomotives to the LNER, and of these, more than half were 0-6-0s.

The need to move heavy coal trains also meant that an important element in the LNER's locomotive fleet was the 0-8-0, and these came mainly from just three companies, the GNR, NER and the GCR, which had started to introduce them in the early years of the 20th century. These were never the most attractive of locomotives, although the neatest was the GNR series with inside cylinders while the others with outside cylinders looked ungainly. The NER 0-8-0s were further developed and became larger, nicknamed 'Long Toms', while Gresley started to build 2-8-0s of a completely new design, initially with two cylinders and later with three. Robinson on the GCR also developed a 2-8-0 with a neat and straightforward appearance and of these 666 were either taken up by the army from the GCR or ordered from a number of builders for service with the Army abroad during the First World War.

At the bottom of the locomotive pecking order was the freight shunting locomotive. In fact, the duties varied enormously from work in the ports, where small 0-4-0 tanks, including saddle tanks, would handle small groups of wagons, through the more usual 0-6-0T or 0-6-2T configuration for sidings, and on to the large, eight-coupled locomotives needed for the new hump shunting yards. The different companies had their individual approach to this latter task. The GCR had some large 0-8-4Ts, known as 'Daisies', while the NER had exactly the opposite configuration with 4-8-0Ts, while the GNR had 0-8-2Ts developed out of Ivatt's 0-8-0 goods engine. These had originally been intended as suburban passenger locomotives, but they handled empty carriage workings at King's Cross and shorter trips from the collieries of the Nottinghamshire coalfield, on which they were joined by 4-6-2Ts. Some of the six-coupled shunters on the GNR were in fact 0-6-0STs which, at the trials mentioned earlier, proved to be the best of the inherited designs, and from which Gresley developed into the J50 for the LNER, with the saddle tanks replaced by side tanks with sloping front ends to aid visibility. The GCR and NBR used 0-6-2Ts, which could also be used to bank trains.

An oddity was that the LNER inherited two petrol-engined shunting locomotives with one each from the North British and the Great Eastern.

While the suburban services on North Tyneside were electrified, as were some freight lines, the overwhelming mileage of suburban workings in 1923 was by steam. Here again, a wide variety of locomotive was to be found as not only did the London, or strictly speaking, Southern Area, suburban services vary widely, but the LNER also found itself with suburban services in other places as well, including Tyneside, Edinburgh and Glasgow, and with less-dense patterns of service around smaller regional centres such as Nottingham and Aberdeen.

Both the GNR and the GCR operated 4-4-2Ts, with the tank engine design ideal for short suburban journeys with a fast turnaround at each end. Ivatt followed the GNR 4-4-2T design with a 0-6-2T design, later further developed by Gresley with superheating and many of

The length of the A2 Pacifics is clear in this view of No. 2401 *City of Kingston-upon-Hull,* at Gateshead shed in 1927. (*HMRS AAB205*)

these survived into the 1960s. Robinson on the GCR took a slightly different course with his 4-4-2Ts developed into 4-6-2Ts for outer suburban traffic. The NER usually preferred the 0-4-4T configuration but also introduced three-cylinder 4-4-4Ts for the longer distance services, although these suffered from poor adhesion, and were later joined by 4-6-0Ts with 5ft 1¼in driving wheels for the gradients on the North Yorkshire coast lines: both classes were eventually rebuilt as 4-6-2Ts.

The GER favoured a variety of tank engines, including 0-4-4Ts, 2-4-2Ts, 0-6-0Ts and 0-6-2Ts, all with good acceleration which was more important than a higher top speed as stations were close together.

North of the border, the NBR had two classes of 4-4-2T for its Glasgow and Edinburgh suburban services, and the Great North of Scotland coped with Aberdeen's local traffic using a stud of just nine 0-4-4Ts.

Chapter 7

Atlantic to Pacific

The big problem facing Nigel Gresley when he took up his appointment as the first chief mechanical engineer of the LNER, was not just that he inherited more than 200 different classes of steam locomotive, many of them elderly, so that standardisation was important in order to contain costs, but that the LNER did not have the funds available to embark on a grand scheme of what might be described as 'scrap-and-build'. In addition, the first chairman, William Whitelaw, had come from one of the smaller constituent companies, the North British, and as mentioned earlier, the NBR was notorious for its strict economy. It is also possible that Whitelaw had no idea of the enormity of the task that faced the company's senior officers, indeed, he almost certainly did not as there was no precedent for mergers on the scale of the LNER, still less its bigger rival on the Anglo-Scottish routes, and between London and Southend, the LMS. Although on Grouping the prospects were not very bright, no one could have foreseen just how bad the world economy was to become, or the impact of the poor industrial relations of the 1920s.

The famous A1 Pacific No. 4472 *Flying Scotsman* at Potters Bar in 1923, although even if the train is the 'Flying Scotsman', at the time the name was unofficial. (*HMRS AAZ 421*)

A Pullman train headed by C1 4-4-2 No. 4444 during the mid-1930s. (*HMRS ABZ 611*)

The new company had 7,423 steam locomotives, 13,467 carriages and 281,748 goods wagons and vans. This required the attention of around 50,000 workshop employees which, on Grouping, were scattered around Darlington, York, Shildon and Hull on the NER alone; as well as at Doncaster on the GNR; Gorton and Dukinfield on the GCR; Stratford on the GER; Cowlairs on the NBR and Inverurie on the Great North of Scotland Railway. Both Doncaster and York had been badly damaged by fire during the First World War, but production was maintained after the facilities were reorganised and naturally, priority was given to reconstruction.

While 1922 was largely spent organising the new grouped railway companies and filling key appointments, a committee chaired by Sir Vincent Raven of the NER looked at the provision of new locomotives and also renumbering of rolling stock, as well as the urgent need to standardise brakes and corridor connections. To a great extent, the prior existence of the East Coast group of companies and their joint coaching stock was a great help, but away from the main lines and on the GCR and GER, other traditions and methods prevailed.

Raven was retained as a consultant after Grouping and an early task was to report on the company's workshops. His prime recommendation was to concentrate all locomotive production on Doncaster and Darlington, while he estimated that on an assumed life of 40 years, the company would need to build 185 new locomotives annually. This, of course, overlooked the fact that many of the inherited locomotives needed replacing as soon as possible and others would reach their 40th year within the next 20 years, or even less. Needless to say, the LNER failed to produce anything like 185 new locomotives a year until 1947, when it actually built 193, spurred on by the need to make up for wartime restrictions and losses. In fact, 1923 saw just 126 locomotives built; all pre-Grouping designs and ordered by the constituent companies, although these orders had to be confirmed by the LNER. By the early 1930s, 1923 must have looked like a busy year, for in 1932 just 34 locomotives were built, and only half this number in 1933.

A comprehensive system of locomotive classification was introduced, using a system from the Great Northern which consisted of a letter denoting the wheel arrangement followed by figures indicating the series. Under this scheme, 'A1' was used for the GNR Pacific and 'A5' the

GCR 4-6-2T, while 'J27' was the largest of the NER's 0-6-0s. Power classifications varied from area to area without any attempt at standardisation, while it was not until 1940 that a route availability classification was started.

Raven introduced a fog signalling apparatus, but this does not seem to have produced the results that the LNER expected as it was abandoned in 1933.

The Gresley Era

Once Gresley was appointed as chief mechanical engineer, plans were laid for central control of locomotive building in 1924, which naturally included Gresley designs that would be introduced wherever they were needed on the LNER. Some of the pre-Grouping designs continued to be built. It was not until 1925 that the LNER started to prepare an annual programme for building locomotives, wagons and carriages, which were first approved at a joint meeting of the area locomotive and traffic committees and then presented to the LNER board for approval.

Gresley's Pacific designs were already in service as Grouping took effect, and the design changes to those delivered in 1924/25 were such that wider route availability was achieved, including operation over the former NBR lines. Many of the locomotives were given the names of famous racehorses, although some were no longer prominent in the public mind, and so names such as *Sandwich* or *Spearmint* must have seemed odd. That apart, the new locomotives provided much needed extra power for the increasingly heavy trains on the East Coast, and no less important, allowed what would today be described as a 'cascade' of older and smaller engines, most of them 4-4-2 Atlantics, for use elsewhere on the LNER. The day of the 4-4-0 was not past, however, and there was still a demand for these, especially in Scotland, but Gresley had not had time to produce his own design and so the LNER authorised 24 of the former GCR 'Director' class rather than further examples of the former NBR's 'Scott' class.

It was another Gresley design, the three-cylinder 2-6-0 K3, that was selected as the standard mixed-traffic locomotive, with no fewer than 60 being built at Darlington in 1924/25. The early examples look dated with their NER-style cabs, but later engines were fitted with cabs with side windows, giving them a more modern appearance. A new standard design of tender was introduced for the third K3 to be built, with 4,200 gallons of water and 7½ tons of coal. The initial batch was allocated mainly to the GNR routes, cascading the earlier K2 class to other routes, including the busy Liverpool Street and Southend line, as well as on to the West Highland line. The K3 remained in production until 1937, with 193 built.

The new 'standard' tender was in fact not one but three standard tenders of different sizes which the LNER introduced. Originally with a stepped-out coping, the standard tenders were later given straight sides. Deviations from the standard included an eight-wheel 5,000-gallon capacity tender for the Pacifics, including some with a corridor and connection for non-stop services, and a smaller 3,500-gallon tender for locomotives on short-haul work. Economy, or parsimony, also dictated that not every new locomotive had a new tender, and as tenders required much less maintenance than a steam locomotive and fewer major overhauls, it was steam railway practice to have fewer tenders than locomotives.

Meanwhile, heavy mineral trains, mainly coal but including iron ore and aggregates, were catered for by eight-coupled locomotives, the most prominent of which were the former GCR 2-8-0 series which had been adopted by the Ministry of Munitions with many of these being offered for sale as war surplus. These were a bargain to the cash-strapped LNER, which bought 273 between 1924 and 1927, with the last batch costing just £340 each! Added to these were another 148 inherited from the GCR, of which 17 had larger boilers that were later replaced by the standard pattern. This total of 421 locomotives was the largest single class on the LNER.

Gresley was allowed to build two 2-8-2 Mikados, designated Class P1, which were fitted with booster engines to power the trailing wheels or pony truck, just as had been attempted with the Atlantics. They also adopted features from a Pennsylvania Railroad's locomotive, although in this case it was a 2-8-2, and they were intended to haul 100-wagon coal trains between Peterborough New England yard and Hornsey Ferme Park, but operating restrictions meant that trains of this length could not be handled. The first of these two large locomotives was available for the big centenary of the Stockton & Darlington Railway in 1925.

Another heavy locomotive which entered service was the even larger 2-8-0+0-8-2 Beyer-Garratt articulated locomotive, which combined the wheels of a 2-8-0 with a single massive boiler. It spent its life on the Worsborough Bank near Barnsley until electrification, when it was transferred for trials on the Lickey Incline in 1949/50 and 1955, but without success, despite conversion to oil firing in 1952. Many believe that it was actually intended for Wath–Immingham coal trains.

Lower down the scale, Gresley N2 0-6-2Ts were built for the King's Cross suburban services, allowing Ivatt's N1s to be sent to Nottingham and to Yorkshire, in turn releasing 4-4-2Ts to be cascaded on to country branches and allowing Stirling 0-4-4Ts to be withdrawn. N2s were also sent to Edinburgh, Glasgow and Dundee for use on suburban services. A few were allocated to the Liverpool Street suburban services, but for the most part these were handled by a further build of 112 N7s, which had originated as a Great Eastern design. At Marylebone, Robinson's capable 4-6-2Ts, designated as A5s by the LNER, did not need replacing and indeed, a further 13 were built for services in the North East, and later the unsatisfactory former NER 4-4-4Ts were rebuilt as 4-6-2Ts, in which configuration they displayed a considerably improved performance.

In 1930, Gresley introduced the first of his V1 2-6-2Ts, of which 92 were eventually built, with later versions having higher boiler pressure and the earlier examples later being rebuilt to this standard. These were spread around the system, and in many cases replaced the N2s in Scotland.

Given the importance of goods traffic, and especially coal, to the LNER, there was a need for 0-6-0s, and these were built with both 5ft 2in coupled wheels, Class J39, allowing them to work shorter distance passenger trains, and 4ft 8in wheels, Class J38, for coal trains, especially in areas such as Scotland with severe gradients. There were 35 Class J38s and 289 of the J39s. Doubtless there would have been even more but for the continued existence of many pre-Grouping 0-6-0s.

One oddity introduced during the Gresley era but not of his design, was the product of an independent locomotive builder, Sentinel, which applied its experience of building steam lorries to the lighter end of locomotive building. The four grouped companies all undertook trials with the Sentinel CE, for centre engine, but only the LNER ordered this locomotive. Unlike the conventional steam locomotive, the CE used a vertical boiler and a chain drive, both as used in

For a period, there was a fashion for Sentinel steam shunters with vertical boilers, engines and chain drive, which was kinder to the track than conventional steam traction. These tiny four-wheeled locomotives tended to have long lives. This is No. 54 in departmental service. (*LNER*)

steam lorries. Trials showed that the CE was capable of hauling a considerable load and the chain drive was much kinder to the track than the traditional locomotive motion, which in effect gave the track hammer blows. The CE series could be used wherever track was poor, such as on some branch lines and in the smaller goods yards. The LNER ordered 15 CEs as Class Y1, and when Sentinel produced a centre engine, double geared, variant as the CEDG, no fewer than 32 were ordered as Class Y3, all during the late 1920s, with a further 20 ordered in 1930 on the grounds of economy as the odd-looking locomotives used just 15lb of coal per mile and could be operated by just the driver. Unusual these may have been, but most survived at Nationalisation.

Coal was important to the LNER not just as part of its traffic but as its fuel. The Miners' Strike of 1926 had come as a shock to the economy, but it had not been the first stoppage at the pits in the years following the war. In 1927, 30 locomotives at Stratford shed were converted to oil burning to provide an alternative source of fuel. The old Great Eastern had been amongst the first of the railway companies to experiment with oil burning locomotives prior to Grouping, with the first conversions as early as 1897, which may be why Stratford was chosen by the LNER as home to its small stud of oil-burning locomotives. Locomotives on the longer distance services of the LNER, mainly on the former Great Northern and North Eastern lines, would have needed to retain the flexibility of coal firing for which the inherited infrastructure was well suited.

Water was as essential to the steam railway as coal, perhaps even more so, as one could use oil instead of coal but there was no substitute for water. Hard water had the same impact on the boilers and boiler tubes of a steam locomotive as it did on a kettle, only it was far more expensive and time-consuming to remove the limescale and as it built up, the performance of a locomotive fell away. During the 1930s, Henry Turner, the LNER's chief chemist and metallurgist, oversaw the introduction of water-softening plants, with £600,000 earmarked in 1932 for the construction of 18 plants on the former Great Northern lines, reducing the costs of boiler maintenance and extending the intervals between major overhauls as well as improving performance and fuel consumption.

The problem was not universal throughout the system, with most of the former North British lines running through areas with soft water.

As traffic fell during the years of the Great Depression, many locomotives were withdrawn, selected in many cases because they were non-standard, although inevitably there were also those that were less successful designs, perhaps lacking power or reliability, or suffering from heavy coal consumption.

Inter-company Trials

Locomotive engineers did not work in isolation. From the Victorian era onwards they had enjoyed a steady flow of technical information about developments on other railways, and not necessarily just in the British Isles. In addition, senior railwaymen of all disciplines moved more frequently between companies than was the case in many other industries at the time. This was sometimes necessary if an ambitious young engineer was not to waste many years waiting to step into dead man's shoes.

Taking this process a stage further was the decision in 1925 to exchange locomotives with the Great Western, so that the two companies could compare the relative performance of their star performers on a particular route. While the Gresley Pacifics were undoubtedly powerful performers, they were also great consumers of coal, but Gresley was reluctant to listen to suggestions that short-travel valves inhibited their performance. There is still uncertainty over whether Gresley himself or the new Southern Divisional Manager Alex Wilson initiated the trials. Wilson was certainly keen to show off the A1s to the GWR.

The trials attracted keen public interest. The two routes chosen were between King's Cross and Doncaster on the East Coast route, and between Paddington and Plymouth on the GWR. In each case, an A1 was set against a 'Castle' class 4-6-0. On the line to Plymouth, the A1, No. 4474, later named *Victor Wild*, with its longer wheelbase struggled with the tight downhill curves of the line so that it had to work hard on the uphill sections to keep to time. On the former Great Northern line the Castle showed its superiority, with better timekeeping allied to lower coal consumption. While the LNER team retired disappointed, the lessons were taken to heart, and work started on an improved valve design with longer travel while higher boiler pressures were adopted for new construction, with 27 locomotives introduced by 1935 and designated A3. Nevertheless, limited finance meant that while all of the 52 Gresley Pacifics in service in 1925 were converted to the new valve design within six years, just five received new boilers and the remainder had to wait until their boilers were judged incapable of further repair, with some not receiving the new boiler until the war years.

Most importantly, the new features worked well, allowing non-stop running between King's Cross and Edinburgh Waverley, once tenders had been modified with a corridor and connection to allow a change of footplate crew en route. What, with hindsight seems a wasted opportunity, as from 1 May 1928, the 'Flying Scotsman' train began its non-stop runs, but still had to stick to the 8½-hour schedule agreed in the wake of the 19th-century races, until the service was accelerated in 1932.

Three locomotives at Grantham in 1932, with, left to right: C1 4-4-2s No. 4405 and 3286 and A3 4-6-2 No. 4474 *Victor Wild*. (*HMRS ABZ 605*)

Motive Power Experiments

The proponents of the steam locomotive placed much faith in higher boiler pressures to ensure a long-term future for steam. This was understandable up to a point as the electric trains had shown vastly improved performance on services with many stops, but struggled to match steam in top speed and in any case the railways had, over a century, built a massive infrastructure devoted to the needs of the steam locomotive. This was being developed further with large new coaling plant to improve productivity and reduce the time and number of men needed to coal a locomotive.

Both the LNER and the LMS invested in experimental steam locomotives. The LNER candidate was a 4-6-4, classed W1, and numbered 10000. This was a high-pressure locomotive at 540lb per square inch, three times that of an A3. It was built in secret at Darlington using a boiler built by Yarrow, the Clyde shipbuilder. Within the company, the locomotive was known as the 'Hush-hush' because of the secrecy; although the *LNER Magazine* noted with amusement that a journalist had written that its name meant that it was intended to be much quieter than other steam locomotives!

Unlike the LMS locomotive, *Fury*, withdrawn from service after a fatal explosion and rebuilt with standard pressure, after completion in late 1929, No. 10000 did at least see passenger service, although it was never completely reliable. It handled the 'Flying Scotsman' non-stop and was present at many of the 'exhibitions' which the LNER presented at points around its network over the years. It was rebuilt in 1937 as a conventional three-cylinder locomotive. The outward appearance of 10000 was also different, with sheeting fitted around the firebox, and this was one of the best features of the locomotive as it lifted smoke and improved the view from the footplate. Amongst the many problems with 10000 was that it was difficult to keep the boiler tube ends tight as she had many times the number of tubes of a conventional locomotive. When one senior manager asked a well-regarded fitter-boilermaker at one depot what was his favourite view of this locomotive, he was told in no uncertain terms that: 'The very best view of her was the back of the tender, when the bloody thing was going away...'

As can be seen, Gresley has been credited with not imposing his designs on suburban tank locomotive construction as long as the existing locomotives were capable performers. This could be because of his interest in the upper end of locomotive performance, whether it be high-stepping express locomotives or heavy freight engines, or it could be simply that time and financial pressures inhibited much further work. Certainly, the abundance of inherited tank engines and especially 0-6-0 and smaller meant that there was little need for new building. His plans for 2-6-2T and 2-6-4Ts were rejected, often because they would be too long for the platforms at Moorgate, but also because there were tender locomotives that could be cascaded onto these services.

On the former Great Eastern, the pre-Grouping 4-4-0s and 4-6-0s were given new boilers and rebuilt incorporating Gresley features wherever possible. More than fifty of the 4-6-0s ran for many years with feedwater heating equipment to enhance their performance, while others had the conventional piston valves replaced by Lentz poppet valves.

The Other Gresley Express Locomotives

This is to jump ahead somewhat, because in the meantime, Gresley had to meet demands for new locomotives elsewhere on the system that could not be met either by his new Pacifics or by the cascading of smaller locomotives from elsewhere on the LNER. While the period between the wars has been viewed as one of economic difficulty and industrial decline, East Anglia was proving to be something of an exception, and the former GER lines needed new locomotives for the expresses and boat trains. Gresley built a new 4-4-0, Class D49, at Darlington with three cylinders driving the leading coupled wheels, with 36 built during 1927–29, bearing the names of English and Scottish Shire counties. Although tried at King's Cross where one example handled duties normally allocated to an Atlantic, they were not needed on the old GNR lines. The later 'Hunt' class was a modified and up-dated version of the Shires.

Gresley's design principles could not be adopted easily for a new 4-6-0 needed by the Liverpool Street expresses, while also keeping within the weight limits set by the divisional civil engineer, who had to contend with many weak bridges on his network. The design work went to Doncaster, but the team struggled to reach a workable compromise while the need for the new locomotives became more pressing. Eventually, ten new locomotives of the Holden design were built by Beyer Peacock, while a design-and-build contract was awarded to the North British Locomotive Company for new 4-6-0s, with a split drive with the centre cylinder driving the leading coupled wheels. The first ten, known as 'Sandringhams', named after country estates, and classed as B17, were ready by the end of 1928. Further examples were later built at Darlington, giving a total of 73, with some of the later examples, named after football clubs, being sent to the former GCR lines.

Most of the steam railcars were single vehicles, but *Phenomena*, seen here at Blyth in 1938, was a two-car articulated set. (*HMRS ACW 127*)

Steam Railcars

Unlike the Southern, the LNER did not invest heavily in electrification, and unlike the Great Western, it did not see diesel rail cars as the solution to the problems of running branch lines economically. The LNER instead placed its faith in steam railcars, of which eventually 92 were operated. As with every attempt to produce an economical railway vehicle, regardless of the system of propulsion used, these suffered from poor capacity and a limited ability to handle overcrowding, but they were also less reliable than one might have expected given the 'mature' steam technology used. Most used 100hp two-cylinder engines, although a few had more power, and in an attempt to address the issue of capacity, there was even an articulated twin-carriage model.

The first example arrived in 1926 from Sentinel, which built most of the railcars, although a few were also built by the Clayton Wagon Company, while Sentinel also built 58 small shunting engines, mainly for departmental use, as mentioned earlier.

Unlike rail motors, which clearly had in most cases, a small steam locomotive sitting on the frame of a passenger carriage, the Sentinel and Clayton railcars had the steam locomotive boxed in so that they looked at first glance as if they were powered by diesel or electric, except when the smoke and steam gave the game away.

Chapter 8

The Streamliners

The A1/A3 Pacifics became an undoubted success, once boiler pressures were raised and long travel valve gear introduced. Nevertheless, more was needed as trains were getting heavier, for a variety of reasons. One of these was the introduction of third-class sleeping accommodation in 1928, which proved very popular and meant longer and heavier trains, so that even the mighty Pacifics needed double heading on the gradients between Edinburgh and Aberdeen. More catering vehicles also meant extra carriages.

It was not just passenger trains that required more power. Faster freight trains were one way in which the railways could counter competition from road haulage, unregulated until 1930. Parcels, mail, milk and fish all required faster trains, as did other perishable traffic such as bananas. A good mixed-traffic locomotive was the answer, one that could handle secondary expresses as well as fast, fully fitted goods trains. The locomotive would have to be a successor to the K3s. As an interim measure, conversion of some of the more modern Atlantics to 2-6-0 configuration with an articulated tender had been considered, but the idea was abandoned, in 1932.

A4 class 4-6-2 No. 4902 *Seagull* was amongst the last of the A4s to enter service, in 1938, and is seen here, near Offord, in 1939. (*HMRS AEU 527*)

PRINCIPAL TRAINS BETWEEN LONDON AND SCOTLAND

LM&S

1193a

L&NE

Week Days

	mrn SC	mrn RC	mrn RC	mrn RC	mrn RC	mrn N	mrn PC	mrn RC	mrn PC	mrn S	mrn RC	mrn RC	mrn A	mrn RC	mrn P	mrn S
LONDON (Eus) 412..dep.	1220	SC	..	..	..	RC	..		10 0	10 10	..	..	RC	10a5	..	RC
" (King's Cr) 810 "	..	1 5	4 45	..	7†25	9 20		10 0	..	RC	..	10 5	1010	..	1120	1150
" (St. Pan) 642 "	..	..	..	4 25	..	..	9 5	..	..	..	10 9	..	..	..	..	..
EDINBURGH (Prin St.) arr.	..	..	..	..	..	..	..	..	5E5	5J45	..	..	..	..	..	..
" (Wav).. "	..	9 36	1 35	3f43	3 50	4 45	5 45	5 0	..	..	..	5F25	5 50	..	7 5	7 30
GLASGOW (Central). "	..	..	..	..	..	..	5U42	..	5g0	..	..	..	..	..	..	..
" (Queen St.) "	..	11 6	2 58	..	5 1	6 3	..	..	..	..	..	6 45	7 22	..	8 13	8 43
" (St. Enoch) "	9 38	..	..	3*15	..	..	..	..	..	..	6 48	..	..	..	..	..
PERTH (General)..... "	..	11 33	3 29	5U23	5 50	..	7 13	..	..	..	..	7 13	..	7 25	..	..
DUNDEE (Tay Bridge) "	..	11b32	3 29	6 16	6 16	..	8 58	6 37	..	..	..	7 11	..	..	8 58	1030
" (West)...... "	..	..	..	6U0	..	..	..	..	..	..	..	..	..	8 21	..	..
ABERDEEN .... "	..	1b23	5 20	8 15	8 15	..	9U52	8 15	..	..	..	9 0	..	9 52	1045	..
INVERNESS.......... "	..	3 36	7 55	9 35	9 35	..	..	..	..	..	..	..	..	..	..	..

	non RC	aft S	aft S	aft RC	aft G	aft W	aft S	aft RC	aft E	aft S	G RC	aft E	aft E	aft E	aft E	aft
LONDON (Eus) 412..dep.	..	PC	1 15	..	1 30	1 30	1 30	1 35	2 0	RC	H	7 25	RC	RC	7 40	..
" (King's Cr) 810 "	..	1 10	RC	1 20	C	RC	PC	..	SC	2 30	4 0	RC	7 25	7 40	RC	8 25
" (St. Pan) 642 "	12 0	..	..	..	RC	..		..	..	..	..	SC	SC	SC	SC	..
EDINBURGH (Prin St.) arr.	..	..	..	..	..	..	9 46	..	9 45	..	..	..	..	..	..	..
" (Wav).. "	9 1	8 40	..	8†45	..	..	..	..	..	1020	10 0	..	3 35	3 50	..	6 6
GLASGOW (Central). "	..	..	9 12	..	8 0	9 5	..	..	..	..	..	..	..	..	..	..
" (Queen St.) "	..	9 55	..	9 57	..	..	..	..	..	1157	1139	..	5 29	5 29	..	7N33
" (St. Enoch) "	8 48	..	..	..	..	..	..	..	..	..	..	..	..	..	..	..
PERTH (General)..... "	1058	..	..	1058	..	..	..	1041c	..	..	..	4 46	4 55	..	..	8N30
DUNDEE (Tay Bridge) "	..	..	..	..	..	..	..	..	..	..	..	..	..	5 25	..	8N41
" (West)...... "	..	..	..	..	..	..	..	..	..	..	..	..	..	..	6 50	..
ABERDEEN .... "	..	..	..	..	..	..	..	3 0	..	..	..	7 10	..	7 20	..	..
INVERNESS.......... "	5N25	..	..	5N25	..	..	..	5N45	..	..	..	8 45	8 45	..	..	..

Week Days—Continued

	aft F	aft SC	aft N	aft D	aft SC	aft RC	aft RC	aft E	aft S	aft E	aft Y	aft RC	
LONDON (E) 412dep	9 15	..	9 25	9 25	..	SC	SC	1050	1050	1055	1135	1145	..
" (K's C) 810 "	SC	..	SC	..	..	10 25	1035	RC	RC	RC	RC	SC	..
" (St. P) 642 "	..	9 15	..	..	9 30	..	..	SC	SC	SC	SC	..	..
EDINB'GH (P. St.). arr	..	..	..	..	..	..	..	7 43	8 5	..	..	..	..
" (Wav.) "	..	7 6	..	..	..	..	7 30	..	..	..	..	..	..
GLASGOW (Cen.).. "	6 19	..	6 25	6 45	..	..	..	..	..	..	9 30	9h35	..
" (Q. St.) "	..	..	..	SC (3rd class only)	..	8 49	9q38	..	..	..	..	..	..
" (St. En) "	..	..	..		7 31	..	..	..	..	..	..	..	..
PERTH (General) "	..	8u55	..		..	8u55	..	..	9 18	9 11	..	..	..
DUNDEE (Tay B) "	..	9U18	..		..	9U15	..	..	10 3	..	..	..	..
" (West).. "	..	..	..		..	..	..	..	..	10 0	..	..	..
ABERDEEN ...... "	..	11d18	..		..	11d12	..	..	1130	1129	..	..	..
INVERNESS....... "	..	1K40	..		..	1K40	..	..	1§47	1§40	..	..	..

Sundays.

	mrn RC	mrn RC	mrn RC	mrn Z	mrn RC	mrn PC	aft PC	aft RC	aft RC	aft RC	aft RC	aft	aft SC	aft SC	aft SC	aft RC		aft RC	aft RC	aft RC
LONDON (E) 412dep	..		..	1110	1120	1135	..	7 20	SC	7 30	SC	..	..	9 30	..	SC	..	SC	1050	1145
" (K's C) 810 "	..	11 0	1110	RC	..	..	1 0	SC	7 25	SC	7 40	8 25	..	..	..	1025	..	1035	SC	SC
" (St. P) 642 "	1030	..	..	..	..	..	..	..	..	..	..	..	9 15	..	9 30	..	..	..	..	..
EDINB'GH (P. St.). arr	8U35	..	..	..	..	8 35	..	..	..	..	..	..	..	..	..	..	..	..	7 48	..
" (Wav.) "	..	6 0	7 0	..	..	..	8 20	..	3 35	..	3 50	6 6	7 6	..	..	..	..	7 30	..	..
GLASGOW (Cen.).. "	..	..	..	7 7	7 20	8 35	..	..	..	..	..	..	..	7 15	..	..	..	..	..	9 35
" (Q. St.) "	..	7 29	8 36	..	..	..	9 38	..	5 29	..	5 29	7 33	..	..	..	8 49	..	9 38	..	..
" (St. En) "	8 25	..	..	..	..	..	..	..	..	..	..	..	..	..	7 31	..	..	..	..	..
PERTH (General) "	..	..	..	..	..	d 1239	1037	4 46	4 55	5 33	..	8 30	8 55	..	..	8 55	..	..	9 11	..
DUNDEE (Tay B) "	..	8 9	9 8	..	..	..	1055	..	..	..	5 25	8 41	9 18	..	..	9 15	..	..	..	..
" (West).. "	..	..	..	..	..	..	..	..	..	6 50	..	..	..	..	..	..	..	..	10 0	..
ABERDEEN ...... "	..	..	11 5	..	..	2d50	..	..	..	7 40	7 20	..	1112	..	..	1112	..	..	1129	..
INVERNESS....... "	..	..	..	..	..	5d25	5 25	8 45	8 45	9 50	..	..	1§40	..	..	1§40	..	..	1§40	..

A or A On 16th, 23rd & 30th inst.
a 5 mins. later on 23rd & 30th inst.
B Arr. 9 5 mrn. on Suns.
b 13 mins. earlier on Sats.
C The Coronation Scot. Limited accommodation.
c Arr. 12 10 ngt. on Sats.
D Sats. only (except 30th inst.)
d Via Glasgow (Cen.), leaving there at 11 0 aft.
E or E Except Sats.
F Fridays and 30th inst. On 30th inst. arr. Glasgow 5 45 mrn with 3rd class sleeping accommodation only.
F Except 16th, 23rd and 30th inst.
f 12 mins. later on Sats.
G Except Sats. and 29th inst.
g Arr. 5 40 aft. on Sats.
H The Coronation. Extra charge. Limited seating accommodation. Seats bookable in advance.
H Arr 6 37 aft. on Sats
h Arr. 9 25 mrn on Suns
J On 23rd and 30th inst., dep. Euston 10 5 & arr. Edinburgh (P.St.) 5 48 aft.
K Arr. 1 47 aft. on Suns.
N Except Fridays and Saturdays.
N Except Sun. morns.
n Arr. 11 3 mrn on Suns.
P or P Pullman Cars only. Supplementary Charges.
q Arr. 10 48 mrn on Suns.
RC Restaurant Car whole or part of journey
S or S Sats. only.
SC 1st & 3rd cl. Sleeping accommodation.
U Change at Carlisle.
u Arr. 9 2 mrn. on Suns.
W On 29th inst. only.
Y On nights of 29th and 30th inst. Arr. Glasgow (C.) 8 43 mrn on 31st inst.
Z On 31st inst. only.
* 10 mins. later on Sats
† 5 mins. later on Sats
§ Afternoon Time.

Services to Scotland improved out of all recognition between 1922 and 1938, largely because of the ending of the restrictive agreement that kept day trains to an 8½-hour journey time. Also noticeable are named trains, such as the 'Flying Scotsman' for example, which previously had simply been known officially as the 'East Coast Luncheon and Dining Car Express'. The 'Flying Scotsman' is the sixth column from the upper right, taking six hours against 6½ hours for the LMS flagship 'Coronation Scot', twelfth column from the upper right. *(Bradshaw)*

In short, the LNER needed two completely new locomotive types, with one a powerful but fast locomotive capable of working between Edinburgh and Aberdeen without double heading. The other would be a fast and competent mixed-traffic locomotive with wide route availability, much the same specification as led to the Stanier 'Black Five' on the LMS. In fact, there was a need for three new types, with the continuing need to develop the standard Pacific locomotives, and for this there would be the logical successor to the A3, the A4.

Gresley ensured that the two new locomotives shared certain features. First, both had 6ft 2in driving wheels, although the configuration varied with 2-8-2 for the Aberdeen trains and 2-6-2 for mixed traffic; next, both had the wide firebox of the A3s, although enlarged still further to 50sq ft for the Aberdeen trains, and, finally, they shared the same boiler design as the enlarged higher pressure boiler being introduced on the Pacifics, albeit 2ft shorter in the mixed-traffic locomotive.

The Aberdeen locomotives were classed as P2, and when the first appeared, No. 2001, named *Cock o' the North*, in May 1934, it also adopted Lentz valves and the cladding first seen on No. 10000. It was the largest and most powerful British express locomotive at the time, and after making an impression when first seen on trials at King's Cross, it was sent to the testing station at Vitry-sur-Seine in France, which provided much useful information. The second locomotive of the class did not appear from Doncaster until October, and this used piston valves with

Walschaerts gear. The next four appeared in 1936, and were streamlined using the wedge shape more usually association with the A4s, with the first two being modified to this design later. In fact, No. 10000 was also rebuilt with a streamline front end in 1937, but showed no real improvement over the Pacifics, and no further 4-6-4s were built and the design itself was not developed further.

The big problem with the P2s was that they were supposedly ideal for the task for which they were designed, and there were economies as well as efficiencies in no longer having to double head expresses between Edinburgh and Aberdeen, but they were too large and heavy, and used too much coal, for other work. In truth, there were just a few trains for which they were ideally matched. In fact, their eight-coupled wheels also resulted in them having difficulty with the tight curves on this demanding stretch of line. This meant that for much of the time these excellent locomotives either could not be used, or were a costly means of working even a day express. After Gresley's death, Thompson ensured that these were rebuilt as Pacific locomotives and became Class A2/2, although they were still long overall and appeared ungainly, as well as having poor adhesion with six coupled wheels.

Streamlining was not applied to the new mixed-traffic locomotives, which from the outset looked like slightly shortened A3s, even to having a 'banjo' steam collector instead of a dome, as introduced on the final four A3s built in 1935. These were designated as V2s, with a standard 4,200 gallon tender and a P2 wedge-shaped spectacle plate. The first was named *Green Arrow*, but of 184 V2s built between 1937 and 1944, only eight were named. In fact, *Green Arrow* was named for the sake of expediency to help publicise a new fast freight service.

This was another successful class that could, if necessary, replace a Pacific, but this was usually done in an emergency and more often they replaced the Atlantics and relieved the K3s to be cascaded from the fast freight trains. When the second batch of B17s, mentioned earlier and named after football clubs, proved to have insufficient power for the express services over the former GCR lines, it was the V2s and cascaded earlier Pacifics, displaced from express work on the East Coast by the new A4s, that were drafted in to take over the Marylebone expresses. The high axle loadings of the V2s nevertheless precluded their use on the Liverpool Street services.

The A4s

In the popular mind, Sir Nigel Gresley will be associated with the famous streamlined A4 Pacifics more than any other locomotive. This is understandable, but as we have seen, other classes were also successful, especially the V2s.

The ending of the restriction on journey times between London and Scotland meant that the LNER was freed to consider higher speed running. In the early 1930s, a fast express would spend much of its time running at speeds not much higher than 50mph. The LNER started to experiment with running shorter and lighter trains at much higher speeds. The untapped potential of even the A3s was soon shown when, in November 1934, No. 4472 *Flying Scotsman* reached a speed of 100mph, the first time that this was officially authenticated.* Shortly afterwards, the same driver, W. Sparshatt, was also given his head with a seven carriage train from Newcastle to King's Cross when, driving another A3, *Papyrus*, he set a new record of 108mph and completed the journey in less than four hours.

While the 1935 locomotive programme had included another four A3s, Gresley was already hard at work further developing and refining the design. He shortened the boiler by a foot and lengthened the combustion chamber by the same amount, as well as raising the steam pressure to 250lb per square inch, but the most important change was visual, with the entire exterior covered in silver cladding, including valences over the motion and the coupled wheels. This

* The much earlier record set by the *City of Truro* on the Great Western in 1904 was not official, and for many years doubt was cast on the validity of the claim, although in recent years it has generally been regarded as genuine.

A3 class 4-6-2 No. 2752 *Spion Kop* appears in fine condition at Doncaster in 1939. It is named after a Derby-winning racehorse (sired by *Spearmint*, another Derby winner, commemorated by A3 No. 2796, later No. 100), rather than the Boer War battle. (*HMRS AAN 612*)

was the new A4 class, designed for the new high-speed 'Silver Jubilee' express introduced in 1935 between King's Cross and Newcastle to mark the silver jubilee of King George V that year. Not surprisingly, the locomotive was named *Silver Link*,* and the next few locomotives of the same class also had 'silver' name, with the second being *Quicksilver*.

In contrast to the stately pace of construction for the P2s, *Silver Link* took just eleven weeks to build. Despite this, she was no troublesome prototype, and on the inaugural press trip for the 'Silver Jubilee' she reached 112½mph and then maintained an average of 100mph for 43 miles. In addition, for the first three weeks of the new service, she was the only A4 available and ran the return journey each day, 537 miles in total, without any trouble.

Government-backed low-interest loans under the New Works Programme of 1935 were used to build a further 17 A4s, as well as many other locomotives, making a total of 43 altogether after the low level achieved of just 17 in 1933. A similar number of older locomotives was withdrawn and scrapped, but given the 1935 total of 6,802 locomotives, it is clear that building a thoroughly modern and efficient locomotive stock for the LNER was going to take a very long time.

A total of 35 A4s was built, and initially the first four were painted silver to match the carriages of the 'Silver Jubilee'. Later locomotives were painted green, but in 1937 five were painted garter blue to work the new 'Coronation' express between King's Cross and Edinburgh, with these named after the dominions in the British Empire. One of these locomotives, No. 4489 *Dominion of Canada*, was easily recognised from a distance with a North American-style bell fitted to the front of her smokebox.

Streamlining the A4s was not simply a publicity measure, but was intended to save fuel at high speeds, while an important side effect was that smoke was lifted clear and the view from

* Perhaps we should be relieved that the locomotive was not also named 'Silver Jubilee', as the giving of the same names to locomotives and express trains has doubtless been a contributing factor in many today being incapable of distinguishing between a locomotive and a train, as with the *Flying Scotsman* and the 'Flying Scotsman'.

the footplate much improved. The same treatment was given to two of the 4-6-0 'Sandringham' class locomotives working out of Liverpool Street, and in this instance, largely to gain publicity as the maximum speed of these locomotives was far below that at which streamlining would have a beneficial impact.

Looking as if in need of some tlc is this ex-GNR K2 class 2-6-0, No. 4651, at Derby Slack Lane in 1936. (*HMRS AAK 814*)

The A4 was also to benefit from further development before the series came to an end. The last four were given a Kylchap double exhaust system and chimney to ease the flow of steam and exhaust gases, reducing pressure in the cylinders. It was this advance that encouraged the LNER to once again attempt a speed record in 1938, when the Gresley A4 Pacific No. 4468 *Mallard* set an unbeaten speed record for steam of 126mph running down Stoke Bank on the ECML. Despite being an official speed record attempt and the locomotive employing the latest in steam railway technology, this was a greater achievement than generally realised, not just because it has never been beaten anywhere, but because far from being specially prepared, *Mallard* had worn valves and was driven hard by a driver, Duddington, known for thrashing his locomotives. Had she been properly prepared and all valve clearances correct, the record might have been set even higher. As it was, the locomotive had to be withdrawn afterwards for a major overhaul.

Had war not intervened, Gresley would almost certainly have produced further improvements to the A4s, and it is known that he did plan, amongst other things, a development of the A4 with boiler pressure of 275lb per square inch.

Gresley's Final Work

Knighted in 1936, Gresley's last designs to enter production were mixed-traffic locomotives and as such, were definitely not streamlined. During 1937/38, a 2-6-2, designated K4, emerged from Doncaster. This had 5ft 2in wheels to work heavy trains on the West Highland line, and just six were built. Next, came the V4, based on the V2 but with 5ft 8in wheels, a wider firebox and 250lb per square inch boiler pressure. The maximum axle load of just 17 tons meant that it could run almost anywhere on the LNER, although some have argued that it was an overly sophisticated and complicated design for the role it was intended to play. Just two were built.

As war approached, one modification to a former NER J72 tank engine held the promise of one-man-operation of smaller steam locomotives, one of the attractions of the diesel shunter. In May 1939, a 'Nu-Way' mechanical stoker was fitted to No. 2331. This used two revolving spirals driven by a steam turbine to carry coal from the bottom of the bunker to the firebox. In September 1939, a thermo pump was fitted to automatically control the boiler feed water. The equipment worked well and was not removed until 1947, but there were no further conversions, partly due to the lack of materials and skilled manpower during the war years, but also because of trade union resistance.

After Gresley

Gresley's untimely death in April 1941 left a void in the LNER's management structure as he never had a designated deputy, and the man most likely to have succeeded him from his team had been Oliver Bulleid, who left to become chief mechanical engineer of the Southern Railway in 1937. The choice fell on Edward Thompson, a man of broad experience who had worked for the GNR and NER and who was the mechanical engineer for the Western Section of the Southern Area at Doncaster.

Many orders for steam locomotives were cancelled and electrification went into abeyance. Class O2 locomotives for mineral trains remained in production until 1943, while the V2s remained until 1944. The workshops were increasingly diverted from railway use to become shadow factories for the production of tank traps, guns, and components for aircraft and armoured vehicles.

Thompson and Gresley had not worked well together. Apart from differences in character, Thompson had quietly disagreed with much that Gresley had espoused, and once in charge he made no secret of his views. He objected to three cylinders except for the largest and most powerful locomotives, and took the same view of complicated conjugated valve gear that required constant attention if it was to provide the optimum performance. His views were in fact endorsed by many in the running sheds and maintenance depots, especially as wartime shortages of spares and skilled labour became acute.

The point was, of course, that Gresley was operating in a peacetime environment when high-stepping steam locomotives were the order of the day, while Thompson was working in a wartime situation when speed was less important than reliability and ease of maintenance. Thompson also favoured concentrating on fewer classes of locomotive with greater standardisation on both new and rebuilt engines. Much of this was sound, especially in the prevailing conditions, but he distanced many of those who had been close to Gresley and in so doing, generated much resentment. One appointment that he made was to make Arthur Peppercorn his assistant chief mechanical engineer.

Thompson's plans were indeed sound, if much less exciting than those of Gresley. The most important locomotive for which he was responsible was a mixed-traffic 4-6-0, the LNER equivalent of the Stanier 'Black Five' and the GWR's 'Hall' class. He did not approve of the V4 2-6-2, which is why no more were built. His first new locomotive was the B1 class 4-6-0, based on standard parts with a 'Sandringham' class boiler strengthened to a pressure of 225lb, coupled wheels of 6ft 2in and the outside cylinders of the K2 2-6-0. The result was a handsome locomotive with the first appearing in December 1942, and named *Springbok*, with all of the first 41 being named after breeds of antelope. This was a numerous class by LNER standards with a total of 410 eventually built.

CMEs of the day spent much of their time rebuilding existing locomotives to match their company standard, and the LNER had been no exception. Nevertheless, Thompson's next project was to attempt to improve the operating performance of the 2-8-2 P2s, and he converted one of these into a Pacific. This was a step too far, as to use the existing short connecting rods, the leading bogie had to be located ahead of the cylinders, making the locomotive look ungainly and losing the smooth flowing lines of the original Gresley design. The wheelbase was also lengthened in the process, reducing route availability and the new configuration also resulted in poor adhesion, essential for a class of locomotives designed to cope with severe gradients and heavy trains.

Undeterred by criticism, he converted the rest of the class (A2/2), as well as having the last four V2s built as A2/1 class 4-6-2s, and using the result as the basis of a new design of mixed-traffic 4-6-2, Class A2/3, which started to emerge from Doncaster in late 1946, with the first named *Edward Thompson*. To the dismay of Gresley's admirers, he also rebuilt the first Gresley Pacific, *Great Northern*, although retaining the 6ft 8in wheels.

All but one of the highly successful A1s were rebuilt as A3s. This is No. 2598 *Blenheim*, believed to be at Derby Slack Lane in 1936. *(HMRS AAK 814)*

The boiler and cylinders of the B1 were also used for a new 2-8-0, Class O1, which incorporated frames and wheel centres cannibalised from Robinson O4s. A shortened version of the same boiler resulted in a new 2-6-0, the K1, but while one locomotive was converted to this design before his retirement, the rest were built by the North British Locomotive Company and delivered after Nationalisation. A new 2-6-4T, the L1 class, also appeared and shared the same 5ft 2in coupled wheels specified for the K1.

Making do was very much the order of the day with the Ministry of Supply laying down strict rules and insisting on standardisation for completely new designs. To provide a new 0-6-0, Thompson rebuilt a Robinson design that dated back to 1901, with piston valves and a higher pitched boiler, while Robinson's 0-8-0s were rebuilt into 0-8-0Ts, using parts held for a batch of 0-6-0Ts and releasing tenders so saving steel.

A number of other classes were also rebuilt, one locomotive at a time so that the result could be evaluated. Just three of these efforts resulted in more than one locomotive being rebuilt, the 4-4-0 D49, the 2-6-0 K3 and ten 4-6-0 B17s, reclassified B2N

At the time of his retirement in late June 1946, Thompson had been working on a programme to build 1,000 steam locomotives, and he nearly achieved this because the number of locomotives built to LNER design and entering service before and just after Nationalisation reached 952. The company's urgent need for locomotives to replace those lost during the war years or which had simply become worn out through intensive use and arrears of maintenance was also met by buying surplus locomotives from the Ministry of Supply, which provided 200 of a Riddles 2-8-0 design nicknamed 'Austerities' by 1947 (LNER Class O7), and also 75 0-6-0 saddle tanks (Class J94).

Thompson's successor as CME for the final 18 months before Nationalisation was another complete change in personality. This was Arthur Peppercorn, described as having an outgoing and genial personality. He continued Thompson's work, but as an admirer of Gresley, did much to restore the Pacific design to that envisaged by its creator, albeit without the complication of the conjugated valve gear. He also changed the profile of the cab, improving its appearance. There were a further 15 Pacifics built with 6ft 2in coupled wheels before 49 of another version with 6ft 8in wheels was introduced, designated A1. The Peppercorn Pacifics were noted for their reliability, with an average of 100,000 miles being run between heavy overhauls, although five built with experimental roller bearing axleboxes did even better than this.

At the same time, Peppercorn was involved in plans to introduce a large fleet of diesel-electric shunting locomotives and express diesel-electric locomotives for the East Coast route, as we will see in the next chapter.

Chapter 9

Electrics and Diesels

The early electrification schemes of the Great Central and the North Eastern railways have already been mentioned in Chapter 1. The result was that the LNER inherited three separate electrified sections from the North Eastern with a total of 58 route miles, 126 multiple unit motor coaches and trailers, and 13 locomotives of three classes, as well as the 4½ miles of the Grimsby District Light Railway with its 16 single-deck tramcars from the Great Central. This was little when set against the total 6,307 route miles of the new company.

The North Eastern under Sir Vincent Raven had considered electrifying the line between York and Newcastle, but not beyond. The northwards extension would have required the North British to electrify, and southwards would have needed the Great Northern to do the same. Many have expressed surprise that the project was dropped, but without electrifying the entire route between London and Edinburgh, the locomotive changes at York and Newcastle would have resulted in delays.

The NER's early electric locomotives had a distinctive Continental appearance, and the influence of steam locomotive design on the wheel configuration can be seen here. No. 13, described as 4-6-4, is seen at the Stockton & Darlington Centenary Exhibition. (*HMRS AAB 619*)

Today, the case for electrification is proven, but at the time, many locomotive engineers objected and worked hard to ensure that steam locomotives could produce the power and acceleration needed. Some drivers maintained that the powerful tank engines built for services such as those to Southend could match the acceleration of an electric train, especially if the track was slippery. Whether or not this was the case, it is certainly true that many railwaymen viewed the Southern Railway's electric multiple units as being nothing better than trams, and as well as the cost of scrapping the vast infrastructure created for the steam locomotive, there is the feeling that there was a certain amount of inbuilt conservatism. It is also easy to forget that the very best and most powerful steam locomotives were the advanced technology of the day.

The Great Debate

There was considerable debate and examination of the case for and against steam and electrification, or even the use of diesel on the railways, not just in the railway press but even in the house magazines of the railway companies. One big argument in favour of the new technology was that the number of men required to work a train fell from three to two. Another was that the lengthy period of preparation for a steam locomotive to start its day was ended. This took several hours, with the locomotive sheds having personnel who would prepare and light the fires from five or six hours before the day's work was to begin, and the locomotive fireman would take over an hour or so before the engine was required. A third reason often advanced was that diesel and electric locomotives only consumed power while working, something which comes as a surprise to those of us who have seen diesels sitting stationary for hours, engines throbbing! Many also argued that steam locomotives were very fussy about the quality of coal they used, with bad coal resulting in poor steaming, but electric power stations were more consistent.

The driving trailer of a steam-powered auto train at Alexandra Palace station in 1947. The driver would spend half his time in the locomotive and half in the driving trailer. (*HMRS ABZ 308*)

H.A. Watson, the NER's general superintendent came up with another reason for electrification, which was that on a steam railway the timetable had to allow for trains moving at seven different speeds, but on an electric railway, just three speeds were required. These were 60mph for expresses, 30mph for stopping passenger trains and fast goods, and 15mph for slow goods.

On the other hand, the railways had a massive infrastructure for the steam age. There were locomotive sheds, coaling plants, water (supplied at the station platform or in water troughs to be picked up by locomotives moving at speed), and a whole works system, some owned by the railway companies, others independent of them, to build steam locomotives. At the time, most braked rolling stock used the vacuum brake, which utilised steam and so electric or diesel power had to include a boiler or the carriages and wagons be converted to air-braking. Conversion of steam locomotives to air-braking was possible, and locomotives transferred to the former GER lines had this done. One reason why so many of the first generation of electric trains were multiple units was that these could be 'turned around' at the terminus so much more quickly, but it was also the case that they were complete in themselves with compressors for air-braking and electric motors for propulsion. In these circumstances, changing power from electric to steam en route would have been more difficult than changing from electric to diesel.

The early electric trains showed a massive improvement in timings for stopping services compared with steam due to their better acceleration, and were even an improvement on semi-fast services, but struggled to match the steam locomotive on the fast expresses for which speeds were already rising above 60mph. One problem was that there were so many different modes of electrification, with different voltages, even on third rail dc, as well as the option of overhead with direct or alternating current. The LNER alone had three different systems on its small mileage.

This led to three government-sponsored committees looking at electrification in 1920, 1927 and again in 1931. This was over and above the consultant's report commissioned by the Southern Railway. The first two committees, with Gresley a member of the second, proposed that all future electrification should be at 1,500V dc overhead or 750V dc third rail, depending on circumstances. The third committee was charged with looking at main line electrification and was chaired by Lord Weir and had Sir Ralph Wedgwood as a member. It commissioned the consultants, Merz & McLellan, to cost a scheme for the LNER's East Coast Main Line from King's Cross to Doncaster, including the Leeds offshoot and the major branches to Nottingham and March. The consultants found that this would cost £8.6 million and give a 7.22 per cent return on the capital cost. Weir recommended a programme of main line electrification and a Royal Commission on Transport agreed, advocating that priority be given to electrification of all suburban lines.

Recommending priority be given to the suburban lines made sense. After all, with the exception of the outer reaches of the Metropolitan Line, the London Underground was completely electric, and so too were all the inner and outer suburban lines of the Southern Railway by this time, with its general manager, Herbert Ashcombe Walker already planning the company's first main line electrification to Brighton.

Experiments

As early as 1928, Gresley approved a plan to convert one of the electric engines used between Shildon and Newport to diesel-electric so that it could be tested on the coal trains between New England and Ferme Park. In 1932, an attempt was made to modify an Ivatt 0-8-2T to diesel. These steps may seem bizarre to us today, especially the conversion of an 0-8-2T to diesel, but locomotive designers were feeling their way forward. One of the early LMS diesel shunting locomotives was also a steam to diesel conversion, and even today, diesel shunting engines are often 0-6-0s, similar to their steam forebears. Despite this, neither of these projects proceeded beyond the drawing board.

An Armstrong Whitworth 0-6-0 diesel shunter was obtained in 1932, but after trials was returned to the manufacturer the following year. One reason for this may have been reliability, but the LNER also found that it had inherited many 0-6-0Ts and did not order many shunting locomotives during its existence.

Amongst the inherited locomotives were small, four-wheeled shunters with petrol engines, which the LNER initially designated as Z6, but changed this to Y11 in 1943. There had been a brief fashion after the First World War for small 'Simplex' petrol-engined shunting locomotives. These were very low-powered but replaced horses that were used, and continued to be used in

LNER days, in the smaller yards where often only one or two wagons needed to be shunted. The LNER petrol-engined shunters came from the NBR and the GER, but the company also bought a second-hand shunter in 1925 that had been used by Preston Water Works. The GER example must have been one of the smallest locomotives to be named, called *Peggy*, after the horse it replaced, although the name is believed to have been removed by 1933. Little is known about the reliability of these locomotives but they must have earned their keep as all three survived beyond Nationalisation, with the NBR and GER examples converted to diesel and not withdrawn until 1956.

An attempt to overcome the poor pulling power of the early diesel locomotives at low speed was the Kitson-Still steam locomotive, which switched from steam to diesel power as speed increased. Although it worked well, the bankruptcy of the manufacturer left the locomotive without support and it was eventually returned. *(LNER Magazine)*

One project that did reach completion was the Kitson-Still steam-diesel hybrid locomotive. This was an attempt to improve the performance of the early diesel locomotive which, before the advent of diesel-electric transmission, lacked pulling power at low speeds. The locomotive builder Kitson took the Still system that had enjoyed some success for stationary and marine use. The system involved using a diesel engine with double acting pistons which were propelled by steam on one side and by diesel on the other. The engine was started by steam, and as speed built up to 5mph or more, switched to diesel, although steam and diesel could be used together when extra power was needed, and the diesel's exhaust heat also helped to heat the steam. In trials, the locomotive was found to use just one fifth of the weight of fuel needed by a steam locomotive, but had relatively little power for its size. Nevertheless, on trials in 1928, one of these locomotives hauled a 400-ton goods train from Darlington to Starbeck and back, despite being checked by signals and restarting on a 1-in-33 gradient.

The prototypes of the Kitson-Still hybrid were completed in the early 1920s and displayed at exhibitions, including at least one mounted by the LNER. A developed example spent most of its operational life on loan to the LNER, and while initially limited to 43mph, it gradually improved to achieve 55mph. By 1933, the locomotive was sufficiently reliable to operate a daily return goods train between York and Dairycoates. Despite showing considerable potential, diesel-electric technology was advancing while the extensive trials were proving expensive for the manufacturer, and doubtless contributed to the receivers being appointed in 1934. Without the manufacturer's support, the locomotive was laid up at York North shed until summer 1935, when it was returned to the manufacturer.

The alternative to the steam railcar was the diesel-electric, and this Armstrong Whitworth example was used by the LNER, proving reliable in trials, but more temperamental in regular service. (*LNER*)

The GCR had enjoyed considerable success with a petrol-electric railcar introduced around 1912, in contrast to the experience of the NER which also had two petrol-electric railcars. Possibly the NER examples were too heavy as the GCR one was lighter and smaller, yet still carried fifty passengers, almost as many as the NER examples. It did suffer a spell of poor reliability in cold weather, for which the only cure was to drain the radiator at the end of each day in the winter, and refill it the following morning. This was retained by the LNER and numbered 50179. In 1921, to counter increased competition from road transport, it worked the branch between Macclesfield Central and Bollington, earning itself the nickname of the 'Bollington Bug'. It was withdrawn in 1935.

The LNER did conduct trials with two diesel locomotives and four diesel railcars or railbuses supplied by independent builders, but some reports suggest that these were not sufficiently reliable. Contradicting this was an article in the *LNER Magazine* about the performance of the diesel-electric rail coach *Tyneside Venturer* which was built by Armstrong Whitworth and began working the Hexham and Blackhill branches on 11 April 1932. It was later transferred to Middlesbrough where it handled the passenger service to Guisborough, which involved a 1-in-44 gradient at Nunthorp Bank, and which occasionally meant handling a passenger carriage to provide extra capacity at peak periods. The author, one C.M. Stedman, the locomotive running superintendent for the North Eastern Area, commented that the controls were simple so that a steam locomotive driver could take control after a very brief period of tuition, and that the rail coach '...has proved to be thoroughly reliable during trials which have covered 34,000 miles. This mileage was covered without failure or loss of time.'

The rail coach was painted green and cream. It included power-operated doors. Its end appearance was plain and uncluttered, similar to electric multiple unit cab ends of the day. It was moved the following year to work the Scarborough–Whitby–Saltburn service, where it took turns with Sentinel steam rail coaches so that performance could be compared.

A more streamlined railbus, *Lady Hamilton*, was introduced on 6 July 1933, again using diesel-electric traction and also supplied by Armstrong Whitworth. The initial run was from Newcastle to Hexham, as with the rail coach. The streamlining of the ends was similar to that used on the LMS prototype diesel articulated multiple unit, and to that of the prototype Northern Line '1937' rolling stock. This was a lighter weight vehicle, built to carry 57 passengers with a luggage compartment or up to 71 without, weighing 17½ tons, and at the time was '... claimed to be the lightest 60-seater self-propelled coach for railway service made in Great Britain'. The entrance vestibule in the centre of the vehicle also provided access to the underfloor engine through trap doors. Seating was two and three abreast. The railbus was said to be able to run at up to 70mph. A number of independent accounts refer to the railbus needing steam locomotives as a substitute 'during its many repairs.' In fact, even the sturdier rail coaches seem to have been reliable while running on trials, doubtless with the manufacturer's representatives on call, but much less so when cast into the hard grind of daily operations. This may simply have been a foretaste of the British Railways experience, where diesels shared maintenance facilities with steam locomotives, and did not appreciate the grime and heavy engineering of the steam shed.

The rail coaches recorded fuel consumption of just over six miles per gallon, while the less heavily-built railbus managed 8mpg.

While the railbus seems to have been troublesome, possibly because it was lightly built, there is little doubt that the performance of a diesel-electric locomotive, also provided by Armstrong Whitworth, was hardly likely to endear itself to any railway, especially one so wedded to the concept of improvement in steam locomotive technology as the LNER.

One diesel-electric trial that ended abruptly when the engine crankcase blew up was with the Armstrong Whitworth 1-Co-1 locomotive, seen here with a train of cattle wagons. (*LNER*)

In 1933, AW supplied a diesel-electric mixed-traffic locomotive to the LNER. This was basically a 2-6-2 wheel arrangement in steam terms, but as it had six driving wheels, in diesel and electric terminology it became a 1-Co-1. There was a driving cab at each end, and was designed so that two locomotives could be coupled together with just one driver. It was designed for a maximum speed of 70mph, and the locomotive was intended to haul an 800-ton goods train or a 260-ton passenger train. The diesel was an Armstrong-assembled Sulzer eight-cylinder in-line unit and Crompton-Parkinson electric motors were installed. Initial trials started on 6 July 1933 between Newcastle and Alnmouth, with a number of trips to Newcastle, all presumably on passenger trains. Later that year, tests were made with goods trains of up to sixty wagons between Newcastle and both Berwick-on-Tweed and York. The LNER may have been a reluctant user of this prototype, but a crankcase explosion in June 1934 led to the locomotive being returned to the manufacturer.

The LNER experimented with diesel shunters in the 1940s, later than the other companies. This is one of four built at Doncaster Works in 1944–45 with 350hp English Electric power units. Originally No. 8002 it was renumbered by BR as 15002. All four were withdrawn in 1967 and broken up. (*BR*)

The LNER did not begin to order diesel shunting locomotives until after the outbreak of the Second World War, when the lack of a building programme for shunting engines since Grouping started to be felt. A Board meeting on 18 February 1941, not long before Gresley died, ordered four locomotives to be built at Doncaster using English Electric propulsion. They differed from similar locomotives built for the LMS by being slightly longer and by being able to be used as mobile generators in an emergency. Despite evidence of some urgency, they were not delivered until 1944 and 1945, initially classified as J45, but later this was changed to DES1, diesel-electric shunting.

A fifth engine, with Brush traction equipment, as the new chairman of the LNER was also chairman of that company, was ordered post-war, and delivered in November 1947, virtually on the eve of Nationalisation.

The LNER's Plans

The LNER Board ignored the prospect of an electrified ECML completely, despite the high return promised and despite the NER's earlier work, and despite Sir Vincent Raven being on the board. Instead, the company played safe and as early as 1923, started to examine a Great Northern suburban electrification in detail, going as far out from King's Cross as Hitchin, an outer suburban destination, at 1,500V dc, with 650V dc for inner suburban services to be compatible with the Metropolitan. Express passenger and fast fish trains would run through with steam traction, but for other trains, a changeover would be made at Hitchin, with 20 electric locomotives replacing 60 steam engines. It seems strange that they did not consider instead, the lines from Liverpool Street, and in addition to inner and outer suburban electrification, think of going all the way to Southend, which offered the prospect of off-peak holidaymaker traffic as well as peak period commuters.

Unfortunately, the economy remained in a difficult state and the plans were shelved until 1930, when the LNER decided to electrify as far as Welwyn Garden City with the High Barnet and Hertford North branches. The Southern was using the money gained from capitalisation of the Passenger Duty, abolished in 1929 by the then Chancellor Winston Churchill. This was on the condition that the railways invest the money in modernisation, not to benefit the passenger, but to help ease unemployment, and to extend its electrified network from the outer suburbs to Brighton.

By contrast, for its first post-Grouping electrification the LNER imposed conditions, the most important being that the government provide a grant. The government refused, no doubt considering that it had done enough. The delay was to affect the LNER's suburban traffic further, as the Piccadilly Line reached Cockfosters in 1933, attracting passengers, and revenue, from the LNER. The spread of commuterland meant that elsewhere the LNER was gaining traffic, but without electrification, it could not cope, so the High Barnet branch was transferred to what would become the Northern Line of the newly established London Passenger Transport Board. The revenues of the grouped railways in the London area and the London Passenger Transport Board were pooled, with the LNER getting 6 per cent. This was the second highest of any of the grouped companies, but less than a quarter of the Southern Railway's share.

Meanwhile, the LNER had returned to considering the problems raised by congestion on the Liverpool Street suburban services. As early as 1927, plans were conceived for electrification as far as Shenfield on the main line to Colchester, and the Ongar branch, which, with a new station at Crowlands, was estimated would cost £7.5 million and give a return of 5.1 per cent. This was followed in 1929 by a much-reduced plan with electrification as far as Gidea Park and converting existing rolling stock, which would have cost £4.9 million and produced a handsome return of 11.9 per cent. For both projects, there would have had to be additional tracks and a flyover at Ilford.

Once again, the London Underground came to the rescue, with the extension of what became the Central Line to Ongar, but neither this nor the electrification as far as Shenfield was completed until after the war and Nationalisation.

Electrification in the North

Strangely, despite the pressing need for electrification in the London area and the larger market, it was in the north that the LNER pursued electrification. The first scheme was a joint project with the LMS on the jointly owned Manchester, South Junction & Altrincham line, which was converted to 1,500V dc overhead and new rolling stock obtained built to an LMS specification. This was completed in 1931.

The Tyneside electrified network was extended in 1938 by ten miles to South Shields, using the rolling stock built for the pre-Grouping North Tyne network, suitably refurbished. For the North Tyne lines, 128 new all-steel carriages in articulated pairs were introduced plus four motor parcel cars. A new livery of red and cream, once used briefly by the NER, was applied to the new rolling stock at first, but in 1941, they were repainted in blue and grey after warnings from the RAF about their high visibility livery. But nothing could be done about arcing, which immediately drew attention to third-rail electrification at night! The new rolling stock was unpopular from the start and compared unfavourably with the older carriages built for the North Tyne electrification, with passengers disliking the bucket-style seats which were fashionable, but uncomfortable.

Meanwhile, the freight line between Shildon and Newport reverted back to steam in 1935, by which time the volume of traffic had fallen to just 15 per cent of the 1913 figure.

Relief for the LNER's hard-pressed financial situation came with the 1935 New Works Programme and low-cost Treasury loans. Again, the needs of London or of the East Coast Main

NEWCASTLE, YORK, CHURCH FENTON, NORMANTON, and LEEDS.—North Eastern.

Week Days.

Miles from York	Up.	aft	mrn	mrn	mrn		mrn	mrn	mrn (Through Train, York to Manchester.)	mrn		mrn	mrn	mrn (Through Train, York to Manchester.)	mrn	aft (Through Train, York to Manchester.)	aft	aft	aft	aft (Through Train, York to Manchester.)	aft		aft (Through Train, York to Manchester.)	aft		aft	aft
	731 NEWCASTLE (Cen.) dep.	1112	1 37						7 35	7 35			9 30	9 30	1020	1210	1210				2 45		2 45				4 55
	731 DARLINGTON (B. T.) "	1220	2 12				6 28		8 40	8 40			1035	1035	1121	1 14	1 14				3 43		3 43				5 57
	York dep.	1 40	4 15	6 47	7 35		8 25	9 25	9 55	10 5		10 35	12 0	12 5	1 25	2 40	2 40	3 30	3 14	3 53	5 10		5 14	6 5		6 8	7 0
3¾	Copmanthorpe			6 55	7 43							10 43							3 22							6 16	
7⅛	Bolton Percy			7 2	7 50							10 50							3 29							6 23	
8¾	Ulleskelf			7 6	7 54							10 54							3 33							6 27	
10¼	Church Fenton 770 arr.			7 10	7 58				1011			10 58							3 37				5 29	6 20		6 31	
—	Church Fenton dep.			7 16					1013										3 40				5 30	6 22		6 50	
12¾	Sherburn-in-Elmet			7 21															3 45							6 55	
15½	Monk Fryston			7 27															3 51							7 1	
16¼	Burton Salmon ‡			7 31															3 55							7 5	
21	Castleford * 371			7 42					1031					1227		3 10			4 5				5 46	6 41		7 12	
24½	Normanton 518, 616 arr	2 15		7 50					1038					1243		3 18			4 13	4 24			5 52	6 50		7 21	
75¼	518 MANCHESTER (Vic.) arr	5 16		1012					1217					2 15		4 40				6 5			7 39				
106¼	518 LIVERPOOL (Exch.) "	8 7		1111					1 20					3 20		6e15				7 15			9g23				
—	Church Fenton dep.				8 0							11 0						X								6 33	
15¾	Micklefield †				8 11							11 11														6 44	
18¼	Garforth †				8 17							11 17														6 50	
21	Cross Gates				8 25							11 24														6 57	
24¾	Marsh Lane [750, 751, 771				8 37							11 35														7 9	
25½	Leeds § 489, 672, 682, arr.		4 55		8 40		9 0	10 0		1040		11 38	1235		2 0		3 24	4 11			5 45					7 12	7 35
68¾	489 MANCHESTER (Ex.) arr.		8 8				1055	1152		1240			2 23		4 48		5 50	6 57			8 35						9 20
100	489 LIVERPOOL (Lime St.) "		9 19					1245		1 45			3 15		5 42		6e57	7 52			10d20						1043

Week Days—Continued. / **Sat.** / **Sundays.**

Up.	aft (Dining Car Train, Newcastle and York to Manchester and Liverpool.)	aft	aft	aft	aft	Sat. aft	mrn	mrn	mrn	mrn (Through Train, York to Manchester and Liverpool.)	Sun. mrn		mrn	aft		aft	aft	aft	aft	mrn
731 NEWCASTLE (Central) dep.	4 55		5 7	7 0	8 3	1112	1 37			6 18	1030		1030	2 5		2 5		7 8	1112	1 16
731 DARLINGTON (Bank Top) "	5 57		6 48	8 13	8 59	1220	2 12			8 23	1146		1146	3 1		3 1		8 11	1220	2 12
York dep.	7 7	8 8	9 14	9 35	9 53	1 40	4 15	7 58		1035	1 0		1 10	4 15		7 0	9 8	9 35	1 40	4 15
Copmanthorpe		8 16				Sun		8 6								7 8			M'n	M'n
Bolton Percy		8 23				mrn		8 16								7 17			mrn	mrn
Ulleskelf		8 27						8 20								7 21				
Church Fenton 770 arr.		8 31						8 24								7 25				
Church Fenton dep.		8 42						8 36								7 42				
Sherburn-in-Elmet								8 41								7 47				
Monk Fryston		8 50						8 47								7 53				
Burton Salmon ‡								8 51								7 57				
Castleford * 371		9 4						8 59		11 1						8 5				
Normanton 518, 616 arr.	7 38	9 12				2 15		9 6		1110	1 35					8 12			2 15	
518 MANCHESTER (Victoria) arr.	9 30							1147		1 29	4 52					11 8			5 16	
518 LIVERPOOL (Exchange) "	1020							1 59		2 58	6 29								8 7	
Church Fenton dep.		8 40							8 41							7 35				
Micklefield †		8 51							8 52							7 46				
Garforth †		8 57							8 58							7 52	Z			
Cross Gates		9 4							9 6							8 0	Z			
Marsh Lane [751, 771		9 15							9 18							8 12	9 57			
Leeds § 489, 672, 682, 750, arr.		9 18	9 50	1020	1028		4 55		9 21				1 45	4 50		8 15	10 0	1020		4 55
489 MANCHESTER (Exch.) arr.					1225		9 15		2 30				7 20					1225		8 8
489 LIVERPOOL (Lime St.) "					3A2		1120		4 15				10 0					3 2		9 19

Cross-country services were not neglected, and important routes such as York to Manchester showed a considerable saving in time between 1922, above, and 1938, below. (*Bradshaw*)

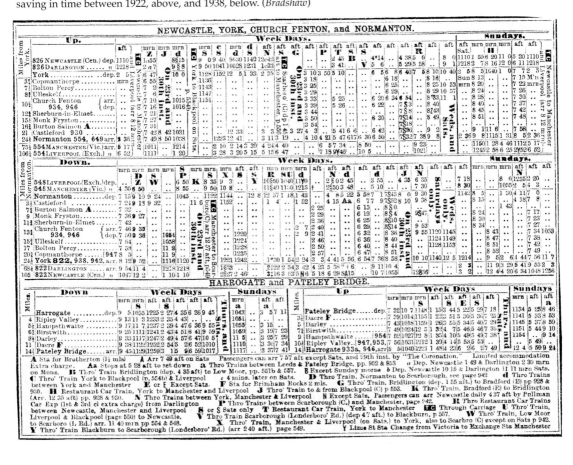

NEWCASTLE, YORK, CHURCH FENTON, and NORMANTON.

Up. — Week Days.

Miles from York	Up.	aft (TC Newcastle to Manchester and Liverpool (arr 8 12 mrn))	mrn Z	mrn J (On 23rd and 30th inst.)	mrn d	mrn S (TC York to Blackpool on Sats. p. 554b)	c S	mrn d	d S	aft N	aft S (TC Scarboro' (C) dp 1 45 aft to Manchester, p.556)	aft G (On 23rd and 30th inst.)	aft	aft P	aft T	aft S B	aft S V	aft	aft	aft	aft R	aft	aft (Weds. and Sats.)
	826 NEWCASTLE (Cen.) dep.	1110	1a55		8§15	9 0	9 40	9b30	1140	12c42			..	..	2 45	B	..	4*14	..	4 38	5 0	..	8 0
	826 DARLINGTON "	1218	2a7		9§8	9 50	1041	10b28	1231	1c33			..	..	3 41	..	V	5 6	..	5 29	5 58	..	9 1
	York dep.	2 5	6 47		10 0	1128	1152	12 5	1 33	2 35			3 10	3 50	5 10	..	..	6 5	6 8	6 40	7 5	8 10	10 40
3¾	Copmanthorpe	mrn	6 55		..	1136	..	..	..	..			3 18	..	..	..	..	..	6 18	..	..	8 18	..
7⅛	Bolton Percy	..	7 2		..	1143	..	..	..	..			3 25	..	..	..	..	..	6 25	..	..	8 25	10 53
8¾	Ulleskelf	..	7 6		..	1147	..	..	..	..			3 29	..	..	..	..	..	6 29	..	..	8 29	10 57
10¼	Church Fenton 934, 946 arr.	..	7 10		1015	1151	..	..	..	..			3 33	..	5 25	..	..	6 20	6 34	6 54	..	8 33	11 1
	Church Fenton dep.	..	7 16		1016	..	..	..	..	..			3 39	..	5 26	..	..	6 22	..	7S3	..	8 40	
12¾	Sherburn-in-Elmet	..	7 21		..	..	..	..	..	..			3 44	..	..	..	..	..	..	7S8	..	8 43	
15½	Monk Fryston	..	7 27		..	..	..	..	..	..			3 50	..	..	..	..	6 30	..	7S14	..	8 49	
16¾	Burton Salmon A	..	7 31		..	..	..	..	..	..			3 54	..	..	..	..	..	..	7S18	..	..	
21	Castleford 930	..	7 42	8 42	1031	..	..	12 33	..	3 3		3 27	4 3	..	5 41	6 6	..	6 42	..	7S26	..	9 2	
24½	Normanton 554, 649 arr.	2 36	7 49	8 50	1038	..	1223	12 41	..	3 11	3 19	..	4 10	4 21	5 47	617	6 30	6 50	..	7S32	7 38	9 8	
75¼	554 MANCHESTER (Vic.) arr.	5 17	1011	..	1214	..	2 10	2 14	3 39	4 24	4 40	..	..	6 5	7 34	..	8 50	..	..	..	9 23	..	
106½	554 LIVERPOOL (Exch.) "	6 52	1111	..	1 20	..	3 28	3 20	5 15	5 15	6 47	..	..	7 18	9Y46	..	10 5	..	..	..	1021	..	

Up. — Sundays.

Up.	aft Sat.	mrn	mrn H	mrn	aft	aft (TC Newcastle to Manchester and Liverpool (arr 8 12 mrn))
826 NEWCASTLE (Cen.) dep.	1110	1 55	6 20	11 0	5 20	1110
826 DARLINGTON "	1218	2 7	8 16	12 0	6 11	1218
York dep.	2 5	8 5	1040	1 0	7 7	2 5
Copmanthorpe	Sun	8 13	..	..	7 15	M'n
Bolton Percy	mrn	8 20	..	..	7 22	mrn
Ulleskelf	..	8 24	..	..	7 26	..
Church Fenton 934, 946 arr.	..	8 28	..	..	7 30	..
Church Fenton dep.	..	8 40	..	..	7 37	..
Sherburn-in-Elmet	..	8 45	..	..	7 42	..
Monk Fryston	..	8 51	..	..	7 48	..
Burton Salmon A	..	..	..	..	..	..
Castleford 930	..	9 1	11 6	..	7 58	..
Normanton 554, 649 arr.	2 36	9 8	1115	1 31	8 5	2 36
554 MANCHESTER (Vic.) arr.	..	1150	1 28	4 46	1112	5 17
554 LIVERPOOL (Exch.) "	..	1245	2 58	6 25	2Y52	6 52

Down. — Week Days.

Miles from Normanton	Down.	mrn	mrn D Z	mrn S W	mrn	S P	mrn K (On 23rd and 30th inst.)	mrn S (TC Manchester to Scarboro(C) arr 12 57 aft, p549)	mrn X	aft S	aft S Y	mrn R	mrn S U	mrn d	aft	aft N	aft d	aft	aft d	aft	aft J (On 23rd and 30th inst.)	aft N	aft (Saturdays only.)	aft (Weds. only.)	aft
	548 LIVERPOOL (Exch.) dep.	..			..	6 50		8 35	9 3	..		10§50	1040	11Y0	..	2§0	2 45	..	3 55	..	4 35	6 35		..	7 18
	548 MANCHESTER (Vic.) "	4 30	6 50	..	..	8 55	..	9 50	10 8	..	..	11§40	1130	1215	†	2§50	3 48	..	5 10	..	..	7 30		..	8 30
	Normanton dep.	7 15	9 10	9 24	..	1045	..	1122	1144	..	12 8	12 57	1 18	1 43	..	4 8	5 22	5 58	7 1	7S45	8 0	9 30			1142
3¼	Castleford	7 24	9 13	9 32	..	..	11 6		1152	..	..	1 4	..	1 52	..	4 15	Aa	6 7	7 9	7S52	8 10	9 38			..
7¼	Burton Salmon A	7 32	..	..	..	..			..	..	..	..	..	..	2 25	..	..	6 15	..	8S0		..			..
9	Monk Fryston	7 36	9 27	..	..	..			..	..	..	..	..	..	2 29	..	..	6 19	..	8S4		9S47			..
11¾	Sherburn-in-Elmet	7 42	..	..	..	..			..	..	..	..	..	..	2 36	..	..	6 25	..	8S10		..			..
13¼	Church Fenton 934, 946 arr.	7 46	9 35	..	..	..			..	..	..	..	..	2 7	2 40	..	..	6 29	..	8S14		9 53			..
	Church Fenton dep.	7 50	9 36	..	1054	..			..	1220	..	..	..	2 9	2 41	..	..	6 32	..	8 36		9 55	1120	1145	..
15¾	Ulleskelf	7 54	..	..	1058	..			..	1224	..	..	..	..	2 46	..	..	6 36	..	8 40		..	1124	1149	..
17	Bolton Percy	7 58	..	..	11 2	..			..	1228	..	..	..	..	2 50	..	..	6 40	..	8 44		..	1128	1153	..
20¾	Copmanthorpe [947	8 5	..	..	11 9	..			..	1235	..	..	..	..	2 57	..	..	6 47	..	8 51		..	..	..	..
24½	York 822, 938, 942, arr.	8 12	9 52	..	1116	1120			1221	1242	..	1*30	1 54	2 24	3 3	4 41	5 56	6 54	7 36	8 58		10 10	1140	12 5	1214
68¾	822 DARLINGTON arr.	9 54	11 4	..	1218	1218			1§33	..	..	2†22	2 54	3 42	4 23	5 38	7†6	..	9 11	10 4		..	..	..	2 3
105	822 NEWCASTLE (Cen.) "	1047	12 2	..	1 10	1 10			2§27	2 46	..	3†16	3 53	5N6	5 18	6 29	8A15	..	10 7	1055		12§56	..	..	3 2

Down. — Sundays.

Down.	mrn	mrn	mrn	aft N	aft	aft
548 LIVERPOOL (Exch.) dep.	..	..	8 0	1235	2 20	..
548 MANCHESTER (Vic.) "	..	..	1055	2 5	4 3	..
Normanton dep.	8 5	..	1 30	4 11	7 0	..
Castleford	8 15	..	..	4 18	7 8	..
Burton Salmon A	..	..	1 43	..	..	..
Monk Fryston	8 24	..	..	..	7 17	..
Sherburn-in-Elmet	8 30	..	..	..	7 23	..
Church Fenton 934, 946 arr.	8 34	..	..	..	7 27	..
Church Fenton dep.	..	8 43	..	..	7 34	1053
Ulleskelf	..	8 47	..	..	7 38	..
Bolton Percy	..	8 51	..	..	7 42	..
Copmanthorpe [947	..	8 58	..	..	7 49	..
York 822, 938, 942, arr.	..	9 5	2 6	4 44	7 56	11 7
822 DARLINGTON arr.	..	11 9	3 29	5 41	9 53	2 3
822 NEWCASTLE (Cen.) "	..	12 4	4 20	6 34	1048	1256

HARROGATE and PATELEY BRIDGE.

Miles	Down	mrn	mrn S	aft	aft S	aft	aft	aft (Thurs. and Sats.)	Sun. mrn a		aft a	aft
	Harrogate dep.	9 5	1055	1225	2 27	4 35	6 26	9 45	1043	..	3 5	7 11
4	Ripley Valley	9 13	11 3	1233	2 35	4 43	..	..	1051	..	..	..
5½	Hampsthwaite	9 17	11 7	1237	2 39	4 47	6 36	9 55	1055	..	3 15	..
6½	Birstwith	9 25	1111	1241	2 43	4 51	6 41	9 59	1059	..	3 19	7 23
9½	Darley	9 33	1117	1247	2 49	4 57	6 47	10 5	11 5	..	3 25	7 29
11	Dacre F	9 38	1122	1252	2 54	5 2	6 52	1010	1110	..	3 30	7 34
14½	Pateley Bridge arr.	9 45	1129	1259	3 1	5 9	6 59	1017	1117	..	3 37	7 41

Miles	Up	mrn	mrn	mrn S	aft	aft S	aft E	aft S	aft (Thurs. and Sats.)	Sun. mrn	aft	aft a
	Pateley Bridge dep.	7 32	10 7	1148	1 15	3 44	5 22	5 29	7 18	1134	5 25	8 46
3½	Dacre F	7 39	1014	1155	1 22	3 51	5 30	5 36	7 25	1141	5 33	8 53
5	Darley	7 43	1018	1159	1 26	3 55	5 34	5 40	7 29	1145	5 37	8 59
7¼	Birstwith	7 49	1024	12 5	1 32	4 7	5 46	5 46	7 35	1151	5 44	9 10
9	Hampsthwaite [954	7 52	1027	12 8	1 35	4 10	5 49	5 49	7 38	1154	..	9 14
10½	Ripley Valley [947, 953,	7 56	1031	1212	1 39	4 14	5 53	5 53	..	..	5 49	..
14½	Harrogate 933a, 946, arr	8 5	1040	1221	1 48	4 23	6 2	6 2	7 49	12 4	5 59	9 24

A Sta for Brotherton (1½ mls) A Arr 7 49 aft on Sats Passengers can arr 7 57 aft except Sats, and 29th inst. by "The Coronation." Limited accommodation Extra charge. Aa Stops at 5 28 aft to set down a Thro Trains between Leeds & Pateley Bridge, pp. 952 & 953 a Dep. Newcastle 1 49 & Darlington 2 30 mrn on Mons. B Thro' Train Bridlington (dep. 4 35 aft) to Low Moor, pp. 551b & 557. B Except Sunday morns b Dep. Newcastle 10 15 & Darlington 11 11 mrn Sats. C Thro' Train York to Blackpool (p. 554b) & Liverpool c 4 mins. later on Sats. D Thro Train, Normanton to Scarborough, see page 942 d Thro Trains between York and Manchester E or E Except Sats. F Sta for Brimham Rocks 2 mls. G Thro' Train, Bridlington (dep. 1 55 aft.) to Bradford (E) pp 928 & 930. H Restaurant Car Train, York to Manchester and Liverpool J Thro' Train to & from Blackpool (C) p 553. K Thro' Train, Bradford (E) to Bridlington (Arr. 12 35 aft) pp. 928 & 930. N Thro Trains between York, Manchester & Liverpool N Except Sats. Passengers can arr Newcastle daily 4 37 aft by Pullman Car Exp (1st & 3rd cl extra charge) from Darlington P Thro Trains between Scarborough (C.) and Manchester, page 942. R Thro Restaurant Car Trains between Newcastle, Manchester and Liverpool S or S Sats only T Restaurant Car Train, York to Manchester TC Through Carriage U Thro' Train, Liverpool & Blackpool (page 550) to Newcastle. V Thro Train Scarborough (Londesboro' Rd.) (dep 4 7 aft.) to Blackburn, p 557. W Thro' Train, Low Moor to Scarboro (L Rd.) arr. 11 40 mrn pp 554 & 548. X Thro' Train, Manchester & Liverpool (on Sats.) to York, also to Scarbro (C) except on Sats p 942. Y Thro' Train Blackburn to Scarborough (Londesboro' Rd.) (arr 2 40 aft.) page 549. Y Lime St Sta Change from Victoria to Exchange Sta Manchester

Line were ignored and the company opted for electrification of the former Great Central line from Sheffield Victoria to Manchester London Road, and Wath Yard, near Mexborough. This was an arduous route across the Pennines, mainly used by slow-moving coal trains but with worthwhile passenger traffic and the reason it was chosen was that electrification would increase the line's capacity. It would also end the unpleasant journey through the three-mile long Woodhead Tunnel amidst the unpleasant reek of smoke. Overhead electrification was chosen, and costed at just £1.6 million, with a projected return of 10 per cent. Unfortunately, with overhead electrification no-one realised at first that a new tunnel would have to be built under the Pennines as the existing one lacked sufficient headroom for the overhead wires and the pantograph on top of the locomotives.

To keep, costs under control, the ten ex-Shildon Bo-Bo electric locomotives would be used for the scheme, which would need 25 passenger, 64 freight and 32 banking and shunting engines in total, but would replace 196 steam locomotives. The coal wagons were unbraked and it was intended that they remain so, which meant that a special design of 41 40-ton brake vans would have to be built to augment the braking capacity of the locomotives. Fortunately, it was then realised that by running shorter, but more frequent trains, both the need for the brake vans and the banking locomotives would be removed and operations would be safer and more efficient.

Gresley designed the new locomotives, specifying a 2,700hp Co-Co passenger locomotive and a 1,868hp Bo-Bo mixed-traffic locomotive for the freight trains, with one of the latter completed just before his death in 1941. The Bo-Bo configuration was chosen by the LNER on the grounds of economy, but resulted in problems with adhesion when accelerating away from a stand in slippery conditions. Designated EM1, for 'electric mixed-traffic', it underwent trials on the MSJ&A line and then into storage as electrification of the line was not completed until 1952, well after Nationalisation. Between 1945 and 1947, it was loaned to Netherlands Railways, and the experienced gained resulted in modifications to the rest of the class, once production resumed during the early 1950s.

Before Gresley's death, he had plans approved for four 350hp diesel-electric shunting engines, although these were not delivered until late 1944. Built at Doncaster with English Electric equipment, they were also equipped to be used as static power plants in an emergency.

During the Peppercorn period, the LNER laid plans to purchase an additional 176 diesel-electric shunting engines and for 25 diesel-electric locomotives that would work in pairs on the Anglo-Scottish expresses, and be maintained in new depots at the main termini. Nevertheless, time was running out, and orders were left for the new owner of the LNER.

The London Area

While the LNER had been slow to electrify its many lines in the London area, plans were laid for the transfer of some of these lines to the London Passenger Transport Board, which took over the High Barnet and Mill Hill branches in 1939 as part of the Northern Line. The take-over of the Epping and Ongar branch was delayed until after the Second World War, indeed until after Nationalisation, due to delays in completing the extension of the Central Line. These extensions were part of the New Works Programme for 1935 to 1940, essentially intended to stimulate the economy and reduce unemployment.

One result of the plans was that the lines were electrified on the LPTB four-rail system, and 289 carriages of London Transport's 1938 rolling stock were delivered while the lines were still in LNER ownership. These carriages were marked on the solebar as being owned by the company, even though they were maintained by the LPTB and driven by their personnel. In fact, this was simply an accounting measure while transfer of the lines was awaited, and as a result, many of the carriages ended up on the Bakerloo Line, with which the LNER had no physical or operational connection!

Chapter 10

The Named Expresses

The practice of naming trains had its origins in the late 19th century. There were two kinds of named train, the descriptive, and the formal. The former included such trains as the Blackpool, Llandudno and Windermere club trains, while the others were inspired by marketing considerations and included the 'Flying Scotsman'. This is because, in considering titled trains, specials such as 'Excursion' or descriptive terms such as 'Limited' or 'Mail', are generally excluded here. Purists also reject informal titles, but it can surely be argued that these gain credibility through constant use. In fact, early editions of Bradshaw did include a number of titled trains that were descriptive, and also justified their status with accelerated timings, and by 1877, there were already a number of these, mainly mail trains. Titled trains did not have to be daily or year-round, but could include summer specials, and indeed, the use of a title was a marketing tool that could promote a train that ran along a route that was seasonal.

Contrary to popular opinion today, the fragmented pre-Grouping railway did not preclude efficient through-running and in fact, from the early days of the Anglo-Scottish expresses, collaboration between the companies was essential. Post-Grouping, the LNER and the GWR collaborated on the longest-distance train ever to run wholly within Great Britain, the service between Aberdeen and Penzance. The railway practice of describing services as 'up' and 'down' as they ran to and from London had a particular twist on the Anglo-Scottish services, as trains would run down from London to the border, and up to Edinburgh (or Glasgow) and then, if they continued would run down to Inverness or Aberdeen.

Our interest centres on the titled trains operated by the LNER, and these follow in alphabetical order. As a rule, titles did not include the definite article. There were relatively few titled trains in existence by Grouping for many of those that had been created were dropped under the austerity measures of the First World War.

Gresley produced some fine carriages for the fastest expresses of the late 1930s. Adding to the feeling of civilised travel was the facility to send one's heavy luggage in advance. This meant that the luggage could be collected from your home and delivered to your destination, with the same service available for the homeward journey, or there was a slightly cheaper service, from departure station to destination station, or any variation of home, station and destination.

The 'Aberdonian'

Although born of out of the East Coast contender in the races of 1895 to see which group of railways could provide the first train to reach Aberdeen from London, the 'Aberdonian' of later years was far from the fastest. It is incredible to think that as early as the night of 21/22 August 1895, the overnight sleeper from King's Cross reached Aberdeen in just 8 hours 40 minutes having covered 523.7 miles in 520 minutes, including stops and locomotive changes involving no fewer than five engines. Actual running time was just 8 hours 26½ minutes. The following night the West Coast companies were first, but there have been accusations of their train being allowed to leave the intermediate stops early.

In 1923, the running time from King's Cross to Aberdeen was 11 hours 5 minutes. In truth, very high speeds were not important on overnight trains as passengers wanted a civilised departure and equally civilised arrival time. The train left London at 8pm or 8.15pm, as the times varied over the years, and although passengers could alight at Edinburgh, the arrival here was too early for most and passengers for the city would have taken a later train.

The train was given its title for the first time in 1927. Just before the outbreak of the Second World War, it was leaving King's Cross at 7.30pm and passengers had the use of a composite dining car attached to the London end of the train and taken off at York, reached at 11.15pm, so allowing reasonable two or even three sittings for dinner. Edinburgh was reached at 3.50am, where the train was divided with carriages and sleeping cars for Fort William, Perth and Inverness taken off. The Fort William portion was taken to Glasgow, where a restaurant car was attached for breakfast, with Fort William reached at 9.54am. The Perth and Inverness portion was taken to Perth, reached at 5.28am, where in a further example of inter-company collaboration, it was attached to the LMS 'Royal Highlander' that had come from Euston. Inverness was reached at 9.50am.

The need to work heavy trains over the difficult line between Edinburgh and Aberdeen led to the P2 class 2-8-2 Mikados of which the first was No. 2001, *Cock o' the North*, the name given to a Scottish duke. This is the locomotive in original form, but it was later rebuilt as a semi-streamlined Pacific. (*HMRS ABZ 727*)

Some accounts indicate that the original name proposed for the train was the 'Moray Firth Sleeper', but this was rejected. This was a wise decision as Aberdeen is not on the Moray Firth and the closest any part of the train came to the Moray Firth was the Inverness portion.

First away from Edinburgh was the Aberdeen portion, with stops at Dundee, Arbroath, Montrose and Stonehaven, reaching its destination at 7.30am, having taken a straight 12 hours from King's Cross. This was much slower than the racing best of 1895, but that train had weighed just 105 tons, while the 1939 train was far heavier. The Fort William portion was a composite sleeping car and a composite brake, while that for Perth and Inverness was a first-class car and a third-class car, with a composite brake. The Aberdeen portion was the largest, with an articulated twin first-class, one or two third-class cars, a composite sleeping car and a composite brake. The train often had parcels vans added, and with the restaurant car between London and York, weighed at least 500 tons. It could be more, especially on Friday evenings.

In summer, the train ran as two or even three sections. The first left King's Cross at 7.25pm and was given its own title, 'Highlandman', and consisted of the Fort William and Inverness portions, much strengthened and with an additional portion for Nairn, which was detached at Aviemore from the Inverness portion. The 'Aberdonian' itself left King's Cross at 7.40pm. In addition to extra carriages and sleeping cars for Aberdeen, it also had a through section for Elgin and Lossiemouth. Between London and Edinburgh at this time, the train was hauled by a Pacific, but between Edinburgh and Aberdeen, a P2 2-8-2 locomotive such as *Cock o' the North* or one of her sisters would be used, specially designed by Gresley for this arduous stretch of line. North from Aberdeen, 4-6-0 haulage was used.

The return journey always departed at 7.35pm by 1939, and took ten minutes less than the northbound journey. By the time the train left Aberdeen, the portion from Fort William was well on its way having departed at 4.7pm, picking up further sleeping cars at Glasgow and being attached to an earlier express at Edinburgh, so it wasn't really the 'Aberdonian'. Southbound to Edinburgh, the 'Aberdonian' made the same stops as northbound, but once over the border, Grantham replaced both Doncaster and Peterborough.

The 'Aberdonian' was one of just four named expresses to retain its title during the Second World War. The service was rationalised, running between King's Cross, Edinburgh and Aberdeen only, with the other pre-war stopping points served by connections. The departure was advanced to 7pm and the journey time extended to 13½ hours. This was a feature of wartime operation with overnight trains sent away earlier than in peacetime in the hope of missing the bombing raids. Trains were also slower because of speed limits, and because they were often lengthened, while the quality of the coal used often varied.

Post-war, no acceleration of the schedule was possible before Nationalisation, and in fact for some years afterwards.

'Antwerp Continental'

See Boat Trains below.

Boat Trains and the 'Continentals'

The former Great Eastern Railway was one of the railway packet steamer operators between England and the Continent, and established a well-deserved good reputation both for its ships, which have been described as 'miniature ocean liners', and its boat trains, which in LNER days, became the 'Continentals'. For the professional railwayman, the remarkable feature was the way in which these trains were slotted into the heavily congested route between Colchester and Liverpool Street, especially as the up-trains had to operate in the midst of the morning peak. It is also worth remembering that the railways during the first two thirds of the 20th century were always fitting slow-moving heavy coal trains between their other traffic, as not only almost every home, but many offices and other establishments relied on coal for heating, and what was known as 'town' gas was extracted from coal.

The boat trains originated with the service from Parkeston Quay in Essex to the Hook of Holland, with trains to Amsterdam or further afield, with services through to northern Germany and from Berlin to what are now Poland and Russia. The service became the principal route between London and the Netherlands and Germany, and soon required its own special railway services. In 1904, the GER introduced a specially-built corridor train for the service with restaurant cars amidst the nine bogie carriages, while there were three six-wheel trucks and one four-wheel truck for the registered luggage and mails. This train weighed 287 tons and was allowed 85 minutes for the 69-mile down journey. The schedule was eased to 87 minutes, but in 1912, with the introduction of the 1500 class 4-6-0 locomotives, the schedule was tightened to 82 minutes.

The following year, the GER provided a corridor restaurant train for the service between Parkeston Quay and Antwerp. This also doubled up as a summer holiday season train between Liverpool Street and Clacton-on-Sea, filling in the time between its morning arrival at Liverpool Street and the evening departure to Parkeston Quay. During the late 1930s, the restaurant cars on this train were replaced by three Pullman cars, which made sense as the journey time only allowed one mealtime sitting, while there was also a Pullman car of the 'drawing room' type for those not wanting a full meal. This was a lighter train, but even so, could amount to twelve bogie carriages, at peak times, including the Pullmans, when it weighed 390 tons.

Just before the First World War, Henry Thornton, who had been trained in the United States, took over as general manager of the GER. Wartime restrictions prevented any great improvement in the service, but once peace returned, he added two first-class Pullman cars to the Hook of Holland, and these remained with it until the outbreak of the Second World War.

The Hook of Holland and Antwerp services were joined by a summer-only service to Zeebrugge in Belgium after the end of the First World War.

Parkeston Quay soon became the most convenient English port for packet ships carrying passengers and mails between northern Europe and London. The Zeeland Shipping Company, that had first operated between Flushing in the Netherlands and Queenborough on the River Thames, had for a while, operated to Folkestone to avoid the fogs in the Thames. However, this was a longer passage and in 1927, the service switched to Parkeston Quay, which also attracted a service from Esbjerg in Denmark. With the opening of the Little Belt Bridge in 1935, the latter service connected with a diesel express that connected Esbjerg with Copenhagen.

The Parkeston Quay services were of sufficient importance to receive early attention from the new LNER. In 1924, the company provided a new train of standard LNER rolling stock and allocated dedicated footplatemen to the link, with four drivers and four firemen from Parkeston shed covering the boat trains. By this time, the weight of the train had grown to 430 tons empty, 455 tons loaded, consisting of 13 bogie carriages including two Pullmans. The average speed between Liverpool Street and Parkeston Quay may have seemed low at 50.4mph, but this included a steep gradient rising to Bethnal Green, Brentwood bank, and slacks through Stratford, Chelmsford and Colchester, and a very slow turn off the main line at Manningtree before another climb. The 1500 class 4-6-0s continued to work the train.

In 1927, the train was named the 'Hook Continental', and for most of the next decade was booked to depart Liverpool Street at 8.30pm, and to reach Parkeston Quay at 9.52pm, but in the mid-1930s, this was eased with an 8.15pm departure and a 9.42pm arrival, back to 87 minutes. This was despite receiving new locomotives, Gresley's 4-6-0 'Sandringham' class, although many doubt whether these were a big improvement over the 1500 class once they had been given new boilers. At least the evening down train ran after the evening peak had ended, but the morning train had to cope with peak traffic. The up train was booked to leave Parkeston Quay at 6.20am, but from Gidea Park onwards was delayed by the start of the morning peak period (the so-called 'rush hour' was of much greater duration before the Second World War), and was not booked to arrive at Liverpool Street until 7.53am.

In 1936, a new and even more luxurious train was provided for the service, weighing 443 tons empty and 500 tons fully loaded. From the locomotive backwards in the down direction this consisted of a third-class brake, two second-class compartment carriages, open second, open second restaurant, kitchen car, first restaurant, semi-open first, compartment first, the two Pullman cars and two bogie brakes, making 13 vehicles in all, but sometimes increased to 14.

By this time, the service to Antwerp was also given the title of 'Antwerp Continental', departing Liverpool Street at 8.40pm and had the same timings to Parkeston Quay, where the 'Hook Continental' had to be cleared from the platform to allow for its arrival. The train was titled the 'Antwerp Continental' during the 1930s, but continued to Dovercourt Bay and

Harwich, so also carried domestic passengers. During the summer, when the Zeebrugge service was also operating, the 'Antwerp Continental' also carried the Zeebrugge passengers. Despite this encouraging growth, traffic dropped so severely during the height of the depression years that for a while, the two trains were combined to become the 'Hook and Antwerp Continental'.

There was a third 'Continental', the 'Flushing Continental', but the schedule varied widely. By the late 1930s, it was leaving Liverpool Street at 9.30am to reach Parkeston Quay West at 10.55am, but in summer it departed at 10am, and arrived at 11.30am for the day sailing. In the up direction, the train departed Parkeston Quay at 6.30pm and Parkeston Quay West at 6.45pm, reaching Liverpool Street at 8.13pm in winter, while in summer it left Parkeston Quay West at 7.55pm to reach Liverpool Street at 9.30pm.

The Esbjerg sailing must have been less well patronised as the passengers for Scandinavia simply had a portion attached to the 3.10pm buffet car express to Great Yarmouth, which was detached at Manningtree and shunted from there to Parkeston Quay West to arrive at 4.45pm. Nevertheless, in the years just before the war, the train had an independent existence with Pullman restaurant cars, scheduled to depart from Liverpool Street at 4.10pm and run non-stop to reach Parkeston Quay West at 5.45pm, before continuing to Harwich. Up trains ran at varying times depending on tidal conditions and spare paths were left in the working timetable to allow for variations in the arrival time of the incoming packet ships, or, in railway parlance, 'boats'.

The outbreak of war in September 1939 saw all of the LNER's boat trains withdrawn. The 'Hook Continental' was the first to be reinstated with the return of peace, running three times weekly from November 1945, and returning to daily operation in November 1946 once sufficient shipping was available for a daily sailing. At first, the scheduled journey time was 100 minutes, with an 8pm departure from Liverpool Street.

This is P1 class 2-8-2 No. 2394 at one of the LNER's exhibitions, in this case at Cambridge in 1938. Behind the locomotive is a German train ferry van, so clearly business customers were in mind, while closer to the camera is a historic railway carriage. (*HMRS AEU 231*)

Cambridge Buffet Expresses/Garden Cities

Cambridge Buffet Expresses was more of a collective title than that of a single named train, the Cambridge Buffet Expresses dating from May 1932, when the LNER decided that additional traffic could be generated between Cambridge and London if the train service were to be improved. The main obstacle to any improvement was the route to Liverpool Street, so it was decided that the new service would operate to King's Cross.

Smartly turned out, as one would expect, since this is the locomotive assigned to head the Royal Train, D16 4-4-0 No. 8787, at Cambridge in 1939. *(HMRS 816)*

The new trains included two third-class corridor coaches with armrests dividing the seating into three on each side, making the LNER the first railway in Britain to do this. The buffet placed between the two carriages was an open car with a counter at one end, and seating for those taking meals at the other. As intermediate stops were made in each direction at Welwyn Garden City and Letchworth, as well as Hitchin, the trains were named after the garden cities. In 1932, the trains took 82 minutes down and 77 minutes up, but the following year these timings were reduced to 75 minutes down and 72 minutes up. Cambridge undergraduates ignored these titles and the trains became known to them as the 'Beer Trains'.

The experiment showed an almost immediate improvement in patronage, with the trains doubling in length over the next couple of years, and at very busy times, often reached nine carriages. By 1939, the trains departed King's Cross at 9.35am, 12.40, 2.10, 8.10 and 11.40pm, and in the up direction they left Cambridge at 9.25am, 12.30, 3.30, 5.25 and 10.10pm; all of which suggests that the London commuter market was not what the LNER had in mind.

A variety of locomotive power was to be found on these trains, with engines drawn from the former Great Northern, Great Eastern and Great Central. The trains were withdrawn on the outbreak of war, but reinstated shortly after it ended.

The 'Clacton Belle'

This train had a short life, being named soon after Grouping and relating to a summer Pullman excursion train from Liverpool Street to Clacton using rolling stock from the 'Antwerp Continental', which otherwise would have lain idle between its morning arrival from Parkeston Quay West and the evening departure. The name was dropped after a few seasons.

The Continentals

See Boat Trains above.

The 'Coronation'

Named to mark the coronation of King George VI and Queen Elizabeth in July 1937, the 'Coronation' was an attempt to capitalise on the success of the earlier 'Silver Jubilee' that had shown that the travelling public appreciated high-speed railway travel.

While journey times between London and Scotland had fallen over the years, development had also been constrained by agreements between the East and West Coast companies. For many years, trains had taken as long as 8½ hours, while the best performance during the 'Race to Aberdeen' in 1895 had been King's Cross to Waverley in 6 hours 19 minutes, although the train weighed just 105 tons. Yet, the 'Silver Jubilee' had set a four-hour schedule between King's Cross and Newcastle without difficulty, and the idea occurred to the LNER's management in 1936 that a six-hour schedule to Edinburgh should be achievable.

The objective was more difficult than the LNER had anticipated. The 'Silver Jubilee' was just seven carriages in length, although replaced with a new eight-carriage set, while the planned 'Coronation' was to have nine carriages, making it 26 per cent heavier than the new 'Silver Jubilee'. The intention was that the A4 class 4-6-2 streamlined Pacific should work through from King's Cross to Waverley without a locomotive change.

The two sets of rolling stock for the train were specially built and broke with the LNER style of teak-panelled carriages, having an enamelled finish with light blue upper panels and dark, or 'garter', blue lower panels. Each set consisted of four articulated twins plus a distinctive end carriage with a 'beaver tail' observation car at the end with a wedge shape to emulate the streamlined design of the locomotive: the idea being to reduce the air resistance of the suction effect by a normal square-ended carriage as the train travelled at high speed.

While the observation car was turned and always at the rear of the train, the rest of the carriages, running from the London end, consisted of a third-class brake, third-class and kitchen, followed by two first-class carriages, a third, a third and kitchen, third and brake. The two kitchens meant that passengers had meals served at their seats, as with a Pullman. All of the carriages had electrically operated air conditioning for the first time in the British Isles, and windows were double-glazed and non-opening to reduce draughts and noise. Cutlery had flat handles to avoid rattling. First-class seats were arranged in alcoves and were swivelling with the table tapered from the window so that passengers could turn their seats and enjoy the view. The interior styling was modern, with aluminium and coloured panels.

Similar rolling stock was built for the 'Silver Jubilee' and the 'West Riding Limited' although without an observation car. These two trains could provide a daily return journey with one set of rolling stock, but commercial considerations dictated that the departure times for the 'Coronation' should be late afternoon in each direction and two sets were needed. A fifth set was built as a substitute for the regular sets when they visited the workshops for overhaul.

The observation car was open to both classes of traveller on payment of a supplement of one shilling for an hour, and was fitted with loose armchairs. This was in addition to the supplement paid by passengers of 4 shillings third class and 6 shillings first class for the through London–Edinburgh journey. In the winter months, with almost the entire journey made in darkness, especially in the up direction, the observation car was not attached to the train.

A stud of five streamlined A4s was allocated to the 'Coronation': Nos 4488 *Union of South Africa*, 4489 *Dominion of Canada*, 4490 *Empire of India*, 4491 *Commonwealth of Australia*, and 4492 *Dominion of New Zealand*.

In addition to offering higher speed, the departure time was also set to be as attractive as possible to the business traveller, with a 4pm departure time from King's Cross so that passengers could spend most of the working day in London, yet be home in Edinburgh by 10pm. Rather than interfere with the 4pm departure to Leeds, both trains started at the same time, but with the 'Coronation' departing from Platform 5 and taking the fast line, while the humbler Leeds train left Platform 10 and took the slow road as far as Finsbury Park. The 'Coronation' covered the 188.2 miles to York in 157 minutes, with an average speed of 71.9mph start-to-stop making it the fastest run in the UK. After a three-minute stop at York, the train continued to Edinburgh, which at first was run non-stop but it was soon realised that the traffic potential of Newcastle was too important to be missed. The 80.2 miles from York to Newcastle were run in 77 minutes, and after a three-minute stop at Newcastle, which was left at 8pm, the train had an exact two hours for the remaining 124.5 miles to Edinburgh.

The down train left Edinburgh at 4.30pm and although it stopped at Newcastle, it then ran non-stop to King's Cross, where it arrived at 10.30pm.

An almost immediate success, the train was soon filled to capacity.

The outbreak of the Second World War saw the service suspended and the five sets of rolling stock were stored in remote places to await the return of peace. Post-war, the train was not reinstated and the sets were split and the carriages allocated to other trains.

The 'East Anglian'

The Coronation of King George VI and Queen Elizabeth in 1937 gave the railways one of the busiest years since the return of peace, although it was short-lived and 1938 was to be another bad year. Optimistic about the future and with the success of the 'Silver Jubilee' showing that the public responded well to speed and special rolling stock, the LNER decided to improve their services into East Anglia. The outcome was that a six-coach train was built with similar facilities to those on the King's Cross streamliners, and two B17 class three-cylinder 4-6-0 locomotives, Nos 2859 and 2870, were streamlined and named *East Anglian* and *City of London* respectively.

The formation in the down direction from the locomotive was third-class brake, first-class and kitchen, open first, open third, third and kitchen, and third brake. All the carriages were open and passengers were served meals at their seats. No supplements were payable in recognition of the train not providing a comparable performance to the King's Cross expresses.

This was an ambitious idea, but the reality of operations on the busy lines out of Liverpool Street meant that true high-speed running was out of the question. Once again departure times were set to allow for the needs of the business traveller, and with the shorter distances involved, this could be even later, with departure from Liverpool Street at 6.40pm, which was also as the evening peak was easing off. The train reached Ipswich at 8pm and left four minutes later to arrive at Norwich Thorpe at 8.55pm. This meant that the average speed was just 51.5mph to Ipswich and only rose to 54.5mph to Norwich.

In the up direction, departure from Norwich was at 11.55am, with another four-minute stop at Ipswich which was reached at 12.46pm, and arrival at Liverpool Street at 2.10pm.

In 1938, the schedule was tightened by five minutes with the call at Ipswich reduced to two minutes and a further three minutes shaved off the schedule between Ipswich and Norwich,

LONDON, CHELMSFORD, COLCHESTER, IPSWICH, and NORWICH.—Great Eastern.

Offices—Liverpool Street Station, E.C.2. Sec., G. F. Thurston. Gen. Man., Major-Gen. Sir H. W. Thornton, K.B.E.

Down. — Week Days.

Miles	Down.	mrn	mrn	mrn	mrn	1&3	mrn	mrn	1&3	mrn	mrn	mrn	mrn	mrn	mrn	mrn	mrn	1&3	mrn	mrn
	LIVERPOOL ST....dep.	5 0	...	...	...	6 54	8 15	8 18	8 46	...	9 50	9 55	10 0	1012	10 20	1023	1026	1047	11 30	1&3
4	Stratford (W. Ham) „	...	...	...	...	7 6	8 26	8 30	8 57	...	...	...		...	...	1034		1058	...	1142
29¾	Chelmsford „	5 47	5 55	...	...	8 14	9 3	9 12	9 48	...	...	...		11 3	11 10	1123		1156	12 16	[illegible]
36	Hatfield Peverel	...	6 5	...	...	8 24	...	...	9 59	...	...	...		...	...	...		12 6	...	...
38¾	Witham 279, 282	...	6 10	...	...	8 32	9 18	9 27	10 7	...	...	...		...	...	...		1214	12 31	...
42¼	Kelvedon † 324	...		...	...	8 40	...	9 36	1016	...	...	...		...	...	...		1222	...	...
46½	Mark's Tey 290	u	Stop	...	...	8 50	...	9 46	...	...	...	...	11 9	...		...		1235	12 45	...
51¾	Colchester ‡ 280....arr.	6 19	...	...	...	8 59	9 37	9 55	1030	...	...	...	...	1131	11 39	1153		1244	12 54	1 4
70½	280 CLACTON-ON-SEA* arr	8 5	mrn	...	...	1014	...	1035	12 1	...	...	...		...	...	1238	1218	...	2 9	1 47
—	Colchester ....dep.	6 23	6 43	7 40	...	9 3	9 40		1033	1125	...	...		1135	11 43			1248	12 57	
56	Ardleigh	...	...	7 49	...	9 12	...		...	...	...	...		...	11 52			...	1 6	
59½	Manningtree 279	...	6 55	7 58	...	9 22	...		1047	1137	...	...		...	12 3			1 2	1 16	
68¾	279 HARWICH (P.Q.) arr.	...	7 24	8 46	...	9 54	...		1116	1232	...	...		...	12 32			...	1 47	
70¼	279 „ (Town) „	...	7 34	8 55	...	10 3	...		1126	1244	...	...		...	12 44			...	1 57	
63¼	Bentley 284	...	...	8 7	...	9 31	...		1056	...	...	...		...	...			1 11	1 25	
68¾	Ipswich 278, 280..arr.	6 45	...	8 17	...	9 41	10 2		11 6	...	1116	...	1140	1159	12 18			1 21	1 35	
117¾	278 LOWESTOFT (C.) arr.	9 13	...	1052	...	...	11 35		...	...	...	1248	...	1 43	2 25			...	...	
121¾	278 YARMOUTH (S.T.) „	9 20	...	11 0	...	...	11 38		...	...	...	1252	...	1 50	2 32			...	...	
—	Ipswich ....dep.	6 54	...	8 21	9 0	...	10 7		...	...	1121	...	1145		12 25			...	...	
71¼	Bramford	...	...	...	9 6	...	...		...	...	...	...	1151		...			...	...	
73½	Claydon	...	...	...	9 11	...	...		...	...	...	...	1156		...			...	...	
77¾	Needham	7 7	...	...	9 19	...	...		...	...	...	...	12 4		12 38			...	...	
80¾	Stowmarket	7 16	...	8 38	9 27	...	10 25		...	...	1139	...	1213		12 47			...	...	
83	Haughley 287, 311	7 24	...		9 34	...	...		...	...	...	...	1221		12 53			...	...	
86½	Finningham	7 33	...		9 43	...	...		...	...	...	...	1230					...	...	
91½	Mellis 319	7 42	...		9 51	...	...		...	...	...	...	1239					...	...	
95	Diss	7 50	...		9 58	...	10 48		...	...	12 3	...	1247					...	...	
97½	Burston	7 56	...		10 4	...	...		...	...	...	...	1253					...	...	
100½	Tivetshall 288	8 5	...		1012	...	...		...	...	...	...	1 [illegible]					...	...	
104	Forncett 286	8 13	...		1020	...	...		...	...	1219	...	1 10					...	...	
106¾	Flordon	8 19	...		1026	...	...		...	...	...	...	1 16					...	...	
109¾	Swainsthorpe	8 26	...		1033	...	...		...	...	...	...	1 23					...	...	
114	Trowse 296, 324	8 35	...		1042	...	...		...	...	...	...	1 32					...	...	
115	Norwich (Thorpe) 288, arr	8 43	...		1046	...	11 17		...	...	1237	...	1 37					...	...	
139	288 CROMER ....arr.	1024	...		...	...	12 19		...	...	1 35	...	...					...	...	
143½	288 SHERINGHAM ... „	1038	...		...	...	12 39		...	...	1 40	...	...					...	...	

Arrives Bury St. Edmunds at 9 1 mrn., see page 287. — Restaurant Cars, London to Yarmouth, and 1st & 3rd class Pullman Cars, London to Cromer. — Through Train, London to Walton-on-the-Naze and Clacton-on-Sea. — Restaurant Cars, London to Cromer. — Ilford at take up. — Calls at 10 16 mrn. to — 3rd class Pullman Car, London to Yarmouth. — Arr. Bury St. Edmunds at 1 17 aft., see page 287. — Third class Pullman Car, London to Clacton-on-Sea. — Sats. only. — Through Train, London to Clacton-on-Sea. — Saturdays only. Restaurant Car, Stratford to Clacton-on-Sea.

Down. — Week Days—*Continued*.

Down.	aft	aft	aft	aft	aft	aft	aft	aft	aft	aft	aft	aft	aft	aft	aft	aft	aft	aft	aft	aft	1&3	1&3
LIVERPOOL ST. ....dep.	1225	1230	1233	...	1236	1256	1 0	1 30	1 33	1 38	2 5	...	2 15	...	3 10	...	3 15	3 18	3 23	...	3 26	4 [illegible]
Stratford (West Ham) „	...		...	...	...		...	...	...	1 48	2 16	...	2 26	...		...	...	...	...	...	...	...
Chelmsford „	...		...	...	1 23		–	2 17	2 32	2 54	2 57	...	3 3	3 40		...	...	4 4	4 11	...	4 32	[illegible]
Hatfield Peverel	...		...	...	...		...	...	2 42		...	...	3 13	...		...	...	...	...	...	4 42	[illegible]
Witham 279, 282	...		...	...	...		...	...	2 50	3 7	...	...	3 21	3 53		...	...	...	...	...	4 50	[illegible]
Kelvedon † 321	...		...	...	...		...	...	2 58		...	...	3 29	...		...	...	...	...	...	4 59	[illegible]
Mark's Tey 290	...		...	...	1 47		...	...	3 8		...	3 26	3 39	...		...	...	...	...	...	5 9	5 47
Colchester ‡ 280 ....arr.	...		...	...	1 56		...	2 45	3 17		3 25	3 36	3 48	...		...	...	4 31	4 40	...	5 18	Stop
280 CLACTON-ON-SEA *..arr	...		...	...	2 37		...	3 23			4 0	...	4 59			...	...	...	5 22	...	6 25	
Colchester ....dep.			...	...			...						3 53			...	...	4 35		4 50	5 22	...
Ardleigh			...	...			...						4 2			...	...	...		4 59	5 31	...
Manningtree 279			1 57	...			...						4 11			...	...	...		5 6	5 40	...
279 HARWICH (P. Q.) ..arr.			2 22	...			...						4 43			...	...	...		5 37	...	...
279 „ (Town).. „			2 34	...			...						4 52			...	...	...		5 49	...	...
Bentley 284			...	...			...		...				4 20			...	...	...		...	5 50	...
Ipswich 278, 280 ....arr.			2 11				2 31		...				4 30		4 40	...	4 52	4 59		...	6 0	...
278 LOWESTOFT (C.)....arr.			...			3 39	4 18		...				...		...	...	6 17	7 15		...	...	...
278 YARMOUTH (S.T.).. „		3 12	...			...	4 22		...				...		...	...	6 22	7 23		...	...	aft
Ipswich ....dep.		...	2 16	2 22		...	...		...				...		4 45	4 50				...	...	...
Bramford		...		2 28		...	...		...				...		...	...				...	...	...
Claydon		...		2 33		...	...		...				...		...	4 59				...	...	...
Needham		...		2 41		...	...		...				...		...	5 7				...	...	...
Stowmarket		...		2 50		...	...		...				...		...	5 16				...	...	...
Haughley 287, 311		...		2 58		...	...		...				...		...	5 24				...	...	...
Finningham		...		3 7		...	...		...				...		...	5 33				...	...	...
Mellis 309		...		3 16		...	...		...				...		...	5 42				...	...	...
Diss	...	...		3 24		...	...		...				...		...	5 50				...	...	...
Burston	...	...		3 30		...	...		...				...		...	...				...	...	...
Tivetshall 288	...	...		3 39		...	...		...				...		...	6 6				...	...	...
Forncett 286	...	...		3 47		...	...		...				...		...	...				...	...	...
Flordon	...	...		3 53		...	...		...				...		...	...				...	...	...
Swainsthorpe	...	...		4 0		...	...		...				...		...	...				...	...	...
Trowse 296, 324	...	...		4 9		...	...		...				...		...	6 2[illegible]				...	...	...
Norwich (Thorpe) 288, arr.	...	...	3 15	4 13		...	...		...				...		5 44	6 29				...	...	...
288 CROMER ....arr.	3 28	...	4 22	5 30		...	...		...				...		6 43	7 51				...	...	...
288 SHERINGHAM ....„	3 42	...	4 38	6 4		...	...		...				...		6 59	...				...	...	...

Restaurant Car, London to Cromer. — Restaurant Car, London to Yarmouth. — Restaurant Cars, London to Cromer. — Through Train, London to Walton-on-the-Naze and Clacton-on-Sea. — Restaurant Car, London to Lowestoft. — Saturdays only. Restaurant Cars, London to Clacton-on-Sea. — Saturdays only. — Except Saturdays. — Saturdays only. — Through Train, London to Walton-on-the-Naze and Clacton-on-Sea. — Saturdays only. — Fridays only. Through Train to Braintree, see page 279. — Restaurant Cars, London to Cromer. — 1st & 3rd class Pullman Cars, London to Yarmouth. — Restaurant Car, London to Felixstowe (Beach). — Through Train, London to Walton-on-the-Naze and Clacton-on-Sea. — Arr. Bury St. Edmunds ... aft., see page 287.

☞ **Harwich Route to the Continent, via Hook of Holland or Antwerp, see page 929.**

Services increased on the lines to East Anglia, with named trains such as the 'Flushing Continental' in 1938 (overleaf), when the service was faster and more intense than in 1922, as shown above. (*Bradshaw*)

LONDON, CHELMSFORD, COLCHESTER, IPSWICH and NORWICH.

Down. — Week Days.

Miles	Down.	mrn	mrn	mrn	mrn	mrn	mrn	mrn	Y	mrn	mrn	mrn	mrn	mrn	Z	H	mrn	mrn	mrn	mrn	mrn	mrn	mrn
—	LONDON (L'pool St.) dep.	5 0	530	D	..	..	6 55	7 30	8 15		8 18	.	8 45	9 36	9 48	9L48	10 0	10 3	10 3	10 6	x	10 9	10 12
4	Stratford (West Ham) "	..	..	..	..	..	7 5	7 40	8 26		8 29	8 48	8 56	..	..				d				..
29¼	Chelmsford "	5 50	..	6 1	..	..	8 9	8 46	9 5		9 12	9 36	9 45	..	..								11 4
36	Hatfield Peverel	..	..	610	..	..	8 2	..	..		9 22		9 56	..	..								
38¾	Witham 880, 882	..	..	615	..	..	8 29	8 50	9 19		9 28		10 4	..									
42½	Kelvedon A 876	..	..		..	..	8 37	..	..		9 36		1011	..									
46¾	Mark's Tey 867	6 13	..	Stp	..	..	8 48	..	..		9 45		..	..				1110				1119	
51¾	Colchester B 870 .. arr.	6 21	638	..	..	.	8 56	9 17	9 37		9 55		1023	..				1119				1123	
70¼	870 Walton-on-Naze arr.	7 39	854	..	..	A	1023	10 6	..		1047		1129	..				..			..	..	
69¾	870 Clacton-on-Sea ☾ "	7 22	751	mrn	..	A	1014	9 52	..	B	1032		11 5	1128				..			..	..	
—	Colchester dep.	6 24	641	650	7 48	..	9 0		9 40	9 45	Stop		1028					1121			1124	1131	
56	Ardleigh	..	..	658	7 56	..	9 9		..	9 53			1035					..			..	..	
59½	Manningtree 872	..	..	7 4	8 2	..	9 16		..	9 59	..		1042					..			..	..	
68¾	872 Harwich (P. Q.) arr.	..	..	a729	8 50	..	9 54		..	1021	..	..	1114			Y	1130	..	1145	..	..	..	
70¾	872 " (Town) "	..	..	a739	8 58	..	10 2		..	1028	..	‡	1122			E	1150	..	..	..	..	..	
63½	Bentley	..	..	..	8 11	..	9 28		..	..	..	..	1051			..		..	..	..	..	..	..
68¾	Ipswich 864, 873 .. arr.	6 45	7 2	..	8 20	..	9 38		10 2	..	..	1025	11 3		1110	11 25		1144	..	1142	1147	1156	11 55
117¾	864 Lowestoft (C.) .. arr.	9 17	917	b	1047	..	..		1140	..	..	1250	..		1 22	1 31		1 22	..	..	..	1 31	Stop
121¾	864 Yarmouth (S.T.) "	9 18	918	..	1056	c	1120		1138	..	mrn	1150	..		1 23	1 0		1 23	.	1 9	..	1 34	aft.
—	Ipswich dep.	6 55	.	..	8 25	9 0	9S45		10 7	..	1015	1057	..	..	1115	11 30				..	1151		12P8
71¼	Bramford	..	..	..	..	9 6	9S51		..	..	..	..	..	..	..	..				..	..		12P14
73¾	Claydon	..	..	..	..	9 11	9S56		..	..	1024	..	..	..	..	..				..	..		12P19
77¾	Needham	7 8	.	..	..	9 19	10S1		..	..	1032	..	..	..	..	..				..	..		12P27
80¾	Stowmarket	7 18	..	..	8 40	9 26	10S9		1025	..	1038	1113	..	..	1134	11 49				..	12 7		12P35
83	Haughley 867a, 877	7 25	..	..		9 32	..		..	..			..	..	..	..				..			12P42
86¼	Finningham	7 33	..	..		9 40	..		..	..			..	..	..	..				..			12P50
91¼	Mellis	7 42	..	..		9 48	..		..	..			..	..	..	..				..			12P59
95	Diss	7 49	..	..		9 54	..		1046	..			..	..	1157	12 13				..			1P6
97½	Burston	7 54	..	..		9 59	..		..	..			..	..	..	..				..			1P11
100¼	Tivetshall 875	8 2	..	..		10 6	..		..	..			..	..	..	..				..			1P19
104	Forncett 867a	8 10	..	..		1014	..		..	..			..	..	1212	12 30				..			1P27
106¾	Flordon	8 16	..	..		1020	..		..	..			..	..	..	..				..			1P33
109¾	Swainsthorpe	8 22	..	..		1028	..		..	..			..	..	..	..				..			1P39
114	Trowse 884	8 32	..	..		1035	..		..	..			..	..	..	..				..			1P47
115	Norwich (T) 864a, 875 arr.	8 38	..	..		1039	..		1111	..			..	..	1230	12L50				..			1P53
139	864a Cromer arr.	1021	..	..		..	..	..	1214	..			..	..	1 35	1L45		..	..	..		..	..
143½	864a Sheringham .. "	1035	..	..		..	..	..	1239	..			..	..	1 49	2 38		..	..	..		..	..
	Notes				Arr. Bury St. Edmunds 9 1 mrn., page 877.			Weds. and Sats. until 23rd inst., daily afterwards.		Mondays only.	Arr. Bury St. Edmunds 11 3 mrn., page 877.	Saturdays only. Arr. Bury St. Edmund's 11 38 mrn., page 877.		Saturdays only.	Except Saturdays.	Saturdays only.	Parkeston Quay arr. at 11E38 mrn. The Flushing Continental (see note H) Pullman Restaurant Cars.	Except Sats. Calls at Ilford 10 19 mrn.	Saturdays only. Continental Express. Pullman Restaurant Cars.	Saturdays only.	Sats. only. RC to Sheffield and Manchester, page 877.	Sats. only. Calls at Ilford 10 27 mrn.	Mons., Fris. and Sats.

Down. — Week Days—*Continued.*

Down.	mrn	mrn	mrn	mrn	mrn	mrn	mrn	mrn	mrn	e	mrn	aft	aft	aft	aft	aft	aft	aft	aft	aft	aft	J	aft
LONDON (L'pool St.) dep.	10 20	[illegible]	1026	1023	1035	..	1046	1046	1115	1130	1135	1215	1225	1228	1230	1233	..	1236	1252	1256	1255	1 0	
Stratford (West Ham) "	..	RC	..	1035	..	1035	1058	1058	..	..	1146	RC	..	RC	RC	..	..	..	RC	RC	..		
Chelmsford "	11X9		..	1120	1127	1132	1151	1154	..	1217	1233					..	..	1024			1 55		
Hatfield Peverel	..	..	..	..	..	..	12 1	12 4	..	..	..					..	..	..			2 5		
Witham 880, 882	..	..	..	1134	1142	1147	12 8	1212	..	1231	..					..	..	..			2 13		
Kelvedon A 876	..	..	..	..	..	..	1215	1220	..	..	..					..	..	..			..		
Mark's Tey 867	..	..	..	..	..	.	1224	1232	..	1244	..					..	..	1047			..		
Colchester B 870 .. arr.	11X38	..	..	1152	12 0	12 6	1232	1240	..	1252	1 0					1012	..	1 56			..		
870 Walton-on-Naze arr.	..	..	..	1241	1251	1 2	..	..	..	2024	1 49		..			..	..	2047				..	
870 Clacton-on-Sea ☾ "	..	1215	1223	1232	1252	1252	..	..	1 20	2011	1 43		..			..	..	2036				..	
Colchester dep.	11X41						1236	1248		1255						1045	105	Stop				..	
Ardleigh	11X50						1244	..		1 E 3						..	..					..	
Manningtree 872	11X57						1251	1257		1 8						..	2 0 2					..	
872 Harwich (P. Q.) arr.	12 34						..	..		2 1				..		..	2018		..	..		..	
872 " (Town) "	12 43						..	..		2 10				..		..	2027		..	..		..	
Bentley							1 1	1 7		..				..	..	..	..		..	..		..	
Ipswich 864, 873 .. arr.	12n14						1 11	1 17		1 25				..	..	2 0 8	..		..	..	2 30		
864 Lowestoft (C.) .. arr.	2n15			..			..	..				..		..	..	3n52	..		3 41	3 36	4 28		
864 Yarmouth (S.T.) "	2n22			..			..	..				3 0		..	3X0		..	aft		..	4 13		
Ipswich dep.	12n25		..	..	..	..	..	..	..			..		..	..	2013	..	2 18	..	..			2 18
Bramford	..		..	..	..	..	..	..	..			..		..	..		..	2 24	..	..			..
Claydon	..	..	..	..	..	..			..		..	..		..	..		..	2 29	..	..			..
Needham	12n38	..	..	..	..	..			..		..	..		..	..		..	2 37	..	..			..
Stowmarket	12n46	..	..	..	..	..			..		..	..		..	..		..	2 45	..	..			3 5
Haughley 867a, 877	12n51	..	..	..	..	..			..		..	..		..	..		..	2 52	..	..			..
Finningham		..	..	..	..	..			..		..	..		..	..		..	3 1	..	..			..
Mellis		..	..	..	..	..			..		..	..		..	..		..	3 9	..	..			..
Diss		..	..	..	..	..			..		..	..		..	..		..	3 16	..	..			..
Burston		..	..	..	..	..			..		..	..		..	..		..	3 22	..	..			..
Tivetshall 875		..	..	..	..	..	..	..	..		..	..		..	..		..	3 30	..	..			..
Forncett 867a		..	..	..	..	..	..	..	..		..	..		..	..		..	3 37	..	..			..
Flordon		..	..	..	..	..	..	..	..	..	..	..	..	..	..		..	3 43	..	..			..
Swainsthorpe		..	..	..	..	..	..	..	..	..	..	..	..	..	..		..	3 50	..	..			..
Trowse (875, 884		..	..	..	..	..	..	..	..	..	..	..	..	..	..		..	3 59	..	..			..
Norwich (T.) 864a .. arr.		..	..	..	..	..	..	..	..	..	..	..	..	..	..	3 0 9	..	4 3	..	..			..
864a Cromer arr.		..	..	..	..	..	..	..	..	..	..	..	3/22	..	..	4 07	..	5 25	..	..	..		..
864a Sheringham .. "		..	..	..	..	..	..	..	..	..	..	..	3/36	3 45	..	4021	..	6 17	..	..	..		..
Notes	Arr. Bury St. Edmunds 1/13 aft., p. 877.	Saturdays only.	Saturdays only.	Except Saturdays.	Saturdays only.	Saturdays only.	Saturdays only.	Except Saturdays.	Saturdays only	Buffet Car. Liverpool St. to Ipswich	Saturdays only.	Saturdays only.	Mons., Fris., and Sats. RC Liverpool St. to Cromer	Saturdays only.	Mons., Fris. and Sats.	RC Liverpool St. to Cromer.		4 mins. later on Sats.	Saturdays only.	Mondays and Fridays.	Saturdays only. To Maldon (East) and Heybridge, page 880.	Except Sats. RC Liverpool St. to Ipswich on Mons. and Fris.	Arr Bury St. Edmunds 3 27 aft. p. 877

LOCAL TRAINS & Intermediate Stations between Liverpool Street and Chelmsford, page 1014.

setting a new record for former Great Eastern lines of 57.9mph. In the new timetable, the train departed Norwich at noon.

Some commentators believe that the schedule could have been tightened further, especially as there were just six carriages, and that two hours between Liverpool Street and Norwich should have been possible. Certainly, on occasion the train managed to run between Norwich and Ipswich in just 44½ minutes and 42 minutes in the down direction for the 46.3 miles, while between Ipswich and Liverpool Street took as little as 72 minutes up and 70¼ minutes down. Perhaps more to the point, while the timings made an afternoon in London possible, with lunch in the up direction and dinner in the down direction, no attempt seems to have been made to attract people needing to spend a day in London. This was before the advent of the long-distance commuter, but there were those who needed to visit London from time to time.

The train ran only on Mondays to Fridays, and never on a Saturday. It was withdrawn on the outbreak of war in September 1939, and was reinstated on 7 October 1946, reverting to the old departure times in each direction, with the Norwich departure later brought forward to 11.40am.

The 'Eastern Belle'

These were summer Pullman excursion trains from Liverpool Street to East Anglian resorts, using rolling stock from the 'Antwerp Continental' which otherwise would have lain idle between its morning arrival from Parkeston Quay West and the evening departure.

The famous 'Hush-Hush' No. 10000 was used on many regular duties, such as the 'Flying Scotsman', although it was a difficult locomotive to maintain. The nickname resulted from the secrecy that surrounded the start of the high-pressure locomotive project, but one newspaper assumed, wrongly, that it was because she was very quiet! The 4-6-4 is at King's Cross with Sir Nigel Gresley on the platform and the crew on the bufferbeam. (*SCM 11502/74*)

The 'Flying Scotsman'

No other train has such a long history as the 'Flying Scotsman', which can trace its origins to a train introduced in June 1862, leaving King's Cross at 10am every weekday for Edinburgh Waverley. The name was in use unofficially for many years, although the East Coast Group of Railways officially described the train as a 'Special Scotch Express'. It was a major participant in the 'Race to Edinburgh' held in 1887 and revived in 1888, with the best timing in the earlier year being 7 hours 26¾ minutes, of which 26 minutes was the York luncheon stop. Locomotives were changed at Grantham, York and Newcastle. Afterwards, from 1895, racing ceased and by agreement between East and West Coast companies, the overall journey time between London and Edinburgh became a more relaxed 8½ hours.

One would have expected such a long-distance service to have been amongst the first to have dining cars, but these did not appear until 1900, more than two decades after the Great Northern Railway, one of the East Coast Group of Companies, had first introduced this amenity.

Bradshaw's Railway Guide in 1922 does not show the train having a name at all, and it was left to the LNER to introduce this officially as part of its marketing for the train. In 1924, a pair of new trains entered service with both including three new articulated restaurant cars, amongst the first to be equipped for cooking by electricity. The through schedule continued to be constrained by the agreement that had ended the races, despite massive improvements in locomotive power over the preceding thirty years, but the LNER decided to run the train non-stop from May 1928. Yet another pair of new trains was then introduced, and to allow for a change of crew without stopping, special tenders were built with a corridor connection to the leading carriage.

The new trains included a carriage, always marshalled next to the restaurant cars, with a cocktail bar, a retiring room for ladies and a hairdressing salon with a barber. This was the longest non-stop railway journey in the world at the time, and some of these novelties were to enable passengers to pass the time on a train that had the pitifully generous allowance of 8½ hours for the journey, giving an average speed of 47.6mph. A later train that made a number of stops took exactly the same time!

This ludicrous situation ended in 1932 as railway schedules throughout Great Britain were being tightened. The through journey was cut to 7 hours 50 minutes, but this was only the beginning. In July, the train started to run in portions as it always did during the busy summer months. The first portion ran non-stop and the end-to-end time was cut even further to 7½ hours, with the average speed rising to 52.3mph. In the years that followed, the average speed rose and the schedule tightened to 7¼ hours in 1936 and 7 hours in 1937. During 1938 and 1939, with stops included, the through journey time was 7 hours 20 minutes.

What made this pre-war spurt all the more notable was that in 1938 a pair of new trains was introduced, with air-conditioning in each carriage, and this increased the weight of the train so that it could be as much as 504 tons with 14 carriages, although at peak periods this could be 600 tons with 16 fully laden carriages. Northbound, the formation from the locomotive was a brake third and a composite coach intended for Glasgow, a composite with luggage compartment for Perth, three thirds, a buffet car, a triple articulated restaurant set and a first for Edinburgh, and a composite, third and brake third for Aberdeen. The buffet car was an innovation based on US practice, with the entire vehicle given over to the service of drinks and light refreshments.

The Aberdeen carriages were taken off at Edinburgh and attached to the 5.40pm restaurant car express, which called at Kirkcaldy, Cupar, Leuchars Junction, Dundee, Broughty Ferry, Arbroath, Montrose and Stonehaven to reach Aberdeen at 8.15pm. The Glasgow carriages were transferred to the 5.43pm to Queen Street, where they arrived at 6.45pm. The Perth carriage was transferred to the 5.55pm and reached its destination at 7.13pm. London-bound, the Aberdeen portion departed at 6.40am attached to an express with a breakfast car, while the Glasgow portion left Queen Street at 8.35am and the Perth carriage left at 8.25am. This must have made for a hectic spell of shunting at Waverley so that everything was in correct order for a 10am departure.

The train continued to run during the Second World War, but was confined to London King's Cross–Edinburgh Waverley, so that passengers wishing to go further had to change. Extensive and costly shunting manoeuvres were a peacetime luxury. A relief was sent forward from King's Cross at 9.40am, before the main train departed at 10am, with an additional stop at Peterborough before reaching York, and north of York there were stops at Newcastle and Berwick-on-Tweed, with arrival at Waverley at 6.55pm. London-bound, the train left at 10am, as in peacetime, but stopped at Berwick, Newcastle, Darlington, York and Grantham, to arrive at King's Cross at 6.45pm. Wartime loads in the early years could exceed 20 carriages, with as many as 23,

The predecessor companies of the LNER were great users of 4-4-2 Atlantic locomotives, as seen here with Class C7 No. 2212 heading the 'Harrogate Pullman'. This was one of a number of trains that used the Pullman cars that the GER had contracted, but was unable to use profitably. (*HMRS AAB 135*)

weighing as much as 780 tons as there were many standing passengers, with no restaurant cars. Later in the war, poor coal and indifferent steaming meant that a limit of 18 carriages had to be laid down, and later still this was reduced to just 15.

Post-war, a new timetable on 1 October 1945 saw restaurant cars reintroduced. The wartime stopping pattern was retained, but the through journey time was cut by 50 minutes, reaching Waverley at 6.5pm. The London train arrived at King's Cross at 6pm. A year later, the call at Peterborough was replaced by one at Grantham, after which the train ran non-stop to Newcastle and then to Berwick, reaching Edinburgh at 6.10pm. The southbound service was unaltered.

The 'Harrogate Pullman'

When Henry Thornton, later Sir Henry, became general manager of the Great Eastern after working in the United States, he was surprised to find that there were no Pullman cars, especially as these were already in service in the south. He quickly established an arrangement with the Pullman Car Company which supplied new cars for the Great Eastern. The cars soon proved very popular on the boat trains between Liverpool Street and Parkeston Quay, but when placed on other services there was not the same demand as other railway companies had found. The LNER inherited the Pullman cars on Grouping, and an arrangement with the Pullman Car Company that still had many years left to run.

While a small number of cars were left at Liverpool Street for the boat trains, the rest were transferred to King's Cross and formed into an all-Pullman express, the 'Harrogate Pullman', introduced in Summer 1923, running between King's Cross, Leeds, Harrogate and Newcastle. The section between King's Cross and Leeds took just 3 hours 25 minutes, the fastest service between London and Leeds at the time, while the time to and from Harrogate was four hours.

Two rakes were formed, each with four second-class cars and two first-class cars. Departure from King's Cross and from Harrogate was at the same time each day, 11.15am. A reversal was necessary at Leeds. In the down direction, the train reached Leeds at 2.40pm, and after reversing it continued to Harrogate, which it left at 3.20pm, and continued to Newcastle with stops at Ripon and Darlington before reaching its destination at 5pm. In the up direction, it left Newcastle at 9.20am and reached King's Cross at 3.15pm.

For Summer 1925, the service was extended to Berwick-on-Tweed and Edinburgh, with a through journey time of 8 hours 35 minutes. While the down departure from King's Cross was unaltered, Edinburgh was left at 8.30am, which meant that the departure from Harrogate was put back to 1.5pm and that from Leeds was at 1.40pm, with arrival at King's Cross at 5.5pm.

This timetable was very short-lived, and changed in September 1925. Another all-Pullman train had been trialled using a variety of routes to discover which would be the most popular. This later became the 'West Riding Pullman', running to Leeds and Bradford, of which more below. The opportunity was taken to schedule the 'Harrogate Pullman' as a non-stop train, leaving King's Cross at 11.20am and running the 198.8 miles to Harrogate to arrive at 3.3pm. This meant an unusual route including more than four miles of LMS track. Arrival in Edinburgh was brought forward to 7.35pm, cutting 20 minutes off the summer schedule. The service continued to depart from Edinburgh at 8.30am, so that it still left Harrogate at 1.5pm, but arrival at King's Cross was at 4.45pm.

The service settled down, and must have been successful as in May 1928 it was provided with a new set of seven all-steel Pullman carriages and was renamed the 'Queen of Scots', whose history is covered further on.

The 'Highlandman'

See the 'Aberdonian' above.

The 'Master Cutler'

This train had its origins in a breakfast car express introduced by the LNER that left Sheffield at 7.30am and with stops at Nottingham and Leicester arriving at Marylebone at 10.40am. This involved some fast running, especially south of Leicester to cover the 103.1 miles to Marylebone in 109 minutes despite some difficult gradients. There were usually eight or nine carriages and at first the locomotive power was a former Great Central 'Director' class 4-4-0, but later, a LNER B17 4-6-0 was allocated.

The train disappeared at the start of the Second World War but was reintroduced post-war and was granted the title of the 'Master Cutler' with the introduction of the 1947 winter timetable; just in time for Nationalisation.

The 'Night Scotsman'

This was a title given to a northbound train only until the Second World War. Dating from the early years of the 20th century, by 1914 it was taking eight hours to reach Edinburgh, leaving King's Cross at 11.30pm and arriving at Waverley at 7.30am. Between the wars the departure time became earlier, so that by 1939 it was 10.25pm with arrival at 7.15am. Stops were made to pick up passengers at Grantham, York and Newcastle. The train became so busy before the Second World War, that even with 13 or 14 carriages and sleeping cars, reservations were confined to those wishing to continue their journey to Glasgow, Perth or Aberdeen. On arrival at Waverley, the train was divided into three portions for these three cities and each was added to a breakfast car train, with that for Perth having a Pullman restaurant car. Passengers reached Glasgow Queen Street at 8.49am, Perth at 8.55pm and Aberdeen at 11.12pm. Edinburgh passengers were carried by the 10.35pm sleeper from King's Cross.

The unnamed southbound train was the 11pm from Edinburgh Waverley, which consisted of coaches and sleeping cars that had left Dundee at 9pm, Inverness at 4.15pm and Perth at 8.10pm, and which stopped at Berwick-on-Tweed, Newcastle, York and Grantham, before arriving at King's Cross at 7.15am.

The train retained its title during the war years, with the southbound working being named for the first time. The service was cut back to run between London King's Cross and Edinburgh Waverley, with a northbound departure at 10.15pm and arrival at Waverley at 7.42pm. A relief left King's Cross at 10pm, calling only at Grantham and Newcastle, although there was a brief stop at York to change the driver and fireman, to reach Edinburgh at 6.57am.

Post-war, the Edinburgh arrival of the 'Night Scotsman' was brought forward to 7.5am, and the start from Waverley was changed to 10pm, with a 6.30am arrival at King's Cross.

The 'Norseman'

The 'Norseman' had a brief history, starting in 1937 and operating on certain specified days only from King's Cross to Tyne Commission Quay at Newcastle, to connect with steamer sailings to Oslo. The operation ended with the outbreak of the Second World War.

The 'North Briton'

This train originated in the early 1900s in a plan to provide a daytime express aimed at the business traveller that would run from Leeds to York, Newcastle and Edinburgh, where it would wait for five hours before performing the return working. Although the route was less direct than the competing Midland Railway service, the North Eastern Railway knew that the West Riding to Newcastle market was sufficient to make the train viable, while it would also provide the fastest train of the day between Newcastle and Edinburgh. The train left Leeds at 8.50am, reaching York in 35 minutes where it waited for 13 minutes, before continuing to Newcastle over the tortuous Gateshead route as the more direct King Edward Bridge was still to open. At Newcastle, a composite dining car was added and the train reversed, and continued to Edinburgh Waverley where it arrived at 1.30pm.

The southbound journey started from Waverley at 6.25pm, reaching Newcastle at 9.5pm, where the dining car was detached, and continued to reach York at 10.55pm, and Leeds at 11.45pm.

By 1910, the train was running on to Glasgow, although still basically with five coaches, plus the restaurant car that was only part of the rake north of Newcastle. The train was officially named by the LNER, and received new carriages, while it also grew in length so that north of Newcastle it was hauled by a Pacific northbound, and southbound had a Pacific as far south as York. The northbound timings did not change much, but southbound the departure from Glasgow was at 4pm, Edinburgh at 5.10pm, an additional stop was made at Dunbar, and eventually reached Leeds at the more civilised, and commercially attractive, hour of 10pm, with a reduction of 50 minutes in the through journey time.

The train was stopped during the Second World War, but reinstated with the return of peace and after Nationalisation became the first post-war mile-a-minute train.

The 'North Country Continental'

The Great Eastern was forever anxious to develop its port and shipping services at Parkeston Quay, but these were only reached conveniently from London. It was clear that a new train was needed to tap the potentially lucrative markets of the Midlands and the North. At first the title was unofficial, but when it was introduced in 1885 the train was amongst the first long-distance cross-country trains in Great Britain. In 1891 it is also believed to have been the first train in the country to admit third-class passengers to the 'dining saloon', although it is likely that there was scant comfort as the GER was slow to introduce bogie carriages and travellers had to endure the rough riding of six-wheel carriages.

New rolling stock was provided in 1906, with modern corridor carriages. Of necessity, this was a portioned working, with Manchester, Liverpool and Birmingham each having two bogie carriages, while there was a six-wheel brake for York. The main part of the train consisted of a set of six carriages including a composite kitchen car sandwiched between an open third-class carriage and a semi-open first-class carriage.

Leaving Parkeston Quay at 7.2am, the train ran on the main line towards Norwich as far as Haughley, where it took the line to Bury St Edmunds, and then a single-track branch from Newmarket to Ely, and then across the Fens to March. There, the two rearmost carriages were dropped and taken on over the LNWR to Market Harborough, Rugby and Birmingham. The train continued to Spalding and Sleaford to Lincoln, which was reached at 10.56am, where the Liverpool and Manchester carriages were dropped to be taken on as two separate trains by the Great Central. The remainder of the train continued through Gainsborough to Doncaster, and onto the Great Northern line to York. Arrivals were at Birmingham at 12.11pm, Manchester at 1.38pm, Liverpool at 2.45pm and York at 12.32pm, where there was a connection with the northbound 'Flying Scotsman'. In the opposite direction, the train left York at 4pm, and its portions left Liverpool at 2.30pm, Manchester at 3.20pm and Birmingham at 4pm, to arrive at Parkeston Quay at 9.35pm.

After the First World War, the restaurant cars were transferred to the Liverpool and Manchester portion, which worked as a single train via Manchester Central. After Grouping, the departure from Parkeston Quay was put back to 7.25am, and Lincoln reached at 11.20am. Between Doncaster and York, the train used the old Knottingley line so that if it was late it would avoid delaying the 'Flying Scotsman'. The connection with the Anglo-Scottish express remained, but only if the 'North Country Continental' was running on time or no more than a few minutes late. Despite accelerations elsewhere on the network, the train was 11 minutes slower from Parkeston Quay in 1939 than in 1914 as far as York! The run through to Liverpool was 25 minutes quicker. The train by this time was far heavier, with 13 or 14 carriages and on summer weekends a duplicate train was often provided.

The train was cancelled on the outbreak of the Second World War.

The 'North Eastern'

To those of us today accustomed to clockface departures and long-distance day trips on business, the fact that as late as 1904, the last through evening service to Newcastle from London King's Cross was the 2.20pm departure to Edinburgh comes as a surprise. In the autumn of that year, the GNR and NER decided that a later departure terminating at Newcastle would be an improvement. Before this, Tynesiders had to catch the 6.15pm to Bradford and change at Doncaster to arrive in York at 10.15pm and Newcastle at 12.24am. No wonder a departure from King's Cross at 5.30pm that reached York at 9.5pm and Newcastle at 10.42pm was so widely welcomed in Yorkshire and the North East.

Nevertheless, this was not a completely new train. The GNR had for many years run trains to Nottingham and Sheffield, and it was to a Nottingham train that a portion for Newcastle was attached. The Newcastle portion initially consisted of just four carriages, and those wishing to take a meal had to do so before the train divided at Grantham. This inconvenience didn't last long as by the following year, the Newcastle portion of the train was by far the busier and acquired extra carriages including a restaurant car. For a while the train ran with two restaurant cars, but in Summer 1905, the GNR put on a new train to Sheffield and Manchester running non-stop to the former. From 1905 onwards, the Newcastle train became an entity in its own right with six carriages, including a restaurant car, built at York for the combined use of the GNR and NER. The train became one of the fastest on the East Coast Main Line, and between York and Darlington it was one of the rare trains that achieved a mile-a-minute status in 1905, covering the 44.4 miles in 44 minutes.

The First World War saw the train slowed considerably, not reaching Newcastle until 11.25pm. Shortly before Grouping, it was decided that too many trains stopped at York, and the 5.30pm from King's Cross should be one of the trains to run non-stop through the city, although there still had to be a stop just to the north of the station at Clifton, to change engines! The same applied to the 8am up departure from Newcastle. The LNER endorsed this decision with trains running non-stop between Grantham and Darlington. This was not an economic arrangement as Gateshead engine crews had to work as far south as Grantham and from there to Newcastle, which left the locomotive idle for eight hours and required the footplatemen to travel as passengers to pick up their train.

By this time, the 5.30pm for Newcastle needed nine carriages, but despite the poor economic climate, by 1928 it needed at least eleven and often thirteen, with a weight of 405 tons light and as much as 430 tons gross. Pacific locomotives became usual traction and the schedule was tightened slightly, while in 1931 the call at York was reinstated. In 1932, the timings were tightened further and Newcastle was reached at 10.37pm.

The 'North Eastern' was displaced from its 5.30pm departure from King's Cross in autumn 1935 with the introduction of the 'Silver Jubilee', the new streamlined train that immediately cut the London–Newcastle schedule to a flat four hours with just one stop, Darlington. Its place in the timetable was lost, along with its traffic, to the dashing newcomer, which ran at an average speed of 70.4mph between King's Cross and Darlington, and the train was put back to 5.45pm and merged with the departure normally made at that hour for Hull, with the train stopping at Doncaster to divide. Newcastle was reached at 10.55pm. Despite an interval of just 15 minutes between the departure of the 'Silver Jubilee' and the 'North Eastern', the latter still had its attractions for those not in a hurry as they did not have to pay the surcharge levied on the faster train. In the up direction, the train left Newcastle at 8.15am, and in London at 1.15pm, with stops at Durham, Darlington, York and Grantham.

Wartime saw another reduction in speed and at first passengers had to be content with a 4pm departure from King's Cross and a seven-hour journey to Newcastle. In January 1940, relief came with a 5pm departure for Newcastle, making the stops of the old 'North Eastern' and reaching its destination at 10.50pm. The balancing working in the up direction left Newcastle at 8am and reached King's Cross at 1.55pm. This was not to last. By 1945, the train was back to a 5.30pm departure, and did not reach York until 9.50pm, and with numerous stops then took until 12.20am to reach Newcastle. The up journey left Newcastle at 8.5am and reached London at 2.5pm, while passengers prepared to risk losing their seat, could change onto the 8.50am from Darlington and reach King's Cross at 1.50pm, having just stopped at York and Peterborough.

The train was not reinstated after the end of the war, although at first there were rumours that the 'Silver Jubilee' would be back.

The 'Northern Belle'

Not an express train but a more leisurely 'land cruise' pioneered by the LNER from 1933. The train provided a week-long tour of beauty spots and resorts in the north of England and Scotland, with a different itinerary each week. It seems to have run only in June, and no doubt was one way of extending the summer holiday season, which at the time was shorter and more concentrated than today. The train consisted of first-class day, sleeping and restaurant carriages with 60 passengers being looked after by a staff of 27. Including staff accommodation, the train could include as many as 15 carriages. Up to four week-long land cruises were made each June from 1933 to 1939.

The 'Ports-to-Ports Express'

A strictly unofficial name coined for a railway service that initially ran between Newcastle and the port of Barry in South Wales.

The Great Central had taken a massive step forward when it opened its new line to London in 1899. The following year, a short spur was opened from Woodford & Hinton, 34 miles to the north of Leicester, to Banbury on the Great Western, and this allowed new opportunities for services to be introduced between the North-East of England and the South West. The trains that started to use the new line almost all ran on to Oxford, but the one exception was the 'Ports-to-Ports Express', which instead ran using a little-used branch line that started south of Banbury, at King's Sutton, and ran through the Cotswolds to Cheltenham, where the main line to Gloucester and Cardiff was joined.

When the 'Ports-to-Ports Express' was first introduced in 1906, it terminated at Barry, and while it was a joint venture between the NER, GCR and the GWR, it was handed over to the Barry Railway for the journey westwards from Cardiff. After Grouping, it became a joint venture between the LNER and the GWR, along with the Aberdeen to Penzance service. By this time, the train was running beyond Barry to Swansea, although it avoided the direct line between Cardiff and Swansea, and at the northern end a through carriage from Hull and Goole was attached at Sheffield for the southbound journey, and where it was also detached northbound.

By 1939, the train departed Newcastle at 9.30am and stopped at Durham, Darlington and Northallerton to reach York at 11.32, spending part of the run on the slow line to allow the 'Silver Jubilee' to pass. Leaving York at 11.42am, it ran non-stop to Sheffield, where it arrived at 12.51pm and the carriage from Hull and Goole was attached before the train reversed, as it left at 1pm. The train then ran over the old GCR line to Nottingham, Loughborough, Leicester and Rugby and finally reached Banbury at 3.30pm. Up to this point, a Pacific had been used and the running had been fast, but Banbury to Cheltenham had a weight restriction and until the GWR 'Manor' class 4-6-0s were introduced, the train was taken forward by a 2-6-0 Mogul. High speed running was interrupted for this stage of the journey with 82 minutes allowed for the 44¾ mile run to Cheltenham. After Cheltenham, the train stopped at Gloucester and Chepstow before it reached Newport at 6.30pm, and Cardiff at 6.51pm. Swansea was reached at 8.45pm, at the end of a 397-mile journey that had taken 11¼ hours; an average speed of 35.3mph.

Northbound, the GWR in the late 1930s cut out the Barry loop so that the train left Swansea at 8.15am and ran with stops at Neath, Briton Ferry, Port Talbot, Bridgend and Llantrisant to Cardiff, which it left at 9.40am, followed by a 10am departure from Newport. Banbury was reached at 12.40pm, and after a four-minute stop and locomotive change, the train then continued to Sheffield, missing the Loughborough stop and taking 2 hours 19 minutes for the 107¼ miles. The Hull coach was detached at Sheffield and reached its destination at 4.45pm. Reversing again, the 'Ports-to-Portss Express' reached York at 4.19pm for an eleven-minute stop, and with the same stops as southbound, reached Newcastle at 6.15pm, just ten hours after leaving Swansea.

The train normally consisted of six coaches including a restaurant car, while there was also a composite corridor coach for the Hull connection. The LNER and GWR each provided a set of carriages, so the lineside observer would have seen the rolling stock of the two companies alternating on successive days, with one working northbound while the other worked southbound.

On the outbreak of war, the train was cancelled, but it was revived in October 1946, but between Banbury and Swansea it was diverted to the longer route via Oxford, Swindon and the Severn Tunnel, while except on summer Saturdays, the most northerly point served was York. The Welsh-bound departure would be from York at 12.20pm, with Swansea reached at 9.8pm, while departure from Swansea was at 8.15am, with arrival in York at 5.12pm.

The 'Queen of Scots'

This train originated as the 'Harrogate Pullman', which is covered in detail above, but was renamed 'Queen of Scots' in May 1928 to mark the arrival of a new set of seven all-steel Pullman carriages, which gave an overall weight of 290 tons laden. The down departure of the 'West Riding Pullman' was put back to the afternoon in the new timetable, and so the 'Queen of Scots' went back to the original route and departure time for the 'Harrogate Pullman', leaving King's Cross at 11.15am and ran to Harrogate via Leeds once again. A further change was that it was extended from Edinburgh to Glasgow, where it arrived at Queen Street at 8.45pm having run 450.8 miles. The service was clearly meant to cater for two different markets, travellers between London and Yorkshire and those travelling between Yorkshire and the North East of England, Edinburgh and Glasgow, rather than the through London to Edinburgh or Glasgow business.

The service again settled down until the Anglo-Scottish services enjoyed a general acceleration in May 1932. Departure from King's Cross became 11.20am, and Leeds was reached at 2.31pm, allowing just 191 minutes for 185.7 miles, giving an average speed of 58.3mph. Harrogate was reached in 3¾ hours, Edinburgh in another four hours, and Glasgow in 8 hours 53 minutes from London. In the London-bound direction, the train left Glasgow at 10.15am, Edinburgh at 11.20am, Harrogate at 3.23pm and Leeds Central at 3.55pm, with an additional stop in this direction only, at Holbeck, just a half-mile from Leeds Central, reaching King's Cross at 7.5pm.

The demanding run saw several different types of locomotive in service. The former GCR 4-6-0s were not up to the task, and the same company's 'Director' class 4-4-0s were more successful, but had hardly anything in reserve to recover from delays. Most of the time, ex-GNR Ivatt 4-4-2 Atlantics were the locomotive of choice until sufficient Pacifics were available to take over.

The service was withdrawn at the outset of the Second World War, but reinstated after Nationalisation.

The 'Scarborough Flyer'

Originally, Scarborough was viewed as a resort for holidaymakers from the north of England and later the Midlands as well, and train services from London were not very attractive. This all changed with Grouping as the new LNER considered Scarborough would be attractive to people from London and started to publicise the resort. The timing was opportune with the growing availability of bogie carriages with corridors and refreshment facilities, making longer-distance travel by rail more comfortable.

No time was lost, and in 1923 a through summer-season express was introduced, leaving King's Cross at 11.50am and running non-stop to York, covering the 188.2 miles in 3½ hours, and after calling at York, running non-stop to reach Scarborough at 4.20pm. The balancing up express left Scarborough at 3pm, ran non-stop to York, and then again made a non-stop run from York to London, which was reached at 7.30pm. At first, the train was combined with a portion for Glasgow, and later for Newcastle.

The service was clearly a success as it survived the difficult years that followed and an entire train was required, with a composite brake for Whitby behind the locomotive in the down direction. For the 1933 summer season, the train was rescheduled to reach York in just 3¼ hours and the through journey to Scarborough took 4 hours 10 minutes. In 1935, the schedule was tightened still further, with King's Cross to York cut to just 3 hours, with five minutes spent at York and then 50 minutes was allowed for the 42 miles between York and Scarborough, which was reached in 3 hours 55 minutes. The timing between London and York required an average speed of 62.7mph, and made the 'Scarborough Flyer' one of the fastest trains on the LNER at the time. In the up direction, the train now left Scarborough at 10.40am and reached York at 11.30am, where it picked up the carriage that had left Whitby at 9.40am, and left York at 11.35am, to reach King's Cross at 2.35pm.

In addition to the Whitby carriage, which continued as part of a train leaving York at 2.15pm, the 'Scarborough Flyer' consisted of ten carriages, including two restaurant cars, although the number of carriages varied according to demand, and all in all, the eleven carriages weighed 365 tons tare and up to 390 tons fully laden. Between King's Cross and York, Pacific locomotives were always used, but for the shorter run between York and Scarborough, an Atlantic or a 4-4-0 would be used.

The service was so successful that immediately before the outbreak of the Second World War, the 'Scarborough Flyer' left King's Cross at 11am, but at 10.50am a restaurant car express also left for the Yorkshire resort, stopping only at York to change engines although the public timetable showed the train as running non-stop to Scarborough, which arrived there at 3.7pm. On these occasions, the 'Scarborough Flyer' was much slower to York, with an extra 20 minutes added to the schedule. At the same time, a through restaurant car train was run to Whitby, departing King's Cross at 11.25am, and stopping at Selby to drop a portion for Bridlington, and then again at York to change locomotives, although neither stop was shown in the public timetable, before continuing to Whitby.

Needless to say, the outbreak of war brought these fast-growing through services to an end, and the service was not reinstated until some time after Nationalisation.

The 'Sheffield Pullman'

A short-lived Pullman train that ran between Sheffield and King's Cross from May 1924 to late 1925, when it was withdrawn.

The 'Sheffield Special'

The Great Central Railway was the last of the major companies to reach London and did so when the railway system was virtually complete. This meant that in the major cities served there was almost always an alternative to its services and it had to woo customers away from their well-established usual route. On many of its routes, the GCR line was less direct than that of its rivals, but it had two big advantages. The first of these was that it had the latest carriages, all of which were corridor stock with vestibules and corridor connections, and at the very least a buffet car on every fast train. The second was the quality of its track, which was well laid and allowed for fast running with water troughs to permit more non-stop running.

The line between Quainton Road and Harrow was difficult and did not allow fast running on the approaches to Marylebone, but from Quainton Road northwards beyond Nottingham, the track was laid for high speed running. It was in short, a modern railway for the day whereas its competitors had many lines that dated back to the beginning of the Victorian era, or even earlier.

Marylebone was closer to the West End than many of London's termini, but at first it lacked an underground connection until the Bakerloo Line reached it and a station was opened.

In 1903, a new express was introduced between London and Sheffield. Departing in the down direction at 3.25pm, it was scheduled to run the entire 164.7 miles non-stop in just 3 hours 8 minutes. The following year, this was cut to 2 hours 57 minutes and in 1905 the schedule was tightened further to 2 hours 50 minutes. This meant that the GCR was matching the best times offered by its rivals the Midland and the Great Northern, despite having a longer route. A balancing service left Sheffield for Marylebone every morning at 8.50am and also ran non-stop.

Although not named in the timetable, these trains with their fast non-stop running became known as the 'Sheffield Special'. Initially, the train consisted of just three carriages and a Robinson 4-4-0 locomotive was adequate, despite the keen timings. As traffic grew, four carriages were pulled by a Robinson 4-4-2 Atlantic, and in the down direction a non-corridor coach was added to be slipped at Leicester where it was worked through to Grimsby and Cleethorpes.

Strangely, having tightened the schedule to gain a competitive edge over its rivals, the through timing was allowed to ease back to 2 hours 57 minutes and remained at this until the outbreak of the First World War, while the up departure was advanced to 3.15pm. A further carriage was added and slipped at Penistone for Bradford, while at Sheffield a carriage off a through train from Bournemouth to Newcastle was attached. The run was extended to Manchester London Road with an intermediate stop at Guide Bridge, arriving at 7.25pm with a connection to the 7.30pm for Liverpool.

The train continued throughout the First World War and while speeds were eased in the interests of fuel economy and wear and tear on rolling stock and track, there was no significant reduction. Stops were introduced at Leicester and Nottingham, with Sheffield reached at 6.37pm and after an additional stop at Penistone, arrived at Manchester at 8pm. The stopping pattern continued post-war with a down departure at 3.20pm.

After Grouping, the LNER eventually allocated its standard carriages to this express which grew to a formation of seven vehicles, one of which was an LMS composite brake for Bradford, which brought up the rear of the train. The formation from the locomotive in the down direction was a third-class brake, third corridor, third restaurant car, first-class restaurant and kitchen car, composite and third brake, plus the LMS vehicle already mentioned. This amounted to 243 tons, or 260 tons fully loaded, and usually a B17 'Sandringham' class 4-6-0 was allocated to the train. Still unnamed, by this time there was no obvious balancing working from Sheffield in the morning.

The 'Silver Jubilee'

Britain's first streamlined train with specially built carriages and the streamlined A4 Pacifics, the 'Silver Jubilee', was intended to revolutionise railway travel and could even be said to have had as much impact on the British travelling public as did the High Speed Train four decades later.

Named in honour of the silver jubilee of His Majesty King George V in 1935, the start of the service was preceded by a test run as the increase in speed was unprecedented. On 27 September, the train was taken by the A4 locomotive No. 2509 *Silver Link* on a trial run to Grantham and back. Even climbing the 1-in-200 ascent to Potter's Bar, the speed rose to 75mph, and after Knebworth 100mph was reached and exceeded for the next 30 miles, with 112.5mph reached on two occasions, setting a new British speed record. The 76.4 miles to Peterborough was covered in 55 minutes 2 seconds, 8½ minutes less than allowed in the timetable.

The following Monday, 30 September, the first departure was from Newcastle Central at 10am. The 36 miles between Newcastle and Durham suffered from heavy gradients, for which 40 minutes was allowed, followed by a two-minute stop before the train ran the remaining 232.3 miles to King's Cross non-stop, in 3 hours 18 minutes, to reach London at 2pm with an average speed of 70mph. The down journey left King's Cross at 5.30pm, reaching Darlington at 8.48pm, and arriving in Newcastle at 9.30pm.

This was a demanding schedule for the time, necessitating speeds of 90mph over long stretches, while between Hitchin and Huntingdon only 19 minutes was allowed for 27 miles, giving an average of 85.3mph including a 70mph speed restriction at Offord. There were also speed restrictions at Peterborough, Selby and York. Stretches of track which had never needed speed restrictions to be posted were given speed limits of 70mph or 80mph. Locomotives used on the route were the first to have a 'spy in the cab', a primitive form of tachograph, which not only showed the driver his speed at a time when most railway locomotives did not have speedometers, but also recorded the speed on a paper tape powered by a clockwork mechanism so that the speed could be checked at the end of each journey. Safety also required that, instead of the block signalling section ahead of the train being kept clear, two block sections had to be kept clear allowing for the extra braking distance of the new train.

A4 class 4-6-2 No 2510 *Quicksilver* in silver livery for the 'Silver Jubilee' express to Newcastle, just pulling away from King's Cross in 1935. (*HMRS ABJ 029*)

Not surprisingly, the train was an instant success and was almost always fully booked, with an average load factor of 86 per cent in its first year, despite a supplement of 5 shillings first class and 3 shillings second class. Running only on weekdays, nevertheless, the supplements alone paid for the cost of building the train in two years.

Initially, the train ran with three articulated sets of carriages, two doubles and a triple, giving seven carriages in all. On the down run from the locomotive, this meant a twin articulated set with a corridor brake third and a third-class carriage; next was the catering triplet with an open third-class car and an open first-class car sandwiching a kitchen and pantry car; then furthest from the locomotive in the down direction, was the other twin consisting of a first-class carriage that was half open and half corridor, and a first-class corridor brake. The demand was such that the northern twin had to have another third-class carriage added, making it a triple. In this form, the train had eight carriages and weighed 248 tons empty.

To match the speed and the new vehicles, the 'Silver Jubilee' was painted in silver-grey with stainless steel fittings, while at first, four A4 locomotives were assigned to the service, all painted in the same colour scheme. The locomotives were Nos 2509 *Silver Link*, 2510 *Quicksilver*, 2511 *Silver King* and 2512 *Silver Fox*. This didn't last, and as more A4s entered service, they were painted garter blue and these locomotives were painted in the same livery, so that any A4 could be rostered to work the service.

The service was withdrawn on the outbreak of war and not reinstated afterwards. Post-war, the restaurant car triple returned to service between King's Cross and Newcastle, but post-Nationalisation the other carriages worked the relatively humble 'Fife Coast Express' between Glasgow and St Andrews.

The 'West Riding Limited'

Following the success of the 'Silver Jubilee' and the 'Coronation', a third streamlined service was introduced in October 1937, the 'West Riding Limited'. The route was one that had been pioneered by a Great Northern service and later developed by the 'Queen of Scots', whose calling pattern varied to fit in with another unnamed express to Leeds and Bradford. As early as November 1934, a return trial run between King's Cross and Leeds was made by a four-carriage train weighing 147 tons and headed by the famous A3 Pacific No. 4472 *Flying Scotsman*, which covered the 156 miles from London to Doncaster in 2 hours 2½ minutes, with Leeds reached in 2 hours 32 minutes. In the up direction, another two carriages were added to the trial train, making a load of 208 tons, yet the through journey to King's Cross was completed in 2 hours 37¼ minutes, and at Essendine, 100mph was achieved.

The 'West Riding Limited' was a train of eight carriages consisting of four articulated sets, and was scheduled to run to Bradford in 3 hours 5 minutes in each direction, while to Leeds the time was 2 hours 44 minutes in the down direction and 2 hours 43 minutes in the up direction. The unladen weight was 278 tons. As with the 'Silver Jubilee', locomotives were assigned to the train, initially these were the A4 Pacifics Nos 4495 *Golden Fleece* and 4496 *Golden Shuttle*, but as with the Newcastle train, later, any locomotive of this streamlined class could expect to be rostered for the train.

The down departure from King's Cross was set at 7.10pm, reaching Leeds Central at 9.53pm, where the train reversed and was taken by double-headed N2 0-6-2Ts for the run to Bradford Exchange, which was reached at 10.15pm. This was a sparkling performance with a difficult gradient out of King's Cross and a 1-in-150 ascent to Hemsworth and severe speed restrictions at Wakefield, another gradient and a difficult stretch between Holbeck and Leeds Central, while the tank engines were needed for the severe gradient out of Leeds Central towards Bradford.

The up departure at 11.10am from Bradford Exchange also used the 0-6-2Ts, and arrived at Leeds Central at 11.28am. The A4 Pacific would back on to the other end of the train and departure was at 11.33am. From Doncaster southwards, the 'West Riding Limited' ran 15 minutes behind the up 'Silver Jubilee', and reached King's Cross at 2.15pm.

At the time, day trips on business to London were almost unheard of over these distances, but the timings allowed the Yorkshire businessman to spend a couple of hours in his office, and then have almost five hours in London for meetings.

The train was withdrawn on the outbreak of the Second World War, and not restored afterwards, although some of its two-car articulated sets were used by a post-Nationalisation train, the 'West Riding'.

The 'Yorkshire Pullman'

Encouraged by the success of the all-Pullman express to Harrogate, launched in 1923, the LNER introduced a five-car 'Sheffield Pullman' in June 1924. This left King's Cross at 11.5am, ahead of the 'Harrogate Pullman', and ran via Nottingham Victoria and then over what had been Great Central lines to Sheffield. Nottingham was reached at 1.28pm and the train left at 1.32pm, and arrived at Sheffield at 2.20pm. In the up direction, it left Sheffield at 4.45pm and reached London at 8pm.

The service was almost immediately judged a failure, and in July the timetable was changed, with the train becoming Sheffield-based, leaving in the up direction at 10.30am and reaching King's Cross at 1.45pm. This time it provided a worthwhile amount of time in the Capital for the Yorkshire businessman and departed King's Cross at 6.5pm, and arrived in Sheffield at 9.20pm. The hopes of attracting a significant traffic from Nottingham were once again disappointing, and in April 1925, it was cut from the timetable and the train was diverted to the main line and ran non-stop from King's Cross via Retford to Sheffield. It then ran non-stop from Sheffield to Manchester Central, becoming the 'Sheffield and Manchester Pullman'. This meant a much shortened journey time between King's Cross and Sheffield of 2 hours 57 minutes against 3 hours 15 minutes via Nottingham. Manchester was reached at 10.12pm, 4 hours 7 minutes, from London.

Success still evaded the LNER and in September 1925, with the 'Queen of Scots' serving Harrogate, it was decided to introduce a new Pullman service to Leeds and Bradford, using the cars from the 'Sheffield and Manchester Pullman'. The train left King's Cross at 11.10am, and ran non-stop to Leeds where it arrived at 2.35pm, with two cars being detached and taken on to Bradford, where they arrived at 3pm. The Leeds cars, meanwhile, were taken empty to Harrogate, where they spent the night before leaving the following day at 11.15am for Leeds Central. There, they joined the two cars that had left Bradford at 11.20am, before leaving Leeds at 11.50pm and again running non-stop to arrive at King's Cross at 3.15pm. This gave Harrogate a daily train from London, but two towards London.

To modern eyes accustomed to intensive working, this was hardly economic as two sets of Pullman cars were needed for the train, as well as another two sets for the other Harrogate train, the 'Queen of Scots'. It was not surprising that further changes came in May 1928, when the 'Queen of Scots' was diverted to serve Leeds once more, while the Leeds and Bradford Pullman was named the 'Yorkshire Pullman' for the first time. Once again, the London departure was changed, being switched to 4.45pm, and the train diverted to serve Leeds, Bradford, Harrogate and Newcastle, all of which now had two fast Pullman trains to and from London daily. By this time the Bradford portion was detached at Wakefield to run more directly to the city, after which it continued to Halifax, giving a service to London in just over four hours. The new timings also meant that just one set of Pullman cars was needed.

This arrangement lasted longer than the earlier attempts to establish the service, but in 1935, it was decided to work some of the Pullman cars through to Hull, giving that city a 3½-hour journey time to and from London. This required a call at Doncaster, which gained a mile-a-minute service from London with the 4.45pm down from King's Cross taking just 156 minutes for the journey, while the up train in the mornings took a minute less. This was no longer purely a West Riding service, and the train was renamed the 'Yorkshire Pullman', but the Harrogate portion stopped running through to Newcastle with the launch of the 'Silver Jubilee'. When the 'West Riding Limited' was launched in September 1937, the four-car Harrogate portion was diverted to run via York to Doncaster, where it joined the two cars from Hull and the two from Halifax via Bradford. At weekends in the summer, the train grew from eight cars to twelve. Pacifics were normally used on what had finally become a busy train, but V2 class 2-6-2 locomotives also handled it successfully.

The train was withdrawn on the outbreak of the Second World War, but reinstated on 4 November 1946, with a down departure from King's Cross at 3.50pm, and from Harrogate at 10.20am. Further changes followed Nationalisation, including a change to accommodate the new 'Tees-Tyne Pullman'.

Chapter 11

Carrying the Goods

None of the four grouped railway companies was as dependent on goods traffic as the LNER. No less than two-thirds of the company's annual turnover came from freight,* leaving just one-third of its turnover from passengers, despite its heavily used commuter services. Of the various forms of freight traffic, by far the most important in terms of tonnage was that of coal, both for the home market and for export. It is difficult for anyone born in the last fifty years to fully appreciate how important coal was. It was the prime source of heating in the home and in many offices and factories, with the bigger ones having large boiler rooms. It was used to produce gas, more usually known as town gas, as well as electricity, and was needed for most merchant shipping and, of course, for the railways themselves. Any lengthy journey by rail would be punctuated by the express racing past long lines of coal wagons, sometimes moving slowly along the slow line, but more often sitting in a siding waiting for the express to pass.

In 1923, the first year of Grouping, the total output from all of Britain's coalfields (there were none in Ireland), amounted to 273 million tons, with more than a third of this being for export. Of this, the share the LNER carried amounted to 102 million tons, with only the Great North of Scotland and the Great Eastern running through areas that did not have coalfields, but of course, the communities both railways served still needed coal. The GNR and GCR had long coal trains running slowly southward, while the latter also had a considerable east-west trade across the Pennines from Yorkshire to Lancashire, as well as an eastward flow with export coal to Immingham. In the North East, many collieries had their own railway systems and coal staiths for loading into ships, usually known as colliers.† For those that didn't, the NER moved coal from colliery to factory or port, or to the many small sidings in which coal merchants would bag the coal ready for distribution to their smaller customers. Further north, the NBR moved coal from the large Fife coalfield to the docks at Methil and Leith, on the Forth, and to Aberdeen.

While the railway companies competed for this traffic, and competition for coal from the East Midlands coalfields was especially keen between the LMS and LNER at first, there was also competition from shipping, as there was a very heavy coastal traffic at the time. In 1923, there were twice weekly sailings from Leith to London, and twice weekly from Newcastle to London, which increased to three times a week in 1927, the year after the General Strike and the Miners' Strike.

All of this shows how important coal traffic was, and how disastrous it was when the miners, who had had a number of largely localised and relatively short strikes in the years following the First World War, went on a prolonged strike in 1926, which for a while, was accompanied by the General Strike. The loss of coal traffic during the strike was bad enough, but what hit the LNER worse than any other railway was that a very large proportion of the export traffic was lost for

* While most of us consider 'freight' to be an American term and 'goods' British, not only the LMS with its penchant for American practices and terminology, but also the other railways used the term 'freight'.

† This is a confusing term. At the time, it generally meant a coal miner rather than a ship specifically designed to carry coal, while today, coal would be moved by a bulk carrier.

ever. This was before the years of the Great Depression took effect. Despite desperate efforts to encourage coal traffic after the strike, even by 1930, the coal traffic of the LNER was still down at 88 million tons, and on the eve of Nationalisation, it was 63 million tons.

The Common Carrier

These statistics have to be put in context. The railways were very much caught on the back foot by the tremendous growth in road haulage following the First World War as well as being hampered first by their 'common carrier' obligation that ensured that they had to carry any freight offered, and then by the Railway Rates Tribunal, which governed how much they could charge for any of the railways' traditional traffic. The range of goods carried by the railways at the time was far wider than today, with the railways able to cherry pick and have lost traffic such as parcels and sundries, for example. If you wanted to move the contents of a house, or even move a whole farm, you contacted your local station. There were even instances, not at all uncommon, of a circus being moved by train. New forms of traffic, often requiring express freights, were more profitable. The railway companies employed salesmen, at the time known as 'canvassers', to sell their freight services. Incentives were offered to customers, including a number of free passes for their directors or senior managers, with the number dependent on the volume of business provided.

The period after the Grouping coincided with growing industrial instability while traffic fell from the artificial peaks of the war years. Anxious to stimulate traffic, in 1923 freight rates were reduced from 112 per cent above the pre-war rate to 75 per cent above. Nevertheless, costs had risen considerably during the period of state control, and traffic was falling. Estimates for Britain's railways as a whole suggest that the total of railborne freight, reached 367 million tons in 1913, and then went on to peak at more than 400 million tons during the First World War, and then, except for a recovery during the Second World War, went into steady decline from 1919 onwards.

For most of Britain's railways freight was the main business, with the only exception amongst the 'Big Four' being the Southern Railway.

Freight brought many problems to the railways. The common carrier obligation and the intervention of the Railway Rates Tribunal meant that there was nothing so simple as a charge of X per ton per mile travelled, as different rates applied to different categories of goods. This common carrier obligation was to become an increasing burden as road transport competition developed, able to charge what it liked and carry whatever suited that mode of transport most, often leaving the railways with the less economic loads. It is hard for us today to fully understand the importance of freight to the railways and of the railways to freight. Virtually every railway station (halts were another matter) had its own goods yard, often shared by one or more of the local coal merchants who would bag and distribute coal to their customers from the premises.

Almost every station had its own goods yard for these were the days when the dominant form of household heating, and in some cases cooking as well, was coal. Offices would have coal fires, so would schools. Even larger establishments would have a coal-fired boiler room for the central heating. Most households that had an electric supply had one strong enough to provide lighting, but not strong enough for cooking or heating, let alone be able to power the range of electrical appliances to be found in the modern home.

If a farmer wished to move farms, his entire stock of animals and equipment would travel in a train specially hired for the purpose. People moving house over anything other than a short distance would often have their belongings loaded into a demountable container aboard a lorry, which would take it to a railway station where it would transfer to a flat truck for the rest of the journey. The circus usually arrived by rail rather than by road, with the final procession from the railway station being through the streets. In 1923, the new LNER carried 7.5 million animals, but due to road competition, this had halved by 1939. It is hard to see how the railways could have retained this traffic as the road haulier could carry the consignment from doorstep to destination without any transhipment, and although traditionally many farmers had herded their animals along the highway to railway stations or goods depots, this practice was becoming dangerous as the volume of traffic on the roads grew.

Freight, or goods, traffic was classified either as 'full load' taking a whole wagon or goods van, and what was variously known as 'smalls' or 'sundries', smaller consignments but different from parcels, which were carried by passenger train and charged at a higher rate. The smalls traffic suffered delays while waiting to be consolidated into mixed loads, in which a van or wagon full of these smaller consignments would be grouped together, all travelling to the same goods station or depot, but for a number of different consignees. Bulk traffics such as coal often provided a full train load rather than just a wagon or two, and many goods wagons were owned by industrial customers of the railways and could be seen around the system carrying their owner's names and in some cases their colours as well. The coal mines were major owners of goods wagons, but so too were many of the larger coal merchants.

A mainstay of the mineral trains was the O1 class 2-8-0. No. 6624 is seen here with a four-plank wagon, doubtless the first of many on a long mineral or coal train. (*HMRS 417*)

Agricultural traffic was important, so much so, that the company found it worthwhile providing a sack-hire business. Newer traffics included sugar beet, much of it grown in East Anglia, but there were also processing plants in Yorkshire and Scotland to be served. More traditional traffic included grain, both home grown and imported.

Private Owner Wagons

Private owner wagons were the bane of many a railway manager's life. They could not be used for other traffic and had to be returned to the premises of the owner, as well as being generally looked after by the railway while away from their owners' premises. Long trains of empty coal wagons that could not be used for anything else did little for railway productivity, the railwaymen would argue, although having sent a train of fifty or more coal wagons to a coal merchant, it is hard to see what could be sent back.

There was another problem with private wagons, which was that they were built to the specification of the owner, rather than the railway. So while the railway companies might want to increase the size of its goods wagons and introduce continuous braking to permit higher

V2 class 2-6-2 No. 4808 heads a fitted fish express at Stannington in 1939. (*HMRS ACW 112*)

speeds, a typical wagon owner such as a coal mine would want to persist with short-wheelbase two-axle wagons because of the tight curves on their premises. Many wagon owners wanted the cheapest and simplest wagon possible. Handling in many industrial sites, and especially collieries with tight curves and limited clearances above the mines (the surface goods wagons were too big to go underground), was often primitive and only the unbraked wagon, operated loose-coupled, was acceptable. When larger coal wagons were introduced, the mine owners largely ignored them as they were too big for the lines in their collieries.

It would be wrong to assume that the private owner wagon was the sole preserve of the coal industry. A new and increasingly important traffic using such wagons was the fast-growing oil industry with private tanker wagons for petrol and, increasingly, diesel fuel.

While special arrangements were made for whole trains for a particular freight customer, and some of these had regular timetables, for wagon-load and less than wagon-load freight, a steam locomotive and guard's van would operate what was known as a pick-up freight, calling at station sidings and collecting whatever wagons or vans that were ready to move. There were also other goods trains that went from one station to another dropping off wagons and vans. Unless the station was busy enough to justify its own shunting locomotive, the locomotives of

A mixed goods, including a cattle truck, headed by an ex-GNR J3 class 0-6-0 near Grantham in 1929. The variety of wagons suggests that this could be a pick-up freight, visiting smaller goods yards to drop off and collect wagons. (*HMRS AEU 521*)

these goods trains would spend much of their time shunting wagons, something that was made more difficult and time-consuming as they always had to ensure that the guard's van was at the back of the train before continuing with their journey, just in case a wagon coupling failed so that guard would have time to alert the nearest signalman and place detonators on the track to protect the train.

Obviously, the wagons collected by the pick-up freight would need to be sorted and sent onwards to their destinations. This was done in marshalling yards, and between the wars the railway companies attempted to introduce a new style of marshalling yard, with humps so that wagons could role down the hump using gravity and be directed into different sidings, depending on their final destination. In the older yards, locomotives would push the wagons into sidings, often letting them roll away. Wagons were stopped by simply bumping into another wagon. Damage to wagons was often severe, and their contents often fared badly as well, but measures were put in hand between the wars to minimise this damage, with growing use of steel wagons and even shock-absorbing underframes.

Another mixed goods running near Grantham, this time headed by an ex-GNR D3 class 4-4-0 in 1929. (*HMRS AEU 523*)

Goods trains were classified as either fully fitted, that is with many of the vehicles having vacuum-brakes that could be controlled by the locomotive driver, or unfitted, that is with no continuous braking system. On unfitted goods trains, each wagon had only a simple handbrake that could be applied in a siding or if the train was checked on a steep gradient, otherwise braking was left entirely to the locomotive and, in an emergency, the guard's van. Such trains ran at speeds of around 5–10mph. Stopping would be accompanied by a clatter as the wagons ran into one another. Fully fitted freight trains were allowed to travel much faster, provided that the rolling stock could do this safely, and the permitted speed depended on the proportion of wagons or vans fitted with the vacuum brake, which automatically applied the brakes once the vacuum was broken, as would happen if the wagon became uncoupled from the rest of the train. Not all wagons were necessarily fitted with vacuum brakes on express goods trains, and there were some variations with those trains having between one-third and one-half of the wagons fitted with vacuum brakes allowed to run at speeds of up to 45mph, while with less than one-third of the wagons fitted with vacuum brakes, the speed was reduced to 35mph. This was still an improvement over the speed of an unfitted goods train.

Many smaller customers had their goods collected or delivered from the goods station or depot by the railways' own fleet of vehicles, and even between the wars, many of these were

A mixed goods, possibly one of the slow pick-up freights, headed by E4 class 2-4-0 No. 2784, and a passenger train meet at Long Melford in 1947. (*HMRS ABD 120*)

still horse drawn although petrol and diesel vehicles were steadily taking over. Two of the most practical of the new vehicles were designed with handling railway work in mind. This was the Scammell Mechanical Horse and the Karrier Cob, both of which were three-wheeled tractors with incredible manoeuvrability introduced in 1930. On Nationalisation, the new British Railways inherited some 6,000 of these vehicles from the 'Big Four' railway companies. Other vehicles introduced at this time were 10cwt (or half-ton) light vans supplied by the Yorkshire-based car and van manufacturer Jowett, as well as 6-ton Albion lorries. By 1934, the collection and delivery motor fleet was covering 20 million miles annually. Nevertheless, by the end of the Second World War, the LNER still had a sizeable number of heavy horses for its collection and delivery work.

In common with the other railways, the LNER employed salesmen, known as canvassers, who sought business from firms that were likely to become freight customers. The through running of trains or wagons between the different companies produced a fair volume of accounts to be settled, and as with passenger traffic, this was done by the Railway Clearing House. There was overlap and competition at various points on the LNER's network with the London Midland & Scottish in particular, and with the GWR to a much lesser extent, so an agreement was reached between these companies that they should coordinate their activities as far as goods business was concerned. The Southern Railway was not a party to these arrangements, as it was a comparatively minor player in the freight business.

The Railways Act 1921 which created the 'Big Four' laid down what it described as 'standard revenues', or what would be described as profits, which each of the companies could make each year. In common with the other companies, the LNER never ever achieved its standard revenue. The first year of its existence was the best, while 1937 was good for passenger traffic, but was followed by another bad year in 1938. The Railway Rates Tribunal was in theory supposed to be able to remedy this by allowing the company to adjust its charges, but was unable to do so adequately due to the weakness of the economy.

Seeking a Competitive Edge

There were four ways in which the railways could re-establish their competitive edge. The first was to speed up the longer distance goods trains, which also required them to increase the number of vehicles that could be braked by the locomotive, with trains either being unfitted or unbraked (except by hand), partly fitted with a number of wagons having vacuum brakes, or fully fitted, meaning that most and ideally all vehicles could be braked. The second way was to introduce containers that could be easily and quickly transferred between road and railway vehicles. The third was to modernise the goods yards, creating large marshalling yards with a

A selection of goods vans and wagons in 1936, with an LMS van prominent, while one of the NE vans is intended for bananas – premium traffic. (*HMRS ABH 514*)

'hump', so that wagons could be sorted as they ran down the slope on to different tracks so that longer-distance goods trains could be assembled. The fourth way was to improve the collection and delivery of goods, and from its inception until the outbreak of the Second World War the railway companies continued the mechanisation of this activity which in 1923 was for the most part dependent upon horse-drawn vehicles: magnificent, but hardly productive.

The LNER stated to accelerate its goods trains, and in 1932 replaced a daily coal train of 80 wagons between Peterborough New England yard and Hornsey Ferme Park with two trains each of 56 wagons, but completing the journey in half the time. The overnight fish train from Aberdeen to King's Cross had tighter timings over parts of its route than the pre-1932 'Flying Scotsman', despite consisting almost entirely of four-wheel vans. Complementing a service for sending small packages by passenger train, called the 'Blue Arrow' service, was a service using fast parcels trains called the 'Green Arrow', and as mentioned earlier, this name was also applied to the first of the V2s to publicise the service. Fast freights such as the 3.35pm 'Scotch Goods' from King's Cross ran at speeds of around 50mph, while there were frequent fast goods trains to Leeds, Liverpool, Manchester and Nottingham, leaving King's Cross late in the evening at half-hourly intervals. Overall, the company's services were sufficiently competitive for it to attract and retain traffic from Luton to Manchester and the West Riding, despite the LMS route being more direct.

One of the innovations introduced was a number of express goods trains. One of these was introduced in 1927, and was called informally the 'Aberdeen–King's Cross Meat Express', which

A bogie fish van is at the head of a train approaching King's Cross station in 1937. (*HMRS ABH 722*)

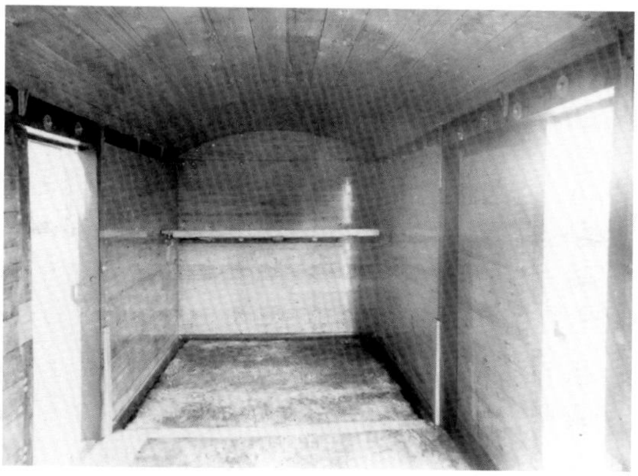

Fish was an important traffic for the LNER as it needed fast freight trains and showed the railway at its best when much traffic was being lost to road. *Above left* is a brand-new 10 ton fish van, No. 229903, just outshopped from the works in 1938, posed for an official photograph. (*HMRS AAN 035*) *Above right* is the interior of the fish van, clean and uncluttered, at least for the time being! (*HMRS AAN 034*)

left Aberdeen on Tuesdays, Wednesdays and Thursdays at 10.40am, reaching Newcastle at 5.8pm, where it left after a two-minute stop, and continued to reach York at 7.4pm, where there would have been an engine change as the train did not resume its journey until 7.15pm, reaching Grantham at 8.58pm, stopping for four minutes, and reaching King's Cross at 11.10pm. The train also ran on other days if demand was sufficient. This was 523.3 miles in 12 hours 30 minutes, an average speed end-to-end of 41.9mph.

There was new traffic, even at a time of economic difficulty. The formation of the Central Electricity Generating Board in 1926 led to a programme of power station construction, with much of the coal carried by rail, as indeed was the electrical machinery required for the new stations, albeit at some considerable disruption to other traffic if the load was 'out of gauge'. Two years later, the opening of a large aluminium refinery and mill at Fort William meant that bauxite became another new traffic for the railways. The 1930s saw goods traffic beginning to increase in the face of road haulage competition, but it was not until the late 1930s that this became significant with rearmament.

One innovation introduced shortly after Grouping, in an attempt to improve the management of goods traffic, was the creation of a freight wagon control centre at York. This required every goods depot to submit a daily return of the wagons held, so that a shortage at one depot could be rectified by transferring wagons from elsewhere. This was augmented by an occasional stock-take, conducted over a weekend, which was necessary because the 'common user' approach to railway-owned wagons meant that many got lost in the system and could even disappear into another company's area. There were also those damaged, but not reported, and some railwaymen maintained dark suspicions about wagons being taken by private owners and repainted in their colours. Even so, the LNER managed its freight, as with everything else, on a divisional basis with a goods manager for each division.

New marshalling yards were also built to improve operations, notably at Hull, March and Mottram.

Some of the traffic was seasonal, with fresh fruit being carried to the major cities, with the fruit pickers, who were often industrial workers taking a paid working holiday, were also conveyed to the farms and orchards by train. While deep water fishing provided traffic for regular fast goods trains every night, the herring fishery moved around the coast, so the originating point for this traffic changed as the season continued, keeping the traffic schedulers busy. Again, Scottish fisher girls would travel from their homes to process the catch when it was landed at Lowestoft or Yarmouth. Even large agricultural shows created a considerable business, with equipment, stands animals and feed being taken to and from each show, and of course these also stimulated passenger traffic.

All of the railway companies became involved with the use of the container, originally introduced by the LMS in 1926. These, of course, were not the containers that we are used to seeing today, being much smaller and looked like an enclosed goods wagon body, so that they could not be stacked. The container not only speeded transhipment between road and rail or railway and ship, it also reduced damage and pilferage, which was a problem even though the 1920s and 1930s were amongst the most law-abiding decades in British history. It became increasingly common for open wagons to be sheeted with tarpaulin to protect their contents. Pilferage resulted in losses of up to 1 per cent of revenue during the 1920s, while during the Second World War, many of the goods finding their way onto the 'black market' were those stolen in transit. The LNER's stock of covered wagons almost doubled between 1923 and 1947 from 25,994 to 50,614, while open wagons fell from 125,596 to 89,937, excluding mineral wagons. As an indication of the way in which traffic changed over these years, while the number of wagons for heavy or bulky loads rose from 1,282 in 1923 to 9,696 in 1947, the number of cattle trucks fell from 6,720 to 2,826, and horse boxes from 1,767 to 828.

One means of improving productivity was to build larger locomotives, and the LNER-built two P1 class 2-8-2 'Mikado' locomotives with a booster fitted to the rear pony truck to enhance pulling power. These locomotives were supposed to be able to handle trains of up to 1,600 tons, but there was one flaw, which was that siding capacity was insufficient for such trains, especially when they needed to be moved into a siding en route to allow an express passenger to pass.

Unusual Traffic

The role of common carrier also meant that the railways had some unusual loads to carry, and those that were out of gauge, that is wider or higher than the standard for railway vehicles, and must have been a nuisance. Typical of such loads would be lifeboats for major passenger liners, which required the adjoining line to be closed to traffic. Such trains were run at quiet periods, but daytime was favoured over night because of the need to be able to see problems if they arose.

The *LNER Magazine* was often very coy about explaining what such loads were for. Lifeboats would be described as being for a 'new Cunarder', or Cunard liner, without mentioning the name, even though by the time such items were needed, the ship would have been named and launched some time earlier. One of the more easily accommodated loads, although they required longer wagons, were 16in guns for warships, although again the magazine did not let on that they were for either HMS *Rodney* or her sister *Nelson*, the only two British battleships to have guns of this calibre. Wartime would have justified such caution, but this was during the winter of 1926/27.

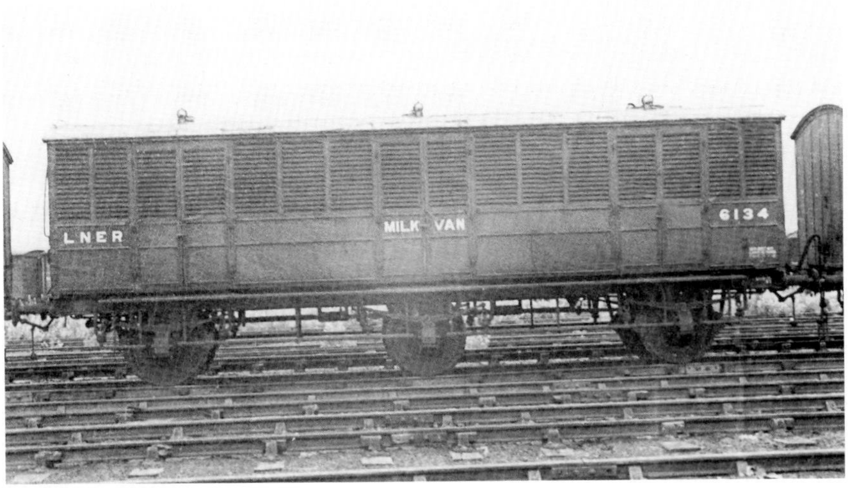

A six-wheeled louvered milk van, No. 6134 in 1935. (*HMRS ABH 835*)

Chapter 12

The Passenger Business

Although primarily a freight railway, passenger traffic was still significant for the LNER, accounting for around a third of annual turnover. Not only in London, but around Edinburgh and Glasgow, on Tyneside, and around Manchester, Nottingham and Leeds, commuter traffic was important. The long-distance expresses were augmented by boat trains from Liverpool Street, while there were the inevitable cross-county and branch line trains.

The LNER shared with the Great Western the distinction of running Britain's longest-distance train, from Aberdeen to Penzance, although for much of the year this was just a single through carriage. Other through inter-company trains ran from Newcastle to Swansea and to Bournemouth. The company also had important trans-Pennine expresses and was a major user of the Cheshire Lines. A through train ran from Liverpool to Parkeston Quay, known, albeit unofficially, as the 'North Country Continental', with no attempt to follow the development of more recent years of packet ships sailing from Hull to Rotterdam and Antwerp. There were also through carriages from Glasgow to connect with sailings from Parkeston Quay.

Retail and other commercial premises at railway stations are clearly nothing new, as this 1936 view of Maryland Point, on the ex-GER line, between Stratford and Ilford, shows. There are 'Frequent trains to the City', so doubtless this was a reasonably affluent area. (*HMRS ABC 712*)

While the restrictions on passenger services during the Great War were far less than those imposed during the Second World War, there were reductions in services as trains became less frequent and heavier, while making more stops. By the time of Grouping, many of the wartime restrictions had been reversed. Nevertheless, one major problem that was not tackled immediately, even after Grouping, was the artificially lengthened journey times between London and the major Scottish cities adopted in the late 1890s. This was as a result of the last 'races', and timings were simply badly outdated by 1923, but still allowed to persist for some time longer.

Even in 1938, six-wheeled, four-compartment carriages were still in use; these are ex-Great Central examples. (*HMRS ABJ 512*)

In fact, it was not until 1932, no less than 37 years after the end of the 'race' to Aberdeen, that the East Coast route was accelerated. There were some ridiculous situations in the meantime. From summer 1923, the night sleeper from King's Cross to Edinburgh Waverley took just 7¾ hours, making it three-quarters of an hour faster than the day 'Flying Scotsman'. When Nigel Gresley introduced corridor tenders in 1928 allowing non-stop running between London and Edinburgh, the train kept to the same 8½-hour schedule, so the average speed was just 47.6mph! The sheer nonsense of this, as stated earlier, was underlined by the fact that the following train, which made four stops, also took exactly the same time!

Despite this, in 1923, the LNER was Britain's fastest railway, with the 44.1 miles between Darlington and York on the East Coast route being run at an average speed of 61.5mph. The same high average speed was also to be found between Leicester and Nottingham in former Great Central territory. This distinction was short-lived, as in Summer 1923, the Great Western accelerated its service from Cheltenham to run at 61.8mph between Swindon and Paddington. One factor that reduced end-to-end journey speeds was the practice, as will be noted in Chapter

A four-compartment six-wheel composite carriage at Doncaster in 1938. (*HMRS ABJ 514*)

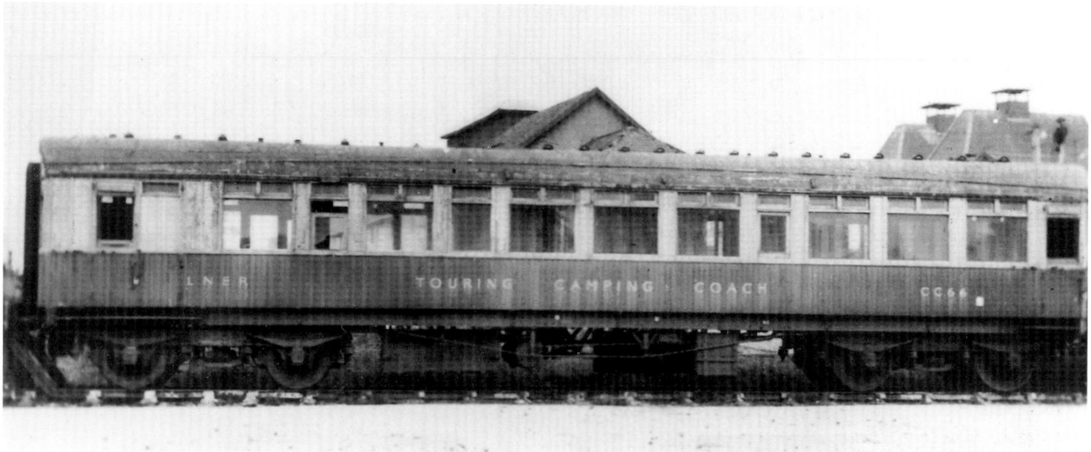

The LNER was the first railway to introduce the camping coach as a means of utilising redundant passenger carriages. This matchboard-sided coach, No. CC66, looks as if it needs some attention, despite being much grander than the old six-wheeled conversion. It is marked as a 'Touring Camping Coach'. (*HMRS ABC 214*)

10, was that many trains were in fact portioned workings, dropping off a number of carriages at one station, and in some cases even taking on others, although for the most part, the further from London the fewer carriages were left on an express.

Slip carriages were inherited by the LNER on a number of trains to save the down train making an extra call. Two came from the Great Central, with slips being made at Finmere and Woodford, and another two from the Great Eastern, at Marks Tey and Waltham Cross. These were withdrawn in 1936/37 after a slip carriage caught up with the rear of its parent train and collided with it.

The General Strike

The passenger business was affected by the General Strike that lasted from 3 to 12 May in 1926, but with the aid of railwaymen who ignored the strike call, managers and others who took up the work of the strikers, and volunteers, the railway kept some trains running. On the first complete day of the strike, 4 May, 148 trains were run, but this more than doubled the following day to 305, and by 11 May, 1,154 trains were being run, with 1,245 trains on the last day of the strike. Speed

Elderly clerestory carriages still remained in service, as with this ex-GER composite at Cambridge in 1936. There is a toilet compartment between the first- and third-class compartments. (*HMRS ABJ 108*)

limits were introduced in case of sabotage, but trains were also operated on the time-interval basis that had been a cause of so many accidents during the early days of the railways.

There was no option as the absence of signalmen meant that it was either time-interval running or no running at all. Fears over sabotage were soon confirmed when, on 6 May, the locomotive *Flying Scotsman* was derailed at Cramlington whilst working the 10am from King's Cross to Edinburgh. This could have been a disaster and it was fortunate that only two passengers and the fireman were injured, with the latter, a volunteer, being scalded. More serious was the accident at St Margarets, Edinburgh, where a train running under the time-interval system entered the station and collided with goods wagons, killing three passengers. That same day, at Bishop's Stortford, two trains running on the time-interval system collided and a passenger was killed and another injured when part of the roof fell on to the platform.

Accelerating the Services

Until the 'Flying Scotsman' became a non-stop service, the LNER lagged behind the Great Western's 'Cornish Riviera Express' which made the longest non-stop run in the British Isles, between Paddington and Plymouth, a distance of 225.7mph with an average speed of 54.8mph. The best the LNER could do was the 188.2 miles between King's Cross and York at an average speed of 53.8mph.

Many of the railway companies had congested approaches to the London termini, but both King's Cross and Liverpool Street were particularly bad examples of this. The situation at King's Cross was made worse by the number of double track bottlenecks between London and York, with the tunnel and viaduct at Welwyn being problems that persist to this day. The only way of coping with this problem was to run the fast expresses in groups, with several trains leaving mid-morning, then again at lunchtime, in the late afternoon and late evening. This would have been a problem on some railways, but the very long distances covered by many LNER expresses meant that the type of clockface departure favoured on the Southern was not necessary, although eventually this was introduced for shorter distance trains. An example of how this worked in practice comes from the summer timetable for 1939, after a three-hour interval from the departure of the 'Flying Scotsman' at 10am, there were departures from King's Cross to Newcastle at 1.5pm, Edinburgh at 1.20pm, West Riding at 1.30pm and Harrogate at 1.40pm, followed by a long interval until 4pm before more fast services departed. The gaps between these 'flights' of departures were needed for slower trains and especially freight traffic.

Many of the camping coaches were old, six-wheeled stock, as with this example, No. CC11 at Stratford in 1938. It was probably waiting to be taken to a suitable holiday location. (*HMRS ABJ 002*)

EDINBURGH, LINLITHGOW, POLMONT, FALKIRK, and GLASGOW.—North British.

Mls. frm E'burgh.	Down.	Week Days.																	
		Sleeping Car, and Through Carriage, London (K.C.) to Glasgow and Fort William. Through Carriage, Penzance to Glasgow, commencing on 10th inst., see pp. 9, 19, 78, 692, 668, 729, 734, and 776.				Sleeping Car & Thro' C'g's from London.—Restaurant Car Express.	Leaves N. Berwick at 8 5 & Gullane at 8 mrn. Lothian Coast Express, see page 776.		Leaves Grangemouth at 10 12 mrn., see page 778.	Express, Leith and Edinburgh to Glasgow.				Saturdays only. Thro' Train to Helensburgh.	Restaurant Car Exp., Leith & Edinburgh to Glasgow.		Restaurat Car Express, Leeds to Glasgow.	Leaves Grangemouth at 2 54 aft., see page 778.	
		aft	mrn	mrn	mrn	aft	aft	mrn	mrn	mrn	mrn	aft	aft	aft	mrn	aft	mrn	aft	aft
	776London (K. C.) dep.	7V30	....	8 25	....	1020	1030	....	....	....	....	....	....	....	....	....	4 45		....
	776York .... "	11V30	....	1 9	....	2 40	2 54	....	....	....	....	....	....	....	3P57	....	9 38		....
	776Newcastle (Cen.) "	1X17	....	3 15	....	4 34	4 52	....	....	....	....	....	....	....	9 15	....	1118		....
		mrn	mrn	mrn	mrn	mrn	mrn	mrn		mrn	mrn	aft	aft	aft	aft	aft	aft		aft
	Leith (Central)...dep.	....	5 30	6 5	....	7 25	....	8 49		9 50	10 53	....	....	1229	1245	....	1 32		....
—	Edinbro' (Waverley) "	4 30	5 50	6 25	....	7 40	8 50	9 5		10 5	11 30	....	....	1250	1 0	....	2 0		2 20
1¼	Haymarket	....	5 55	....	....	7a45		9a10		10a10	11 35	....	....	1255	1a5	....	2a5		2 25
5½	Gogar	....	6 4	....	....	....		....			11 44	....	....			....	....		2 38
8¾	Ratho	....	6 11	....	....	....		....			11 51	....	....			....	....		2 47
12	Winchburgh	....	6 19	....	....	....		....			12 0	....	....			....	....		2 53
14½	Philpstoun	....	6 25	....	....	....		....			12 6	....	....			....	....		3J25
17½	Linlithgow	....	6 33	....	....	8 10		....			12 13	1227	....			....	....		3 32
19¾	Manuel 791, 811	....	6 40	....	....	8 16		....			12 20	....	....			....	....		3 39
22¼	Polmont 779, 791	....	6 45	6 54	7 30	8 23		....		10 40	12 26	1238	1246			....	2 35		3 46
25½	Falkirk (High) ‖	....	....	7 1	7 39	8 30		....	H1022		Stop	1245	1253			....		3H4	3 53
28¾	Bonnybridge	....	....	....	7 47			....	....		....	....	1 0			....		....	4 0
31¾	Castlecary § 788	....	....	....	7 54			....	1039		....	....	1 7			....		3 23	4 7
34½	Dullatur §	....	....	....	8 2			....	1044		....	....	1 14			....		3 29	4 12
35¾	Croy	....	....	....	8 7			....	....		....	....	1 19			....		3 33	4 21
41	Lenzie 805	....	....	....	8 17			....	....		....	....	1 28			....		3 42	4 27
44	Bishopbriggs	....	....	....	8 23			....	....		aft	....	1 35			2 11		3 48	4 34
45¾	Cowlairs	....	....	....	8 31			....	....		12c35	....	1 42			2 19		3 53	4 40
47¼	Glasgow (Qu. St. †). arr.	5 30	....	7 32	8 37	9 0	9 50	1010	11 5	11 15	12e41	1 16	1 48	2*5	2 5	2 25	3 10	3 59	4 40
70¾	796 Helensburgh .. arr.	7 41	....	8 51	....	10 4	....	1117	....	12 33	2e7	....	....	3 7	3L31	4 19	4 45	5 28	5 51

Down.	Week Days—Continued.								Sundays.		
	Restaurant Car Express.				Restaurant Car Express, London (K.C.) to Glasgow.	Leaves Grangemouth at 7 3 aft., see page 778.		Through Carriages, Southampton and Scarbro' to Glasgow' see pp. 56, 76, 690, 668, 753, 728, 734, & 777.—Restaurant Car. York to Glasgow. Commences on the 10th instant.	Sleeping Car and Through Carriage from London (K.C.) and Penzance (on 16th, 23rd, and 30th inst.) to Glasgow, see pages 28, 9, 19, 78, 692, 668, 730, 734, and 777.		Through Express, London (K.C.) to Glasgow.
	mrn	aft	aft	aft	mrn	aft	aft	mrn	aft	aft	mrn
776London (K. C.)..dep.	....	....	....	....	10 0		....	1120	10T30	....	1130
776York .... "	10 5	....	....	....	2 2		....	3 40	2 54	....	4 3
776NewcastleCen.) "	1223	....	....	....	3 50		....	5 45	4 52	....	5 55
	aft	aft	aft	aft	aft		aft	aft	Sun mrn	aft	aft
Leith (Central)...dep.	3 48	4 15	4 51	....	6 0		7 28	8 25		....	....
Edinbro' (Waverley) "	4 0	4 39	5 5	....	6 45		8 0	8 55	8 25	7 10	8 45
Haymarket	4a5	4 44	5a10	....			8 5		....	....	
Gogar		....	....	....			8 14		....	....	
Ratho		4 57	....	....			8 21		....	....	
Winchburgh		5 6	....	....			8 29		....	....	
Philpstoun		5 12	....	....			8 36		....	....	
Linlithgow		5 19	....	....			8 45		8 50	7 35	
Manuel 791, 811		5 25	....	....			....		....	....	
Polmont 779, 791		5 31	5 40	5 45			8 57		....	....	
Falkirk (High) ‖		....	....	5 52	a	7H12	9 4	9 29	9 4	7 49	9 19
Bonnybridge		....	....	5 59		....	....		....	....	
Castlecary § 788		....	....	6 5		7 33	....		....	....	
Dullatur §		....	....	6 12		7 40	9 17		....	....	
Croy		....	....	6 17		7 44	....		....	....	
Lenzie 805		....	c	6 26		7 53	9 28		....	....	
Bishopbriggs		....	....	....		....	....		....	....	
Cowlairs		....	....	6 37		8 4	....		....	....	
Glasgow (Qn.St. †)..arr.	5 5	....	6 15	6 43	7 45	8 10	9 41	10 0	9 35	8 20	9 50
796 Helensburgh..arr.	6 39	....	....	8 29	9 5	1018	1150	....	....	....	....

NOTES.

- a Stop to take up.
- a Stops at Falkirk (High) to set down from England.
- c Stops when required.
- e Except Saturdays.
- H **Grahamston** Station.
- J Arrives Linlithgow at 3 aft.
- L Arrives at 3 7 aft. on Saturdays.
- P Leaves 3 50 mrn. on Mondays.
- T Saturday night time.
- V Except 2nd and 9th inst.
- X Except 3rd and 10th inst.
- * Low Level.
- † High Level.
- § Station for Cumbernauld (1¾ miles).
- ‖ Nearly 1 mile to Falkirk (Grahamston) Station, Caledonian.

The growth of paid summer holidays also meant that the summer season began to expand, although not as long as today, while the pressure at weekends meant that many of the expresses had to run as several parts, each in fact a full length train running closely behind the principal train. This worked well as long as no problems were encountered, but the schedules had no slack left for any delays, and so if a locomotive or carriage failure occurred, punctuality suffered and normal working and good timekeeping could not be resumed until the following day.

Post-Grouping, the company moved quickly to rationalise some of its workings. All trains from Manchester and Sheffield were concentrated on London Marylebone, while those from Hull were concentrated on King's Cross, although boat trains for Orient Line cruises from Immingham continued to use Marylebone, almost certainly because the bottlenecks at King's Cross and Welwyn made it difficult to fit in these extras.

Punctuality was a problem, as we will also see in the next chapter. As late as 1928, a table in the *LNER Magazine* showed punctuality as improving, but slowly, for the first four weeks of each year, with in each case the average number of minutes late:

Year:	*1926*	*1927*	*1928*
Southern Area	2.5	3.3	1.9
North-Eastern Area	1.5	1.6	1.4
Southern Scotland	0.3	0.3	0.2
Northern Scotland	0.7	0.5	0.5
Inter-Area	4.9	5.1	3.9

EDINBURGH, LINLITHGOW, POLMONT FALKIRK, and GLASGOW.

Down. — Week Days.

Down.	mrn	mn	mn	mn	mrn	mrn	mrn	mn	mrn	mrn	mrn	aft	aft	aft	aft	aft	S	aft	aft	aft	aft	aft	aft	aft	aft
Edinbro' (Wav.) dep.	4 28	6 3	625	..	7 27	7 35	8 28	9 5	10 0	1035	11 0	Sats. only.	1210	Sats. only.	Except Saturdays.	1 0	1 26	1 47	1 55	255	..	3 23	4 3	428	4 55
Haymarket	..	6 7	..	..	7 31	7L39	8 32	9L9	10L4	1039	11L4		1214			1L 4	1 30	Weds., Sats.	1Y59	..	..	3 27	RC	433	4L59
Ratho	..	617	..	..	..	RC	R	..		1049	..		..			RC	1 40			..	..	3 36	..	443	R
Philpstoun	..	628	..	..	..	..	..	..		11 0	..		..			..	1 51			..	..	3 46	..	453	..
Linlithgow	..	634	..	..	..	8 1	8 53	..		11 6	..		1236	K		..	1 57			..	..	3 52	..	459	..
Manuel	..	640	..	..	..	..	..	..		1112	..		..			..	2 3			..	..	3 57	..	5 4	..
Polmont 986, 992	..	645	652	731	..	8 10	..	..	1031	1117	1130	12 38	1245	12 51	1256	..	2 8	2 14	2 23	..	341	4 3	..	5 9	5 25
Falkirk (High)	..	..	659	738	8 1	8 17	9 6	..		1127	T	12K57	1252	12T59	1 3		2T16			..	348	4T10	..	..	..
Bonnybridge	..	..	..	744	Mondays only.	..	..	..	TC from Leith (C.) dep. 9 47 mrn.	..	Buffet Car.	1 3	Saturdays only.	..	1 9	TC from Leith (C.) dep 12 45 aft.	Stop	Tues., and	RC from Leeds and TC from Shef-field	..	354	..	..	..	..
Castlecary B 997	..	..	..	750		..	..	..		..		1 9		1 15	1 15		..			..	4 0	..	..	..	..
Dullatur B	..	..	..	756		..	..	..		..		1 14		1 21	1 21		..			..	4 6	..	..	..	..
Croy	..	..	..	8 0		..	..	..		..		TC from Boness.		1 25	1 25		..			..	410	..	..	..	..
Lenzie Junc. 1003	..	..	..	8 8		..	..	..		..				1 33	1 33		aft	..		..	418	..	..	..	5 50
Bishopbriggs	..	..	..	814		..	..	..		..				1 39	1 39		2 13	..		..	424	..	..	..	..
Cowlairs	..	..	..	821		..	..	..		..				1 44	1 44		2 18	..		Dd	430	..	..	..	..
Glasgow (QnSt) C ar	129	..	733	827	8 33	8 49	9 38	106	11 6	..	12 5		1 24	1 50	1 50	2 1	2 24	2 49	2 58	353	436	..	5 1	..	6 3

Down. — Week Days—Continued.

Down.	aft	aft	aft	aft	aft	S	aft	S	S	aft	aft	aft	aft
Edinbro' (Wav.) dep	..	525	5 43	6 20	7 10	7 40	755	835	8 48	8*55	9 45	1030	1040
Haymarket	..	528	RC	RC	P		759	..		..	9 49	1034	1044
Ratho	..	538	..	..	..	RC from King's Cross, page 823.	8 9	..	RC from King's Cross, page 823	..	..	..	..
Philpstoun	..	548	..	..	..		821	..		..	..	..	11 3
Linlithgow	..	554	..	..	..		827	..		..	1011	..	11 9
Manuel	..	559	..	..	..		833	..		..	..	..	..
Polmont 986, 992	533	6 5	6 10	6 47	..		839	9 2	9 18	9*22	1020	11 0	1118
Falkirk (High)	540	612	T	..	7 41	8 11	846	9 9		..	1027	11 7	1125
Bonnybridge	546	..	..	..	The Queen of Scots.		852	..		..	..	Except Saturdays.	Saturdays only.
Castlecary B 997	552	..	..	..			858	..		..	..		
Dullatur B	558	..	..	..			9 4	..		..	..		
Croy	6 2	..	..	..			..	..		..	..		
Lenzie Junc. 1003	610	..	Zz	..			913	..		Vv	..		
Bishopbriggs	616	..	..	..			919	..		..	..		
Cowlairs	621	..	..	..			925	..		..	..		
Glasgow (QnSt) C ar	627	..	6 45	7 22	8 13	8 43	931	941	9H55	9*57	1059	1139	1157

Down. — Sundays.

Down.	mn	mrn	mrn	mrn	aft	aft	aft	aft	aft	aft	N	aft	aft
Edinbro' (Wav.) dep	740	9 40	1025	11 0	2 32	5 0	615	715	835	9 10	1030	1042	1057
Haymarket	..	..	1030	11 4	..	..	619	719	Y	..	..	RC	RC
Ratho	..	..	RC	..	..	..	..	Y	..	..	..	..	..
Philpstoun	..	..	..	..	..	..	..	..	..	..	..	..	..
Linlithgow	8 3	10 3	1051	1126	..	..	641	741	..	..	1053	11 5	..
Manuel	..	..	..	..	..	..	..	..	..	..	..	..	..
Polmont 986, 992	..	..	..	..	..	..	..	..	..	..	..	..	..
Falkirk (High)	816	1016	11 5	1139	Buffet Car.	..	654	754	9 6	9 41	11 6	1118	1129
Bonnybridge	..	..	To Fort William, page 1001.	..		..	..	..	..	..	From Dunbar page 832.	Dep. Whitley Bay 7 7 aft.	Newcastle dep. 7 58 aft.
Castlecary B 997	..	..		..		..	..	..	..	..			
Dullatur B	..	..		..		..	7 7	..	..	..			
Croy	..	..		..		..	..	..	..	..			
Lenzie Junc. 1003	..	..		..		..	..	..	..	..			
Bishopbriggs	..	..		..		..	..	..	..	..			
Cowlairs	..	..		..		..	..	..	..	..			
Glasgow (QnSt) C ar	848	1048		1211	3 32	558	727	826	938	1013	1138	1150	12 1

Up. — Week Days.

Up.	mn	mrn	mn	mn	ZV	¶	mrn	mrn	mrn	S	mrn	mrn	aft	aft	S.J	aft	aft	aft	X	aft	aft	aft	aft	aft	aft	aft	aft
Queen St., Glasgow C..dep	630	7 42	..	838	8 55	9‡25	9 55	1015	11 0	11 6	1116	1155		12 8	1214	1224	1248	1 0	1 7		159	2 5		230	315	354	4 0
Cowlairs	636	RC	..	..	..	..	..	P	..	1112	1122	..	Except Saturdays.	Sats. only.	RC	L		RC	Saturdays only.	Sats. only.	..	212	Sats. only.	236	..	..	RC Glasgow to Leeds
Bishopbriggs	641	..	..	..	..	..	R	..	..	1117	1127	..			Q		Saturdays only.	..			..			240	..	..	
Lenzie Junction	647	7 55	..	851	..	Saturdays only.	10 8	..	..	1123	1133	..			..	RC except on Sats.		..			212	Buffet Car		246	..	..	
Croy	655	..	..	..	..		..	..	..	1131	1142	..			..			..			Sats. only.			254	..	..	
Dullatur B	659	..	..	..	..		..	The Queen of Scots.	..	1135	1146	..			..			..		2 5				258	..	..	
Castlecary B	7 4	..	..	..	..		..		..	1140	1152	..			..			..		210				3 3	..	..	
Bonnybridge	710	..	..	..	..		..		..	1146	1158	..			..			..		216				3 9	..	..	
Falkirk (High)	716	8 18	..	..	..		..		1132	1153	12 5	1227			..			..		222		239	2T48	315	..	..	
Polmont 986 992	724	8 25	829	916	9 31		1033		..	12 0	1211	1234	1238	1243	1249	1259		..		228	237	246	2 56	321	349	..	
Manuel	730	..	834	..	..		..		..	12 5	Except Saturdays	..	1243	..	..	..		..				..	3 1	..	..	..	
Linlithgow	736	8 33	840	..	..	..	1041		..	1211		1242	1249	..	..	..	1 28	..				254	3 7	..	..	..	
Philpstoun	742	..	846	..	..	..	..	..	..	1217		..	1254	..	..	..	..	..				..	3 13	..	..	..	
Ratho	752	..	856	..	..	..	..	..	..	1227		..	1 5	..	..	..	..	..				..	3 23	..	..	..	
Haymarket 838	8 2	8 54	9 6	941	..	..	11 2	..	..	1237		..	1 15	..	..	..	..	1S57			3 1	315	3 33	..	..	..	456
Edinbro' D arr.	8 6	8 58	910	945	10 3	1023	11 6	1113	12 2	1241		..	1 19	1 9	..	1 25	1 50	1F58	2 15		3 5	319	3 37	..	415	452	5 0

Up. — Week Days—Continued.

Up.	aft	aft	aft	aft	aft	S	aft	aft	aft	aft	aft	aft	aft
Queen St., Glasgow C..dep.	455	..	532	6 0	6 6	7 0	..	745	825	9 10	10 0	10 6	10 40
Cowlairs	..	..	..	RC	..	TC & Buffet Car, Glasgow to Newcastle (arr. 11 5 aft.).	..	..	834	u	W	Weds., Sats.	..
Bishopbriggs	..	..	542	..	..		..	..	R		..		..
Lenzie Junction	..	..	548	..	..		..	759	..	Fris. only.	..		..
Croy	RC	..	556	..	625		..	8 8	..		..		..
Dullatur B		..	6 0	..	629		..	812	..		..		11S1
Castlecary B	..	..	6 6	..	..		..	817	..		..		..
Bonnybridge	..	..	612	..	..		..	823	..		..		11S11
Falkirk (High)	528	5T46	618	6 32	..		8T12	830	9 2	..	..		11*13
Polmont 986, 992	535	5 53	625	..	645		8 20	837	9 9	9 45	1036	1041	11*20
Manuel	..	5 58	630	..	..		..	842	..	..	..	Tues., and	..
Linlithgow	..	6 3	645	a	653		8 28	848	..	..	..		11*28
Philpstoun	..	6 9	651	..	..		8 34	854	..	..	..		..
Ratho	..	6 19	7 1	..	..		8 44	9 5	..	..	..		..
Haymarket 984.	6 0	6 28	710	7 1	714		8 54	914	..	..	..		11*49
Edinbro D 977 arr	6 4	6 32	714	7 5	718	7 56	8 58	918	935	1011	11 4	11 9	11*53

Up. — Sundays.

Up.	mrn	mrn	mrn	mrn	N	mrn	aft	aft	aft	aft	aft	RC	aft
Queen St., Glasgow C..dep.	9 45	9 55	10U25	10U35	1045	1145	230	610	825	850	9 25		10 0
Cowlairs	..	RC U	RC to Whitley Bay.	RC to Newcastle (arr. 2 48 aft.).	To Dunbar, page 835.	..	..	..	..	..	..	From Fort William p. 1001	..
Bishopbriggs	..	..				..	..	..	..	..	..		..
Lenzie Junction	..	..				..	..	..	..	..	..		SC and TC to King's Cross p. 829.
Croy	..	..				..	..	..	..	..	..		
Dullatur B	..	..				12 6	..	..	..	..	..		
Castlecary B	..	..				..	..	..	..	..	..		
Bonnybridge	..	..				..	..	..	..	..	..		
Falkirk (High)	..	1028	10U59	11U8	1118	1220	..	643	858	Buffet Car.	9 58	10 5	1032
Polmont 986, 992	..	..	..		..	..	..	..	..		..	..	
Manuel	..	..	..		..	..	..	..	..		..	..	
Linlithgow	..	1040	11U12		1131	1232	..	655	910		1010	1015	
Philpstoun	..	..	..	..	..	..	..	..	..	..	..	..	
Ratho	..	..	..	..	..	..	..	..	..	..	..	..	
Haymarket 984.	..	..	..	..	..	1253	..	716	..	..	..	1038	
Edinbro D 977 arr	1043	11 2	11V34	11V42	1156	1257	328	720	932	950	1032	1047	11 2

a Arr. 6 36 aft. B Sta for Cumbernauld (1¼ miles). C High Level. D Waverley Dd Calls when required to set down for North of Arrochar & Tarbet on informing Station Master, Edinburgh (W.). E or E Except Sats. F Arr. 2 1 aft. Sats H Low Level. J TC Glasgow to Swindon (p. 834). K Calls Falkirk (Camelon) 1 3 aft. K Arr. at 12 44 aft. L TC Except Sats. to King's C., Scarbro & Swindon, p. 834. L Stops to take up. N On 17th, 24th, & 31st inst. P Pullman Car Train (1st and 3rd cl. extra charge) between King's Cross and Glasgow, pp. 822 to 829. Q Conveys Passengers for Berwick and beyond only. R Pullman Restaurant Car. RC Restaurant Car. S or S Sats only. SC 1st and 3rd cl. Sleeping accommodation. T Falkirk (Grahamston). TC Thro Car. U TC to King's C., p. 828. U On 17th, 24th, and 31st inst. conveys passengers for Berwick and beyond only. u SC and TC Glasgow to King's Cross, p. 828. V RC & TC to King's C., p. 827 V 10th inst. only. Vv Stops when required to set down from Newcastle & South thereof

North of the border, frequencies and timings improved between 1922, above left, and 1938, above, with the service on the direct line between Edinburgh Waverley and Glasgow Queen Street much improved. (*Bradshaw*)

What is most interesting about this table is the bottom set of figures, showing that the problems of time-keeping for longer distance trains running across several areas, be they companies or regions, were much more severe than with more localised services.

New Rolling Stock

The LNER soon showed that it wanted its prestige expresses to be the most modern in terms of locomotives and carriages. The 'Flying Scotsman' received new carriages in 1924, then again in 1928, and in 1938, as well as being amongst the first trains to enjoy new rolling stock once the Second World War ended when it was updated again in 1946.

Some improvements were planned, but others came by accident. The LNER inherited the contract between the former Great Eastern and the Pullman Car Company, which had not proved as successful as the GER's general manager, Henry Thornton had hoped. A suggestion by the Pullman Car Company that a service between King's Cross and Harrogate would also be popular for business travellers to and from Leeds and Bradford failed to inspire the LNER's passenger managers, but fortunately they were overruled by the chief general manager, and the service started on 9 July 1923, running via Harrogate to Ripon and Newcastle.

This is a first-class compartment, seen from the corridor, which is in marked contrast to the third-class open interior, although there are no head supports between the seats. (*HMRS AAC 115*)

This is the interior of a third-class articulated twin carriage used on 'tourist' services. The travelling public found the bucket seating uncomfortable and it was not a great success. (*HMRS AAC 102*)

Not all of the new services using Pullman carriages were so successful, but the 'Queen of Scots' proved to be another success, with new rolling stock provided in 1928. Pullman cars continued to be used on the Liverpool Street services, with the 'Hook Continental' having both a first-class Pullman and standard LNER restaurant cars. Unlike the other major user of Pullman carriages, the Southern Railway, the LNER also used these on excursion trains, with the 'Eastern Belle' running to different destinations on summer holiday weekends.

Not all of the special trains were provided by the LNER as many were chartered by other organisations, including travel agents, some of whom acted more as tour operators, just as today they might charter aircraft for a package holiday. Nevertheless, the LNER was responsible for one major innovation, the land cruise. This was meant to capitalise on the growing trend for sea cruises by providing a railborne equivalent, the 'Northern Belle', as described in Chapter 10, which provided a tour of beauty spots and resorts in the north of England and Scotland, with the train having first-class day carriages, restaurant cars and sleeping cars, with the staff of 27 looking after the 60 passengers, about the same ratio of crew-to-passengers as a good cruise ship. This started in 1933 and as many as four cruises were held in June of each year up to 1939, with a different itinerary for each.

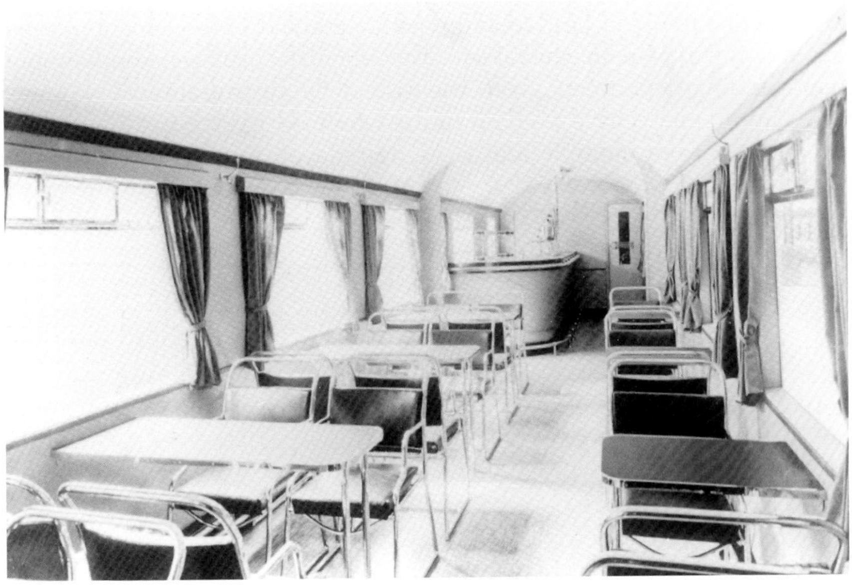

Despite the spartan interior, the buffet cars introduced by the LNER were very popular and introduced many people to the concept of having a snack or, once the concept was proven, even a meal aboard a train, as prices were much lower than in the traditional dining car. (*HMRS AAC 103*)

On Grouping, the LNER inherited more than 200 restaurant cars, including the GER's Pullmans. Most were for first-class passengers on the longer-distance trains, but even at the time, more casual eating was beginning to appear in addition to the company's practice of providing a five-course table d'hôte menu for a set 6s (30p). An innovation was the introduction of the buffet car in 1932, initially serving just drinks and sandwiches, although hot meals were later introduced. One advantage was that it became possible to provide catering on many shorter journeys, with services between King's Cross and Cambridge being amongst the first, and the move was so popular that by 1939, the LNER had 306 restaurant and buffet cars, with some longer distance expresses such as the 'Flying Scotsman' having both conventional restaurant cars and buffet cars.

Another modern feature introduced in September 1930 as an experiment was the provision of radio in certain carriages, for which the passengers hired headsets. The early trials were between King's Cross and Leeds, but the service did not seem to become widespread, whether because of reception problems or the availability of rolling stock is not clear.

Not all of the new rolling stock was regarded as an improvement. In special carriages built for tourist trains, the LNER introduced 'bucket seats', similar to those provided on tourist motor coaches, but these proved to be unpopular and uncomfortable.

One initiative taken by the LNER and followed by the other three grouped companies was the camping coach. As older rolling stock was retired, the problem was what to do with it. As many had wooden bodies, scrap value was minimal, especially during the Depression years. Many were sold off and converted by private owners into garden sheds, but the LNER decided to convert some of its surplus rolling stock into camping coaches, with self-catering family living accommodation for six people, and priced at £2 for a week. Painted green and cream, these were located in unused sidings at country stations, and proved to be so popular that by 1939 there were more than a hundred. Unfortunately, few survived the war as they were requisitioned for military use.

Articulated Sets

Even before Grouping, Gresley had started to build articulated sets of carriages, reducing the weight of the train and also improving the ride. The rolling stock incorporating this feature was usually in two or three-car sets, but a five-car dining set introduced in the early 1920s was also the first to use electric cooking, with a marked improvement in safety compared with the gas stoves that were in general use. The articulated sets were not without some controversy in the operating department, or in the case of the decentralised LNER, operating departments, as a fault in one vehicle resulted in the whole set having to be withdrawn. This, of course, is no different from multiple unit working today, but at the time it was seen as being a major disadvantage.

Under Gresley, the LNER became the leading advocate of articulated sets, usually in pairs or doubles, but the kitchen and dining car sets consisted of three cars, with the kitchen between the first- and third-class cars. The teak exterior is clear to see in this view. (*HMRS AAC 104*)

The needs of third-class passengers were also catered for in other ways. Until 1928, all sleeping cars were first class, but that year the LMS and the LNER introduced third-class sleeping cars, although initially these were what would now be described as couchettes, easily convertible for day use and with four passengers per compartment. The managements of both railways were concerned that the facility would result in some loss of passengers from the traditional first-class sleepers. Standard third-class fares were charged with a supplement of 7s (35p), for which a pillow and blankets were provided. Within a few years, the LNER, LMS and GWR provided third-class sleepers with permanent beds, with either two or four berths per compartment, with first-class compartments having just one berth. The Southern did not provide sleepers until it introduced the all first-class 'Night Ferry' between London and Paris in the late 1930s.

The care and investment expended on the longer distance services was in contrast to the suburban services, especially in the London area. Both the GER and GNR had heavily used suburban services, especially the former. The mainstay of the GER suburban trains were six-wheeled carriages giving a notoriously poor ride. Gresley's economical means of resolving this problem was to convert the carriages into articulated sets of four or five carriages each. This improved the ride, but the carriages were still notoriously short of legroom in each compartment, with just 5ft 3in between the bulkheads compared with the more usual 6ft 3in on other railways. The result was that there was little room for standing passengers without treading on the feet of those fortunate enough to be seated. On the Ilford branch, bodies from pairs of four-wheel carriages were mounted together on 54ft underframes.

New suburban rolling stock was built, but time and again the LNER hesitated to electrify its busiest suburban routes. The money was just not available. At Liverpool Street, the Enfield and

Chingford branches had what the former GER had claimed to be the most intensive suburban service in the world. Known officially as the 'Intensive Service', it was known popularly as the 'Jazz Service' because of the colours painted on the cantrails of the carriages, being amongst the first to use distinctive stripes to identify classes, with first having yellow lines and second blue, while third, which remained on these lines, was unmarked. The GNR not only provided suburban services out of King's Cross, but used the City Widened lines to reach Moorgate, giving it a foothold in the City.

It was not until 1935 that low-cost government-sponsored loans showed a way forward for electrification, but there was not enough time for anything to be done with war looming, and the first stage of the Liverpool Street to Southend scheme was not completed until after Nationalisation. In the meantime, the new London Passenger Transport Board, that had come into existence in 1933, used the former GNR branches to High Barnet to extend what became the Northern Line and the former GER branches to Epping and Ongar to extend the Central Line, although here too, the eastward advance was delayed until after the Second World War. In the meantime, in 1937, the opposite occurred when the LNER took over the London Transport line between Rickmansworth and Aylesbury.

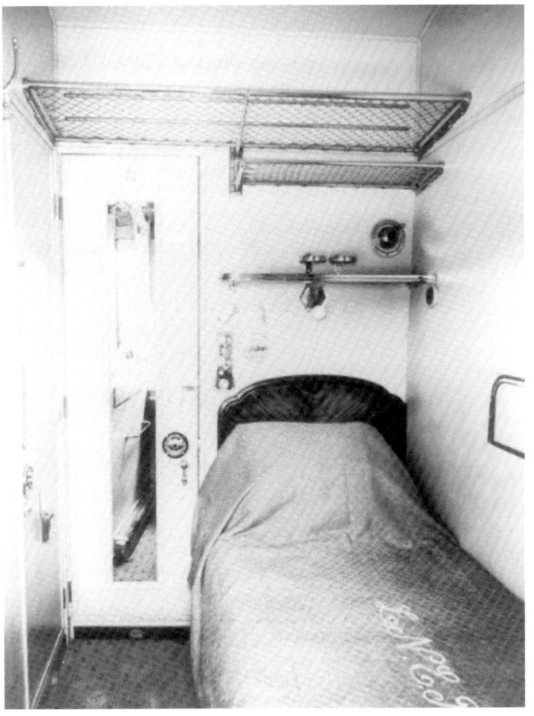

The interior of a first-class sleeper berth in 1930, at a time when third-class sleeper berths were an innovation and more akin to a Continental railway couchette. (*HMRS AAC 100*).

Many of the six-wheel five-compartment suburban carriages were formed into articulated sets by Gresley to improve their riding, but this first-class example seen in 1938 at Stratford seems to have escaped. At least the passengers would have had more legroom as the old GER suburban stock was notoriously tight. (*HMRS ABH 908*)

A detail view of a quad-art (four-car articulated) set for suburban services, showing a composite coach. This is in good condition and may have been just outshopped. The difference in space between first- and third-class compartments can be seen. (*HMRS 033*)

The LNER developed its Tyneside electrification, extending the North Tyneside network inherited from the NER, which had completed the work in 1904 into South Tyneside in 1938, using the same third-rail system to ensure interoperability. Elsewhere, the picture was not so bright, and in 1937 the Aberdeen suburban service was closed due to strong competition from road transport. On the other hand, the LNER, like the NER before it, did little to improve main line services from Gateshead, despite frequent pleading by the local council.

In between the suburban services and branch lines on the one hand, and the long-distance expresses on the other, there were many shorter distance inter-urban services of considerable importance, such as between York and other Yorkshire towns and cities, including Hull and Scarborough, and between Newcastle and Middlesbrough, for example. Branch lines that reached the main junctions or termini also were the source of much useful longer-distance traffic.

The big problem that all of the grouped companies had was that there were many branch lines that offered no hope of worthwhile business. This was a cause for concern. Some branches did at least have a reasonable volume of business on market days, or during the summer holiday

Articulated rolling stock was not just for the main line expresses, and this is a two-car set on the branch line to Ramsey. (*HMRS ABC 218*)

Two coaches of a 'quad-art' set leaving King's Cross in 1928. (*HMRS ABZ 504*)

period, but overall, there were many that had no chance of showing even an operating profit, still less once overheads were taken into account. There was widespread reluctance to countenance closures, partly because these would be unpopular and the railways still enjoyed the image of the common carrier, despite their objections to the pressure that this put upon them to carry any traffic that was offered. There was also a strong sense that the railways were often the lifeline that kept many rural communities alive. Private enterprise they may have been, but the grouped railways had managements with strong feelings of obligation to the community.

The LNER's solution to the problems of branch lines was the steam railmotor, which it found could halve the cost of maintaining a branch line service. The company did not go the whole hog and embrace the internal combustion engine as did the GWR, but favoured steam, possibly because of concerns over servicing. Most of the railmotors operated by the LNER were provided by Sentinel, and while these were usually single carriages, in September 1930 an articulated twin-carriage railcar was introduced. On trials between Scarborough and York, this completed the 42 miles in 47 minutes, despite two signal checks. The Sentinel railcars looked very much like contemporary electric or diesel cars, except, of course, that once in steam, smoke and steam could be seen. In this they contrasted with the traditional auto-train, which while it could be driven from either end, clearly had a very small locomotive at one end.

One problem with the steam railmotors was that while they were fine for the basic daily service, they lacked the capacity to handle peak loads, as on market day, for example, and also lacked the power to pull an extra carriage, let alone two. The railmotors were to prove troublesome and few of them lasted for more than ten years.

In fact the LNER, and the other grouped railways, did have to resort to station closures and on occasion, a branch line would be closed.

In 1930, the company closed the branch from Alnwick to Coldstream, saving £3,965 annually, and that year also saw closure of many of the stations on the branch from York to Scarborough. A few years later, it also closed the station at Turnhouse on the outskirts of Edinburgh, then the site of an aerodrome and Royal Auxiliary Air Force unit, but today, it is Edinburgh's busy airport. One of the first closures after Grouping had been Hull Cannon Street, the former terminus of the Hull & Barnsley Railway, but this was the kind of rationalisation needed if grouping was to produce benefits. There were a few closures in East Anglia, and in 1927 the passenger service was discontinued on the Wisbech & Upwell light railway, although this remained open for goods traffic, including the highly seasonal fruit business.

The boiler end of Sentinel steam railcar No. 2236 *British Queen*, at York in 1935. These were an attempt to reduce the costs of operating the quieter branch lines, but reliability was poor and none survived to Nationalisation. They were painted green and cream. (*HMRS ABX 206*)

In common with most companies, the LNER inherited a two-class system, with second abolished on most lines before Grouping. Exceptions included the Continental boat trains from Liverpool Street, and until 1938 there were also three classes on the inner suburban services from both Liverpool Street and King's Cross, with first class abolished on these in 1941 as a wartime austerity measure.

Wisbech was the junction for the Wisbech & Upwell Tramway, which closed to passenger traffic in 1927. This is an unusual, short post starting signal. (*HMRS ABJ 116*)

Chapter 13

Publicity

All of the grouped railway companies showed a strong appreciation of the value of publicity, but there were marked differences between the approaches used. There were also strong similarities, and in particular all of them spent much effort exhorting their employees to seek business for the company. They realised that simply publishing timetables was not enough, and advertising and public relations were much in evidence.

One of the public relations activities conducted by the LNER was the staging of events, starting with the Stockton & Darlington Centenary Exhibition at Darlington in 1925. Here is Britain's first Beyer-Garratt articulated locomotive, No. 2395, still in works grey. It spent much of its life as the Wath banker. (*HMRS AAB 517*)

One of the distinctive features of the LNER's publicity was that it spent much time and doubtless no small effort, in arranging rolling stock exhibitions around the country. This started in 1925 with a major exhibition at Darlington to mark the centenary of the railways, the opening of the Stockton & Darlington Railway in 1825, which was seen as a direct predecessor of the NER, one of the LNER's constituent companies. The exhibitions appear to have been well-attended, as contemporary photographs show substantial numbers wandering around at track level, and while young boys were much in evidence, many of those present were older and included many women. Steps were provided so that visitors were able to inspect new carriages and, of course a draw for boys of all ages was the ease with which they could gain access to the footplates of locomotives, all safely out of steam!

The NER had taken an initiative in 1922 that continues to this day, albeit now in much grander and more extensive form, with the creation of the first railway museum at York, and this was something else continued by the LNER.

Inevitably, the extent to which the value of publicity had been appreciated by the pre-Grouping companies varied, but both the Great Central and the Great Northern had been early converts. The attractions of the Lincolnshire resorts were clearly the way to ensure that the railway was busy at weekends and during the summer holiday months, and the GNR offered

Also at the Stockton & Darlington Centenary Exhibition was this Q7 0-8-0, No. 902, smartly painted, although given the nature of the duties allocated to the class, this would not have lasted long in this condition when in service. (*HMRS AAB 523*)

cheap tickets. The poster showing the bounding rotund fisherman with the caption 'Skegness is so bracing' instantly became a classic, highly regarded to this day. The GCR was one of the first of Britain's railways to establish a publicity department with its head reporting directly to the general manager.

The LNER lost no time in maintaining the momentum created by the constituent companies. The North Eastern Railway's advertising manager, W.M. Teasdale, was appointed to the same position with the new company and moved to London. His brief included supporting the divisional managers and to this end each division had its own advertising manager with substantial delegated authority, but reporting to Teasdale. For all the railways, local advertising was important, to the extent that prizes were awarded for the best effort by a stationmaster or one of his staff using blackboard and chalk. On the LNER, district officers and stationmasters were able to communicate directly with the divisional advertising manager. At the same time, standardisation was taken to a considerable degree, and included instructions on the mixing of the paste used for posters. It was made clear from the outset that advertising was not simply for passenger business, but for the goods business as well.

One of the most forward-looking measures adopted at a time of severe economic difficulty was the appointment, as early as July 1923, of S.T. Burgoyne, who had worked under Sir Eric Geddes, the first Minister of Transport, as Industrial Agent. This new post was created to lobby major industrial concerns to locate new premises on the LNER network. It is difficult to judge how successful this appointment was as in 1924 Burgoyne was sent north to be an assistant goods manager. Teasdale was promoted to assistant general manager with specific responsibility not only for the work handled by Burgoyne, but also to handle Parliamentary matters. Teasdale seems to have been effective as by 1932, the chairman was able to tell the annual general meeting that no fewer than 24 firms had been attracted to locations on the LNER network in the previous three months, although most of them were in locations south of the Humber and doing little to reverse the long-term industrial decline of Yorkshire and the North East.

Teasdale left in 1932 to join a newspaper group and his successor was C.G.G. Dandridge, originally of the Great Central. One of his first steps was to issue a book, *Selling LNER Transport by the help of the Advertising Department*, which advised personnel on how to get the best value from their advertising. The book was aimed mainly at stationmasters and the managers of goods depots, who would also have had their teams of canvassers to sell the LNER to a wide range of industrial customers, big and small.

The LNER Magazine

Employee communications already existed before the LNER came into being, and indeed, it was a prerequisite of running a railway. Footplatemen had to be aware of speed restrictions, work on the line or other problems before starting their shift. Railways were the business giants of the day, and employees had to be aware of all manner of things, and these had to be communicated centrally at a time when most businesses had the employer on the spot, not several hundred miles away.

As the railways had the whole of 1922 to put structures in place ready for Grouping, it is surprising to find that in January 1923, the employee magazine was the *North Eastern Railway Magazine*, with the masthead incorporating the company's coat of arms. This was possibly made up for by two and a bit pages showing the 'Coats of Arms of Constituent Companies'. On the other hand, one news story was the new North Eastern Pacific!

While the tone of these publications may sometimes seem strange to us today, the magazine was more than work-related. The early issues included 'notes' on allotments and angling, although the modern reader might jibe at an article on 'Personal Efficiency' and the advice to masticate one's food thoroughly! An article on railways in China showed that the LNER like the LMS, took an international view, while closer to home there was an article on the 'Newcastle Meat Trades'. What are we to make of one obituary, stating that a certain Mr A.G. Larard of Hull was: '...a man of somewhat complex character, but never failing courtesy and good nature... conscientious and painstaking in his duties'.

It was the magazine that informed staff of the changes that were taking place, or at least those who read it, as the 40,000 circulation was less than the company's payroll and it was also available to anyone outside the company who wished to subscribe. Early issues explained that green would be the colour for passenger locomotives and black for those handling mineral traffic, but it soon complained that the 'shades of green varied'. By December, the new LNER coat of arms was featured.

Unusually for the railway magazines, the September 1923 issue showed the aftermath of a shunting accident at Heck sidings near Selby.

The standard LNER station running-in board contrasts with the Gothic script of the advertisement for a newspaper. (*HMRS ABJ 211*)

The imposing frontage of the station at Cambridge in 1947. (*HMRS ABC 409*)

It was not until January 1924 that the changes were reflected in a new masthead proclaiming the *North Eastern & Scottish Magazine (London & North Eastern Railway)*. By April, it was reflecting on a 'snowbound winter in the Northern Scottish Area' and complaining of fine powdery snow – perhaps the first recorded mention of the 'wrong kind of snow'. It may have been a relief to engine drivers when they read in a 1928 issue, of a vacuum windscreen wiper which, when fitted to a steam locomotive, had proved 'very effective during rainy and snowy weather'.

'Punctuality is our first duty to the public', Wedgwood himself warned readers in an editorial in February 1926. This was a recurring theme, suggesting that the LNER did have difficulty in maintaining a high standard, but to be fair, these were the days when a train was either on time or it was late, with no five or ten-minute margins before it had to be recorded as an official statistic. The magazine returned to this problem in later years, as mentioned earlier in the previous chapter. In fact, the record for goods traffic was even worse than for passenger trains, and in the North Eastern Area, for example, average minutes late in 1928 varied between 9.3 in Sunderland and 37.4 in Hull. The poorer time-keeping of goods trains is not surprising as these would have to wait while a passenger express was given priority, and for the many slow-moving coal trains, these often ran from one siding to another on double-tracked lines so that passenger trains and fast goods with perishable items could have priority. While such problems were faced head on, what is strange is that there was no mention of the General Strike in any issue of the magazine that year.

In late 1926, the magazine finally became the *London & North Eastern Railway Magazine*, almost four years after Grouping! It cost 2d an issue at a time when a tabloid newspaper would cost a penny.

Looking back, there were oddities. A feature extolling the flexibility and security of containers was illustrated with a container on a wagon, as one might expect, except that the wagon was horse-drawn! Other innovations included experiments with a Kitson-Still combined steam and diesel locomotive.

By 1929, the magazine had doubled in size to 56 pages. One of the highlights of that year was the opening of an office in Rome in collaboration with 'our good friends on the SR'.

One of the innovations announced in the magazine in early 1931 was a staff suggestion scheme, with awards of between one and seven guineas, or in today's usage, between £1.05 and £7.35. The higher figure represented more than twice the weekly wage of a skilled man at the time. In 1933, there was a series of features entitled 'Fifteen Countries for Fifteen Pounds',

An important centre such as Cambridge also had substantial goods and parcels traffic, with the LNER's local fleet of lorries lined up. The station's passenger entrance is in the background. (*HMRS ABC 411*)

just in case anyone winning the higher award had any doubts on how to spend it! By this time, railwaymen not only had cheap fares within their own country, and not just with their own company, but in many countries abroad as well. The company also sought to gain kudos for its investment by representing this as a humanitarian gesture, with advertisements headed: 'For the relief of unemployment', followed by: 'The LNER has agreed to undertake the construction of new works to the value of £3,500,000.'

As with the other railway company magazines, safety was a constant theme, and the LNER approach was to run a series of paired photographs, with one showing readers the right way and the other the wrong way for such matters as lifting heavy loads, crossing a railway line, and coupling or uncoupling wagons. By 1936, there was a new quiz so that readers could discover for themselves whether or not they were railway minded.

The war years saw the magazine become thinner and the quality of paper used was poor as wartime restrictions began to bite, but glossy paper was back during mid-1946, although by this time the price was 3d.

The final issue of December 1947 included an article by someone in favour of nationalisation, while readers were assured that there would be a January 1948 issue and it would continue until new arrangements were put in hand, but this seems to have been an unfulfilled promise as there doesn't seem to have been an issue that month. No doubt the new British Transport Commission or the subordinate Railways Executive, known as British Railways, was determined to stamp out any feelings of nostalgia for the past or loyalty to the old companies.

Public Relations

One of the most important aspects of publicity was public relations, not only because it included the 'free' publicity to be obtained from press and, increasingly, broadcast reports, but also because it was also used defensively when something went wrong, as in a railway accident. Wedgwood exercised considerable personal control in this area, as indeed any responsible person in his position in a large organisation would do, and was given a free hand by the board.

Early decisions included the use of the initials L.N.E.R. instead of L. & N.E.R., which appeared but briefly on an early repaint of some locomotives. This was, of course, taken in conjunction with decisions on the livery to be carried by locomotives, carriages and wagons. For us today, it seems strange that apart from liveries, the coat of arms and the correct use of initials, the rest of what might be described as corporate identity was left until 1929, when a house style was introduced, created by the sculptor Eric Gill for the Monotype Corporation and known as Gill Sans. This was controversial, for while the sum paid for the work was never revealed, many claimed that the company's own draughtsmen could have done as good a job at a much lower price. Having done this, Gresley was allowed to continue using large block characters on locomotives and characters with distinct serifs on passenger rolling stock! New electric multiple units had the initials LNER within a cigar-shaped lozenge.

Looking at the *LNER Magazine*, one is left with the distinct impression that for some years timekeeping was a problem, and the wags sometimes claimed that the initials LNER actually stood for the 'Late and Never Early Railway'. Another claim was that 'Suffolk was a county cut off on one side by the sea and on the other three sides by the LNER!'

While the dirt and grime of the steam age was the cause of much complaint, the company did attempt to improve its stations and generally attempt to make them brighter, but even here, there was a lack of a standard. Marylebone was repainted in green and cream, but at Cambridge the company bowed to the wishes of the University and used light blue! In common with the other companies, the LNER held competitions for the best station gardens with prizes awarded each summer.

As so often happens, there were also wider considerations in statements to the media. In 1934, Wedgwood decided, with the agreement of the board, not to announce that the LNER was going to order a substantial number of new locomotives in one batch. The rationale was that the government was considering its 'New Works' provisions and the company did not want the Treasury to know that the LNER was capable of funding such major investment itself.

The first opportunity for the LNER to display its assets to the public came at the British Empire Exhibition at Wembley, which ran from 1924 through to 1925. The *Flying Scotsman* was presented, in pristine condition with its driving wheels moving slowly. In 1925, the LNER capitalised on the centenary of the Stockton & Darlington with an exhibition of rolling stock in the Faverdale Works, which had just opened, and with a procession of 53 locomotives and trains from Stockton to just outside Darlington. The *LNER Magazine* frequently reported on exhibitions which were held at suitable points throughout the network. Perhaps the one most worthy of mention came in 1938, when to celebrate the fiftieth anniversary of the 'Flying Scotsman' train, Patrick Stirling's 8ft single No. 1 was restored (and survives to this day at the NRM) and a number of Howden's Victorian carriages were gathered to represent a train of the period. A celebration run was made from King's Cross to Cambridge and the train was on show at several of the LNER's exhibitions before the outbreak of war the following year.

With the other members of the Railway Companies Association, the LNER was constantly pressing for an end to the restrictions that prevented them competing on fair terms with the road haulage industry. This culminated in the 'Fair Deal' campaign of the late 1930s.

The 'Fair Deal' Campaign

The pressure by the railways to be released from their onerous restrictions on charges and the common carrier obligation contributed to a growing interest in transport by the government, but when restrictions on competition occurred, they were aimed more at restricting road transport than liberating the railways. The first step was the Road Transport Act 1930, which required road haulage to be licensed, with a system of 'A' licences for hauliers, 'B' licences for manufacturers and traders who also wished to be able to hire out their vehicles, for example after making a delivery so that they did not run home empty, and 'C' licences for manufacturers and retailers to deliver their own goods to customers. The 'C' licences were granted automatically, but a case had to be made for the 'A' and 'B' licences after the initial issue to existing operators under grandfather rights.

Passenger transport legislation and licensing came next, in 1933, with only private hire coaches exempt from the need for a road service licence, which was necessary for stage carriage work, express services and excursions and tours, and again after grandfather rights had been granted to existing operators, these had to be applied for and objectors could seek a hearing. The objectors were often competitors, who would argue that existing bus or coach services were adequate, or even not making enough money, but they could also include the railways. All in all, this was a system of transport rationing.

Finding that the Road Traffic Acts 1930 and 1933 had not helped the situation very much, the 'Big Four' launched a 'Fair Deal for the Railways' campaign arguing against the restrictions. War intervened and state control of the railways for the duration put an end to the campaign, so we will never know for sure what the outcome might have been. The omens weren't good. The public opinion poll to end all public opinion polls was Mass Observation, which started to survey public opinion before the outbreak of war and continued for some years afterwards. One of its first surveys was on public reaction to the 'Fair Deal' campaign, and it found that many were either completely uninterested or believed that the railways were, in effect, protesting too much.

As always, there was scant public sympathy for railway management. At the same time, there is more than a suspicion that at times the railways overdid it on occasions. They had a case, but surely the LNER was going a step too far when it put advertisements headed 'TRAINS IN CHAINS' on the back of restaurant car menus?

Advertising

The LNER's advertising differed from that of its West Coast rival, the LMS. Much of the LMS poster advertising was artistic and fascinating for those who love railways, but the sales message if it existed at all was buried. LNER advertising was no less artistic, and included the work of such famous artists as Frank Mason and, post-war, Terence Cuneo, but it also carried a strong sales message. Exhibitions of LNER posters were held even in such places as the Burlington Galleries in London. The LMS favoured industries, but the LNER chose resorts, regions and the named expresses.

Advertisements for cheap excursions were designed to resemble a music hall bill.

As with the other railway companies, the LNER published its annual *Holiday Handbook*, which eventually consisted of more than a thousand pages and cost 6d, although the low cost is not surprising as the book included advertisements for hotels, camping sites, and resorts, while as with the LMS, magic lantern slides were available on loan and later these were replaced by travel films.

For the enthusiast, there was also a booklet *Locomotives of the LNER*, published in 1929, with illustrations of the more recent locomotives

At a time when foreign travel was for the minority, the LNER was amongst the first to promote the Dutch bulb fields in spring. (*LNER*)

DURHAM
IT'S QUICKER BY RAIL
FULL INFORMATION FROM L·N·E·R OFFICES AND AGENCIES

The 'Big Four' grouped railway companies set great store by publicity and even collaborated when it made sense to do so. However, there was also rivalry over which served the best holiday areas, and cities such as Durham were also worth promoting. (*LNER*)

and with a list of named engines, but it was far from comprehensive and must have left many disappointed.

The push towards developing a more profitable express freight network was assisted by a booklet, *Expressing Freight*.

While wartime saw the end of promotional advertising, and in any case, the railways were all being run by the Railway Executive, which attempted to discourage railway travel, the immediate post-war period saw a resumption of activity. There was little that could be done to promote travel, as the railways found themselves short of rolling stock, in fact, short of everything except demand for their services. In an attempt to discourage nationalisation the LNER indulged in prestige advertising, and publicised its two-stage £50 million plan with a booklet *Forward: The LNER Development Plan*, with an illustrated cover showing a streamlined locomotive named *Enterprise*.

Chapter 14

The Record Setters

The LNER will always be associated with the world speed record set by the A4 Pacific No. 4468 *Mallard*, which remains unbeaten for steam traction to this day. This was the highlight of a series of timetable improvements that started even before 1932, the year in which the agreement was terminated restricting the through journey time of the expresses between London and Scotland. The LNER sought to accelerate its trains first between London and Newcastle, and then over the main part of the East Coast route between London and Edinburgh.

The famous record-setting A4 4-6-2 No. 4468 *Mallard* heads a lengthy express. Her achievement was all the more notable because the decision to attempt a record was made on the spur of the moment. (*HMRS AEU 528*)

The first significant step forward was on 11 July 1927 when the LNER inaugurated the world's longest non-stop railway service by running the 268 miles between King's Cross and Newcastle Central in a scheduled 5½ hours. Leaving King's Cross at 9.50am, the train headed by A1 Pacific No. 4475 *Flying Fox*, reached Newcastle on time at 3.20pm, giving an average speed of 48.7mph. An even better performance was achieved on 14 July when No. 2569 *Gladiateur* managed the same down run in six minutes less than the schedule. Five locomotives were assigned to the

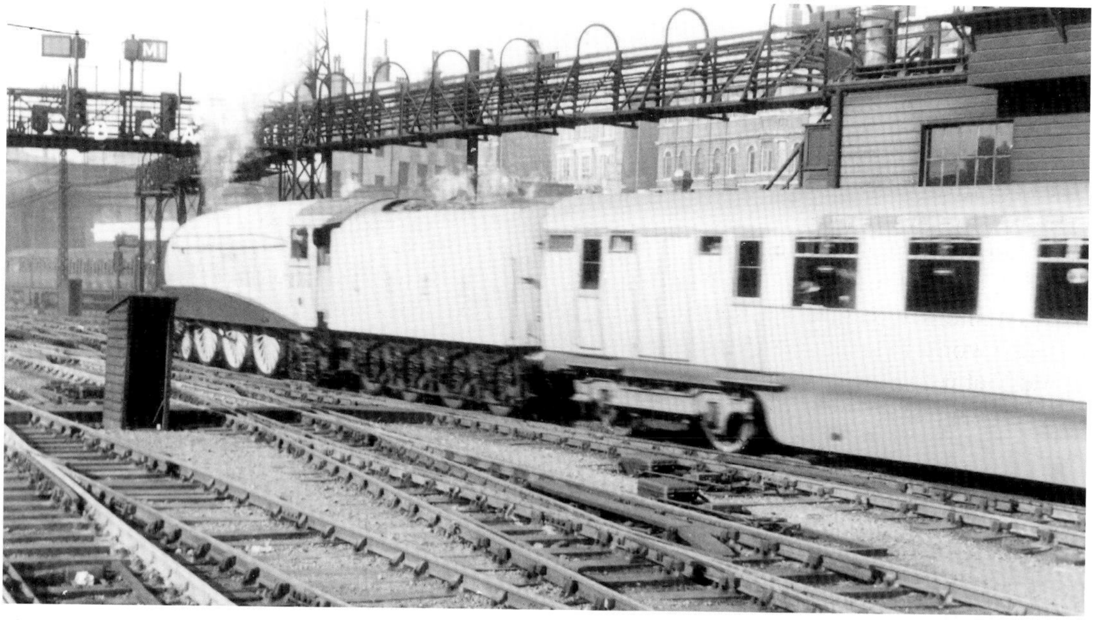

The streamlining of the locomotive on the 'Silver Jubilee' and other LNER high-speed trains was followed through on the carriages with skirts to reduce drag. (*HMRS ABJ 030*)

service, three from King's Cross depot, including *Flying Fox*, and two from Gateshead, of which *Gladiateur* was one. The speeds achieved were not tremendous, even by the standards of the day, but these were heavy service trains rather than speed record breakers and the schedule was one that had to stand the problems of everyday operation. The achievement lay in running non-stop, and as an advance portion of the 'Flying Scotsman' on Mondays, Thursday, Fridays and Saturdays, when demand was at its heaviest.

The following year, through non-stop running between King's Cross and Edinburgh Waverley started, setting a fresh record for distance with 392.7 miles, but not for speed, as this was an average of just 47.6mph, with a following train making four stops taking the same time. Despite this, the start of the service on 1 May 1928 was accompanied by a civic send-off at both ends of the route with the trains leaving the termini at exactly the same time, 10am. On arrival at King's Cross, the LNER's chairman, William Whitelaw, was there to greet the

The end of the three-car articulated catering set on the 'Silver Jubilee', with the end of the leading car of a two-car compartment set. (*HMRS 031*)

footplatemen of the arriving train, while at Waverley, senior officers of the Scottish Area were present.

Services were accelerated in 1932 and again in the years that followed, but a major step forward came in 1935 with the introduction of the 'Silver Jubilee', running on weekdays between King's Cross and Newcastle Central in exactly four hours with a stop at Darlington in each direction. This train was Britain's first streamlined train, with a stud of locomotives assigned to it and painted in the same silver livery as the carriages. Named to celebrate the silver jubilee of King George V, it provided people in the North East with the opportunity of a return trip to London within the day. The through average speed was 67mph, but between London and Darlington, over the 232 miles, the average speed increased to 70.3mph, at the time the world record for a non-stop run of more than 200 miles. Always anxious to remind the world that it could trace its ancestry to the first railway, the Stockton & Darlington, the LNER made much of the fact that it was celebrating its 110th birthday!

The Railway World Speed Record

On Sunday, 3 July 1938, during a series of high-speed brake trials on the main line between Peterborough and Grantham, the opportunity was taken to make an attempt on the world speed record for railways, using the A4 locomotive No. 4468 *Mallard*. Although the load was far less than a full train, it was no light weight either, with three twin-articulated carriages from the spare 'Coronation' set and the company's dynamometer car, making seven vehicles in all with an empty weight of 236.5 tons, or 240 tons with officials and equipment aboard. *Mallard* was chosen because she was one of three A4 locomotives to have the Kylchap exhaust arrangements, which included a double blast-pipe and chimney.

The decision to find out how fast the locomotive could run with the seven-vehicle load seems to have been almost a spur of the moment decision, and it is notable that no-one from the *LNER Magazine* was aboard, leaving the publication to reproduce an account from the *Railway Gazette*.

Mallard took her rake of carriages through Grantham station at just 24mph because of permanent way work, and then accelerated to almost 60mph over the next 2½ miles up a rising gradient of 1 in 200, eventually reaching almost 75mph over the next mile-and-a-half to Stoke summit, again over a further stretch at 1 in 200. Descending Stoke Bank, the speed rose to 116mph, and then to 119mph, and then crossed the 120mph mark where it stayed for the next three miles, reaching a maximum of 126mph. The locomotive maintained a speed of between 123mph and 126mph for nearly two miles. The record-breaking run was then curtailed as the opportunity was taken to conduct a brake test from such a high speed and the train was approaching the curve at Essendine, which also included several sets of points, and it was thought unwise to take these at such a high speed.

This was a greater achievement than generally realised, not just because it has never been beaten anywhere, but because far from being specially prepared, *Mallard* had worn valves and was driven hard by a driver, Driver J. Duddington of Doncaster, known for thrashing his locomotives. Had she been properly prepared and all valve clearances correct, the record might have been set even higher. As it was, those on the footplate could smell the machinery as it overheated and the locomotive needed major workshop attention afterwards.

Many claim that locomotives of the day operating in the United States and Germany could have matched or even exceeded this record, but the point is that they didn't. One would have expected the Germans, whose dictator had a thirst for propaganda, to have set a new record if they had been able. Others have also suggested that the LMS 'Duchess' class could have matched or exceeded the record, but again, this did not happen. It might be pertinent to note that while the LNER cut the London to Edinburgh journey time of the 'Flying Scotsman' to just six hours, the rival LMS service to Glasgow took 30 minutes longer.

Chapter 15

Shipping

Without exception, all of the grouped railway companies were major shipowners. This stemmed largely from the fact that Great Britain is an island, but not entirely, as the totals often included river steamers or ferries, and pleasure steamers on lakes or lochs. It was also the case that Parliament had been reluctant and slow to grant the railways the powers to become involved in maritime activities, and it was not until 1863 that powers to operate widespread shipping were granted, although before that Parliamentary powers could be sought provided that a specific route or routes could be specified. The power to operate ships was so extensively exercised that many ferry or packet services were operated almost as an extension of the railway service. With the Southern Railway, the LNER was one of just two companies to operate train ferries, but the LNER confined this operation to freight.

Through running to Europe did not wait for the Channel Tunnel, and the LNER was one of two railways with train ferries, although it confined its ships to carrying freight. Here is an SNCF van in 1938 with details of running restrictions, which included not running on the Metropolitan Line or the Southern's Whitstable branch, which had height restrictions. (*HMRS ABJ 429*)

All of the grouped companies were also major owners and operators of ports, many of which were very large, while those on the LNER included a number that specialised in coal traffic and in another case, at Lowestoft, fish. The company had the distinction of being the world's largest operator of railway-owned docks. There were river ferry and canal interests as well.

Just two of the constituent companies had no involvement with shipping, the Great Northern and the Great North of Scotland. The North British Railway had paddle steamers on the Clyde, increasingly used for pleasure, but at one time an important part of the river's transport links, as well as Loch Lomond pleasure steamers. The Great Central, Great Eastern and Great Northern all had important North Sea shipping operations.

On 1 January 1923, the LNER inherited 22 ships of 250grt and above, plus another 18 smaller vessels as well as an assortment of tugs and dredgers.

Ships

The most prominent of the LNER's shipping interests were those of the former GER, which had introduced a packet service from Harwich to the Hook of Holland as early as 1867. In 1887, the GER opened its own specialised port facilities at Parkeston Quay, which it named after its chairman, Sir Charles Parkes. This grew into the main port for services to the Netherlands, with the traveller able to journey by rail to Amsterdam and beyond, while there was competition for services to Belgium from both Tilbury and Dover. The crossing was longer than the short crossings from Dover and Folkestone to France, and so the ships were built with a higher standard of accommodation, including cabins for the overnight crossings.

On Grouping, the GER provided nine passenger ships and two cargo ships, including three new passenger vessels, the *Antwerp*, *Bruges* and *Malines*, with broadly similar capabilities with gross tonnage of between 2,947 and 2,968, and passenger capacity of between 758 and 776, all built in 1920. There was also the older *St George*, acquired from the Canadian Pacific Railway in 1920, but built in 1905, which was 2,676grt and had accommodation for 700 passengers. Her spell with the LNER was brief as she was sold in 1929. The best ships were assigned to the Hook of Holland service, with the older ships operating to Antwerp and a cargo-only service was provided to Rotterdam, then much less important than today.

The LNER was proud of its ships, as this advertisement shows. They were the largest railway-owned ships, partly because the service was overnight. Although the Southern had overnight services from Southampton and Newhaven, much of their emphasis was on the short sea crossings. (*LNER*)

As with the Southern Railway, the LNER soon found that its European ferry services were facing competition from air transport, and the newly established Imperial Airways was able to offer a seven-hour first-class flight from Croydon to Berlin for £8 10s, compared with 23 hours by railway and sea for £7 10s first class. Fortunately, air transport had still to make its presence felt and was generally regarded as unreliable, with the catchphrase 'If you've time to spare, go by air.'

Just as the railways were able to buy ex-War Office steam locomotives, in 1924 the LNER was able to purchase the train ferries used to transport rolling stock between Richborough in Kent and Dunkirk. The LNER and Belgian State Railways formed a joint company to operate these as La Société Belgo-Anglaise des Ferryboats, which the LNER acquired outright in 1933. The ships used a new train ferry berth at Harwich. Little thought was given to their names as they entered services as *Train Ferry No. 1*, *Train Ferry No. 2* and *Train Ferry No. 3*, although *No. 1*, the only ship to survive war service returned to the LNER to be renamed *Essex Ferry*. She was joined in 1947 by a new ship, *Suffolk Ferry*.

The cargo service was up-dated with an older ship being replaced by a new vessel, the 1,088grt *Sheringham* in 1926.

In 1927, the Zeeland Shipping Company transferred its Flushing service from Folkestone to Harwich, forcing the LNER to expand the facilities at Harwich, which in turn attracted a Danish operator with a service from Esbjerg in 1934.

During 1929/30, the ships on the Hook of Holland service were replaced by three new identical vessels, the *Vienna*, *Amsterdam* and *Prague*, all of 4,220grt and with accommodation for 716 passengers, while the older ships were transferred to the Antwerp service. As just two vessels were required for the regular service, the third was transferred to cruising, which resulted in the Vienna being appropriately refitted for this purpose. These ships carried fewer passengers than those they displaced on the Antwerp service, despite a significantly higher tonnage, and this trend continued when, on the eve of Nationalisation, a new ship was commissioned, the *Arnhem*, with accommodation for just 422 passengers in a one-class ship of 4,891grt.

The company magazine waxed lyrical about the new ships, and especially the *Vienna*, saying that '...hot and cold water in every cabin gives an idea of how up-to-date the ship is'.

The Great Central's predecessor, the Manchester, Sheffield & Lincolnshire Railway, first became involved in shipping in 1865. The GCR had operated out of Grimsby to Hamburg, Rotterdam and Antwerp, primarily with small cargo ships of around 1,400grt which had limited accommodation, for no more than twelve people. The most recent of these ships had been completed in 1911, and the LNER did not invest in any replacements, even for the Hamburg mail service.

The North Eastern's shipping interests lay in two shipping lines, the Wilson's & North Eastern Railway Shipping Company, and the Hull & Netherlands Steamship Company. The W&NERSC was a joint venture with the Ellerman Wilson Line, Hull's main shipowners, and had just seven small ships, six of which dated from before the First World War. The H&NSC was even smaller, with just two small ships and another three chartered, with one of these dating from 1874. Surprisingly, it was the latter company that made the most money for the LNER! The NER seems to have ignored the possibilities of shipping apart from these small, even half-hearted investments. The company had powers to operate shipping to the Scandinavia countries, but

Train Ferry No. 1 at Harwich. These ships only received real names when they were requisitioned by the War Office during the Second World War, this being HMS *Princess Iris*, but then *Essex Ferry* after the war, surviving until 1957. (*HMRS AEU325*)

The line to nowhere! The linkspan for the train ferry at Harwich in the up position, 1939. (*HMRS AEU 326*)

left this to other companies, with services generally based on Newcastle, the most convenient port for such routes.

The years of the Great Depression saw fluctuating currency values and a growing trend to impose import tariffs, none of which helped trade, while the mid-1930s saw growing political friction with Germany and Italy in particular, resulting in trade embargoes. In 1935, the railway shipping interests on the Humber, including the W&NERSC, the H&NSC and the LNER's ex-GCR services, as well as those of the LMS, were combined into a consortium, Associated Humber Lines, rationalising services to use fewer ships, but continuing to serve eight European ports from Goole, Grimsby and Hull.

Separate from these North Sea services were the ferry operations across the Humber, for which three new paddle steamers were built, two in 1934 and one in 1940.

Six small Clyde paddle steamers, named after characters created by Sir Walter Scott, and two Firth of Forth ferry services were the mainstay of the North British fleet. The Forth services included a cargo service from Leith to Burnt Island and a passenger and car service operating in the shadow of the Forth Bridge from South Queensferry to North Queensferry. In addition, a joint venture with the Caledonian Railway operated six paddle steamers on Loch Lomond, and this became a joint LNER/LMS service on Grouping. During the 1930s, two new ships were built by the LNER for the Clyde services, one of which had diesel-electric propulsion, while in 1947, the famous paddle steamer *Waverley* was introduced to replace a ship lost in war service.

The LNER Harwich–Hook of Holland ferry *Vienna*, one of three ships built for this service. (*LNER*)

The need to replace war losses was important as these had reduced the LNER fleet to 13 large and eight small ships by 1946, although three new ships followed in 1947.

Even less than the railway, the LNER did not coordinate its shipping interests and manage them as a single entity. The Continental traffic manager was one of the company's chief officers, but operations were controlled by the area managers. To some extent there was logic in this, as the operations varied so widely and there was little attempt to maintain packet services from, say, Newcastle. What seems strange in retrospect is that there was no attempt to create a single smokestack or funnel colour to denote an LNER ship, but instead, pre-Grouping colours remained. This meant that the Harwich steamers had yellow smokestacks, those at Grimsby were white and the Scottish loch and river steamers had red smokestacks with a narrow white band. Even when a house flag was introduced in 1923, with a saltire, or St Andrew's cross, having 'LNER' in the centre, there were local variations permitted. In the dexter canton, that is closest to the mast, there was an emblem for each port, with a bat's wing for Harwich; a white star for Grimsby, and a thistle for the Scottish ships.

Ports and Harbours

No less than 41 miles of quayside and 400 acres of water area were inherited by the LNER. The largest of the LNER's docks were those on the Humber. The former GCR had an extensive system of docks at Grimsby, for the landing or import of fish and the import of timber, and for the export of coal, augmented by the new docks, opened in 1922 at Immingham, which included a dry dock operated by the Humber Graving Dock & Engineering Company, in which the LNER had an interest. Across the river, on the north bank, the NER and the Hull & Barnsley had much more general port facilities at Hull, which handled general cargo, oil and grain as well as coal, fish and timber, and accounted for almost a third of the LNER's port facilities.

While keeping shipping at arm's length, the NER also had extensive dock interests on Teesside, owning Middlesbrough Docks, while Hartlepool exported coal from the Durham coalfield, for which it imported pit props. Further north, Tyne Dock at Jarrow handled iron ore for the steelworks at Consett, while the NER also owned coal staiths at Blyth and Dunston.

The NBR's main port was at Methil in Fife, mainly for the export of coal, but there were other, smaller, facilities at Burntisland, Bo'ness and Alloa. In Cumberland and deep into LMS territory, the NBR had a tidal port at Silloth on the south side of the Solway Firth.

The succession of miners' strikes clearly hit this business very hard, especially after many export markets were lost as a result of the prolonged strike of 1926. Despite this, in 1928,

The North British Railway developed the port at Methil in Fife to serve the many local collieries, and this is the junction off the Fife loop into the Wemyss Coal Company's premises. (*HMRS AAM 334*)

additional facilities for handling fish were built at the St Andrew's Dock and a further oil terminal was constructed at Salt End, while in 1934 £1.7 million was spent on a new fish dock when the facilities at Grimsby were enlarged. At Hull, the Queen's Dock, which was too small and obsolete, was sold to Hull Corporation who filled it in and built a new civic centre there. Further north, the Tyne Improvement Commissioners bought Tyne Dock in 1936. These changes meant that between 1923 and 1947, the total length of quays fell from 41 miles to 36 miles. By which time, the docks were in a poor and war-battered condition, having been an obvious target for the Luftwaffe.

Canals

Britain's canal network was in decline long before Grouping, and it was a burden for the LNER that it inherited 285 miles of canals in England and Scotland. The longest of these was the Chesterfield Canal in the East Midlands, at 45½ miles, but it also had the Union Canal, running 31¼ miles from near Glasgow to Edinburgh. Typical of the financial state of these canals was the Sheffield & South Yorkshire Navigation, which had not paid a dividend since 1899. The LNER could afford to carry out only the most essential maintenance, but nevertheless, this cost the company £50,000 each year, while tolls raised just £12,000 in 1923 and continued to fall in the years that followed, with the company having to employ lock-keepers and toll clerks. The sole value of the canals lay in the properties along their banks, but even this income amounted to a mere £24,000 annually.

The canals had included a few narrow boats owned by the railways, especially the GCR whose employees called them 'Sir Sam's Navy', but few, if any, passed to the LNER.

Closing a canal was even more difficult than closing a railway, with each requiring an act of Parliament, an expensive, slow and uncertain procedure. The first chairman, William Whitelaw, complained about the cost of their upkeep and declared that he would willingly have given them away, had anyone been interested.

Chapter 16

Road Transport

It took around thirty years for the railways to oust the stagecoach while the network expanded, but whenever a new railway line opened, the stagecoach was finished, although many had a temporary reprieve providing feeder services to the new railheads until the railway continued its relentless march. The isolation of some stations from the centre of the town or village they were supposed to serve also meant that some form of transport to and from the station was necessary. For these reasons, the railways had been involved in road transport from early in their history, but their involvement was limited. They could run buses from a town or village to the station, and they could collect goods for shipment and bring them to a goods depot or station, or deliver them to a customer from a station or goods depot, but they could not provide a door-to-door goods service without rail being involved, and could not run buses other than for railway passengers.

As with shipping, the approach of Parliament was that for the railways everything was forbidden unless it was specifically permitted, which has normally been the opposite of British legislation. As the railways were creatures of Parliament, needing an act to authorise their construction, they were relatively easy to control.

On Grouping, the LNER had 29 buses and 58 cars, a surprisingly low figure for such a large railway, as well 20 steam, 25 electric and 153 petrol-engined lorries and vans, all of which faded into insignificance compared with the 6,989 horse-drawn wagons for which the company kept a stable of 5,189 horses, with 547 of these actually used to shunt wagons on the railway. This last aspect of work for the horses was not as harsh as it seems since a railway wagon faces less friction and therefore needs less power to move it than a road vehicle. What seems incredible is that in 1946 the LNER still had 3,369 horse-drawn vehicles and 1,398 horses, of which 118 still found themselves in the goods yards shunting wagons. Nevertheless, from 1930 onwards the railways started to introduce vehicles such as the Scammell Mechanical Horse and the Karrier Cob, three-wheeled tractors that could handle a wagon designed for horse traction. A horse was a cheaper means of moving a single loaded wagon or even two or three empty wagons than a steam or diesel shunting engine.

Railway horses had a short working life – the average was eight years in Scotland, falling to 5½ years in London, where horses cost £55 against £44 in the north of England. Until 1926, the practice was for horses to be bought from dealers and then a group of them would be gathered together for inspection by a company director, but this prolonged process caused some hardship to the horses, leading many of them to fall ill, with a marked mortality rate. Wedgwood resolved this issue by permitting the area horse superintendents to buy animals at country fairs or direct from farmers, saving the dealers' mark-up and also cutting the mortality rate.

The railway companies seem to have taken great pride in their horses, which were often shown at country fairs and won many prizes. There were practical reasons for their continued use, for despite the tremendous growth in the number of men with mechanical and driving skills as a result of the First World War, there were still many who were more familiar with horses.

Investing in Road Transport

The reluctance to give the railways ever greater powers was born out of the belief that they could damage the existing operators, at sea and then on land. There was from the early days a distrust of the railways because the new mode of transport was so superior in terms of speed, reliability and cost to anything that had gone before. The impact of the railways on the canals was noticed, even though some canals survived in railway ownership. There was also the case that the railways became local monopolies competing with their neighbours at the edge of their operating area, and there was concern that this would extend to road transport as well.

On the other hand, the railways felt that they were at the mercy of road transport which boomed after the end of the First World War as many men were demobbed from the armed forces with the ability to drive and maintain road vehicles, while war surplus lorries were also sold off cheaply. The typical ex-army lorry in 1919 could easily be converted into a bus as they usually used the same design of chassis, as passenger vehicles had still to receive the low centre drop axle that would allow floor heights to be lowered.

This changed during the late 1920s, when the railways sponsored legislation that was passed in 1928 and enabled them to invest in road transport undertakings. An oddity of this move was that the railways surrendered their own bus operations, usually using them as at least part of their investment in established bus companies, while in some cases bus companies were purchased outright by the railways. The same practice was not adopted for their collection and delivery road vehicles, which continued to carry the name of the railway company, although in many areas such services were part of the agreement between the LNER, LMS and GWR to pool their freight receipts. Again, when the railways did buy road haulage operations, they did so jointly with all four grouped companies participating in the purchase of the parcels carrier Carter Paterson and the haulage and removals firm, Pickfords in 1933.

The grouped companies were quick to take advantage of their freedom to move into passenger road transport, far quicker in fact than proved to be the case with road haulage. By early 1930, the LNER was able to announce that it had acquired interests in a number of major bus companies. In Scotland these included the Scottish Motor Traction Company, whose subsidiaries included Midland Bus Services (not to be confused with the English Midland Red), W. Alexander & Sons, and the Lanarkshire Group. North Eastern Area bus companies included Northern General, United Automobile Services, East Yorkshire Motor Services and the West Yorkshire Road Car Company, while in the Southern Area companies included Eastern Counties and the Lincolnshire Road Car Company, as well as a firm called Ortona. There were also a number of companies which were owned jointly with the LMS, including Yorkshire Woollen District, Yorkshire Traction, North Western Road Car, East Midland Motor Services, Trent Motor Traction, and Eastern National, the Essex operator whose territory covered the southern area of the former GER as well as the former London Tilbury & Southend Railway.

The goods shed at Woodbridge, with an LNER lorry and barrows. (*HMRS ABD 114*)

Chapter 17

Accidents

Improvements in signalling and in rolling stock design and construction have meant that railway accidents in recent years have been far fewer and less serious than during the first half of the 20th century. By the time of Grouping, the interlocking of signals and points was becoming more widespread, but even so, fog remained a persistent danger and was far worse than today because almost all domestic heating and much industrial production, as well as the railways themselves, were fuelled by coal. Most railway carriages were largely constructed of wood, many were still wooden framed, and offered no protection to their occupants in a collision or derailment. Rolling stock still existed at Grouping that used gas lighting and gas was still the preferred means of cooking, and this was another weakness of the older rolling stock that meant that serious accidents could often be accompanied by fire.

Inevitably there were a number of serious accidents during the life of the LNER, and like any other railway, some accidents highlighted problems hitherto unnoticed or which railway management thought had been resolved. Nevertheless, it is clear that the LNER seems to have been one of the safer railways, with fewer accidents over the period under review.

There were a couple of accidents during the General Strike of May 1926, as mentioned in Chapter 12, which were partly the result of using inexperienced people, some of them volunteers, on the railway. But also, this was because of the absence of signalmen which meant that the railway used the time-interval system, that had been shown to be dangerous in the early days of the railways, but was forced upon the LNER as it was a case of this system or no running at all!

One accident that occurred shortly after Grouping was of a kind that still persists to this day, a collision between a train and a road vehicle on a level crossing. Few details remain of this incident, but on 30 August 1926, a train collided 'with a charabanc' on the crossing at Naworth and eight people were killed on the coach as well as the crossing keeper, who was held to blame. Less than six months later there was a more serious accident at Hull caused by signalling error.

Hull Paragon

Safety features do not always guarantee against an accident. The main passenger station in Hull, Paragon, was protected by the latest safety features of the day, including an interlocking system that should have made it impossible to allow a train to pass unless the selected route was safe. Yet, on 14 February 1927, the 8.22am from Withernsea collided head-on with the 9.5am from Hull to Scarborough, killing twelve passengers and seriously injuring another 24. It was little short of a miracle that the footplate crews of the two locomotives survived.

In the subsequent inquiry, it was found that there were three signalmen in the box and one of them had pulled the wrong lever, setting the points ahead of the Scarborough train when he had intended to set them for the train arriving from Withernsea. All should have been well as locking bars would normally have prevented the points being changed as the signal ahead of the Scarborough train was set at clear. Unfortunately, another signalman was breaking the rules by setting the signals behind the Scarborough train to danger while the train was still passing; disengaging the locking bar on the points and allowing them to be changed when his colleague used the wrong lever. Even so, had the locomotive been just a few feet further forward, its wheels would have prevented the points from moving.

In the sharp impact, the wooden carriages behind the locomotives of both trains either telescoped through each other or simply broke up.

Both signalmen were blamed for this accident.

Penistone

Less than a fortnight later there was another accident, at Penistone, caused by the carelessness of a signalman and the neglect of a locomotive driver and his fireman. This was a rare inter-company accident, but Penistone, high in the Yorkshire moors, and the immediate area, suffered a disproportionate number of railway accidents over the years. The line was a meeting point between the LMS and the LNER.

On 27 February 1927, an LMS locomotive was running around a train obeying a green signal, unaware that this was meant for an express. The LMS locomotive, a radial tank, had worked a train through on the Huddersfield line, and had arrived and its passengers had alighted. It needed to clear the line to allow an empty stock working from Bradford to enter the station and so shunted its rake of carriages in to the other LMS platform. Although not necessary, it was usual for the locomotive to run round to the other end of the train, which required a number of shunts backwards and forwards, ending with a move to the front of the train on the LMS up line. Sending the fireman to brew tea in the porter's room, the driver was on his own, but was given a hand signal by the duty Huddersfield Junction signalman, who promptly forgot to set the points for the LMS line, leaving the locomotive on the LNER line. The driver realised that he was on the wrong line and stopped, but when he saw a signal at the eastern end of the station go to 'off', he thought that this was meant for him and moved forward believing that he would run back on to the LMS line. The signal was intended for the express from Manchester to Marylebone, with five carriages, which had eased to 20mph because of speed restrictions at Penistone, and this prevented the accident from being more serious.

While the Huddersfield Junction signalman was blamed for the accident, the crew of the LMS locomotive was also blamed as the driver should have sent the fireman to the signalbox to remind the signalman of his locomotive, rather than to brew tea.

Darlington

The following year there was another head-on accident, this time at Darlington Bank Top on 27 June 1928. In this case it was a driver's error rather than a signalman. A parcels train was being driven by an inexperienced driver who misunderstood the complicated signalling at the station and went too far past a signal that was only allowing his train to move a short distance. His locomotive fouled the main line and was hit by an excursion train running at around 45mph. Two coaches of the excursion train telescoped and the 25 people killed were all in these two carriages.

Welwyn Garden City

Accidents involving two express trains have the potential for massive loss of life, and it seems incredible that the death and serious injury toll at Welwyn Garden City was not even greater.

On the night of 15 June 1935, three expresses left London King's Cross within 13 minutes, with the first being the 10.45pm for Newcastle, followed at 10.53pm by the second, also for Newcastle, and then at 10.58pm, by a train for Leeds. The first train passed the signals at Welwyn and continued safely on its journey, but the signalman failed to clear the signals for the 10.53, leaving the distant signal at caution so the driver slowed the train in case he had to stop at the home signal. As he approached, the signals were changed to clear, and he started to accelerate, but before his train could recover the lost speed, it was rammed in the rear by the 10.58, travelling at around 70mph. The rearmost carriage was destroyed in the impact and others badly damaged, while two carriages in the 10.58 telescoped, although others with centre buck-eye knuckle couplings stayed in line and doubtless reduced the number of casualties. In the collision, 13 passengers were killed, with the guard of the 10.53, and another 81 seriously injured.

The inspecting officer concluded that the signalman had been promoted beyond his level of competence for such a busy box. He had mistakenly cleared the down-line block instruments for an up train and had not realised that the 10.53 had not passed his box when he accepted the 10.58. The recommendation was that the block instruments should be connected to the track circuits to prevent a recurrence using a system that became known as the Welwyn control. The early adoption of this control could have avoided the next accident on the LNER, at Castlecary in Scotland, although to be fair, the widespread introduction of any new system takes several years.

Castlecary

The final serious accident on the LNER before the outbreak of the Second World War was in Scotland at Castlecary, on the main line between Edinburgh and Glasgow, on the evening of 10 December 1937 in heavy snow that had produced 'white-out' conditions.

At 6pm that evening the 5.30pm Edinburgh Waverley to Glasgow Queen Street express travelling at 70mph ran into the back of the 4.20pm local train from Dundee Tay Bridge to Queen Street. The local train was running late because of the poor weather. The Edinburgh train was headed by A3 No. 2744 *Grand Parade*, and this heavy Pacific locomotive completely destroyed the rear four carriages of the local train and pushed its locomotive forward a hundred yards with the brakes on. The accident occurred despite the signalman at Castlecary operating Regulation 5e that required a double section to be clear ahead for a train to be allowed to pass the previous box, in this case at Greenhill Junction. A set of points had been blocked by snow. In the poor visibility the train from Dundee ran past the home signal at Castlecary, but the Dundee train managed to stop just beyond the signal. The signalman failed to ascertain the whereabouts of the Dundee train, believing that it had not stopped, and accepted the Edinburgh express into the section having set his signals at danger.

The Edinburgh express also ran past the signal and into the rear of the Dundee train. It was believed that the distant signal had been stuck in the off or clear position by the snow, and it wasn't until the driver of the express saw the home signal at danger that he realised he was heading towards another train. In the ensuing accident, 35 people were killed, including seven railwaymen, and another 179 were hurt, many of them seriously. Several carriages on the Edinburgh train rode over the top of its locomotive, although the tender and cab protected the driver and fireman.

The driver of the express was charged with culpable homicide, the Scottish equivalent to manslaughter, but the charge was dropped, and the inspecting officer concluded that the signalman was principally to blame. The accident was made worse by the confined location of the station, set in a cutting.

There was to be a serious accident during the Second World War at King's Cross, which is covered in Chapter 19, but apart from that there were no further serious accidents on the network until 1946, at Potters Bar.

Potters Bar

Errors by both a driver and a signalman resulted in an accident at Potters Bar on 10 February 1946, when the 9.32pm passenger train from Hatfield to King's Cross hit the buffers in a short siding at Potters Bar at 10.8pm and the impact derailed its carriages, which fouled the main line. In the next minute-and-a-half, the carriages were hit by a King's Cross to Edinburgh express and within half-a-minute by a Bradford to King's Cross express, resulting in two fatalities and 17 injured. The driver was held to blame, but the signalman also shared responsibility for moving the points as the train ran over them, derailing the second carriage.

Chapter 18

The Infrastructure

As the country's second largest railway, the LNER inherited 6,714 route miles or 17,271 track miles of railway, with 2,600 stations and depots, plus bridges, tunnels and viaducts. Keeping the track in good order required 60,000 tons of rail annually and 1.25 million sleepers, as well as 500,000 cubic yards of ballast. All in all, the infrastructure accounted for two-thirds of the company's assets. Inevitably, the standard varied considerably, depending on the wealth or otherwise of the pre-Grouping company but also on the territory through which the line ran.

The viaduct over the River Cambus gives a good impression of the high standard of track maintenance on the LNER. (*HMRS AAM 327*)

The former Great Northern Line was very well engineered with a ruling gradient of 1 in 200 but even on this there were sharp curves, such as that at Peterborough North which required trains to slow to 20mph. There was also the steep climb of 1 in 107 through Gas Works and Copenhagen tunnels for trains starting from King's Cross, and three miles at 1 in 178 for up trains from Stoke box. On the North Eastern north of Darlington and on the North British, the country became progressively hilly, with Cockburnspath Bank providing a challenge with its 4½ miles at 1 in 96 for trains running south. Further north, as mentioned earlier, the line between Edinburgh and Aberdeen was hilly and curved with many difficult starts for stopping trains. That said, the former NBR lines were capable of taking the heaviest locomotives, although there were loading gauge restrictions in some places.

Some actually referred to the East Coast Main Line as the 'Bridges Route'. Going north, the line took the Welwyn Viaduct, swing bridges at Selby and Naburn, Durham Viaduct, the High Level

Bridge at Newcastle, which also carried a road, until the King Edward Bridge was completed and the reversal at Newcastle Central ended, then the Royal Border Bridge at Berwick-upon-Tweed, and then the Forth Bridge and finally the Tay Bridge, with a much lesser bridge at Montrose.

The entire infrastructure was not completely in LNER hands. The Forth Bridge had been built by a consortium of the GNR, NER, NBR and the Midland Railway, leaving the LMS as a minority partner on Grouping. The LMS and LNER were also partners on the jointly owned Manchester, South Junction & Altrincham line and, for a while, on the Midland & Great Northern Line until this was taken over completely by the LNER.

Although the extension to London crippled the Great Central financially, both the trans-Pennine main line and the line to Marylebone were well engineered with a generous loading gauge, possibly in anticipation of eventual through working of trains to a proposed tunnel under the English Channel. Nevertheless, it seems almost inevitable that the ruling gradient of 1 in 178 had to be exceeded in the steep climb of 1 in 120 to the summit at Woodhead, while there were several steep gradients to be faced on the London Extension as it ran through the Chilterns.

Of the larger constituent companies, the weakest by far was the Great Eastern. East Anglia had not been a profitable area for railways and while there were few significant gradients, the often low-lying and even marshy landscape in some areas did not lend itself easily to constructing a well ballasted high speed railway with heavy rails. Even on main lines, many underbridges could not accept an axle load in excess of 18 tons. An early post-Grouping assessment of the infrastructure and bridge renewal in particular found that while the GNR needed £118,000 for this work, the GER needed £1.3 million.

The railways have always been very adept at making continued use of redundant rolling stock, often using it for their own service needs. This former six-wheeled clerestory carriage was in use as a hut at Doncaster in 1938. (*HMRS ABJ 519*)

The Great North of Scotland had struggled to raise money as it was being built, and it also had severe weight restrictions on much of its network.

While the economic situation was bleak and the LNER in this as everything else was fondly described as 'poor, but honest', there were three factors that drove railway modernisation from Grouping to the outbreak of the Second World War. First, local authority rating of railway property was changed to reduce the impact on the companies. Second was the removal of the Railway Passenger Duty in 1929 on condition that the sums saved were capitalised by the railway companies and the money used for new investment to help reduce unemployment. Third was the availability of low interest loans backed by The Treasury in the years that followed, which saw the LNER do its best to modernise.

The way in which the grouped companies took advantage of these incentives to modernise differed greatly, as one would expect given that their circumstances varied and a centrally imposed programme of improvements would not have worked. The Southern Railway and the London & North Eastern, for example, were complete opposites with regard to the proportion of their turnover generated by goods and passenger traffic.

Stations

Many of the railway stations on the LNER were pleasing, especially the old NER stations at York and Newcastle Central, both of which retained their cohesion. Being built on a curve also added an extra dimension to their appearance, despite imposing severe speed restrictions on the few trains not stopping. Surprisingly, King's Cross was not the largest station by acreage, this being Edinburgh Waverley, then London Liverpool Street and Newcastle Central, while Liverpool Street was the busiest with more than 1,200 trains daily, a reflection of its dense commuter traffic.

One oddity, a coincidence, was that both Waverley and Liverpool Street were built with platforms below street level, and the stations marked by the impressive structures of the North British Hotel (now renamed the 'New Balmoral') and the Great Eastern Hotel respectively. By contrast to spacious Waverley, the company's station in Glasgow, Queen Street, was cramped, with short platforms and a steep incline in tunnel for departing trains, and was also said to be one of the grimiest on the LNER.

Although money was scarce, the LNER did rebuild stations and also built new ones to attract additional traffic. One of the first to receive attention after Grouping was King's Cross, where additional platforms were built. The fairly low frontage of the station was concealed from the would-be traveller by a clutter of shops and stalls between the building and the Euston Road. There was even at one time, a type of show known as 'The African Village', housed in a brick building. All of this compared badly with the impressive frontage of St Pancras, from which King's Cross was separated by Pancras Road.

Later, a number of stations were rebuilt, including Berwick-upon-Tweed and Clacton. Elsewhere, new stations were built, in many cases to attract commuters, as at Welwyn Garden City, but also for holidaymakers, when Filey Holiday Camp station was built in 1947 to serve a Butlin's holiday camp.

A view of part of the sidings at Peterborough, one of the busiest on the East Coast Main Line, with two ballast brakes beyond the sheds. (*HMRS ABJ 237*)

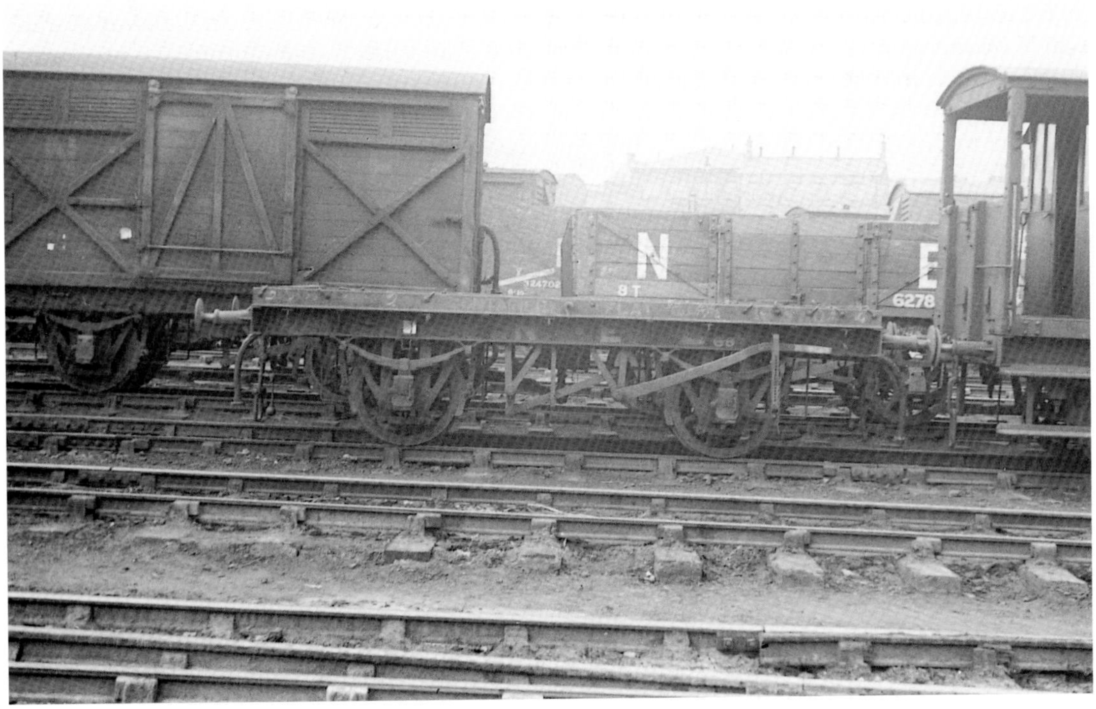

An assortment of wagons, with an empty container truck next to a brakevan, and a fish van on the next road. (*HMRS ABJ 402*)

Goods Depots and Marshalling Yards

By far the most heavily dependent on freight traffic than any other railway, the LNER paid close attention to the development of its goods depots and marshalling yards. Priority was given to those marshalling yards where modernisation could result in both increased productivity providing savings in manpower or damage to railway wagons and vans or to goods in transit, and accelerating the flow of traffic at a time when the competition from road haulage was becoming more intense.

This is a rotating ground signal, used for shunting operations at Bourne in Lincolnshire, photographed in 1934. (*HMRS ABW 129*)

Typical of the yards that were built or modernised was that at March in Cambridgeshire, which became important for the growing agricultural and fish traffic out of East Anglia and the coal traffic into the region. It also handled international traffic heading for the train ferries. Here, the yard incorporated a hump, with wagons and vans shunted to the top of the hump, and then running down unbraked into the right road. In the up yard, braking was by means of hydraulically operated retarders, with steel beams squeezing the wheels as the wagons ran past, but this system damaged Mansell wheels with protruding bolts. The system was not modified, but when the down yard was built, a different system, an eddy current-retarder, was used which spared the wheels. The same system was used in new yards at Mottram, near Manchester, opened in 1935, and at Priory Yard, Hull.

A new goods depot was built at Ardwick East, Manchester. Elsewhere, existing depots were modernised and extended, and here too, productivity was much to the fore. For example, Goodman's Yard, on the former London & Blackwall Railway, was modernised during the early 1930s, with a 30-ton wagon hoist as one of the improvements.

A clear view of a 'cenotaph' coaling tower, showing wagons being hauled up to the top where they would be tipped over to release the coal. This example was at Cambridge. (*HMRS AER 132*)

Just two of the mighty P1 class 2-8-2s were built as limitations on the length of sidings, especially at passing points, meant that their full potential could not be realised. As can be seen from this 1929 view of No. 2394, it still has the booster on the rear pony truck, intended to increase power further. (*HMRS AAM 407*)

Workshops, Running Sheds and Track

In addition to the introduction of water softening equipment from 1932 onwards as mentioned in Chapter 7, productivity was also improved by the introduction of mechanical coaling plants at the most important and busiest locomotive depots. Major termini had carriage washing plants installed nearby, again reducing the manpower required and also improving the standard of cleanliness, a constant challenge for the steam railway.

The interior of the works at Darlington with two V2s under construction in 1939. (*HMRS ACW 120*)

In some cases change was forced upon the company, as with the renewal of locomotive turntables when costly rebuilding became necessary to install 70ft turntables to cope with the growing number of Pacific locomotives, which were also operating over much more of the network as their numbers and route availability increased. Some saving was made when smaller turntables replaced by the larger ones could be relocated, cascaded to less busy depots, but installing a larger turntable meant considerable building work.

The post-Grouping period was one in which the fashionable material for buildings and other structures, such as bridges, was concrete, and the railways often already had concrete fabrication yards; which were enlarged and modernised.

Perhaps the best instance of wider recognition of the high standard of the track throughout much of the LNER, mentioned earlier, came in 1927 after the Sevenoaks railway disaster on the Southern Railway. One of the contributing factors to the accident was the poor ballasting used on the former South Eastern & Chatham Management Committee lines, using smooth round shingle taken from beaches, while another was the poor riding quality of the 'River' class 2-6-4T locomotives, one of which had been handling the ill-fated train. To compare its riding on the Southern with that on another railway, one of these locomotives was taken to the former GNR main line between St Neots and Huntingdon, where it was reported to have reached a speed of 80mph while still running steadily, prompting the Ministry of Transport inspector to comment on the high standard of the LNER's permanent way.

An essential part of every railway's operations was the breakdown crane, and it was standard practice for these to be spread across the system so that there was always one within reasonable distance of an accident or derailment. This is a Ransomes & Rapier steam breakdown crane in 1939. (*HMRS AEU 832*)

One innovation adopted by the LNER was the decision to lay steel sleepers when replacement was necessary, with the company explaining that steel sleepers were home-produced while wooden sleepers had to be imported. Reinforced concrete sleepers were also used instead of wood, but at first these were unsatisfactory as flexing caused cracks, which were made worse by water and heavy frost or snow, but later pre-stressed concrete sleepers were more successful.

Improvements in technology were also applied to the permanent way. Rail weights and lengths were increased, being standardised at 95lb per yard and at 60ft in length. Experiments were made with lengths of 90ft rail at Thirsk and on Welwyn Viaduct, while at Peterborough in 1937, rails were laid at 100lb per yard and 120ft lengths. Starting in 1934, experiments were made with continuously welded rail in lengths up to a quarter mile. Later, in 1939, there were experiments with flat-bottomed rail which was cheaper to lay than the traditional bullhead type keyed into chairs. At busy junctions, such as that at Newcastle Central, cast manganese steel crossing points meant that the life of the points was no longer measured in months, but in years.

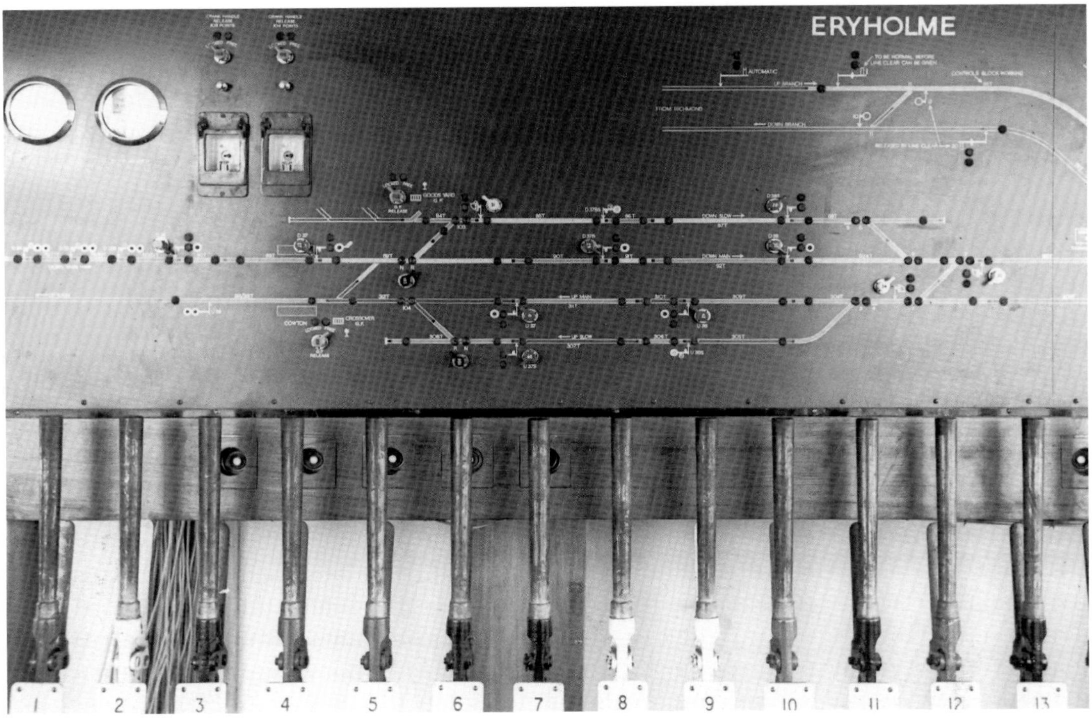

The track layout panel in the signalbox at Eryholme in 1939 – one of the more modern boxes at the time. (*HMRS ACW 227*)

Productivity was also to the fore in track laying, with track, including that at junctions, pre-assembled and laid by crane. Before Grouping, the GNR had used mechanical equipment to record track condition. In 1932, a track laying machine was obtained, reducing the time needed for civil engineering possessions of the line. In 1947, trials were made with a self-propelled ballast tamping machine imported from Switzerland. There were twice-yearly official track inspections and the gangs producing the best-kept sections of track received an award.

There was much to be done on the track as the railways had been taken over by the government on the outbreak of war in 1914 and not released back to the companies until shortly before Grouping. In wartime, little had been done other than the most pressing maintenance as materials and scarce skilled manpower were needed elsewhere. Despite the poor economic outlook, much traffic continued to increase post-war and in any case, improved timings required more stretches to be quadrupled, while in some areas, especially in Scotland, even main lines were single track. More than half the inherited network had double track, with many stretches of quadrupled track, especially in industrial areas or close to the London termini. The LNER had 337 route miles of four-track, of which 133 were on the East Coast route, and by the outbreak of the Second World War, another 41 route miles had been upgraded to four-track. Yet, even the busy East Coast Main Line had sections with just double or triple tracks, and some of these bottlenecks survive to this day, notably Welwyn Viaduct and the associated tunnels.

Before coaling towers became widespread, coaling stages were used, which were slower and also required more manpower, often using wheelbarrows. Left is J69 0-6-0T No. 358E (lettered L&NER, later renumbered 7358) and right, is N7 0-6-2T No. 8001 at Stratford Yard in 1923, with a coaling elevator in the background. (*HMRS ABZ 716*)

One reason why these sections had not been given the attention that they deserved was the cost. The LNER decided that instead of quadrupling between Wood Green and Stevenage, it would be more cost-effective to extend the Cuffley branch via Hertford to Langley, near Stevenage, creating a loop and possibly attracting new traffic. The loop could be used by through goods trains as an alternative to waiting in sidings until fast passenger trains had passed. This was completed in 1924, and was the last extension of the company's own route mileage, apart from the Watford branch opened a year later, as opposed to track mileage and extensions into industrial premises and to wartime airfields and stores depots. The Watford branch, completed in 1935, was a joint venture with the Metropolitan Railway.

The LNER did undertake widening of the route when it was necessary and there was no alternative. Four-tracking was introduced between Huntingdon and Offord, and between Alne and Northallerton at Beningborough. Further quadrupling occurred on the lines from Liverpool Street when four-tracking was extended as far as Gidea Park and then later extended further to Shenfield, where a dive-under or burrowing junction was also built to avoid conflict between Southend trains and up trains on the main line. Costly, because of the terrain through which it ran, was the doubling of the Edinburgh to Aberdeen section of the East Coast line between Arbroath and Montrose, completed in 1932.

One quadrupling that did not take place, even though land was acquired, and as early as 1926 the LNER had recognised the problem of delays in the Southern Area, was between Greenwood box and Potters Bar. However, with other projects accorded higher priority and then the Second World War, the project was not completed until after Nationalisation. Passing loops were provided at other bottlenecks further north.

Overall, the standard of track was sufficiently high that when the first high-speed streamlined trains were introduced in 1935, there was no need to upgrade the track beforehand. Experience showed, however, that some improvements were needed, with the traditional entry to curves being realigned and superelevation introduced, while junctions and crossings also had to be modified. The problems did not arise so much on the downhill stretches, where speeds rose from 90mph to 100mph, but on the uphill, where speeds rose more dramatically from 60mph to 90mph.

Chapter 19

Railways at War

There were two aspects to the story of Britain's railways in wartime. On the one hand, there is the story of the railways struggling to meet their increased wartime commitments and the relationship between the railways and the state, which became both their biggest customer and also their controller, imposing restrictions and effectively taking their revenue and using them as subcontractors. On the other hand, there was the way in which the railways and railway personnel, both men and women, coped with enemy aerial attack.

Government interest in the potential of the railways dated from as early as 1871 and the Regulation of the Forces Act of that year, which allowed the government to take control of the railways in a national emergency. The real interest at the time seems to have been more a concern with internal unrest rather than an external threat. The first major use of the railways for military purposes came later, with the Boer War, but that did not require control of the railways, and indeed it really only affected one company, the London & South Western Railway, one of the Southern Railway's ancestors.

In common with the other companies, the London & North Eastern Railway did not have the benefit of what amounted to a practice run during the Boer War, when the LSWR was the prime mover of men and horses from London and the military training grounds across the south of England to Southampton. The LSWR experience had been unique. When the First World War came, in common with every other railway in Great Britain, the predecessor companies of the LNER found themselves under state control between 1914 and 1918.

A1 class 4-6-2 No. 2576 *The White Knight* heads a passenger express at Stannington in 1940. (*HMRS ACW 007*)

An ex-North British 4-4-0 at Dalmeny, just to the south of the Forth Bridge, after the second carriage, with the clerestory roof, had derailed in 1940. The tender simply has the initials 'NE', a wartime austerity measure. (*HMRS AAC 529*)

The actual basis for state control had occurred in 1912, with the formation of the Railway Executive Committee consisting of the general managers of ten leading railway companies, including the Great Northern, the North Eastern and the Great Eastern. The role of the REC would be to run the railways as a single entity in the case of war. When war came, the main pressure fell upon the companies in the south, especially those serving the Channel ports closest to France.

The railway companies not only had to adapt to centralised control, they also lost some 200,000 of their employees, who numbered around 600,000 in total, to the armed forces. Passenger services were cut back to allow paths for troop trains and to save fuel as well as wear and tear on track and rolling stock. Some minor branch lines were closed to save fuel and manpower, and a number of them never reopened. Nevertheless, it was not until 1917 that cheap fares were abolished and ordinary fares increased by 50 per cent, with even greater restrictions on the number of trains available for civilian passengers. On the other hand, in contrast to the practice during the Second World War, while the availability of restaurant cars was reduced considerably, the facility did not disappear completely during the First World War.

Fortunately, the railways had, for the most part, enjoyed a period of considerable prosperity during the years leading up to the First World War, and so the problems encountered in assessing fair payment for the use of their facilities in the later conflict were not so serious. One or two companies encountered delay in receiving the grants due for abnormal maintenance costs, and there were some disputes that had to go to law. Overall, for the First World War, the government paid the railways £60 million to be shared between the companies.

The attitude of the government towards the railways during the First World War was still remembered by many of those running the railways. After all, the period between the two world wars had amounted to slightly less than 21 years. Directors and senior managers were also painfully aware that the years between the two world wars had not been good ones for the railways, which had not managed to achieve the revenues set out for them by the government on Grouping.

In the case of the companies that amalgamated to form the giant London & North Eastern Railway, in 1912, the Great Eastern managed to pay 2.5 per cent and the Great Northern 4.37 per cent, with 6 per cent on the North Eastern, but the North British had struggled to pay 3 per cent on its preference stock and 1 per cent on its deferred stock, while the Great Central paid nothing. At least the latter's shareholders were prepared for what happened in the years 1935–38, when the LNER could not pay a dividend. Most of the railways had managed to pay a dividend in 1937 when the Coronation of His Majesty King George VI had stimulated passenger traffic, and possibly the wider economy as well, but the freight-orientated LNER did not benefit from this as much as the others. Overall, dividends were less than shareholders would have received had they invested their money in a Post Office savings account!

As any government compensation would be based on average turnover for the years immediately preceding the war, it was with considerable foreboding that the new conflict was anticipated. Added to which, everyone realised that this time the growing potential of the bomber, a nuisance to the railways during the First World War rather than a serious threat, meant that they would be in the front line. The feeling was that the 'bomber would always get through', based on what had been seen of the Spanish Civil War and Japanese attacks in China. There were also problems of administration, with key personnel evacuated to areas where it was hoped that they could continue with their work uninterrupted by heavy bombing.

Preparing for War

Preparation for the wartime operation of the railways was put in hand as early as 1937. In September 1938, the Ministry of Transport warned that as soon as the danger of enemy aggression was imminent, a Defence of the Realm Act would be passed, and that one of its provisions would be for the government to take control of the railways and the railway operations of the London Passenger Transport Board. It was realised that bombing would be a threat, and in 1937, a technical committee laid plans for dealing with the effects. Meanwhile, Lord Stamp, the President of the LMS, as chairman of the Railway Companies Association, was in charge with negotiations with the government over the state's use of the railways in wartime. As expected, in late September 1938, once again a Railway Executive Committee was formed, with the LNER represented by its general manager. Initially, the REC was chaired by Gilbert Szlumper of the Southern Railway, but he later became 'Director-General of Transportation' at the War Office.

One of the early tasks for the Committee was to draw up a list of measures, including protection of employees and their administrative centres, as well as material for emergency repairs, and any additional equipment needed. For the railway companies and London Transport, the total estimate came to £5,226,400, equivalent to some £321 million today, and a foretaste of things to come followed when the Government decided at the end of 1938 to provide a grant of just £4 million, of which £750,000 was to go to the LPTB, with the companies left to fund the balance themselves. The LNER share of this much reduced sum was £764,950, the second highest for any of the grouped companies. The total paid to the railway companies and the LPTB was £3,093,250, with the remainder being spent on equipment that would be pooled between the four railway companies.

Part of the money was spent on relocating the headquarters as it was vital that the railway continued to function no matter what happened. The LNER relocated its chief general manager and his staff to The Hoo, a large country mansion near Hitchin, which officially became 'HQ1 Hitchin', but even with its own decentralised structure, it had to find many more centres for its London staff and these were the most widely scattered of any of the railways.

Stores were created for materials that would be necessary for the railways to remain operational despite heavy aerial attack. The civil engineers received an extra three months' supply of materials to repair and maintain the permanent way, including baulks of timber and strut joists. A three-month supply of locomotive and carriage spare parts was ordered over and above usual needs.

Meanwhile, many employees enrolled in the civil defence and air raid precautions services, while others were already in the Territorial Army, many of them in the Railway Supplementary Reserve of the Royal Engineers, or were planning to join. Air raid precaution (ARP) exercises also began, and the staff magazine carried a photograph of a guard wearing a gas mask. This was understandable as memories of the havoc and hardship created by the use of gas in the First World War were still fresh. Believing that 'the bomber will always get through' meant that steps were taken to ensure that air raid shelters were constructed at all railway workshops and at other centres such as marshalling yards.

Although there were deep level underground lines, the tube lines, at or close to the major London termini at King's Cross and Liverpool Street, there was no intention at first of using these as additional air raid shelters. It was public pressure that eventually forced the authorities to relent and open the tube stations at night to the public as shelters. Unfortunately, official misgivings about their suitability as shelters were justified and there were a number of cases of tube stations being bombed and those sheltering killed.

State Control

On the eve of war, as threatened, the Minister of War Transport, as the Minister of Transport had become, moved quickly to seize control of the railways on 1 September 1939, using powers granted to him under the Defence Regulations Act 1939.

The state also decided what resources could be made available in terms of raw materials and manufacturing capacity to keep the railways running. This was not nationalisation in the true sense of the word, but it was a bureaucratic straightjacket, although it must be borne in mind that the control and direction of labour, raw materials and manufacturing capacity applied to the entire economy and not just the railways.

Despite the haste to grab control of the railways, there was considerable delay in finalising the means of working them. The system of state control meant that the railways effectively became contractors to the government, with all revenue passing to the government which then allocated a share out of a pool, which was set at a guaranteed £40 million. There was little real negotiation, and the inclusion of the London Passenger Transport Board in the scheme was opposed by the 'Big Four' railway companies who believed that passenger traffic would slump in wartime, and that as the only all-passenger operator, London Transport would become a liability for the others. It certainly meant that the allocated funds would have to be spread around more thinly.

The LNER share of the pool was fixed at 23 per cent, while the LPTB received 11 per cent; the GWR received 16 per cent, the same as for the Southern Railway, and the LMS 34 per cent. These percentages were based on the average net revenues for the companies and LPTB in the three years 1935–37, which the government regarded as the standard revenue for each company. Once the guaranteed £40 million had been paid, any balance was allocated to the five train operators on the same percentage terms up to a maximum of £3.5 million. After this, the arrangements became complicated, since if there was a further balance, the revenue over a total of £43.5 million would be divided equally between the government and the pool until the pool total reached £56 million. At this stage, if the revenue share allocated to any of the companies then exceeded its standard revenue, the figure the companies had been expected to earn annually at the time of the Grouping, the excess would be shared out proportionately among the other companies.

Costs of maintenance and renewals had to be standardised, while the cost of restoring war damage would be met up to a total of £10 million in a full year. Privately owned wagons were also requisitioned by the Ministry of War Transport, and the individual companies had to meet the costs and revenue attributed to the wagon owners out of their share of the revenue pool.

This was a 'take it or leave it' type of agreement, with the government leaking threats of nationalisation if the companies failed to agree, although these were officially denied. The years in question had not been good ones for the British economy, although 1938 had been worse

All the railway companies dispersed their head offices on the outbreak of the Second World War, but wherever they were, the railways always tried to continue operations. However, what the reply from these telephone switchboard operators must have sounded like while wearing their gas masks has to be imagined. (*IWM KY3159D*)

and the railways had had to work hard to get the government to recognise this. The difficult economic conditions that had prevailed for almost all of the inter-war period had meant that none of the railway companies had ever achieved the standard revenues anticipated by the Railways Act 1921, the measure that authorised the Grouping.

The best that can be said for the deal was that the government was anxious to avoid inflationary pay claims from railway employees, and no doubt anxious to ensure that it did not play a part in war profiteering since it was likely to be its own single biggest customer. But the inescapable fact was that the railways were having their revenues more or less fixed, while costs were bound to rise as they struggled to meet the increased demands that wartime would place upon them. Placing an upper limit on the cost of making good war damage was another instance of either political expediency to keep the unions quiet, and the Labour Party within the wartime coalition government, or simple naivety since normal insurance measures were not available in wartime.

Nevertheless, within little more than a year, the Ministry of War Transport reneged on the original agreement and left the railway companies to pay for war damage out of revenue. The fixed annual payments were also changed, with the provision for extra payments dropped so that any surplus would be taken by the government, which generously also offered to meet any deficit, which was an unlikely event given the demands placed on the railways. The new deal provided for the following annual payments:

A light load for the famous A4 Pacific No. 4468 *Mallard* in 1940, at a time when train lengths were becoming longer as wartime restrictions began to bite. The plaque, commemorating its record-breaking achievement was a much later addition. (*HMRS AAH707*)

London & North Eastern Railway	£10,136,355
London Midland & Scottish	£14,749,698
Great Western Railway	£6,670,603
Southern Railway	£6,607,639
London Passenger Transport Board	£4,835,705

The railway companies were once again left with little option but to accept. The mood of the times was that any argument was unseemly as it seemed that invasion was a very real danger.

Bus services were not included in the scheme and neither was road haulage. The reasons for this were ones of practicality, as there were so many operators, including a number of owner-driver operations, especially in road haulage and coach private hire, that it would have been extremely difficult. In any case, the state had other means of regulating these modes of transport, by tight controls on the allocation of fuel and vehicles, with the armed forces free to requisition vehicles as necessary, and the Ministry of War Transport was able to allocate vehicles from one operator to another if it thought fit. The irony was that many bus operators in the provinces and especially in what would in peacetime have been resort areas, found wartime demand heavier as new bases for the armed forces were often established in these areas, especially along the southern and eastern coasts of England. Areas in which transport had been heavily affected by the Blitz, such as London and Coventry, often had their vehicles replaced by vehicles from other operators before the limited production of utility vehicles was finally authorised.

Ferry services were badly disrupted as ships were taken over by the Ministry of War Transport, with many needed to help move the British Expeditionary Force (BEF), to France and then to keep it supplied. Other small ships were taken up by the Admiralty as they were needed for the many tasks around the main naval bases.

For all of the grouped railway companies, shipping was part and parcel of their operations. The LNER was no exception and its main shipping routes were those across the North Sea. On the outbreak of war, the government immediately requisitioned the packets used on the services to the Hook and to Antwerp, as well as the train ferries. Unusually, once under state control the ships were renamed, and given ones that were far more imaginative and less stark than those bestowed by the LNER. *Train Ferry No. 1* was renamed *Princess Iris* when requisitioned and *Train Ferry No. 3* became *Princess Daffodil*. *Train Ferry No. 2* was an early casualty, being sunk at Le Havre in 1940, and while *Princess Daffodil* lasted longer, she was sunk in the English Channel in 1945. Of the packet ships, only *Prague* survived to return to LNER service post-war, and even she had a short life after that, being scrapped in 1948 after catching fire during a refit.

The *Amsterdam* had the most distinguished war record, for after taking part in the evacuation of Dunkirk, it was then used as a hospital ship, and later converted to a landing ship for the Normandy landings, then again to a hospital ship, before being sunk by a German mine off Cherbourg later in 1944. Little is known about the fate of the *Vienna*, other than that she was retained by the armed forces after the war ended, possibly to help supply the British Army of the Rhine.

It was not just the ships that had to be given up, the country needed the ports as well and, as in the First World War, Harwich was used as a naval base. The Hook, which had been by-passed by the earlier conflict due to Dutch neutrality, became a German fortress after the invasion of the Low Countries in Spring 1940.

Wartime Operations

There had been much rehearsal of wartime operating conditions on the railways over the previous year or so. Railwaymen had practised working in blackout conditions, which meant that no lights could be shown externally, with all windows screened, while station platforms could only be lit by blue lights or, as there were still many lit by gas, specially shaded gas lamps, and drivers and motormen had to pull up their trains beside oil lamps placed on the platform as markers. Steam locomotives had canvas draped between the engine cab and tender to hide the light of their fires, while the side windows that had appeared on the more modern locomotives were blanked out.

None of this, of course, can truly give a real impression of what it must have been like operating a railway in the blackout, or of the problems of individual railwaymen, and women, having to report for work after a broken night's sleep in a crowded air raid shelter, or of coming off a night shift in the morning to find that their home no longer existed, and perhaps face the loss of family members and neighbours as well. The efficient working of a railway required skill and experience, but under wartime conditions most adults had to be available for either the armed forces or prepared to be directed to essential war work, and as skilled men volunteered or were conscripted into the armed forces, many of their places were taken by women. This may have been a factor in the eventual Allied victory as many historians believe that one factor in the defeat of Germany was that the Germans were reluctant to mobilise the civilian population and instead relied too heavily on slave labour and people conscripted from the occupied territories or Vichy France. No country mobilised its population as thoroughly as the United Kingdom.

Wartime acted as a spur to extending loudspeaker announcements to stations, and while initially station name signs were no longer lit, those under station canopies were allowed to be illuminated later, provided that they were swung round at right angles to the platform. Those stations that had had their names painted on the canopies to help airmen with their navigation had them blanked out. A final safety measure at stations was the removal of glass from roofs and canopies, essential since even a small bomb could create so many shards of broken glass as to be an effective anti-personnel weapon.

Other precautions included repainting the electric multiple units on Tyneside blue and grey as their NER-inspired red and cream livery was regarded as being too visible when the RAF flew missions to assess the levels of camouflage.

There were few serious accidents on the LNER during the war years. Indeed, only that at King's Cross in February 1945 was significant.

The LNER was one of the three railways to continue its magazine during the war, the LMS being the exception. Nevertheless, communications with employees in wartime were also taken over to some extent by the state. The magazines or newsletters provided for employees were subjected to censorship and firm rules were laid down that editors had to follow. Over and above that, the Ministry of Information published hard-hitting posters that were intended to dispel rumours or careless talk. Railway workers were prime targets as the very nature of their work meant that they knew much about the war effort. Troop trains were an obvious example, but they also knew if trains were moving munitions or even large aircraft parts, new wartime traffic for the railways, or armoured vehicles.

Typical of these was a poster intended for railway premises:

If you've news of our munitions
KEEP IT DARK
Ships or 'planes or troop positions
KEEP IT DARK
Lives are lost through conversation
Here's a tip for the duration
When you've got private information
KEEP IT DARK

Another poster was more direct:

YOU
Know more than other people.
You are in a position of trust.
Don't let the fighting forces down.
A few careless words may give something away
that will help the enemy and cost us lives.
Above all, be careful what you say to strangers
and in public.

It was necessary to save paper, so the magazine became thinner and poorer quality paper soon began to be used, with the density of the type increased to make use of every scrap of space. A 'Roll of Honour' was introduced with news of those killed, reported missing or known to have become prisoners of war, as well as details of LNER men who were commissioned in the three armed services and those given awards for distinguished service. In June 1941, the LNER Silver Medal was introduced to award those employees who performed acts of courage or gallantry during their wartime railway service, of which more in the next chapter, but it was not until 1943 that the censors allowed mention of the deaths of employees in air raids.

Evacuation and Emergency Measures

After the false hopes raised by resolution of the Munich Crisis of 1938, it soon became clear that war was inevitable. Preparations made by the railway companies were not helped by threatened industrial action, only averted at the last moment. In anticipation of a surprise attack, evacuation began of children and others, including their teachers and expectant and nursing mothers, to get them away from London and major cities judged to be likely targets. The pressure on the LNER and other railways was such that during the four days of the operation, 1–4 September 1939, only a skeleton service could be provided outside the rush hours.

On 31 August, the order to begin the evacuation was given. Children assembled at their schools and from there either walked or were taken by bus or underground to the station allocated to them. Many had to use suburban stations either because of convenience or because the London termini could not handle all of them. As with the other railway companies, the London & North

Liverpool Street station was bombed in both world wars, and this is a view of the damage during the Blitz of 1940–41. (*IWM HU58785*)

Eastern Railway played its part in the mass evacuation of children from London and other main industrial centres.

One of the two embarkation points for its children was New Barnet station, not perhaps the most convenient as children had travelled from their homes to Enfield West station, now renamed Oakwood, on the Piccadilly Line, and then boarded buses for the few miles to New Barnet. Waiting for them were suburban carriages with a few main line carriages gathered from other routes, leaving no more than a skeleton service for the regular travellers. The use of outer suburban stations was partly to avoid congestion in the central area, but also recognised the fact that war was expected to break out at any moment, and many believed that it would do so without formal declaration and with a massive air raid.

The LNER's other major evacuee handling point was at Stratford, on the lines from Liverpool Street. That the operation was such a success was due in no small part to an LNER man, Sir Ralph Wedgwood, chairman of the Railway Executive Committee, and until his retirement in March 1939, general manager of the LNER.

All four railway companies handled this traffic, although not every parent sent their children away, and some made their own arrangements. Meanwhile, the railways were running evacuation specials in and around the main industrial conurbations and other likely target areas, such as Glasgow, Merseyside, Manchester, Tyneside, Birmingham, Portsmouth and Southampton. While the LNER was the sole railway involved in the Tyneside evacuation, using 271 trains to carry 73,916 evacuees, it shared the Manchester evacuation with the LMS, and between them the two companies provided 302 trains for 115,779 evacuees. While most of the evacuation trains seemed to have an average of around 400–500 passengers, the two trains run from Rosyth must have been very crowded with a total of 2,187 evacuees between them.

Many of the evacuees must have made their own way to the departure stations or been taken on the London Underground as the total carried by the railways from London was 617,480, using 1,577 trains. The railways also had to arrange 34 ambulance trains for the partial evacuation of hospitals in these areas. These measures were not just to move patients to places of greater safety, but to free beds for the bombing when it came, and to empty hospitals near the coast in case of an invasion.

Civilians were also reporting to labour exchanges as they received their call-up papers, meaning that there was yet more travel, albeit most of it over short distances. The achievement becomes still more incredible when it is also borne in mind that, during the evacuation and after it ended, 158,000 men were conveyed to the Channel ports and across the Channel to France, along with more than 25,000 vehicles, over a period of five weeks, while other troops were carried to ports such as Glasgow for passage to the Mediterranean.

The problem was, of course, that at this early stage of the war, no-one knew just how the situation would develop. The fall of France was not anticipated, nor was the invasion of Denmark and Norway or the Netherlands. This was because most members of the military believed that there would be a re-run of the First World War with major fighting for the duration of hostilities on French or Belgian soil. The additional feature was to be heavy bombing, but only of those cities within range of German airfields. Plymouth, which was to suffer badly from the attentions of the Luftwaffe was seen as being 'safe'. In fact, a further evacuation was to be necessary, but that would overlap with the evacuation of British forces from Dunkirk, and in the meantime, as the period of the so-called 'Phoney War' drifted on through the winter of 1939–1940, many evacuees drifted homewards.

Drastic Cuts

On the outbreak of war, excursion and cheap day tickets were withdrawn, but day tickets were reintroduced on 9 October 1939, although with tighter conditions that meant they were not available before 10am and could not be used on trains departing from London between 4pm and 7pm, Monday to Friday.

After the evacuation was over, services had returned to normal but briefly, for on 11 September, drastic cuts were imposed on the train services, meaning great hardship for passengers since, although the late holiday and day tripper traffic had virtually disappeared, normal business travel was still virtually at pre-war levels, especially with large numbers of people commuting to their offices in the City.

The LNER issued a new timetable, cutting crack expresses and inflicting trains that could at best be described as 'semi-fast' in their place. Not only did this lead to unacceptable levels of overcrowding with many passengers left behind, it also meant that station dwell times were extended as passengers struggled to alight from trains or climb aboard. After the uproar that followed, normal services were reinstated on weekdays from 18 September.

Nevertheless, this was simply a temporary reinstatement and indicated nothing more than that the blanket reductions of 11 September had not been properly thought out in the

The signalbox at Ardmore West in 1943, with blackout on most of the window area. (*AAM 331*)

short time available to the timetable planners. Wartime conditions meant that services had to be reduced, both to save personnel, fuel and wear and tear, and to make trains and paths available for the military.

The public uproar was such that the Railway Executive Committee relented, and on 2 October, a new timetable showing improved services was published, largely because of the considerable volume of the LNER's commuter network. On this occasion, better allowances were made for peak-period travel. Off-peak, most main line services lost their usual trains with the service halved, often running to extended timings as trains called at more stations. Off-peak suburban services were hourly. On some lines services were curtailed late in the evening, but others had special late services after midnight for the benefit of shift workers. Nevertheless, the new national maximum speed limit was increased to 60mph during October. Even so, there were fewer trains and these were all slower than those for the same period of the previous year, while amenities such as restaurant cars were missing, and there were just three sleeping car trains.

The 'Flying Scotsman' was replaced by a 10am to Edinburgh that did not reach its destination until 7.30pm, adding three hours to the pre-war schedule. Performance was not helped by lengthy refreshment stops, such as 15 minutes at Grantham and 18 minutes at Peterborough, needed to compensate for the lack of catering facilities on the trains. This was a backward step, to the early days of railway travel, before dining cars appeared.

The cuts at King's Cross were as nothing to those at Marylebone, with just two Manchester trains a day and these taking 6 hours 40 minutes for the journey, and no fast trains out of the station between 10am and 5pm. No doubt, the services from Manchester were seen as expendable, except for traffic to and from intermediate stations, as the city was also served by the LMS from Euston. Throughout the railway system, scheduling was not helped by the 60mph speed restriction.

Catering arrangements were reduced. Pullman and buffet cars were withdrawn and restaurant car service ceased on most routes. These cutbacks must have once again aroused some public reaction and been regarded as too severe, for on 1 January 1940, Pullman cars reappeared as did pantry cars and more buffet cars. There was considerable debate over whether sleeping car services could continue, but a number did, although for the ordinary traveller, the reprieve was short-lived.

Less obvious to the traveller, but another absence from the railways during the Second World War, was the travelling post office trains, withdrawn to free the lines for other more essential traffic and also release manpower for the war effort.

On the London & North Eastern, the Edinburgh service saw the number of trains cut from 15 to just eight, while the journey times for the 393 miles extended from a pre-war best of 360 minutes and an average of 466 minutes, to 608 minutes. The Norwich service was cut from 18 trains daily to 12, and the 115 miles were covered in 206 minutes compared with a pre-war best of 130 minutes and an average of 170 minutes.

Despite the looming shortage of everything, including paper, yet another new timetable was issued on 4 December, with more trains and with the return of a number of restaurant cars and buffets cars, the refreshment stops were also much reduced.

Like the railways, some large companies had dispersed, especially those with strategic importance such as the shipping lines, but it was not possible for everyone to do so, for apart from business considerations, the number of suitable venues outside London and other major cities was limited. The many smaller businesses and professional practice remained in London.

The LNER probably suffered the most from the demands of the British Army for railway locomotives, despite its own limited resources. The Ministry of Supply moved quickly to requisition the company's ex-Great Central 2-8-0 locomotives, which were seen as ideal for heavy goods and troop train operation, and these went to France with the British Expeditionary Force in 1939. Needless to say, the locomotives in France were lost in the German push through the Low Countries and into France, which was doubly unfortunate as the LNER bore the brunt of the so-called 'convoy coal trains' which started in February 1940, initially to restock coal supplies after the severe disruption of December 1939 and January 1940, but then also to compensate for the loss of shipping services along the East Coast.

The Harwich–Hook of Holland ferry *Vienna* on wartime service. (*LNER*)

Meanwhile, carriages were converted for use as ambulance trains for the military and others adapted for the evacuation of civilian casualties in anticipation of widespread disruption by heavy bombing, although the latter were never needed. Locomotives were also modified, with a number fitted with condensing gear and pipes for obtaining water from streams, anticipating widespread disruption to water supplies following bombing. The major stations and depots formed their own volunteer fire fighting forces, while there were also fire fighting trains, able to rush to wherever they might be needed, not only because of the greater speed of the railway than road transport, but also because many fires might be more easily accessible from the railway than from the road.

The spread of rationing, introduced in early 1940, and the difficulty that many had in shopping with so many women working, and many of them working very long hours, led to a growth in the number of staff canteens on the LNER. Rolling stock was also modified and equipped as mobile canteen trains, able to be sent to wherever such facilities were needed, either because the station canteen had been bombed or because large numbers were involved in dealing with the after effects of an 'incident'. The LNER's magazine announced early in 1940 that canteens and rest rooms had been provided for troops travelling by train at 25 stations including King's Cross, Liverpool Street, Sheffield, Doncaster, York, Edinburgh Waverley and Glasgow Queen Street.

Although many railway jobs were classified as reserved occupations, the LNER saw a growing number of its personnel leaving to join the armed forces for the duration of the war. Their work on the railway and in the workshops was taken over by women, who even undertook some of the heavier jobs, including those of porters. At first, the new recruits did not have uniforms, but this was quickly remedied. Uniforms were important on a railway not only because much of the work was dirty, but also for security and so that passengers knew who to turn to for advice and help.

Despite the cut in the number of trains, passenger traffic was 3 per cent higher in December 1939 than for the previous December. As industry got into its stride and was placed on a war footing, general goods traffic rose by 51 per cent while that for coal was up by 41 per cent.

Goods train mileage increased by 18 per cent. In the docks, traffic was up by 31 per cent. All of this happened on a railway which had already lost many skilled personnel for service with the armed forces, as well as losing almost forty locomotives which had been requisitioned and sent overseas. Employees were given the first of a series of wartime advances on their pay in recognition that the cost of living was increasing.

The New Year started badly, with many trains cancelled in what the company magazine proclaimed as the 'Worst Winter Ever', as heavy falls of snow blocked lines and trapped trains.

The first winter of war became what was known as the 'Phoney War' and as spring approached the railway companies started to promote their services for holidaymakers. The bright posters extolling the virtues of the many resorts on the LNER, and on other railways, were soon to be replaced by stern messages from the Ministry of War Transport, demanding to know 'Is your journey really necessary?' The Railway Executive Committee did its bit to discourage travel, raising fares in May 1940 by ten per cent, both to discourage travel and to cover the mounting costs of the railways.

There was to be a constant conflict between the authorities and the public at Christmas and the New Year, and in the summer months during the war years. A war-weary and bomb-battered population would do all it could to get away for a summer holiday, while the authorities made it as difficult for them as possible. At Christmas, people working away from home were anxious to get back for a day or two. To try to help, the armed forces eventually refused to issue forces leave passes at peak periods, which was harsh if the individuals concerned were about to be posted abroad, as so many were, as even before the invasion of Europe, Allied forces waged a long-running campaign against the Axis in North Africa.

Dunkirk

In 1940, the Whitsun holiday was cancelled by the government since the Germans were sweeping through the Low Countries and into France. This ultimately led to the evacuation of the British Expeditionary Force from Dunkirk, along with many French troops and some from Belgium as well.

While the Great Western and the Southern railways provided most of the railway steamers used in the Dunkirk evacuation, several LNER ships were also present as they had been commandeered by the government on the outbreak of war.

Ashore in England, all four railway companies were already hard at work handling special trains, many of them sending trains south, to get the soldiers away from the Channel ports. At 5pm on 26 May, the code-word 'Dynamo' was sent to the railways, warning them that the evacuation was due to start. The railway companies provided a pool of 186 trains, of which the LNER share was 47. A problem arose with finding sufficient locomotives capable of running over Southern metals, with the LNER sending its trains from King's Cross to Blackfriars.

At the outset, the railways did not know how many journeys would need to be made by these trains and just where the troops would land. While the entire operation ran from 27 May to 4 June, the busiest days were 1 and 4 June, when the entire operation was achieved by having holding points for empty trains at Faversham, Margate, Queenborough and Ramsgate. Possibly the railways managed so well because they were used to the demand for special trains caused by major sporting events.

Added to the difficulties of organising the railway end of the Dunkirk evacuation was the sudden realisation on the part of the authorities that a second evacuation was needed of the many children moved from London to the south coast, but who were now too close for comfort to German airfields. Neither the railways nor the military knew how many men to expect from Dunkirk, and in the end, more than 338,000 were carried. This of necessity meant massive disruption to ordinary services with even the slimmed-down wartime timetable suspended in many cases. The trains with the troops from Dunkirk joined the LNER at King's Cross.

Large companies encouraged their employees to contribute towards 'Spitfire Funds' to meet the £6,000 or so cost of a fighter for the RAF. This is one of the LNER's aeroplanes (a Mark Vb, BM202) of No. 222 Squadron, with a plaque carrying the name *Flying Scotsman*. What could be more suitable? (*IWM TR21*)

While in many ways, the whole exercise has since been seen as a masterpiece of organisation and improvisation, it took place in an atmosphere of chaos. No-one knew how many troops would arrive or when, and certainly they had no idea of how many were fit and how many were wounded, and still less, of where to send them when they did arrive. The chaos was such that trains were turned round at Dover and departed before the authorities had any idea where they could send the rescued troops. At least the LNER drivers were spared the instruction: 'Stop at Guildford and ask where you are going to.' This didn't apply to the LNER as trains ran through from Blackfriars to emerge at King's Cross.

Volunteers tried to ensure that the arriving troops were given tea and something to eat, as well as a card so that they could write home to let their families know that they were safe. A collection at one station to provide food and drink for the troops, organised by the stationmaster's wife, raised more than £1,000 from passengers and from people who had been drawn to the station by the continuous flood of the heavily laden troop trains. Inevitably, everything was under unforeseen pressure. One example was that at some stations used as refreshment stops, there weren't enough cups: tins had to be used as improvised cups, and just before a train left from a refreshment stop, the order was given for these to be thrown out so that the volunteers could collect them up and wash them ready for the next train.

Restrictions

Throughout the war years there was an almost constant trimming of services to reduce fuel consumption and eliminate under-used train miles. The trains themselves were lengthened, with a call at a station often requiring two stops as passengers alighted from the front portion of the train, which then had to be moved forward to allow those in the rear part to alight or for others to board. Although the LNER had been used in peacetime to running trains of 15 or

16 carriages, under wartime pressures this rose to 20 or more. These very long trains had the disadvantage that time had to be spent dividing the train on arrival, so that its carriages could be put into two platforms, and then the opposite procedure would happen after it had departed, with the front half being drawn clear of the station and then reversed onto the back half.

Often, journeys were delayed by the need for heavy trains to be given banking assistance, usually requiring a stop while the banker was coupled and then later uncoupled.

Services to the East Anglian ports were cut back as with the Low Countries occupied, there were no ferry services across the North Sea. The location of many RAF bases in East Anglia brought additional traffic, both for leave specials and also to support operations at the airfields. It has been estimated that one of the RAF's famous thousand-bomber air raids against Germany required 28 trains to carry aviation fuel and another eight for the bombs. Fortunately for the controllers, this effort was dispersed amongst many airfields.

The bad winter weather of January 1940 had resulted in a severe shortage of coal at the power stations and factories, as well as for the railways themselves, and for the ordinary householder. This was still a coal-fired society and one that is hard to conceive of today, for those who are not old enough to have experienced it. The difficulties in getting coal to the users were compounded by the fact that coastal shipping was regarded as impossible due to German submarine activity. Later, after the fall of Denmark and the Low Countries, it would be seen that German aerial activity, with bases all the way from the North Cape to just north of Bordeaux, would be the main threat to the colliers that had plied their way down the North Sea coast from the coalfields of Fife, Northumberland, Durham and Yorkshire, to ports in East Anglia and Kent, and to London itself.

February 1940 saw the Mines Department ask the Railway Executive Committee to provide 'convoy coal trains' to replace the convoys and replenish stocks of coal in the South. These were trains each of 50 wagons carrying some 600 tons of coal in all, and once started these continued, so that including an initial 140 trains to replenish the sadly depleted stocks of coal in the South, a total of 7,757 such trains were run in 1940 alone.

Fuel supplies, especially for the Royal Air Force, were another priority. Again, with the North Sea effectively closed to British merchant shipping, the fuel trains had to be run from ports in the West to the East, and this took six oil trains a week fully loaded, and once empty, four trains in the opposite direction. This cross-country operation, difficult enough in itself, had to take place by day and the trains carrying highly flammable fuel had to avoid a 'blanket' area, which was a belt 30 miles deep from the coast, stretching from Plymouth to Newcastle.

After the Blitz, the railways found themselves helping in the preparations for the British response, the bombing campaign against Germany. This required the construction of a substantial number of airfields, mainly in East Anglia, while new fighter airfields were to be built in Kent and Sussex. The new airfields were deliberately sited as close as possible to railway lines, usually near small country stations with sidings. This could mean that the building materials for the airfields, including many hundreds of tons of rubble, could inflate the station's normal goods tonnage by more than ten times. The rubble had to be shipped from all over the country, and naturally enough, much of it came from areas that had suffered badly in the Blitz.

From November 1942, six trains a day had to be routed into East Anglia, carrying on average 440 tons of rubble each, and the following year the number was stepped up to nine trains a day. In addition to the rubble trains, there were another two each day with bricks and a further ten trains a day with other building materials, including tarmac. As with the fuel trains, many of these trains were routed along cross-country routes using lines not usually heavily worked.

At first, the instruction was given to all railways that on an air raid warning being given, passenger trains were to stop and passengers allowed to alight and seek shelter if they wished, after which the train would continue at a maximum speed of just 15mph. As the full impact of the Blitz took effect and air raids became so frequent, this slowed traffic down to an unacceptable extent, and the instruction was revised from early November 1940 with trains allowed to proceed at 25mph. The danger of a derailment of a train running onto bomb-damaged track at high speed during an air raid was obvious, but away from the most heavily blitzed towns, many drivers took a chance and often ignored the speed limit, guessing that the risk of bomb damage was relatively light.

In addition to trimming services, as the war progressed, other restrictions were applied. On 6 October 1941, under the directions of the Minister of War Transport, all London suburban trains became third-class only. This was the definition applied to any train starting and ending its journey within the London Passenger Transport Board's area. The reasons for the move were practical, the idea being not only to make the best use of all accommodation on the reduced number of trains, but also to recognise the difficulty in finding the right class of accommodation in a hurry during the blackout.

To drive the point home, carpets were removed from first-class compartments and the first-class indications on the compartment doors painted out, while timetables and departure indicators described trains as 'Third Class Only'. After the withdrawal of first-class accommodation, blackout or not, regular travellers seemed to be able to find their way to the most comfortable part of the train and gravitated towards the superior legroom and elbow room, and plusher upholstery, of the former first-class compartments, so that these soon became shabby with intensive use.

There was constant debate over whether sleeping cars should or should not be withdrawn. Many felt that passengers needed this facility, which was once again restricted to first class only, but others argued that extra day carriages provided better use of the limited number of trains being run. This was a major problem for the LMS and the LNER with their long-distance Anglo-Scottish services, but from December 1942, these ceased to be available for civilian passengers, but a skeleton service was maintained for those travelling on government business.

While main line trains retained first-class accommodation, after a period of reduced catering facilities with only a limited number of trains allowed to offer this facility, on 22 May 1942, all catering facilities were withdrawn from trains on the LNER. It then became important to discourage unnecessary travel. The lack of sporting events and the fact that the coastal resorts had their beaches wrapped in barbed wire, meant that the normal leisure pursuits were not available. Again, on the instructions of the Minister of War Transport, on 5 October 1942, off-peak cheap returns were scrapped, leaving seasons as the only 'cheap', or discounted, tickets. This gives little idea of the impact of the service on the traveller, since the 'reduced' wartime service included a substantial number of troop trains.

In an attempt to economise, heating was another area in which fuel could be saved, so the pre-war system of switching on full heat on main line trains between October and April when the temperature fell below 48 °F at any one of a number of monitoring points, and half-heat when the temperature fell below 55 °F, had been reduced to having full heat when the temperature fell below 45 °F and half-heat when it fell below 50 °F between November and March.

Shortages of skilled staff in the workshops and the conversion of many of these to war production, as well as shortages of materials, meant that the intervals between routine overhauls were extended. Economy measures resulted in locomotives being painted plain black without any lining-out on being sent for overhaul or repair. The colour of the locomotives soon became immaterial as standards of cleanliness dropped.

Another aspect of railway operation in which standards dropped, aided by poor lighting and encouraged by wartime shortages of everything, was honesty. There was much concern about the rising level of what was described as 'pilferage' on all of the railways.

Nevertheless, some wartime pressures had to be accommodated by investment in improved facilities. With the Port of London crippled by enemy bombing and by the unacceptable risks from attack for shipping in the Straits of Dover and the Thames Estuary, other ports became more important.

The East Coast Main Line also needed attention, especially as this was the route taken by so many of the coal trains carrying traffic displaced from the coasting trade. While the double-tracked line between York and Northallerton had been improved during the 1930s with some stretches of quadruple and triple tracks, and the installation of colour light signalling, a number of bottlenecks remained, including those as Skelton Bridge, Raskelf, Sessay and Thirsk. York was also a bottleneck itself, especially since a major re-signalling programme had been abandoned in 1940 because of the other demands of wartime.

It was also the case that the York re-signalling would have put a lot of authority in a single, vulnerable, control centre. Nevertheless, without the re-signalling, York also featured massive sidings on both sides of the line to accommodate goods trains waiting for a route. Again, main line widening was carried out, initially quadrupling the line between Pilmoor and Thirsk, while there were also further lines built, although in some cases elsewhere in one direction only.

Traffic patterns changed. As the ore fields in Great Britain had to be redeveloped to replace imported ore, a pool of some 9,000 hopper wagons had to be organised early in the war, using 6,000 privately owned and 3,000 railway-owned wagons, later augmented by the temporary transfer of 1,600 hopper wagons from the LNER. Hopper wagons, whatever their source, were only suitable for specialised traffic, being loaded by special machinery and unloaded by opening the hopper doors. This traffic was so important that the British Iron & Steel Federation ordered 1,000 new wagons and the Ministry of War Transport ordered the construction of another 2,500.

From December 1941, anxious to ensure that large numbers of standard locomotives be built, the Ministry of War Transport had decreed that all locomotive production would be of the LMS Stanier 2-8-0 design, of which the LNER built 53 at Darlington and 50 at Doncaster. Nevertheless, these were far from the only steam locomotives built in wartime.

The LNER's obsession with speed and its prestige expresses had meant that it was short of the good mixed-traffic and heavy freight locomotives that were to be so necessary in wartime. This situation was made worse by the requisitioning of many of its useful 2-8-0 ex-Great Central locomotives by the War Office. The V2 series of 2-6-2 locomotives had been very successful and useful, but their axle loadings confined them to the main lines. There were many elderly 4-4-0s, 4-4-2s and 4-6-0s that also needed to be replaced, especially since they dated from the pre-Grouping companies and some standardisation would be an advantage. The answer was the V4 2-6-2, an attractive and sophisticated engine that embodied all of Sir Nigel Gresley's experience. Two prototype locomotives were built, but these were not the simple, rugged, locomotives that wartime austerity required.

They were not wasted, but they became yet another of the many classes of goods locomotives infesting the LNER. Some LNER men believed that, had it not been for Gresley's sudden death, that the V4 could have become the standard locomotive as subsequent experience proved it to be reliable and efficient. Meanwhile, Gresley's protégé Oliver Bulleid had left in 1937 to become chief mechanical engineer at the Southern Railway. This was to misunderstand the thinking of those with responsibility for procurement in wartime, when proven reliability was needed rather than new and untested designs, no matter how brilliant.

The choice of design was influenced by War Office requirements for locomotives capable of handling heavy goods trains with passenger trains receiving a much lower priority. On the other hand, given the extended length of wartime longer distance passenger trains, sometimes a freight locomotive was the best option even for them. The Ministry of War Transport was also reacting to the War Office's need for locomotives to be sent overseas, and at this stage of the war the North African campaign was in full swing.

Like all of the grouped railway companies, the LNER was a major manufacturer in its own right. In fact, the London Passenger Transport Board was the exception amongst railway operators, buying its rolling stock from manufacturers such as Metro-Cammell. The 'Big Four' were not above buying from outside, but they also maintained a steady flow of work through their own workshops. Although not actually intended for the 'Big Four' companies, the North British Locomotive Company produced its WD 2-8-0 design for use by the British Army abroad. Many of these were run on Britain's railways before the invasion of Normandy, doubtless to iron out any problems before sending them abroad, as well as helping them through their own locomotive shortages. The LNER had most of these, doubtless to compensate for the loss of so many of its own locomotives, with 350, while the LMS and the Southern had 50 apiece. Post-war, many of these were brought home and put to work on the railways where some regarded them as the best heavy freight locomotive available.

The S160 class American locomotives, also 2-8-0s, arrived in 1943, and after modification by the Great Western, were put into service on a 'pooled' basis, from which at the end of the year, saw them distributed with the Great Western having 174, followed by the LNER with 168, the LMS with 50 and the Southern with six.

Throughout the war years, routine maintenance at the locomotive sheds was less thorough than it had been in peacetime, while wartime loads were much heavier, and the quality of coal provided could never be guaranteed. Such strenuous operating conditions soon began to expose inherent weaknesses and strengths in the different locomotive classes. The cracking of locomotive frames became a problem, and not just with the older locomotives. During the war years, at least four special trains were prepared, two of which were later transferred to Europe after the Normandy invasion. One of these was code-named 'Rapier' for the then General Bernard Montgomery, and was prepared by the LNER at Doncaster using mainly ex-LNER rolling stock, including a first-class sleeper, which was fitted with the amenity of a bath!

Many companies launched 'Spitfire Funds' to encourage employees to raise the £6,000 or so cost of a new fighter for the RAF. One of the aircraft bought with money donated by LNER staff was named, of course, *Flying Scotsman*.

Wartime Accidents

Most of the incidents on the LNER during the war seem to have been cases that could have occurred in peacetime, although the fact that it was wartime did have an impact on the outcome. Typical of these was the accident on 11 February 1941, close to Beighton station, when a heavy steel plate was displaced on its wagon during shunting, protruding well over the side of the wagon and being hit by the side of a passing troop train, killing 14 soldiers and seriously injuring another 35.

On the evening of 4 February 1945, the 6pm service from King's Cross to Leeds consisted of 17 carriages behind 4-6-2 A4 locomotive No. 2512 *Silver Fox*. It was the practice for heavy trains leaving King's Cross to be boosted by the shunting locomotive that had hauled the carriages into the station, as the train departed and immediately thereafter, as it passed into Gasworks Tunnel and the steep rising gradient before it could build up any speed. Departing five minutes late, the train was not assisted as the rake of carriages had been propelled into the platform and so there was no locomotive at the rear of the train to act as a banker. As it struggled to tackle the gradient in the tunnel, the locomotive came to a stand and then began to slide backwards, wheels spinning, but this was not noticed by the driver or fireman in the darkness.

All might have been well, but the points behind the train had already been set for the 7pm from King's Cross to Aberdeen, whose carriages were already at Platform 10. The rearmost carriage of the Leeds train struck the first carriage of the Aberdeen train and rose into the air, striking the overhead signal gantry which crashed down crushing one of the two first-class compartments in the middle of the composite brake, killing two passengers, one of whom was Cecil Kimber, who had been managing director of MG, the manufacturer that had brought sports cars within reach of the ordinary motorist between the wars. While the carriage was new, having been built in 1941, it had a timber body which shattered.

The signal gantry carried signals, shunting discs and platform indicators. Once the wreckage was cleared, main line trains using Platforms 6 to 17 could be controlled by hand signals, but suburban trains had to terminate at Finsbury Park and it took two weeks to replace the signal gantry, with normal services not resumed until 23 February.

The accident could have been avoided had lights been placed in the tunnel so that the footplatemen could see their speed by reference to the lights. This solution had been applied to the line rising from the City Widened Lines after a similar run-back accident many years earlier.

Chapter 20

Under Attack

The LNER was more than any other largely a freight railway, which may well have been one reason for its inter-war poverty. One the one hand there were its crack Anglo-Scottish expresses and its heavy commuter traffic, especially into Liverpool Street, and its boat trains for passengers to the Netherlands, and even its string of seaside resorts in East Anglia, Lincolnshire and Yorkshire, promoted as being the 'drier side of Britain'. On the other, its health and wealth was determined by the coal mines of Yorkshire, Durham, Northumberland and the east of Scotland, by the agricultural traffic of East Anglia, fish from East Anglia and Humberside, and by the manufacturing industries of eastern England and the east of Scotland. In wartime, it was soon to be discovered that, after the fall of Denmark and Norway, and then the Low Countries, the East Coast would be untenable for coastal shipping and the bulk of this traffic was to be transferred to the railways.

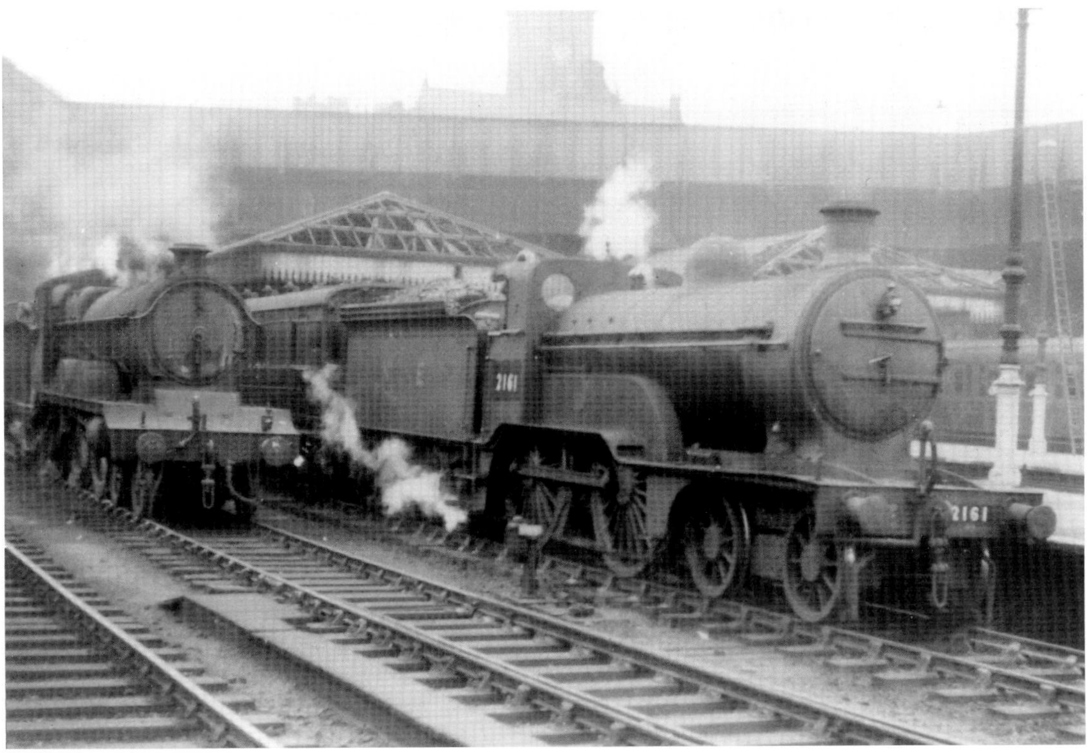

This post-war view of D2 class No. 2161 on a passenger train at Nottingham Victoria suggests the 4-4-0 has recently been renumbered as the numerals stand out from the drab locomotive cabside and bufferbeam. The tender is lettered 'NE', and the station canopy has been damaged by bombing. (*HMRS AAH 803*)

Having had experience of German bombing of London and East Coast towns during the First World War, when one of its predecessor companies, the Great Eastern, had been targeted twice by German bombing at Liverpool Street, the LNER expected to suffer greatly. The first of the earlier bombing raids had caused considerable disruption to services for a brief period, and the second saw serious damage to an express waiting to depart for Hunstanton. Oddly, the other predecessor companies, the Great Northern at King's Cross and the Great Central at Marylebone, were left untouched during the First World War. In 1940–41 the LNER suffered greatly in the London area, but escaped relatively lightly elsewhere, despite its closer proximity to German airbases, though both Sheffield and Hull suffered from heavy bombing.

Given its lack of standardised freight and mixed-traffic locomotives, the one really suitable class that was available was the V2 class 2-6-2. The company did benefit considerably when private owners' wagons were requisitioned, although compensation for this had to come from the LNER's share of the miserly funds made available by a parsimonious Treasury.

Rebuilding was a way of making new locomotives out of old, and this K5, No. 1863, was rebuilt from a K3. Seen here in 1946, the 2-6-0 looks in good condition but still carries the simplified wartime lettering on the tender. (*HMRS AAM 301*)

Bravery on the Line

The air war did not take long to reach the LNER, and Liverpool Street was an early casualty, being badly damaged by bombing soon after the start of the Blitz in September 1940. Later in the war, the station and the carriage works at York were badly damaged by a Baedeker raid.

The raid in September 1940 resulted in several bombs falling on the station, exploding on Platforms 1 and 4, with the former wrecking a train completely, so that it took several days to clear. Platform 18 was also damaged at the concourse end and the booking office also suffered. Perhaps the worst damage was inflicted by an unexploded bomb that landed in the locomotive sidings near Platform 10, and which was surrounded by four wagons full of ballast to absorb any blast should it explode, but when it did explode the morning after, it killed two men. At Broad Street, the terminus next door, a bomb exploded and threw an LMS goods wagon onto the roof at Liverpool Street, where it could only be removed by dismantling. Before the Blitz ended, in May 1940, the offices at Liverpool Street also suffered severe damage.

King's Cross, which had led such a charmed life during the First World War, was far less fortunate during the Second World War. It handled some very long trains with 20 or more carriages commonplace, so that many carriages of necessity stood outside the station. Such trains could often have as many as 2,000 passengers, often with corridors crowded with people standing.

Early on 11 May 1941, towards the end of the Blitz, two 1,000lb bombs, chained together, dropped onto the west side of the station, exploding and demolishing much of the general offices, the grill room and bar, and completely wrecking the booking office. Much of the roof was blown out, although, as elsewhere, fortunately the glass had been removed. Had this happened at a busy time, rather than during the small hours of a Sunday morning, the casualties would have been terrible, but even so twelve men were killed. It was in the nature of wartime railwaymen to overcome such difficulties, and temporary booking and refreshment facilities were soon organised, and no trains were cancelled.

On the other hand, because of damage on the Metropolitan Line, through services from King's Cross to the Metropolitan Line, to reach Moorgate in the heart of the City of London, were suspended from 30 December 1940, and not reinstated until almost a year after the end of the war in Europe had ended. At King's Cross, accident rather than enemy action was to be the major cause of disruption, as we saw in the previous chapter.

Not only major stations were bombed, and this is Partick Central from the footbridge, showing bomb damage in 1943. (*HMRS AAM 311*)

The other LNER terminus in London was Marylebone, the last to be built in the Capital, for the Great Central Railway. Today, after many years as an outer suburban station, it has services reaching as far as Birmingham and Wrexham, but in LNER days it handled a reasonable volume of longer-distance traffic with trains travelling as far as Manchester. The station itself led a charmed life during the Second World War with no direct hits and the few incendiaries that dropped nearby were easily disposed of. Nevertheless, the station was forced to close by enemy action from 5 October to 26 November 1940, the longest closure of a London terminus, when Carlton Hill Tunnel was penetrated by high explosive bombs, and in clearing the debris the tunnel was left as an open cutting with single line working until August 1942. Later, the old Great Central goods depot in London was razed to the ground on 16 April 1941. Towards the end of the war, a flying bomb hit the signalbox at Marylebone, killing two men.

At the height of the Blitz the line south of Blackfriars was disrupted by the bombing of Southwark Bridge and a new connection had to be built running from the LNER at Harringay to Gospel Oak on the LMS, and then on to the Great Western at Acton and then to the Southern Railway by way of Kew Bridge or the West London Extension. The work was regarded as being sufficiently important that it was completed during 1940, just in time for the heavy air raids.

In peacetime, much of the traffic from the Midlands and the North had been routed via Banbury, which handled traffic both from the LNER coming south from Manchester and Sheffield, and from the GWR. Nevertheless, Banbury was not well equipped to handle a massive growth in traffic, especially if lines across London were disrupted. Reading was little better, with the line from Banbury having to cross the busy Great Western main line to reach the Southern Railway.

The solution was to build what amounted to a railway by-pass of London. Of necessity this was some distance from the Capital, both to avoid disruption from heavy air raids and also to utilise existing lines as far as possible. The start of this massive loop was the old London & North Western Line from Cambridge to Oxford, which crossed the LNER from King's Cross at Sandy, the LMS lines from St Pancras at Bedford, the LMS lines from Euston at Bletchley, the LNER lines from Marylebone at Calvert, and the Great Western route from Paddington to Birmingham at Bicester. There were good existing connections in and out of this line at Bedford and Bletchley, but at Sandy and at Oxford, time-consuming shunting movements would be necessary, so here again new connections were hastily installed and opened during 1940. There was no link at all at Calvert, so a completely new connection was created.

The LNER Silver Medal

In the autumn of 1943, the 8.45pm express from Liverpool Street to Harwich was steaming slowly between Shenfield and Ingatestone because of an air raid alert. The driver and firemen noticed a bomb explode in the distance, and this was followed shortly afterwards by a bomb exploding in front of the locomotive. Despite steaming at 25mph or so, there was not time to stop and the locomotive plunged into the crater, with the tender riding up over the footplate killing both men. The carriages of the train, which were full, as this was a popular service for servicemen based at Harwich, were scattered, with some of them tumbling down the embankment, but only one passenger and the forward guard were injured. Restoration of services at this point proved difficult, as a high embankment had to be restored, and that was only after the locomotive and tender had been be retrieved. This was one point on the network where a diversionary route did not exist, so buses had to be used to provide an emergency service between Shenfield and Ingatestone.

It was against this background of railwaymen being exposed to enemy action that as early as 28 November 1940, the LNER board instituted a silver medal for members of the company's staff for acts of bravery in the war, with a design by Gilbert Bayes, bearing the LNER crest on one side and on the reverse, the words 'For Courage and Resource'. During the war years, no fewer than 22 members of the company's staff were to receive this award. Perhaps one of the most notable was for the outstanding bravery that saved the town of Soham, in Cambridgeshire, on 2 June 1944.

Driver Benjamin Gimbert and Fireman James Nightall were handling the 11.40pm goods from Whitemoor to Goodmayes yard, which was diverted to the Colne Valley line to run across country to Ely. The train consisted of 51 wagons of bombs, including one with 40 500lb bombs next to the locomotive, a WD 'Austerity' 2-8-0, No. 77337. Passing the Soham distant signal at around 15–20mph, the driver saw that the first wagon behind the locomotive was on fire. He sounded the whistle to alert the guard, and then stopped the train at the station end of the goods yard. The fireman alighted and uncoupled the first wagon from the rest of the train, and then rejoined the driver as they took the engine forward. The driver intended to get the wagon clear of any buildings and uncouple it before continuing to the next station. As he passed the signalbox at Soham, he called out to ensure that there were no other trains on the line ahead, but almost immediately the wagon exploded, leaving a crater 66ft in diameter and 15ft deep, and damaging 700 houses in Soham as well as demolishing the signalbox and the stationmaster's house. Fireman Nightall was killed and Driver Gimbert seriously wounded. In addition to the LNER medal, both men received the George Cross, although naturally for poor Nightall, both awards were posthumous.

The LNER felt that many of its employees deserved a medal for acts of gallantry not connected with enemy action, but of such a standard that would have warranted government recognition had enemy action been involved. It was a silver medal known formally as the London & North Eastern Railway Medal, with a ribbon of royal blue with three narrow vertical strips in the middle. (*LNER*)

Wagon fires were an accepted hazard of goods train operation for most of railway history, with hot axle boxes being the main cause, and with so much wood in the structure of the goods wagons of the day, a fire could spread very quickly. Given their highly dangerous load, the two men showed outstanding courage, and had they not taken the wagon away from the rest of the train, the explosion would have set the rest of the bombs off and Soham would have been flattened.

Not all of the acts of heroism received the attention they should have done in the company magazine, no doubt due to wartime censorship, and there seems to have been no attempt to provide this information following the end of hostilities.

York no doubt qualified for attack during the so-called Baedeker Raids of 1942 because of the city's historic importance and beauty, but it was also an important railway junction and railway works as well. Early in the morning of 29 April 1942, the full force of an air raid hit York just as the 10pm King's Cross to Edinburgh express arrived. The passengers were advised to leave the train and seek shelter, but many were slow in doing so as they took time to collect their belongings first. A combination of high explosive and incendiary bombs struck the station and its buildings, with a number of incendiaries falling onto the carriages of the Edinburgh express, setting them alight. While many railwaymen set to tackling the burning carriages, others started to separate them from the rest of the train, and managed to save 14 of the 20 vehicles of a typically lengthy wartime express. The remaining carriages, and several other trains in this busy station, were burnt out.

During this incident, a signalman who had already had his signal box put out of action by the bombs, went into the station to help salvage whatever rolling stock he could, and with the help of the crew of a locomotive, managed to save some twenty carriages and goods vans. Others salvaged ticket racks and furniture from the station buildings as well as money from the tills, taking these items to the safety of the Royal Station Hotel. Their action meant that within a few hours of the raid ending, a temporary ticket office was back in service.

The LNER in York still had a substantial number of horses for its collection and delivery services, but all of these were saved from their stable in Leeman Road by two railwaymen and a policeman after incendiary bombs set the building on fire. Less fortunate, the roundhouse engine shed was hit by a high explosive bomb, destroying three of the twenty locomotives inside, including the A4 streamlined Pacific No. 4469 *Sir Ralph Wedgwood*.

Despite the severity of the raid, by the evening of the same day, most of the running lines through York were operational again, and all lines were available by the evening of the following day.

The crew of another LNER express fared rather better. In 1943, the mixed-traffic 2-6-2 V2 locomotive No. 4771 *Green Arrow* was heading a lengthy East Coast express towards Potters Bar, again at the cautionary 25mph judged safe in an air raid as it passed through the tunnel. The driver and firemen saw the tunnel exit ahead silhouetted in the glare of a shower of incendiary bombs, which were normally dropped in large numbers. The driver managed to stop the train with the locomotive just inside the tunnel, before the driver and the firemen jumped down and began to extinguish the incendiaries on the track, some of which had already set fire to the sleepers. This all happened while the air raid continued, but their prompt action saved both the track from further serious damage and also saved the carriages of the train from catching fire. They then walked forward to check that the track was safe, after which the fireman telephoned the next signalbox to explain what had happened. Afterwards, they returned to the locomotive and set off again, steaming very slowly. All in all, this gallant action had taken just half an hour!

The first V-2 rocket to strike the LNER was on 16 September 1944 at Palmers Green, where it damaged the track without affecting any trains, and the line itself was restored to service within 24 hours. The part of the LNER system most seriously affected by the V-2 raids was at Stratford, where track and marshalling yards as well as rolling stock and buildings were badly damaged.

Not all of the heroism resulted from enemy action, as when on 16 May 1945 an RAF Vickers Warwick bomber (a development of the more famous Wellington) crashed into a train on the down Aberdeen–Elgin main line near Dyce station, close to what is now Aberdeen Airport, but at the time was RAF Dyce. Junior porter Morven Taylor was first on the scene, realised that one of the aircraft's crew was trapped in the blazing wreckage, which itself was on top of an overturned goods van. Taylor clambered up on the blazing wreckage and managed to free and rescue the airman, whose boots had trapped his feet in the wreckage. Getting the rescued man to safety, Taylor then realised that a second airman was also trapped, and started a second rescue attempt. This time, some of the aircraft's ammunition began to explode, and the heat became too intense, forcing Taylor back on to the ground, and only just in time as a fuel tank then exploded. Morven Taylor's courage and quick thinking were all the more remarkable as he was just 16 years old!

Running a railway sometimes requires acts of heroism and quick-thinking even in peacetime, and as we will see later, the medal continued to be awarded in such cases, even with the return of peace.

Chapter 21

Peace and Nationalisation

The return of peace was not unexpected as it had been clear even before the Normandy landings almost a year earlier, that the end of the war in Europe was only a matter of time. Britain's railways had all been planning for their post-war reconstruction and development, and indeed, thinking beyond just the railway as they also had the 'Rail Air Plan' that would see them take the lead in developing European air services with a network within the UK and Europe that would produce 20 million miles of flying annually!

Yet, there was little easing of the stress under which the railways were operating. Air raids had ended, and after the blackout of the war years had been replaced towards the end of the war in Europe by what was widely known as a 'dim out', lighting was back to pre-war standards. Employees serving with the armed forces were still away and at first it seemed that they would be likely to remain away for some time as the Allies prepared for the invasion of Japan.

York in 1946, with troops standing on the platform as A3 4-6-2 No. 2504 *Sandwich*, soon to be renumbered as 39, pulls away. Most of this class were named after racehorses. (*HMRS AAL 811*)

Servicemen on the platform at York again, in 1946 as the station pilot, J71 class 0-6-0T No. 237, couples up to a parcels van. This locomotive would probably have been scrapped by then had it not been for the war, as withdrawals started in the 1930s. (*HMRS AAL 812*)

Rolling stock levels were far lower than before the war, and against 19,626 carriages in 1938, the LNER had just 16,935 in 1946. The stud of locomotives had actually risen from 6,533 in 1938 to 6,614 in 1946. Neither of these figures tells how badly worn and neglected the carriages and locomotives of 1946 really were, after six years of intensive use, damage from enemy action and neglect as normal overhauls were skimped, in part to the shortage of skilled labour and the demands on the system, but also because of the use made of the workshops for wartime production.

Just one of the three packet steamers used on the service between Parkeston Quay and the Hook of Holland was released back to the LNER, while two of the three on the service to Antwerp had been lost on war service.

Despite all of this, as soon as peace returned, the British public expected the railways to be able to meet their travel needs. Still operating on reduced timetables with many trains chartered by the armed services, the railways struggled to cope and the London termini were overwhelmed at weekends during the first summer of peace as people queued for the booking office and then for their trains.

The magazine carried an article calling for staggered holidays, pointing out that while people traditionally took their holidays in July or August, the latter was the wettest month of the year and the weather was much better in June and September, while trains were much less crowded. It urged staff to encourage passengers making enquiries to consider an earlier or later holiday, reminding them that parents were allowed to take their children out of school for up to two weeks each year, so that being tied to school holidays was not an excuse. Even in normal times with adequate rolling stock, the campaign made good sense, for one problem with all of the railway companies was that they had substantial quantities of passenger rolling stock used for just six weeks of the year.

Fuel was another problem. Demand for coal was greater than the pits could supply, and the immediate reaction was to start converting locomotives to oil-firing once more, but this was promptly abandoned when a shortage of foreign exchange meant that oil imports had to be restricted.

Peace might have returned, but the railways had another battle on their hands, over and above that of reconstruction or even the daily fight to keep the service going despite the arrears of rolling stock and infrastructure maintenance. The first post-war election, or at least post-European war as fighting continued in the Far East, had returned a Labour government with a large majority and committed to nationalisation of the railways, the canals, road transport and air transport, as well as many other major industries, such as coal mining, iron and steel production, gas and electricity supply.

A decidedly scruffy J3 class 0-6-0 heads a mixed train at Ramsey North in 1947. The wartime neglect of the railway and the heavy demands on cleaning in the steam age shows, as even the locomotive number cannot be seen. A lorry is on the platform, doubtless to load or unload goods from a van on the train. (*HMRS ABC 818*)

'Forward'

All of the 'Big Four' railways emerged from the war intent on fighting nationalisation and on developing their systems. The LNER had accumulated a 'Trust Fund' to meet arrears of maintenance, and in 1947 this stood at £40 million, roughly equivalent to £1,250 million today. It published an illustrated pamphlet outlining the work that the LNER intended to carry out over a period of five years, describing this in an article headed 'Forward' in the magazine as a 'five-year plan' to address arrears of maintenance that would cost £40 million, with another £50 million needed for modernisation, and even that did not cover the cost of widespread electrification.

One of the problems was that the Ministry of Supply still controlled the availability of necessary materials and in 1946 and 1947 none of the railway companies received even its standard peacetime allocation, let alone the extra quantity needed to make up for the arrears. Even so, in that year 579 track miles were either completely or partially replaced, with 300 stations and depots receiving a much-needed coat of fresh paint. New designs of signalboxes, station signs and booking offices had started to appear, while work had resumed on the electrification scheme between Liverpool Street and Shenfield. An ambitious programme to build a thousand new steam locomotives and 5,500 carriages, as well as 70,000 wagon and goods vans, had been started. New ships had been ordered for the services from Harwich and on the Clyde, with two launched and being fitted out. Hotels and refreshment rooms were being revamped. New staff training centres were under construction.

In fact, the opportunity to buy at a low price as many as 200 'Austerity' 2-8-0 goods locomotives and 75 saddle tanks from the Ministry of Supply made a substantial and immediate contribution towards the post-war locomotive strength, but we will never know whether these would have been substitutes for some of the locomotives in the plan, or much-needed additional locomotives, as the LNER had seldom approached its planned rate of construction between the wars.

While there were plans for every part of the network, specific projects outlined in the five-year plan included:

- Alterations to King's Cross, costing an estimated £1,595,000
- Widening at Potters Bar and Hadley Wood costing an estimated £1,023,000
- New station at Peterborough with associated works costing an estimated £1,828,000
- New station at Grimsby with associated works costing an estimated £1,300,000
- New locomotive depot, marshalling yard, etc, at York costing an estimated £3,120,000
- Improvements to stations and depots on Tyneside costing an estimated £1,347,000
- New marshalling yard, etc, at Thornton Junction costing an estimated £1,330,000
- New marshalling yard and other improvements at Edinburgh costing an estimated £3,267,000
- Modernisation of good depots at Ardwick and Sheffield costing an estimated £1,169,000
- New goods and locomotive depot, etc, at Stratford costing an estimated £1,959,000
- Reconstruction of station, etc, at Cambridge costing an estimated £1,290,000

The message was clear: railway management was pressing ahead as if the future was assured. LNER staff were told that: 'Whatever the future may hold as regards the control and management of British Railways, "Forward" must be the motto and the LNER programme forms a most realistic and valuable contribution to railway development in this country.'

More Silver Medals

More awards of the LNER Silver Medal followed the end of the Second World War, and the company clearly intended this to become a permanent feature.

One of these was to a driver, John Ingemells, a goods guard, Arthur Dodman, and a passed cleaner,* Geoffrey Jackson, for heroism on 1 October 1946. A goods train, which included wagons filled with explosives, caught fire between Bardney and Louth. The three men managed to isolate the burning wagon, and in the words of the citation, '...each carried out his part in endeavouring to isolate the burning wagon without regard to his own personal safety'. Both the guard and the passed cleaner were injured, although they recovered later.

Another award of the medal was made to Police Constable Arthur Stanley who was assaulted by three men in Rotherham Goods Yard during the night of 1 November 1946. The men were subsequently arrested and received prison sentences.

Nationalisation

The grouped companies all resisted nationalisation and lobbied hard for the plan to be dropped. They all showed good faith and a belief in the importance of the railways to the nation, and not to simply abandon work on reconstruction and modernisation in favour of distributing the maximum sums in their last years of existence to their shareholders, something not appreciated by many of the shareholders who had lived through the dividend famine of the 1920s and '30s.

To the dismay of some, the LNER attempted to reach a compromise with the government, under which the state would own the railway and the infrastructure but the LNER would manage its system on behalf of the state. This was a scheme put to the Board by the chief general manager

* Passed cleaner refers to the man in question having been passed to act as locomotive firemen, and this was why he was at the scene of the incident. He would have had to work a set number of turns as a fireman before being confirmed in his new grade.

The northern end of the tunnel at Potters Bar with a K5 2-6-0 emerging, running light, in 1947. (*HMRS ADM 604*)

Sir Charles Newton and adopted by them. Known as the 'Landlord and Tenant Scheme', it was dismissed out of hand by the then Minister of Transport, Alfred Barnes.

The plan was an interesting proposal and in some ways similar to the situation on the railways today, where the train operating companies are in effect franchisees, while the state owns the infrastructure through the nationalised Network Rail. Just how well it would have worked is open to question, since not having control over the infrastructure would have meant that the post-Nationalisation LNER would have had difficulty in achieving complete route modernisation with new trains, signalling and track, essential especially with electrification schemes. There was also another problem that would have become acute. For most of its existence, the LNER was over-capitalised, but had fought shy of attempting to remedy this as doing so could have been to the disadvantage of one or more classes of shareholder. Had it become simply a train operating company, the level of over-capitalisation would have become even more acute.

With Nationalisation imminent, when Sir Charles retired, the LNER's chief legal advisor, Miles Beevor, became acting chief general manager, the Board being unable to appoint a permanent replacement with the nationalisation measure going through Parliament.

It is clear that most of the company's employees were in favour of Nationalisation, a programme long advocated by the railway unions. This didn't mean that there was bitterness between the employees and the management. In the December 1947 edition of the *LNER Magazine*, the chairman of the 'Contributors' Committeemen, LNER Superannuation Fund, one J.T. Hinson, wrote:

'The end of 1947 closes an epoch in railway history. I do not think that I shall be the only supporter of nationalisation with some twinges of regret that the LNER must lose its identity in the larger unit of British Railways … When on January 1 the LNER will have been merged in a larger organisation, there will still be room for the genius and enthusiasm of LNE men and women of all grades.'

The magazine itself noted in an editorial that '…within a week or two of this issue of the *Magazine* the London and North Eastern Railway Company will have ceased to exist and its undertaking will have become merged in that of the British Transport Commission'.

That there must have been more than a hint of sadness was evident, and the shame of it was that the LNER, which had celebrated the silver jubilee of King George V in such fine style, was just a year short of celebrating its own silver jubilee in 1948.

Chapter 22

What Might Have Been

Working out just what kind of a railway the LNER would have been had Nationalisation not have happened, or perhaps been reversed by a Conservative government, is more difficult than for, say, the Southern Railway or the Great Western, or even the London Midland & Scottish.

In fact, there are two different 'what might have been' scenarios as we should not ignore Sir Vincent Raven's plans for electrification. His ideas originally centred on the NER's line between York and Newcastle, but had someone like Sir Herbert Walker been in charge of the LNER, he would have almost certainly seen any electrification as extending all the way from London to Edinburgh and possibly on to Glasgow and even Aberdeen. First, Walker would have electrified the suburban network, before embarking on main line electrification, and Southend would have been the next stage before looking to the core East Coast Main Line. Yes, the LNER was poor and did not have money to invest in grandiose schemes, but the savings from wholesale electrification could have changed the picture. The point was, of course, that Raven had retired and was a consultant, and even had he remained, he was an engineer not a general manager, so it would have taken different management to have forced through electrification.

As mentioned earlier, objections to electrification and to diesels was not simply railway conservatism. There was the pragmatic consideration that the infrastructure for steam already existed and represented a heavy investment that would have had to be written off as not all of it was old. There was also the fact that steam technology was still developing and was seen as the advanced technology of the day. At the time of Grouping, speeds of 70mph were not far short of those achieved by commercial air transport. By 1938, for a fair comparison with modern air transport, the relationship between 126mph and the airliners of the day would equate to the railways needing speeds of around 350mph or slightly more today. That shows plainly *Mallard*'s achievement and puts it into perspective.

Nevertheless, we are really interested in what the LNER would have done had Nationalisation not occurred, and the clues in *Forward: The LNER Development Plan* are all we have. There is limited electrification planned between Liverpool Street and Shenfield that would eventually have been extended to Southend, but overall, a commitment to the steam locomotive. This is no surprise, as the steam locomotive was advanced technology between the two world wars and as already mentioned, the railways had a massive infrastructure that existed simply to keep the steam locomotive running. It used home-produced fuel and did not need the costly wiring or third-rail associated with electrification.

The value of home-produced coal was soon underlined, even before Nationalisation, when the Ministry of Supply intervened to stop the railway companies converting steam locomotives from coal to oil-firing as a balance of payments crisis meant that there was insufficient foreign currency to pay for imported oil. It soon turned out to be the case that even after Nationalisation, the British Railways Board continued to build steam locomotives until 1960, so that when steam was finally retired in 1968, some locomotives were less than ten years old and elsewhere on the system, Victorian steam locomotives were still working hard.

No country switched from steam to diesel and electric traction as quickly as Britain, and many have criticised the waste involved. It seems likely that the LNER would have had to switch eventually, but the change would have been more gradual and economical. It is tempting to believe that the LNER could have failed, but at no time did it come close to being bankrupt and it maintained strong reserves. It usually managed an operating profit, but heavy overheads and over-capitalisation meant that this did not translate into worthwhile dividends for all of the shareholders. Given the strong demand for railway services post-war, it is likely that for a few years at least good profits might have been made, and these, with a reform of the common carrier obligation, might have meant that a fresh start could have been made and the bright hopes of Grouping finally realised more than a quarter of a century after it had taken place.

The reduction in costs and the enhanced revenues from the Shenfield electrification could have boosted those arguing for greater electrification and perhaps even convinced the pro-steam lobby that the days of the steam locomotive were numbered. Certainly, as speeds rose even further steam would have struggled and the need for diesel or electric traction would have come by default. The poor acceleration of steam trains would have been their final undoing.

It is certain that the high level of track maintenance for which the LNER was famed would have continued, and possibly the company's fondness for articulated passenger rolling stock. It seems clear that there would have been the need for a wholesale replacement programme for suburban rolling stock, with so much of it pre-Grouping. The problem was, of course, that the company had never achieved the level of locomotive and rolling stock replacement that was judged necessary on Grouping, and this had been made worse by the six years of neglect during the war. This was followed by several years in which the availability of raw materials and fuel was severely restricted so that none of the railway companies received even its normal peacetime requirements, let alone the extra needed to make up for wartime neglect and damage.

It seems unlikely that the LNER's proposal for a 'landlord and tenant' arrangement with the state would have changed matters much, or certainly not for the better. It would have complicated developments and also, as mentioned earlier, made the company even more over-capitalised than was the case between the wars.

Hard decisions would have had to have been made about branch lines and many stations. On the other hand, it is likely that the cuts would have been as severe as they were, and a commercially minded railway would not have made the mistake of leaving some long branches, such as that to Whitby, open only to have a service of just four trains a day. The problems of the bottlenecks on the East Coast route at its southern end had to be addressed, but it is clear that the LNER had this in mind. Extra capacity would also have been released with the steady decline in the popularity of coal, with fewer slow mineral trains to be fitted between the expresses.

The shortening of the peak periods for commuting and the end of widespread working on Saturday mornings would have made the case for electrification of the suburban network more pressing, while at the same time making these services less economic. Given the cramped accommodation of the suburban 'quad-arts', surely the LNER would not have been happy simply to tack an electric engine on to such rolling stock? New purpose-built rolling stock would have been needed. Could the LNER have afforded such investment? Much modernisation could have been covered by the 'trust fund' referred to, and it is clear that the company was gradually coming to realise that electrification was necessary and could offer economies through improved labour productivity and also attract extra traffic.

It would be tempting to think that the switch from steam to electric could have been made in one move, rather than with not one but two stages of dieselisation as in fact happened, with first diesel locomotives and then the High Speed Trains. Nevertheless, tempting though this may be, it ignores the fact that one project for Arthur Peppercorn was the introduction of diesel-electric locomotives to the East Coast Main Line, and this would almost certainly have been the first step forward during the early 1950s had the LNER remained in private hands. The heavy cost of wiring up the entire line between London and Edinburgh, with the reconstruction of bridges and tunnels, would have been too much.

Appendix 1

LNER Locomotive Numbering

A priority for the new London & North Eastern Railway in 1923 was to develop an integrated numbering system for the vast fleet of locomotives inherited from its constituent companies and subsidiaries. This was necessary as there was considerable duplication, especially with the lower numbers as every company had started from number 1. In many cases, the predecessor companies had also allocated numbers randomly and the LNER was keen to introduce some order, with all locomotives in the same class given consecutive numbers, and classes of locomotive to be numbered in blocks.

Nevertheless, as an interim measure the decision was taken by the committee chaired by Sir Vincent Raven, that a suffix letter would be added to locomotive numbers, just as was done for carriages, although instead of 'Y' for York for the ex-NER stock, for locomotives it was 'D' for Darlington, and there was no equivalent of the 'J' for East Coast Joint Stock in the case of locomotives. The other locomotive suffixes were 'N' for GNR; 'E' for GER; 'C' for GCR; 'B' for NBR, and 'S' for the Great North of Scotland.

In 1924, by which time the company had all the locomotives in its possession, a new scheme was adopted with former NER locomotives retaining their numbers, while those of the GNR increased by 3000; GCR by 5000; Great North of Scotland by 6800; GER by 7000, and NBR by 9000. As new locomotives began to arrive, they were allocated numbers at the end of the NER block, although some were allocated vacant numbers within that block. This was confusing enough, but there were many exceptions to this, especially for locomotives likely to be based within the area of a former constituent. In fact, it was not until 1946 that a comprehensive renumbering scheme was introduced, 23 years after Grouping. In the interim, two attempts were made at renumbering, the first in 1942 and the second in 1944. The first system was intended to free up a series of numbers between 8300 and 8900 for new locomotives, but failed, so that by the time it was abandoned early in 1943, just 38 locomotives had been renumbered.

The 1946 renumbering scheme was based on allocating a series of numbers to locomotives of different wheel arrangements and power classifications. This saw express passenger tender locomotives of 4-6-2, 2-8-2 and the larger 2-6-2s numbered between 1 and 999. Six-coupled passenger and mixed-traffic locomotives of 4-6-0, 2-6-0 and smaller 2-6-2s were numbered between 1000 and 1999. Four-coupled passenger tender locomotives (4-4-0, 4-4-2 and 2-4-0) were numbered between 2000 and 2999. Eight-coupled freight tender locomotives of 0-8-0, 2-8-0 and 2-8-2 configuration were numbered between 3000 and 3999, leaving the numbers between 4000 and 5999 for six-coupled 0-6-0 freight tender locomotives. Strangely, electric locomotives were allocated numbers between 6000 and 6999, suggesting that someone expected the LNER to have many more of these.

Passenger tank locomotives of 2-4-2, 0-4-4, 4-4-2, 4-4-4 and 2-6-2T types were numbered between 7000 and 7999, with shunting tank locomotives and diesel shunters numbered in the same series, between 8000 and 8999. Regardless of wheel arrangement, mixed-traffic and freight tank locomotives were numbered between 9000 and 9999, leaving the number 10000 for the experimental Class W1 4-6-4, which it had carried since 1923.

Within each class, the locomotives were numbered in order of construction, but exceptions were made with the A4s named after LNER directors these being numbered 1 to 4.

One problem was that in order to avoid the confusion of having two locomotives carrying the same number, for any progress to be made on renumbering, some locomotives had to be renumbered twice, with a temporary number until their new number became available. Difficulties arose in numbers 1–999, 1xxx, which had to allow for new B1 class locomotives, and 3xxx to make space for locomotives purchased from the War Office.

Appendix 2

LNER Locomotives as at 31 December 1947

This is the locomotive fleet of the LNER on the eve of Nationalisation. In addition, a small number of locomotives were on loan from the Ministry of Supply.

Each 'Big Four' company had its own power classification system. On the LNER, the classification actually referred to the wheel arrangement, with the alphabetical prefix indicating the wheel notation. Thus:

A = 4-6-2	H = 4-4-4	P = 2-8-2	W = 4-6-4
B = 4-6-0	J = 0-6-0	Q = 0-8-0	X = 4-2-2 and 2-2-4
C = 4-4-2	K = 2-6-0	R = 0-8-2	Y = 0-4-0
D = 4-4-0	L = 2-6-4	S = 0-8-4	Z = 0-4-2
E = 2-4-0	M = 0-6-4	T = 4-8-0	
F = 2-4-2	N = 0-6-2	U = 2-8-0+0-8-2	
G = 0-4-4	O = 2-8-0	V = 2-6-2	

When the system was first introduced in 1923, Z was intended for experimental and departmental classes, but this was abandoned in 1927 and from then on it applied to 0-4-2s. There was no 'I', as one would expect for clarity, but one surprise is that there was an 'O'.

The above applied to steam locomotives. Diesel and electric locomotives had prefixes, DE for diesel-electric, DM for diesel-mechanical and E for electric, followed by B for banking, E for express, M for mixed traffic, or S for shunting.

This meant that DES1 was a diesel-electric shunting locomotive, and ES1 was electric shunting. EM1 was electric, mixed traffic.

One weakness of the system obvious to those with a nautical bent, for whom the term 'A1' means the best, is that the higher the number, the more up-to-date the locomotive, so A4s were better than A1s, most of which were modernised to become A3s. Modifications and variations within a class were usually recognised by adding /1 or /2, so one would have an A2/1, A2/2, for example.

Unless stated otherwise, the numbers quoted are those applied in the 1946 renumbering, with earlier numbers in brackets.

4-wheel petrol shunting locomotives

8188/9 (8430/31) Motor Rail 'Simplex' Y11 class petrol shunting locomotives, ex-GER and NBR respectively. Initially classified as Z6 but this was changed to Y11 in 1943. A third Motor Rail was absorbed into LNER stock, acquired from Preston Water Works in 1925. All three survived to be taken over by British Railways and numbered 15097–15099.

0-6-0 diesel-electric shunting locomotives

An Armstrong Whitworth locomotive, not taken into stock, but a demonstrator operated 1932–33.

8000–8003, J45 class, later reclassified as DES1.
8004, DES2 class.

Electric locomotives

1 and 2,ES1 class, 640hp Bo-Bo.
6490–6499 (previously 3–12), EB1 class, 1,100hp Bo-Bo.
6701, EM1 class, 1,360hp Bo-Bo, 24 of which were built after Nationalisation.

Steam locomotives

0-4-0T

8082/3 (7133/4), Y6 class ex-GER.
8086–89 (between 24 and 1800), Y7 class ex-NER.
8090/1 (between 559 and 563), Y8, ex-NER.
8125–8129 (in the range 7210–7229), Y4, ex-GER.

0-4-0ST

8081 (7230), Y5 class ex-GER.
8092–8124 (between 9009 and 10103), Y9, ex-NBR.

A Y9 0-4-0ST, No. 9032, at Polmont in 1935. This locomotive was originally built for the NBR. (*HMRS AEP 021*)

4-wheel vertical boiler
8130–8185 (in the range 19–198), Sentinel Y1/Y3.

4-wheel vertical boiler Tram engine
8186/7 (8403/4), Y10 class 'Super Sentinel' for the Wisbech & Upwell Tramway. Broke away from the 'guard's van' appearance of the original engines, but had cabs at each end and a vertical boiler in between. Unable to cope with heavy loads, with heavy coal consumption and emitting sparks, they were transferred in 1931 after just a year, and spent the rest of the time on dock work at Yarmouth. Both passed to BR.

0-4-2T

8190/1 (6843/34), Z4 class, ex-GNSR.
8192/3 (6830/32), Z5 class, ex-GNSR.

0-4-4
7240–7349 (in the range 149–2100), G5 class, ex-NER.
7505 (sole survivor from range 6884–92), ex-GNSR, withdrawn 1947.

0-6-0T
8200–03 (in the range 5882–93), J62 class, ex-MS&LR.
8204–10 (5060/1, 5089, 5277, 5321, 5538), J63 class, ex-GCR.
8211–15 (in the range 7150–59, 7245–54), J65 class, ex-GER.
8216–26 (in the range 7125–39), J70 class, ex-GER.
8230–8316 (between 27 and 1864), J71 class, ex-NER.
8317–19 (3859, 3908, 4990), J55 class, ex-GNR.
8320–54 (in the range 9066–9847), J88 class, ex-NBR.
8355–64 (544–553), J73 class, ex-NER.
8365 (in the range 2492–2532), J75 class, ex-H&BR.
8366–69 (6408–11), J60 class, ex-GCR.
8370–88 (in the range 7275–7326), J66 class, ex-GER.
8390–8441 (between 15 and 1462), J77 class, ex-NER.
8442–81 (9795–9834), J83class, ex-NBR.
8482–89 (in the range 015–099), J93 class, ex-M&GNR.
8490–8636 (in the ranges 7011–20, 7051–60, 7081–90, 7160–7406), J67/J69 class, ex-GER.
8638–66 (7021–50), J68 class, ex-GER.
8667–69 (N, B, C, D), ex-GER.
8670–8744 (in the ranges 462–1770, 2173–2192), J72 class, ex-NER.
8745–54 (500–581), J72 class, as above but built 1925. 28 further locomotives built by BR.
8757–8889 (in the ranges 3111, 3155A, 3921–4290), J52/J53 classes but all rebuilt as J52; ex-GNR.
8890–8919 (3157–3220), J51 class, ex GNR
8920–29 (3221–3230), J50 class, ex-GNR.
8930–91 (3231–3240, 583–598), J50 class, built by LNER.

0-6-0ST
8006–80, J94 class, Riddles' design for Ministry of Supply.

0-6-0T crane engines
8667–8669 (B, C and D), J92 class, ex-GER.

0-6-0
4105–54 (in the range 3101–4172), J5 class, ex-GNR.
4115–55 (in the range 3177–4173), J3 class, ex-GNR.
4156–63 (081/3/6/8), J3 class, ex-M&GNR.
4157–67 (082/4/5/7/9–092), J4 class, ex-M&GNR.
4170–4279 (3521–3610, 3621–3640), J6 class, ex-GNR.
4280–4453 (5016–6119), J11 class, ex-GCR.
4460–4535 (9038–9348, 9364–81, 9848–57), J35 class, ex-NBR.
4536–4639 (9008–9518), J37 class, ex-NBR.
4640–74 (8140–49, 8240–54, 8260–69), J19 class, ex-GER.
4675–99 (8270–94), J20 class, ex-GER.
4700–4988, (1233–3098, J39 class.
5000–14 (3001–15), J1 class, ex-GNR.
5015–24 (3071–80), J2 class, ex-GNR.
5025–5123 (between 16 and 1820), J21 class, ex-NER.
5126–5209 (in the range 5074–5851), J10 class, ex-MS&LR.
5210–5346 (in the range 9045–9794), J36 class, ex-NBR.

5350–5479 (in the range 7037–7945), J15 class, ex-GER.
5480–99 (3021–40), J5 class, ex-GNR.
5500–89 (8150–8239), J17 class, ex-GER.
5600–44 (in the range 1821–1960), J24 class, ex-NER.
5465–5728 (in the range 1743–2142), J25 class, ex-NER.
5730–79 (in the range 67–1781), J26 class, ex-NER.
5780–5894 (in the range 790–2392), J27 class, ex-NER.
5900–34, (1400–47) J38 class.

A mineral train is headed by J6 0-6-0 No. 3521 past Darlington South signalbox in 1938. (*HMRS ACW 236*)

0-6-2T

9089 (2486), N12 class, ex-H&BR.
9090–9109 (in the range 89–1785), N10 class, ex-NER.
9110–19 (in the range 2405–19), N13 class, ex-H&BR.
9120–9215 (9858–63), N14 class, ex-NBR.
9126–9224 (in the range 9007–9926), N15 class, mainly ex-NBR, but a few LNER-built.
9225–47 (in the ranges 5512–14, 5601–38, 5712–25), N4 class, ex-GCR.
9250–9379 (in the range 5021–5946), N5 class, ex-GCR.
9371–9401 (in the range 14–1168), N8 class, ex-NER.
9410–29 (in the ranges 1617/18, 1640–1705), N9 class, ex-NER.
9430–85 (in the range 3190–4605), N1 class, ex-GNR.
9490–9596 (in the ranges 892–97, 2583–94, 4606–4770, 2662–90), N2 class, ex-GNR, but 2662–90 LNER-built.
9600–9733 (in the ranges 409–475, 826–988, 7990–8011, 2600–61), N7 class, ex-GER, but 2600–61 LNER-built.

0-6-4T

9075–77 (6154–57), M2 class, ex-Metropolitan Railway.
9082 (6153), M1 class, ex-GCR.

0-8-0T

3200–43 (5039–6182), Q4 class, ex-GCR.
3250–3339 (between 83 and 2125), Q5 class, ex-NER.
3340–3459 (between 1247 and 2302), Q6 class, ex-NER.
3460–74 (624–26, 628–34, 901–905), Q7 class, ex-NER.
9925–37 (in the range 5044–6179), Q1 class; Thompson rebuild of ex-GCR Q4 class.

0-8-4T

9900–05 (6170–73, 2798/9), S1 class, ex-GCR but 2798/9 LNER-built.

A former GER E4 class 2-4-0, No. 7492, leaves little room on the turntable at Mildenhall in 1938. As locomotive sizes increased, one of the infrastructure problems was the size of turntables. (*HMRS AEU 601*)

2-4-0

2780–97 (7407–7506), E4 class, ex-GER.

2-4-2T

7093/4 (8308/10), F7 class, ex-GER.
7095–7103 (in the range 5574–5737), F1 class, ex-MS&LR.
7104–13 (5776–85), F2 class, ex-MS&LR.
7114–50 (in the range 8040–99), F3 class, ex-GER.
7151–87 (7071–7800), F4 class, ex-GER.
7188–7217 (in the range 7091–7788), F5 class, ex-GER.
7218–39 (in the range 7001–7790), F6 class, ex-GER.

2-6-0

1720–94 (4630–4704), K2 class; early versions ex-GNR, later LNER.
1800–1992 (various in 38xx and 40xx ranges), K3 class; early versions ex-GNR, later LNER.
1993–96/98 (3441–4/6) K4 class.
1997 (3445) K1/1 class, rebuilt from K4. 70 Peppercorn K1 class later built by BR.
1863 (206) K5 class, rebuilt from K3.

V2 2-6-2 No. 4808 with a goods train near Morpeth in 1939. The train is almost certainly an express given its length and the choice of locomotive. (*HMRS ACW 114*)

2-6-2
800–983, (3641–95, 4771–4899), V2 'Green Arrow' class.
1700/1 (3401/2), V4 class.

2-6-2T
7600–91 (in the range 2897–2933),V1/V3 classes.

2-6-4T
9000, L1 class. The only one out of 100 completed before Nationalisation.
9050–69 (5276–5345), L1/L3 class, ex-GCR.
9070/71 (6158/63), L2 class, ex-Metropolitan Railway.

2-8-0
3000–3199, O7 class, Riddles' 'Austerity' design, based on the LMS 8F, but simplified. Ex-Ministry of Supply.
3475–94 (3456–60/62–76), O3 class, ex-GNR.
3500–3628 (5001–5408, 5966, 6183–6252), O1/O4 classes, ex-GCR.
3629–3901 (6253–6377, 6495–6642), O4 class ex-War Office.
3902–20 (5010–22), O4 class, rebuilt former GCR Class O5.
3931–46 (3461, 3477–3501), O2 class, ex-GNR.
3947–87 (2430–37, 2954–61, 3833–57), O2 class, LNER-built.
7651–7675 (3100–3167), Stanier O6 class (LMS 8F) entered service as the Ministry of War Transport standard heavy goods locomotive with 100 built by the LNER, but all transferred to the LMS before Nationalisation.

2-8-0+0-8-2
9999 (2395), U1 class, Gresley/Beyer-Garratt.

4-4-0
2000 (4075), D3 class, ex-GNR.
2059–72 (between 9036 and 9770), D31 class, ex-NBR.

2100–06 (5268–70, 5852–81), D6 class, ex-MS&LR.
2111–12 (1873 and 1902), D17 class, ex-NER.
2116–2148 (between 4071 and 4359), D3 class, ex-GNR.
2150–2201 (3041–50, 4180, 4305, 4320–40, 4361–99), D2 class, ex-GNR.
2202–16 (3051–65), D1 class, ex-GNR.
2225–56 (6819–6912), D41 class, ex-GNSR.
2260–80 (6825–6915), D40 class, ex-GNSR.
2300–33 (in the ranges 5104–13, 6013–42), D9 class, ex-GCR.
2340–97 (2011–30, 2101–10), D20 class, ex-NER.
2400–15 (between 9243 and 9900), D29 class, ex-NBR.
2416–42 (between 9363 and 9501), D30, ex-NBR.
2443–54 (9882–93), D32 class, ex-NBR.
2455–66 (between 9331 and 9894), D33 class, ex-NBR.
2467–98 (between 9034 and 9505), D34 'Glen' class, ex-NBR.
2500–2620 (8780–8900), D14/15/16 classes, ex-GER.
2650–59 (5429–38), D10 'Director' class, ex-GCR.
2660–94 (5501–11, 6378–6401), D11'Improved Director' class, ex-GCR 2700–2775 D49 'Hunt/Shire' class.

4-4-2

2800–91 (3272–3301, 4300, 4400–61), C1 class, ex-GNR.
2895–98 (5258/9, 5364/5), C5 class, ex-GCR.
2900–25 (5192/4, 5260–67, 5358/60–3, 6083–94), C4 class, ex-GCR.
2930–48 (between 295 and 1794), C6 class, ex-NER.
2950–97 (between 706 and 2212), C7 class, ex-NER.

There seems to be an interesting assortment of items on the flat trucks on this goods train seen near Ruddington in 1936, headed by an O4 class 2-8-0. *(HMRS AEU 506)*

7350–99 (between 4009 and 4550), C12 class, ex-GNR.
7400- 39 (between 5002 and 6066), C13 class, ex-GCR.
7440–51 (6120–31), C14 class, ex-GCR.
7452–81 (between 9001 and 9309), C15 class, ex-NBR.
7482–7502 (between 9438 and 9516), C16 class, ex-NBR.

4-4-4T

7511/2 (6416/7), H2 class, ex-Metropolitan Railway.

4-6-0

1000–09 (8301–10), Thompson B1 class.
1010–1273, Thompson B1 class. 136 further locomotives built by BR.
1346–48 (5052/53, 5416), B6 class, ex-GCR.
1349–59 (5004, 5279/80, 5439–46 , B8 class, ex-GCR.
1360–97 (5031–8, 5072/3/8, 5458–84), B7 class, ex-GCR.
1400–68 (840–9, 906–43, 2363–82, 1371–85), B16, ex-NER.
1469–78 (6105–14), B9 class, ex-GCR.
1479/80 (5195/6), B18 class, ex-GCR.
1481–89 (6095–6104), B4 class, ex-GCR.
1490–93 (5423–8), B19 class, ex-GCR.
1494–99 (6164–9), B3 class, ex-GCR.
1500–80 (8500–80), B12 class, ex-GER, but 1571–80 built by LNER.
1600–2/4–6/8–13/8–31/3–8/40–72 (2800–2/4–6/8–13/8/8–31/3–8/40–72), B17 class. 2859/70 streamlined 1937–51.
1603/7/14–7/32/9/71 (2803/7/14–7/32/9/71), Thompson B2 class rebuilt from B17 class.
1678–90 (5180–87, 6067–72), B5 class, ex-GCR.
1691–98 (beween 782 and 825), B15 class, ex-NER.
1699 (761), B13 class, ex-NER.

4-6-2T

9770–89 (1113–95), A7 class, ex-NER.
9790–99 (686–95) A6 class, ex-NER.
9800–42 (in the ranges 5003–452, 1712–90), A5 class, ex-GCR, except 1712–90 LNER-built.
9850–94 (in the ranges 1326–30, 1499–1531, 2143–62), A8 class, Gresley rebuilds of ex-NER H1 class.

4-6-2

1–34 (2509–12, 4462–9/82–4500, 4900–3. Class A4.
35–112 (2500–8/43–82/95–9, 2743–52, 2743–52/95–99, 4471–81, Gresley A1 (A10)/A3s class.
113 (4470), Thompson A1/1 class rebuild of Gresley A1 class. A further 49 Peppercorn A1 class built by BR.
500/11–24, Thompson A2/3 class.
501–6 (2001–6), Thompson A2/2 class rebuilds of P2 class.
507–10 (3696–9), Thompson A2/1 class development of V2 class.
525, Peppercorn A2 class. 14 further locomotives built by BR.

4-6-4

60700 (10000), W1 class. A 1937 rebuild, with A4-style streamlining, of high-pressure experimental locomotive, nicknamed the 'Hush-Hush' because of the secrecy surrounding it when new.

4-8-0

9910–33 (in the ranges 1350–59, 1656–60), T1 class, ex-GCR except 1656–60 LNER-built.

Appendix 3

Named LNER locomotives

A1/A3 class (Gresley) 4-6-2s

The Gresley A1s, which were almost all later rebuilt as A3s, including the famous No. 4472 *Flying Scotsman*. The first two entered service before Grouping. Many of the locomotives were named after once famous racehorses, as listed below in order of entering service, with the 1946 number, if allocated, and the original 1924-series number in brackets, showing how haphazard the LNER's locomotive numbering system was with no attempt to establish a substantial group of consecutive numbers for an entire class of locomotive.

A1 Pacific No. 4472 *Flying Scotsman* heading the 'Flying Scotsman', near Grantham in 1929, hurrying towards London after the accelerations in this service the previous year. (*HMRS AEU 513*)

– (4470) *Great Northern* (Rebuilt as an A1/1 by Thompson rather than as an A3 in 1945)
102 (4471) *Sir Frederick Banbury*
103 (4472) *Flying Scotsman*
104 (4473) *Solario*
105 (4474) *Victor Wild*
106 (4475) *Flying Fox*
107 (4476) *Royal Lancer*
108 (4477) *Gay Crusader*
109 (4478) *Hermit*
110 (4479) *Robert the Devil*
111 (4480) *Enterprise*
112 (4481) *St Simon*
44 (2543) *Melton*
45 (2544) *Lemberg*
46 (2545) *Diamond Jubilee*
47 (2546) *Donovan*
48 (2547) *Doncaster*
49 (2548) *Galtee More*
50 (2549) *Persimmon*
51 (2550) *Blink Bonny*
52 (2551) *Prince Palatine*
53 (2552) *Sansovino*
54 (2553) *Manna* (renamed *Prince of Wales*, 1926)
55 (2554) *Woolwinder*
56 (2555) *Centenary*
57 (2556) *Ormonde*
58 (2557) *Blair Athol*
59 (2558) *Tracery*
60 (2559) *The Tetrarch*
61 (2660) *Pretty Polly*
62 (2561) *Minoru*
63 (2562) *Isinglass*
64 (2563) *William Whitelaw* (renamed *Tagalie*, 1941)
65 (2564) *Knight of the Thistle*
66 (2565) *Merry Hampton*
67 (2566) *Ladas*
68 (2567) *Sir Visto*
69 (2568) *Sceptre*
70 (2569) *Gladiateur*
71 (2570) *Tranquil*
72 (2571) *Sunstar*
73 (2562) *Sir Gatien*
74 (2573) *Harvester*
75 (2574) *St Frusquin*
76 (2575) *Galopin*
77 (2576) *The White Knight*
78 (2577) *Night Hawk*
79 (2578) *Bayardo*
80 (2579) *Dick Turpin*
81 (2560) *Shotover*
82 (2581) *Neil Gow*
83 (2582) *Sir Hugo*
89 (2753) *Felstead*
90 (2744) *Grand Parade*
91 (2745) *Captain Cuttle*
92 (2746) *Fairway*
93 (2747) *Coronach*
94 (2748) *Colorado*
95 (2749) *Flamingo*
96 (2750) *Papyrus*
97 (2751) *Humorist*
98 (2752) *Spion Kop*
84 (2595) *Trigo*
85 (2596) *Manna*
86 (2597) *Gainsborough*
99 (2795) *Call Boy*
100 (2796) *Spearmint*
101 (2797) *Cicero*
87 (2598) *Blenheim*
88 (2599) *Book Law*
35 (2500) *Windsor Lad*
36 (2501) *Colombo*
37 (2502) *Hyperion*
38 (2503) *Firdaussi*
39 (2504) *Sandwich*
40 (2505) *Cameronian*
41 (2506) *Salmon Trout*
42 (2507) *Singapore*
43 (2508) *Brown Jack*

A2 class (Raven) 4-6-2s

Vincent Raven had built a successful class of Atlantic 4-4-0s for the NER, designated the C7 by the LNER, but even before Grouping it was realised that a more powerful locomotive was needed. Raven therefore developed his A2 Pacific 4-6-2 series from the C7. These were promoted by the NER to counter the publicity received by the GNR for its Pacifics. The first two were delivered in December 1922, so preceded Grouping. LNER numbers are given and the locomotives are listed in order of delivery. None of them survived long enough to be renumbered in 1946.

2400 *City of Newcastle*
2401 *City of Kingston upon Hull*
2402 *City of York*
2403 *City of Durham*
2404 *City of Ripon*

A4 class (Gresley) 4-6-2s

A variety of names was chosen for this iconic class, including those with 'Silver' in the title to provide a stud of locomotives for the 'Silver Jubilee' and, of course, those named after water birds or birds of prey. Unusually, many of this class received second names during their operational life as it was LNER practice to honour prominent company officers and directors.

The locomotives are listed in order of delivery, using the 1946 numbers, except for the original *Sir Ralph Wedgwood*, which was destroyed in the bombing of York in 1942. The original numbers are in brackets, while second names follow the original.

14 (2509) *Silver Link*
15 (2510) *Quicksilver*
16 (2511) *Silver King*
17 (2512) *Silver Fox*
23 (4482) *Golden Eagle*
24 (4483) *Kingfisher*
25 (4484) *Falcon*
26 (4485) *Kestrel / Miles Beevor*
27 (4486) *Merlin*
28 (4487) *Sea Eagle / Walter K. Whigham*
9 (4488) *Osprey / Union of South Africa*
10 (4489) *Woodcock / Dominion of Canada*
11 (4490) *Empire of India*
12 (4491) *Commonwealth of Australia*
13 (4492) *Dominion of New Zealand*
29 (4493) *Woodcock*
3 (4494) *Osprey / Andrew K. McCosh*
30 (4495) *Great Snipe / Golden Fleece*
8 (4496) *Golden Shuttle / Dwight D. Eisenhower*
31 (4497) *Golden Plover*
7 (4498) *Sir Nigel Gresley*
4 (4462) *Great Snipe / William Whitelaw*
18 (4463) *Sparrow Hawk*
19 (4464) *Bittern*
20 (4465) *Guillemot*
6 (4466) *Herring Gull / Sir Ralph Wedgwood*
21 (4467) *Wild Swan*
22 (4468) *Mallard*
4469 *Gadwall / Sir Ralph Wedgwood*
2 (4499) *Pochard / Sir Murrough Wilson*
1 (4500) *Garganey / Sir Ronald Matthews*
32 (4900) *Gannet*
5 (4901) *Capercaillie / Charles H. Newton*
33 (4902) *Seagull*
34 (4903) *Peregrine* (renamed *Lord Faringdon* after Nationalisation.)

A2/1 class (Thompson) 4-6-2s

These were Thompson's Pacific version of the V2, and appeared after his A2/2 rebuilds. The driving themes behind his work were greater standardisation combined with ease of maintenance. The original numbers are in brackets.

507 (3696) *Highland Chieftain*
508 (3697) *Duke of Rothesay*
509 (3698) *Waverley*
510 (3699) *Robert the Bruce*

A2/2 class (Thompson) 4-6-2s

These were rebuilt from Gresley's P2 2-8-2 Mikado locomotives, largely because eight coupled wheels did not cope easily with the tight curves on the lines between Edinburgh and Aberdeen, and also as part of Thompson's move towards standardisation. They retained their original names. The original number is in brackets.

501 (2001) *Cock o' the North*
502 (2002) *Earl Marischal*
503 (2003) *Lord President*
504 (2004) *Mons Meg*
505 (2005) *Thane of Fife*
506 (2006) *Wolf of Badenoch*

A2/3 class (Thompson) 4-6-2s

Built from new and based on the A2/2 above, with 15 delivered in 1946 and 1947. The numbers reflected the renumbering scheme introduced belatedly by the LNER.

500 *Edward Thompson*
511 *Airborne*
512 *Steady Aim*
513 *Dante*
514 *Chamossaire*
515 *Sun Stream*
516 *Hycilla*
517 *Ocean Swell*
518 *Tehran*
519 *Honeyway*
520 *Owen Tudor*
521 *Watling Street*
522 *Straight Deal*
523 *Sun Castle*
524 *Herringbone*

A2 class (Peppercorn) 4-6-2

This was Peppercorn's variation on the A2/3s above, but only one was delivered before Nationalisation, with another 14 delivered to British Railways.

525 *A. H. Peppercorn*

A1 class (Peppercorn) 4-6-2s

All 49 locomotives of this class were built after Nationalisation.

B17 class (Gresley) 4-6-0s

Built 1928–1937, three-cylinder design. Ten rebuilt by Thompson as two-cylinder locomotives and reclassified B2. Listed in 1946 numerical order with original number in brackets.

1600 (2800) *Sandringham*
1601 (2801) *Holkham*
1602 (2802) *Walsingham*
1604 (2804) *Elveden*
1605 (2805) *Burnham Thorpe / Lincolnshire Regiment*
1606 (2806) *Audley End*
1608 (2808) *Gunton*
1609 (2809) *Quidenham*
1610 (2810) *Honingham Hall*
1611 (2811) *Raynham Hall*
1612 (2812) *Houghton Hall*
1613 (2813) *Woodbastwick Hall*
1618 (2818) *Wynyard Park*
1619 (2819) *Welbeck Abbey*
1620 (2820) *Clumber*
1621 (2821) *Hatfield House*
1622 (2822) *Alnwick Castle*
1623 (2823) *Lambton Castle*
1624 (2824) *Lumley Castle*
1625 (2825) *Raby Castle*
1626 (2826) *Brancepeth Castle*
1627 (2827) *Aske Hall*
1628 (2828) *Harewood House*
1629 (2829) *Naworth Castle*
1630 (2830) *Thoresby Park / Tottenham Hotspur*
1631 (2831) *Serlby Hall*
1633 (2833) *Kimbolton Castle*
1634 (2834) *Hinchingbrooke*
1635 (2835) *Milton*
1636 (2836) *Harlaxton Manor*
1637 (2837) *Thorpe Hall*
1638 (2838) *Melton Hall*
1640 (2840) *Somerleyton Hall*
1641 (2841) *Gayton Hall*
1642 (2842) *Kilverstone Hall*
1643 (2843) *Champion Lodge*
1645 (2845) *The Suffolk Regiment*
1646 (2846) *Gilwell Park*
1647 (2847) *Helmingham Hall*
1648 (2848) *Arsenal*
1649 (2849) *Sheffield United*
1650 (2850) *Grimsby Town*
1651 (2851) *Derby County*
1652 (2852) *Darlington*
1653 (2853) *Huddersfield Town*
1654 (2854) *Sunderland*
1655 (2855) *Middlesbrough*
1656 (2856) *Leeds United*
1657 (2857) *Doncaster Rovers*
1658 (2858) *Newcastle United / The Essex Regiment*

1659 (2859) *Norwich City / East Anglian*
1660 (2860) *Hull City*
1661 (2861) *Sheffield Wednesday*
1662 (2862) *Manchester United*
1663 (2863) *Everton*
1664 (2864) *Liverpool*
1665 (2865) *Leicester City*
1666 (2866) *Nottingham Forest*
1667 (2867) *Bradford*
1668 (2868) *Bradford City*
1669 (2869) *Barnsley*
1670 (2870) *Manchester City / Tottenham Hotspur / City of London*
1672 (2872) *West Ham United*

B2 class (Thompson) 4-6-0s

Class B17s rebuilt as two-cylinder locomotives and reclassified.

1603 (2803) *Framlingham*
1607 (2807) *Blickling*
1614 (2814) *Castle Hedingham*
1615 (2815) *Culford Hall*
1616 (2816) *Fallodon*
1617 (2817) *Ford Castle*
1632 (2832) *Belvoir Castle / Royal Sovereign*
1639 (2839) *Rendelsham Hall / Norwich City*
6144 (2844) *Earlham Hall**
1671 (2871) *Manchester City / Royal Sovereign*

* Rebuilt after Nationalisation

B1 class (Thompson) 4-6-0s

Based on the B17 class, but much simplified to ease maintenance. Of 274 B1s built by the LNER, only a minority were named, hence the gaps in the numbers below, and in addition to those shown, British Railways built another 136 of these locomotives, of which only one, No. 6379 was named (*Mayflower*). Those built before the second 1946 renumbering have the original LNER number in brackets.

1000 (8301) *Springbok*
1001 (8302) *Eland*
1002 (8303) *Impala*
1003 (8304) *Gazelle*
1004 (8305) *Oryx*
1005 (8306) *Bongo*
1006 (8307) *Blackbuck*
1007 (8308) *Klipspringer*
1008 (8309) *Kudu*
1009 (8310) *Hartebeeste*
1010 *Wildebeeste*
1011 *Waterbuck*
1012 *Puku*
1013 *Topi*
1014 *Oribi*
1015 *Duiker*
1016 *Inyala*
1017 *Bushbuck*
1018 *Gnu*
1019 *Nilghai*
1020 *Gemsbok*
1021 *Reitbok*
1022 *Sassaby*
1023 *Hirola*
1024 *Addax*
1025 *Pallah*
1026 *Ourebi*
1027 *Madoqua*
1028 *Umseke*
1029 *Chamois*
1030 *Nyala*
1031 *Reedbuck*
1032 *Stembok*
1033 *Dibatag*
1034 *Chiru*
1035 *Pronghorn*
1036 *Ralph Assheton*
1037 *Jairou*
1038 *Blacktail*
1039 *Steinbok*
1040 *Roedeer*
1189 *Sir William Gray*
1215 *William Henton Carver*
1221 *Sir Alexander Erskine-Hill*
1237 *Geoffrey H. Kitson*
1238 *Leslie Runciman*
1240 *Harry Hinchliffe*
1241 *Viscount Ridley*
1242 *Alexander Reith Gray*
1243 *Sir Harold Mitchell*
1244 *Strang Steel*
1245 *Murray of Elibank*

1246 *Lord Balfour of Burleigh*
1247 *Lord Burghley*
1248 *Geoffrey Gibbs*
1249 *Fitzherbert Wright*
1250 *A. Harold Bibby*
1251 *Oliver Bury*

V2 class (Gresley) 2-6-2s

No fewer than 184 V2s were built, although further examples were completed as A2/1 Pacifics by Thompson. Relatively few were named as these were mixed-traffic locomotives and the name *Green Arrow* was in itself used to publicise a new LNER freight service. The 1946 numbers are used with the original LNER numbers in brackets.

800 (4771) *Green Arrow*
809 (4780) *The Snapper, The East Yorkshire Regiment The Duke of York's Own*
835 (4806) *The Green Howard, Alexandra, Princess of Wales's Own Yorkshire Regiment*
847 (4818) *St Peter's School York A.D.627*
860 (4831) *Durham School*
872 (4843) *King's Own Yorkshire Light Infantry*
873 (4844) *Coldstreamer*
964 (3676) *The Durham Light Infantry*

The V2 class 2-6-2 No. 4771 *Green Arrow* was named to publicise a new express freight service. This was one of the few mixed-traffic engines to be named by the LNER and painted in apple green, but even without that, it has the appearance of an express locomotive, as seen at Grantham Yard signalbox. (*HMRS AAH 727*)

V4 class (Gresley) 2-6-2

Intended as a mixed-traffic locomotive for lines requiring a light axle loading, the name *Bantam Cock* was given to the first of class, No. 3401, to highlight the lightweight design. This was the only member of the class to be named officially, although the second locomotive, No. 3402, was unofficially known as 'Bantam Hen'. Under the 1946 renumbering, these became Nos 1700 and 1701.

1700 (3401) *Bantam Cock*

K2 class (Gresley) 2-6-0s

The earlier K1s were not named, but of the 75 K2s, those below were named. In each case the 1946 number is used with the original LNER number in brackets.

1764 (4674) *Loch Arkaig*
1772 (4682) *Loch Lochy*
1774 (4684) *Loch Garry*
1775 (4685) *Loch Treig*
1781 (4691) *Loch Morar*
1782 (4692) *Loch Eil*
1783 (4693) *Loch Sheil*
1787 (4697) *Loch Quoich*
1788 (4698) *Loch Rannoch*
1789 (4699) *Loch Laidon*
1790 (4700) *Loch Lomond*
1791 (4701) *Loch Laggan*
1794 (4704) *Loch Oich*

K1/1 class (Thompson) 2-6-0

This was the sole two-cylinder rebuild of a Gresley K4. None of the Peppercorn K1s, all of which were built after Nationalisation, was named.

1997 (3445) *MacCailin Mor*

K4 class (Gresley) 2-6-0s

The 1946 numbers are used, followed by the original LNER number in brackets.

1993 (3441) *Loch Long*
1994 (3442) *The Great Marquess*
1995 (3443) *Cameron of Lochiel*
1996 (3444) *Lord of the Isles*
1998 (3446) *MacLeod of Macleod*

D49 'Hunt'/'Shire' class (Gresley) 4-4-0s

The original LNER number is in brackets after the 1946 number.

2700 (234) *Yorkshire*
2701 (251) *Derbyshire*
2702 (253) *Oxfordshire*
2703 (256) *Hertfordshire*
2704 (264) *Stirlingshire*
2705 (265) *Lanarkshire*
2706 (266) *Forfarshire*
2707 (236) *Lancashire*
2708 (270) *Argyllshire*
2709 (277) *Berwickshire*
2710 (245) *Lincolnshire*
2711 (281) *Dumbartonshire*
2712 (246) *Morayshire*
2713 (249) *Aberdeenshire*
2714 (250) *Perthshire*
2715 (306) *Roxburghshire*
2716 (307) *Kincardineshire*
2717 (309) *Banffshire*
2718 (310) *Kinross-shire*
2719 (311) *Peebles-shire*
2720 (318) *Cambridgeshire*
2721 (320) *Warwickshire*
2722 (322) *Huntingdonshire*
2723 (327) *Nottinghamshire*
2724 (335) *Bedfordshire*
2725 (329) *Inverness-shire*
2726 (352) *The Meynell*
2727 (336) *The Quorn*
2728 (2753) *Cheshire*
2729 (2754) *Rutlandshire*
2730 (2755) *Berkshire*
2731 (2756) *Selkirkshire*
2732 (2757) *Dumfries-shire*
2733 (2758) *Northumberland*
2734 (2759) *Cumberland*
2735 (2760) *Westmorland*
2736 (201) *The Bramham Moor*
2737 (211) *The York and Ainsty*
2738 (220) *The Zetland*
2739 (232) *The Badsworth*
2740 (235) *The Bedale*
2741 (247) *The Blankney*
2742 (255) *The Braes of Derwent*
2743 (269) *The Cleveland*
2744 (273) *The Holderness*
2745 (282) *The Hurworth*
2746 (283) *The Middleton*
2747 (288) *The Percy*

2748 (292) *The Southwold*
2749 (297) *The Cottesmore*
2750 (298) *The Pytchley*
2751 (205) *The Albrighton*
2752 (214) *The Atherstone*
2753 (217) *The Belvoir*
2754 (222) *The Berkeley*
2755 (226) *The Bilsdale*
2756 (230) *The Brocklesby*
2757 (238) *The Burton*
2758 (258) *The Cattistock*
2759 (274) *The Craven*
2760 (279) *The Cotswold*
2761 (353) *The Derwent*
2762 (357) *The Fernie*
2763 (359) *The Fitzwilliam*
2764 (361) *The Garth*
2765 (362) *The Goathland*
2766 (363) *The Grafton*
2767 (364) *The Grove*
2768 (365) *The Morpeth*
2769 (366) *The Oakley*
2770 (368) *The Puckeridge*
2771 (370) *The Rufford*
2772 (374) *The Sinnington*
2773 (375) *The South Durham*
2774 (376) *The Staintondale*
2775 (377) *The Tynedale*

Class EM1 Bo-Bo electric

Originally numbered 6701, this was changed to 6000 in 1946. Sent to the Netherlands for extensive trials while electrification works continued, the name *Tommy* was given to it by the Dutch. Of the remaining 56 built by British Railways, only the last twelve were named. Class EM2 was delayed by the Second World War and did not appear until after Nationalisation.

Appendix 4

Named Locomotives Inherited by the LNER

Colne Valley & Halstead Railway

2-4-2T F9 class

CVHR No. 4 was withdrawn in late 1923 before it could receive an LNER number, while the others were withdrawn by end-1927.

4 *Hedingham*
8312 *Halstead*
8313 *Colne*

Great Central Railway

4-6-0

B2/B19 class (Robinson) (GCR Class 9P)

Originally classified B2 by the LNER, they were reclassified as B19 in 1945 to make way for Thompson's B2. They were unofficially known as the 'Sir Sam Fay' class after the lead locomotive. Not a truly successful type with only Nos 1494, 1496 *Valour* and 1498 surviving to December 1947. The original LNER numbers are in brackets with the 1946 numbers quoted first, while a dash indicates a locomotive withdrawn before renumbering.

1490 (5423) *Sir Sam Fay*
1491 (5425) *City of Manchester*
1492 (5427) *City of London*
1493 (5428) *City of Liverpool*
1494 (6169) *Lord Faringdon*
1495 (6164) *Earl Beatty*
1496 (6165) *Valour*
1497 (6166) *Earl Haig*
1498 (6167) *Lloyd George*
1499 (6168) *Lord Stuart of Wortley*
— (5424) *City of Lincoln*
— (5426) *City of Chester*

B8 class (Robinson) (GCR Class 1A)

Only four of the eight locomotives to received names passed into LNER stock, while altogether five (of which two were named examples) actually survived Nationalisation, although withdrawn shortly afterwards. The original LNER numbers are in brackets.

1349 (5004) *Glenalmond*
1350 (5439) *Sutton Nelthorpe*
1357 (5446) *Earl Roberts of Kandahar*
1358 (5279) *Earl Kitchener*

4-4-2

C5 class (Robinson) (GCR Classes 8D and 8E)

The original LNER number is in brackets following the 1946 number.

2895 (5258) *The Rt. Hon Viscount Cross, G.C.B. G.C.S.I.*
2896 (5259) *King Edward VII*
2897 (5364) *Lady Faringdon*
2898 (5365) *Sir William Pollitt*

4-4-0

D9 class (Robinson) (GCR Classes 11B, 11C and 11D)

Out of 40 locomotives built, just four were named. The original LNER number is in brackets where the locomotive survived long enough to be renumbered.

2301 (6014) *Sir Alexander*
2307 (6021) *Queen Mary*
5104 *Queen Alexandra*
5110 *King George V*

D10 'Director' class (Robinson) (GCR Class 11E)

All survived to be renumbered in 1946, so the original number is in brackets.

2650 (5429) *Prince Henry*
2651 (5430) *Purdon Viccars*
2652 (5431) *Edwin A. Beazley*
2653 (5432) *Sir Edward Fraser*
2654 (5433) *Walter Burgh Gair*
2655 (5434) *The Earl of Kerry*
2656 (5435) *Sir Clement Royds*
2657 (5436) *Sir Berkeley Sheffield*
2658 (5437) *Prince George*
2659 (5438) *Worsley-Taylor*

D11 'Improved Director' class (Robinson) (GCR Class 11F)

All survived to be renumbered in 1946, so the original number is in brackets.

2660 (5506) *Butler-Henderson*
2661 (5507) *Gerard Powys Dewhurst*
2662 (5508) *Prince of Wales*
2663 (5509) *Prince Albert*
2664 (5510) *Princess Mary*
2665 (5501) *Mons*
2666 (5502) *Zeebrugge*
2667 (5503) *Somme*
2668 (5504) *Jutland*
2669 (5505) *Ypres*
2670 (5511) *Marne*
2671 (6378) *Bailie MacWheeble**
2672 (6379) *Baron of Bradwardine**
2673 (6380) *Evan Dhu**
2674 (6381) *Flora McIvor**
2675 (6382) *Colonel Gardiner**
2676 (6383) *Jonathan Oldbuck**
2677 (6384) *Edie Ochiltree**
2678 (6385) *Luckie Mucklebackit**
2679 (6386) *Lord Glanallan**
2680 (6387) *Lucy Ashton**
2681 (6388) *Captain Craigengelt**
2682 (6389) *Haystoun of Bucklaw**
2683 (6390) *Hobbie Elliott**
2684 (6391) *Wizard of the Moor**
2685 (6392) *Malcolm Graeme**
2686 (6393) *The Fiery Cross**
2687 (6394) *Lord James of Douglas**
2688 (6395) *Ellen Douglas**
2689 (6396) *Maid of Lorn**
2690 (6397) *The Lady of the Lake**
2691 (6398) *Laird of Balmawhapple**
2692 (6399) *Allan-Bane**
2693 (6400) *Rhoderick Dhu**
2694 (6401) *James Fitzjames**

*Delivered after Grouping, the last in late 1924.

Great Eastern Railway

4-4-0

D16 class (Holden) (GER Class S46)

The GER only ever named two of its locomotives. The *Claud Hamilton* name, applied to a new 4-4-0 in 1900, and numbered accordingly, was transferred by the LNER to No. 2546 when the original locomotive was withdrawn in 1947. Class D16 was a Gresley rebuild of Class D15.

8900 (1900) *Claud Hamilton*

Great North of Scotland Railway

4-4-0

D40 class (Pickersgill and Heywood) (GNSR Classes V and F)

The GNSR did not name its locomotives as a rule, but Heywood reintroduced the practice in 1920 and eight of this class of 21 locomotives was named. The original LNER number in brackets follows that of the 1946 renumbering.

2273 (6845) *George Davidson*
2274 (6846) *Benachie*
2275 (6847) *Sir David Stewart*
2276 (6848) *Andrew Bain*
2277 (6849) *Gordon Highlander*
2278 (6850) *Hatton Castle*
2279 (6851) *Glen Grant*
2280 (6852) *Southesk*

Great Northern Railway

4-6-2

See the LNER Class A1 / A3 in Appendix 3.

4-4-2

C2 class (Ivatt)

3990 *Henry Oakley*

Metropolitan Railway

Absorbed named locomotives when the line between Rickmansworth and Aylesbury was transferred to the LNER in 1937.

0-6-4T

M2 class (Jones) (Metropolitan Class G)

The 1946 numbers are used with the original LNER numbers in brackets, although 9075 was withdrawn in 1946 before renumbering, and 6157 *Brill* was scrapped in 1943.

9075 (6154) *Lord Aberconway*
9076 (6155) *Robert H. Selbie*
9077 (6156) *Charles Jones*
6157 *Brill*

North British Railway

4-4-2

C10 and C11 classes (Reid) (NBR Classes I and H)

None of these survived beyond 1939.

9868 *Aberdonian*
9869 *Bonnie Dundee*
9870 *Bon-Accord*
9871 *Thane of Fife*
9872 *Auld Reekie*
9873 *Saint Mungo*
9874 *Dunedin*
9875 *Midlothian*
9876 *Waverley*
9877 *Liddesdale*
9878 *Hazeldean*
9879 *Abbotsford*
9880 *Tweedale*
9881 *Borderer*
9901 *St Johnstoun*
9902 *Highland Chief*
9903 *Cock o' the North*
9904 *Holyrood*
9905 *Buccleuth*
9906 *Teribus*
9909 *Duke of Rothesay**
9910 *The Lord Provost**

* Built as C11 class locomotives.

4-4-0

D29 'Scott' class (Reid) (NBR Class J)

With the one exception which was withdrawn before the 1946 renumbering, the original LNER number is in brackets.

2400 (9895) *Rob Roy*
2401 (9896) *Dandie Dinmont*
2402 (9897) *Redgauntlet*
2403 (9898) *Sir Walter Scott*
2404 (9899) *Jeanie Deans*
2405 (9900) *The Fair Maid*
2406 (9243) *Meg Merrilies*
2407 (9244) *Madge Wildfire*
2408 (9245) *Bailie Nicol Jarvie*
2409 (9338) *Helen Macgregor*
2410 (9339) *Ivanhoe*
2411 (9340) *Lady of Avenel*
2412 (9359) *Dirk Hatteraick*
2413 (9360) *Guy Mannering*
9361 *Vich Ian Vohr*
2415 *Ravenswood*

D30 'Superheated Scott' class (Reid) (NBR Class J)

The original LNER number is in brackets, except for the first of class, withdrawn in mid-1945.

9400 *The Dougal Cratur*
2417 (9363) *Hal o' the Wynd*
2418 (9409) *The Pirate*
2419 (9410) *Meg Dods*
2420 (9411) *Dominie Sampson*
2421 (9411) *Laird o' Monkbarns*
2422 (9413) *Caleb Balderstone*
2423 (9414) *Dugald Dalgetty*
2424 (9415) *Claverhouse*
2425 (9416) *Ellengowan*
2426 (9417) *Cuddie Headrigg*
2427 (9418) *Dumbiedykes*
2428 (9419) *The Talisman*
2429 (9420) *The Abbot*
2430 (9421) *Jingling Geordie*
2431 (9422) *Kenilworth*
2432 (9423) *Quentin Durward*
2433 (9424) *Lady Rowena*
2434 (9425) *Kettledrummie*
2435 (9426) *Norna*
2436 (9427) *Lord Glenvarloch*
2437 (9428) *Adam Woodcock*
2438 (9497) *Peter Poundtext*
2439 (9498) *Father Ambrose*
2440 (9499) *Wandering Willie*
2441 (9500) *Black Duncan*
2442 (9501) *Simon Glover*

D34 'Glen' class (Reid) (NBR Class K)

The original LNER number follows in brackets, except for 9287 which was withdrawn before renumbering.

2467 (9149) *Glenfinnan*
2468 (9221) *Glen Orchy*
2469 (9256) *Glen Douglas*
2470 (9258) *Glen Roy*
2471 (9266) *Glen Falloch*
2472 (9307) *Glen Nevis*
2473 (9405) *Glen Spean*
2474 (9406) *Glen Croe*
2475 (9407) *Glen Bleasdale*
2476 (9408) *Glen Sloy*
2477 (9100) *Glen Dochart*
2478 (9291) *Glen Quioch*
2479 (9291) *Glen Sheil*
2480 (9153) *Glen Fruin*
2481 (9241) *Glen Ogle*
2482 (9242) *Glen Mamie*
2483 (9270) *Glen Garry*
2484 (9278) *Glen Lyon*
2485 (9281) *Glen Murran*
9287 *Glen Gyle*
2487 (9503) *Glen Arklet*
2488 (9504) *Glen Aladale*
2489 (9490) *Glen Dessary*
2490 (9502) *Glen Fintaig*
2491 (9505) *Glen Cona*
2492 (9034) *Glen Garvin*
2493 (9035) *Glen Gloy*
2494 (9492) *Glen Gau*
2495 (9493) *Glen Luss*
2496 (9494) *Glen Loy*
2497 (9495) *Glen Mallie*
2498 (9496) *Glen Moidart*

4-4-0T

D50 class (Drummond) (NBR Class P)

Of three inherited by the LNER, NBR No. 10392 was withdrawn quickly and never received an LNER number, while the remaining two were withdrawn in 1926. The follow-on D51 class had lost their names by 1884.

10390 *Craigendoran*
10391 *Roseneath*
10392 *Helensburgh*

0-6-0

J36 class (Holmes) (NBR Class C)

Out of 168 J36s built, these were named because they were used overseas during the First World War. The 1946 number is given, followed by the LNER original in brackets, except where the locomotive did not survive long enough to be renumbered.

5217 (9176) *French*
9605 *St Quentin*
9608 *Foch*
5268 (9611) *Allenby*
5269 (9612) *Ypres*
9615 *Verdun*
9620 *Rawlinson*
9621 *Monro*
9627 *Petain*
5216 (9628) *Byng*
9631 *Aisne*
9643 *Arras*
5222 (9646) *Somme*
5223 (9647) *Albert*
5224 (9648) *Mons*
5226 (9650) *Haig*
5233 (9657) *Plumer*
5235 (9659) *Gough*
5236 (9660) *Horne*
9661 *Ole Bill*
9662 *Birdwood*
9666 *Marne*
5243 (9673) *Maude*
9676 *Reims*
5253 (9682) *Joffre*

Appendix 5

Locomotives Absorbed at Grouping and Later Acquisitions

Overnight, the LNER found itself with a very mixed fleet of steam locomotives passed on to it by the constituent and subsidiary companies that Parliament decreed should be its lot. The whole of 1922 had been devoted to finalising the arrangements for the Grouping, but the creation of a new management team and some outlines of a structure, were all that could sensibly be achieved.

Records are not always entirely accurate, but below are the locomotives that are recorded as being absorbed on 1 January 1923, and which were renumbered into LNER stock. Later, the LNER took control of the locomotive fleet required for the Midland & Great Northern Joint in 1934, and in 1937 the LNER took over the London Transport Metropolitan Line between Rickmansworth and Aylesbury, and replaced the line's H2 4-4-4Ts with A5 Pacific 4-6-2Ts.

The locomotives are listed in order of the pre-grouping railway company, including the later additions, then by wheel configuration and finally by LNER class, which means that locomotives with a 'higher' class number may actually be older than those with a lower number.

Colne Valley & Halstead Railway

0-6-2T

N18 class, numbered 8314 by LNER. Withdrawn 1928.

2-4-2T

F9 class, numbered 8310–8312 by LNER. The last was withdrawn in 1930.

East & West Yorkshire Union Railway

0-6-0ST

J84 class, with one withdrawn immediately on passing to the LNER and the remaining two numbered 3112 and 3113. Withdrawn in 1928 and 1930.
J85 class, a larger development of the J84, it was numbered 3114 until withdrawn in 1933.

0-6-2T

N19 class; two locomotives that passed to the LNER, numbered 3115 and 3116, but withdrawn by 1928.

Great Central Railway

Petrol-electric railcar

Numbered 51709 by the LNER, withdrawn 1935.

0-4-0ST

Y2 class, originally GCR Class 4, Manning Wardle-built shunters. Withdrawn in 1931.

0-4-4T

G3 class built by Kitson and started life with the Lancashire Derbyshire & East Coast Railway, but taken over by GCR in 1907 as Class C. Withdrawn by 1935.

0-6-0

J8 class (Sacre), originally GCR Class 18, just one survived Grouping and was numbered 309B by the LNER as the Gorton Works shunter. Withdrawn 1924 before renumbering.
J8 class (Parker), originally GCR Class 6AI and based on the 6A (hence '6AI' meant '6A Improved').
J9 class (Parker & Pollitt), originally GCR Classes 9B and 9E. Withdrawn between 1930 and 1936.
J10 class (Parker & Pollitt), originally GCR Classes 9D and 9H with different valve gear from 9B/9E. Withdrawals started in 1933, but many survived Nationalisation.
J 11 class (Robinson), originally GCR Class 9J and developed from the J10, with many later rebuilt by Thompson. Withdrawals did not start until 1954.
J12 class (Sacre), originally GCR Class 6C, one of the first classes to have a cab rather than a weatherboard. Withdrawn between 1922 and 1930.
J13 class (Parker), originally GCR Class 9. Withdrawn 1931–35.

0-6-0T

GCR Class 7 (Sacre). Withdrawn in 1923 before being given LNER classification or numbers.
J60 class, originally GCR Class B, built by Kitson for the Lancashire Derbyshire & East Coast Railway. Withdrawn in 1947 and 1948.
J63 class (Robinson), originally GCR Class 5 and a side tank version of the J62 saddle tank, with some fitted with condensing gear and designated J63/2. All passed to BR.

0-6-0ST

J58 class (Sacre/Robinson), originally GCR Class 18 converted from 0-6-0 tender locomotives. Withdrawn between 1920 and 1930.
J59 class (Sacre), originally GCR Class 18T, altered after 1930 with enclosed cabs. Withdrawn between 1910 and 1929.
J61 class, originally GCR Class 4. An assorted batch of locomotives acquired from contractors, with just two passing to the LNER, which numbered them 5278 and 6469. Withdrawn in 1929–31 as non-standard.
J62 class (Pollitt), originally GCR Class 5, fitted with bells and hooters rather than whistles for dockside working. No. 889 fitted with 4-ton crane in 1903, but removed in 1918. Withdrawn between 1935 and 1951.

0-6-2T

N4 class (Parker), originally GCR Classes 9A and 9B, altered with the larger bunker of the N5. Intended for heavy shunting but undertook a wide range of duties. Withdrawals started in 1932, but a number passed to BR.
N5 class (Parker), originally GCR Classes 9C, 9F and 9O, with a number of boiler variations. Withdrawals started in 1936, but most passed to BR.
N6 class, originally GCR Class A, built by Kitson for the Lancashire Derbyshire & East Coast Railway. Withdrawn between 1933 and 1938.

0-6-4T

M1 class, originally GCR Class D, built by Kitson. Withdrawals started in 1939, but suspended during the war and resumed afterwards so that all were gone by the end of 1947.

0-8-0

Q4 class (Robinson Q4), originally GCR Class 8A; mineral locomotives built as saturated steam but superheating fitted from 1914 and continued under the LNER. Withdrawals started in 1934 but suspended during the war. Thompson started to rebuild them as Q1 0-8-0Ts, but the programme was stopped in 1945. Withdrawals resumed post-war.

0-8-0ST

WMCQR 0-8-0, originally built in 1846, for the London & Birmingham Railway, later the London & North Western, it was sold to the Wrexham Mold & Connah's Quay Railway, which completely rebuilt it in 1880 as an 0-8-0ST, before rebuilding it as an 0-6-2ST and then back again as an 0-8-0ST in 1892. The WMCQR became part of the GCR in 1905, and the locomotive passed to the LNER, but it was withdrawn before a class and a number could be applied.

0-8-4T

S1 class (Robinson), designed as hump shunters. Gresley experimented in 1930 with a booster on the bogie, but these were later removed. All passed to BR.

2-4-0

E2 class (Parker), originally GCR Class 6D. Just three were built.
GCR Class 12A (Sacre), sometimes referred to as LNER Class E3, but all withdrawn before LNER classification could be allocated.

2-4-0T

E8 class (Sacre), GCR Class 12AM. Just two passed to the LNER and withdrawn by January 1925.

2-4-2T

F1 class (Parker), originally GCR Class 3, with all 39 given new boilers by 1929. Several survived until 1949.
F2 class (Pollitt), originally GCR Class 9G. Withdrawals started in 1947.

2-6-2T

L1/L3 classes (Robinson), originally GCR Class 1B, Britain's first 2-6-4Ts, based on the M1 0-6-4T with a boiler similar to that on the 'Director' class 4-4-0s. Nicknamed 'Crabs' because of their unattractive appearance. Built with water pick-up apparatus but this was removed by the LNER in the early 1930s. Initially classified L1 but reclassified L3 in 1945 to make way for Thompson's L1 2-6-4Ts. The first was withdrawn in 1947, but the remainder passed to BR.

2-8-0

O4 and O5 classes (Robinson) (ROD), originally GCR Classes 8K and 8M, mineral locomotives taken up by the War Office for use overseas in both world wars. The LNER also purchased additional locomotives built for the Royal Engineers' Railway Operating Division (ROD) during 1925–27. Used as the basis for Thompson rebuilds 1944–49 (see O1 class in Appendix 2). During WWII, 92 requisitioned for use in Persia, and not returned. Post-war, a small number were acquired for use in Egypt. The remaining locomotives passed to BR.

4-2-2
X4 class (Pollitt), originally GCR Class 13, with six passing to the LNER, which withdrew them between 1923 and 1927.

4-4-0
D5 class (Pollitt), originally GCR Class 11.
D6 class (Pollitt), originally GCR Class 11A.
D7 class (Parker), originally GCR Classes 2 and 2A. All withdrawn by 1939.
D8 class (Parker), originally GCR Class 6DB.
D9 class (Robinson), originally GCR Classes 11B, 11C and 11D, with the first two classes saturated and the 11D superheated.
D10 class (Robinson), originally GCR Class 11E 'Directors'.
D11 class (Robinson), originally GCR Class 11F 'Improved Directors'.
D12 class (Sacre), originally GCR Class 6B. All withdrawn by 1930.

4-6-0
B1/B18 class (Robinson), originally GCR Class 8C; reclassified as B18 in 1943. Just two built and originally numbered 5195 and 5196 by the LNER.
B2/B19 class (Robinson), originally GCR Class I, and known as the 'Sir Sam Fay' class. Reclassified as B19 in 1945.
B3 class (Robinson), originally GCR Class 9P 'Lord Faringdon' class. Robinson Class B4, originally GCR Class 8F.
B5 class (Robinson), originally GCR Class 8, mixed-traffic but popularly known as 'Fish engines' because they spent much time working fast fish trains.
B6 class (Robinson), originally GCR Class 8N, mainly for working freight trains. All withdrawn by the end of 1947.
B7 class (Robinson), originally GCR Class 9Q mixed-traffic engines, known as 'Black Pigs' and 'Colliers' Friends' due to the heavy coal consumption, although ten built post-Grouping performed better.
B8 class (Robinson), originally GCR Class 1A, with four of the eleven built having names – see Appendix 4.
B9 class (Robinson), originally GCR Class 8G, with saturated locomotives classified B9/1, and superheated as B9/2.

4-6-2T
A5 class (Robinson), formerly GCR Class 9N, superheated. Unusually for tank locomotives, these had water pick-up scoops, but these were removed later.

4-4-2
C4 class (Robinson), originally GCR Class 8B.
C5 class (Robinson), originally GCR Classes 8D and 8E. Allocated numbers. 2895–2898 in 1946.

4-4-2T
C13 class (Robinson), originally GCR Class 9K.
C14 class (Robinson), originally GCR Class 9L.

Great Eastern Railway

The name 'Holden' refers to James Holden, with S.D. Holden identified separately.

4-wheel Petrol shunting locomotive

Z6/Y11 class petrol locomotive (built by Motor Rail 'Simplex'). Initially classified as Z6 but this was changed to Y11 in 1943. Numbered 8430 by the LNER in 1930, survived to be taken over by British Railways as No. 8188, but not renumbered again in BR stock. At one time named *Peggy* after the horse it replaced, but this was unofficial and the nameboard was later removed.

0-4-0T

Y4 class (Hill), originally GER Class B74, with coal carried at the back of the left-hand tank. Numbered in 1946 as 8125–8129, and passed to BR.

0-4-0ST

Y5 class, originally GER Class 209. Eight locomotives built by Neilsen, used for shunting and with the unusual feature of coal carried on top of the saddle tank. Four survived to reach the LNER, with three withdrawn between 1926 and 1931, while the fourth was kept for show at LNER exhibitions.

0-4-0 Tram engines

Y6 class (T.W. Worsdell), originally GER class G15, designed for the Wisbech & Upwell Tramway with wooden-bodies and the appearance of a brake van. Numbered 07125, 07126 and 07129 on Grouping. Withdrawn 1931–33.

0-4-4T

G4 class (Holden), originally GER Class S44. Withdrawn by 1938.

0-6-0

J14 class (Holden), originally GER Class N31. All withdrawn by 1925.
J15 class (T.W. Worsdell), originally GER Class Y14, with Holden boilers. One of them set a world record for locomotive assembly of 9 hours 45 minutes in 1913, and then steamed for 5,000 miles before needing a minor overhaul. While withdrawals started in 1920, well over a hundred passed to British Railways.
J16 and J17 class (Holden), originally GER Classes F48 and G58; a goods version of the D14 class 'Claud Hamiltons'. Most passed into BR ownership.
J18 and J19 class (Hill), originally GER Classes E72 and T77; superheated development of the saturated J17 class, with rebuilding of J18s to J19 standard in the late 1930s. All passed to BR.
J20 class (Hill), originally GER Class D81, all of which survived into BR ownership.

0-6-0T

J65 class (Holden), originally GER Class E22, a variant of the J66 class with fewer boiler tubes, often known as 'Blackwall Tanks' because of their work on this line. Withdrawals started in 1930, but five survived to 1947.
J66 class (Holden), originally GER Class T18. Withdrawals started in 1936, but interrupted by the war and a number passed to BR.
J67 and J69 class (Holden), originally GER Class R24, R24 Rebuilt, and S56. Withdrawals started in 1937, but interrupted by the war and a number passed to BR.
J68 class (Hill), originally GER Class C72, some with condensing gear, with one batch as passenger locomotives and the other two as shunters, one was sold for use on the Longmoor Military Railway while the remainder passed to BR.

0-6-0 Tram engines

J70 class (Holden), originally GER Class C53, built as tram locomotives to run on or alongside the public highway on the Wisbech & Upwell Tramway, fitted with cow catchers, wooden bodywork, warning bells, double-ended, and resembled a brake van. Survived to pass to BR.

Ex-GER J68 class 0-6-0T No. 7049 shunts a horsebox at Cambridge in 1939. During the life of the LNER, horseboxes were one of the wagon types that declined steadily, as this traffic was especially vulnerable to road competition. (*HMRS AEU 806*)

A train consisting of former GER carriages is headed by B12 class 4-6-0 No. 8511 through Cambridge in 1939. (*HMRS AEU 812*)

0-6-2T

N7 class (Hill), originally GER Class L77, replacing 2-4-2Ts on suburban duties instead of electrification. Both saturated and superheated examples built. Design adopted by LNER and many more built post-Grouping. All passed to BR.

2-4-0

E4 class (Holden), originally GER Class T26, with withdrawals starting in 1926, but many of this class were retained due to the locomotive shortages of WWII.

2-4-2T

F3 class (Holden), originally GER Class C32. Many fitted with condensing gear. Withdrawn between 1936 and 1945.
F4 and F5 class (T.W. Worsdell), originally GER Class M15. The F4s were known as 'Gobblers' due to their heavy coal consumption, but later versions had different valve gear. F5s had higher boiler pressure. Survived to late 1950s.
F6 class (S.D. Holden), originally GER Class G69, fitted with condensing gear. Survived to late 1950s.
F7 class (S.D. Holden), originally GER Class Y65, with large cabs leading to nickname 'Crystal Palace Tanks'. Withdrawn between 1931 and 1948.

4-4-0

D13 class (Holden), originally GER Class T19 Rebuilt. Mainly withdrawn by 1938, but three retained until 1943–44.
Classes D14, D15 and D16 'Claud Hamilton' (Holden), originally GER Classes S46 and S56.

4-6-0

B12 class (Holden), originally GER Class S69 or '1500s'; passenger locomotives.

Great North of Scotland Railway

0-4-4T

G10 class (Johnson), original GNSR Class R). Withdrawn between 1937 and 1947.

0-6-0T

J90 class (Manson), originally GNSR Class D, built to end the GNSR practice of using redundant tender locomotives for shunting. Withdrawn between 1932 and 1936.

4-4-0

D38 class (Manson), originally GNSR Class Q, numbered 6875 to 6877 by LNER, with all withdrawn by 1937.
D39 class (Cowan), originally GNSR Class C, similar to D47 but with larger driving wheels. Numbered 6801–6803 by LNER.
D40 class (Pickersgill and Heywood) originally GNSR Classes V and F respectively, with the former saturated and the later superheated.
D41 class (Johnson and Pickersgill), GNSR Classes S and T respectively, the latter derived from the former – combined, these became the most numerous GNSR class to enter LNER service.
D42 class (Manson), originally GNSR Class O, similar to earlier D46 below but with larger bogie wheels. New boilers fitted 1915–20.
D43 class (Manson), originally GNSR Class P, similar to D38 above but with smaller driving wheels identical to those of the D42.
D44 class (Manson), originally GNSR Class A. Manson's first 4-4-0s for the GNSR. Most withdrawn by end 1926.

D45 class (Cowan), originally GNSR Class M. All withdrawn by 1932.
D46 class (Manson), originally GNSR Class N, and the first locomotives to be built at Inverurie Works. Numbered 6805 and 6806 by the LNER.
D47 class (Cowan), originally GNSR Classes K and L, with the former known as D47/2 and withdrawn in 1924.
D48 class (Manson), originally GNSR Class G. Numbered 6869–6871 by LNER, and withdrawn by 1934.

Great Northern Railway

0-4-4T

G1 class (Stirling), developed from G2 class below, with many withdrawn before Grouping and the remainder between 1924 and 1927.
G2 class (Stirling), with six out of 16 passing to the LNER but withdrawn by late 1926.

0-6-0

J1 class (Ivatt), originally GNR Class J21. Withdrawals started in 1947 but most passed to British Railways.
J2 class (Ivatt), originally GNR Class J21, based on J1 as above but with larger wheels. Withdrawals started in 1946 but most passed to BR.
J3 and J4 class (Stirling), originally GNR Classes J4 and J5, with many rebuilt by Gresley before Grouping. Out of 160, 41 passed to BR.
J5 class (Ivatt), originally GNR Class J22, with smaller wheels than the J1. Withdrawn after Nationalisation.
J6 class (Ivatt and Gresley), originally GNR Class J22. Gresley versions had the boiler set back. All survived into Nationalisation.
J7 class (Stirling), originally GNR Class J9 and J10. All classed the same by the LNER as they all had the same boiler design. Withdrawn between 1927 and 1936.

0-6-0T

J50 and J51 classes (Gresley), originally GNR Class J23, with 62 built after Grouping. The J51s rebuilt as J50s between 1929 and 1935 with larger boilers. All survived to be taken over by BR.

0-6-0ST

J19 class (Stirling), originally GNR Class J19. Only No. 470 survived into LNER ownership but was not renumbered or given an LNER power classification. Withdrawn 1927.
J52 and J53 class (Stirling), originally GNR Classes J13 and J14, many with condensing gear and also being able to display Southern Railway headcodes. Withdrawals started in 1936, but suspended during war years and most joined BR.
J54, J55 and J56 classes (Stirling), originally GNR Classes J15, J16 and J17. The J15 was the GNR's first saddle tank; J17 being a smaller version and the J16 being rebuilds of both with domed boilers. Withdrawals started in 1902, with most withdrawn by 1939, but a handful survived the war and two J55s joined BR.
J57 class (Stirling), originally GNR Class J18, based on J15 but with small wheels for routes with reduced clearances. Most withdrawn between 1928 and 1933, although one survived to 1938.

0-6-2T

N1 class (Ivatt), also GNR Class N1, built for London suburban trains. Withdrawals started in 1947, but most passed to BR.
N2 class (Gresley), also GNR Class N2, an improved version of the N1 with production continuing after Grouping. All passed to BR.

Although engine sheds were used for maintenance, much of the basic servicing of a locomotive was handled in the yard outside, with pits for ash collection and even basic inspection. The locomotive in the middle of this view at King's Cross is an ex-GNR J52 0-6-0ST. Some sheeted wagons and a goods van are on the left. (*HMRS ABJ 334*)

0-8-0

Q1, Q2 and Q3 class (Ivatt), originally GNR Classes K1 (Q1 and Q2) and K2; mineral locomotives known as 'Long Toms' due to their appearance. Withdrawn between 1926 and 1935.

0-8-2T

R1 class (Ivatt), originally GNR Class L1, built for suburban services. Withdrawn between 1927 and 1934.

2-4-0

E1 class (Stirling and Ivatt), also GNR Class E1; 34 passed to the LNER and all were withdrawn by late 1927.

2-6-0

K1 class (Gresley), originally GNR Class H2, designed for fast goods trains, nicknamed 'Ragtimers' due to their lively ride at speed. Later some rebuilt to K2 standard, modified to run on the former GER and NBR lines with lower chimneys. All passed to BR.

K2 class (Gresley), originally GNR Class H3, designed for fast goods trains, with larger boiler than K1, modified to run on the former GER and NBR lines with lower chimneys. A number were fitted with air braking apparatus to run on the GER. Cabs also modified for Scottish depots. All passed to BR.

K3 class (Gresley), originally GNR Class H4, based on H3, with larger diameter boiler. A fast mixed-traffic locomotive, nicknamed 'Jazzers', largely due to their exhaust beat and rough riding, production continued after Grouping up to 1937. Rebuilding in 1945 resulted in reclassification as K5. All survived to be passed to BR.

2-8-0

O1 class (later Class O3) (Gresley), also GNR Class O1, heavy goods locomotives, nicknamed 'Tangos' because the dance was in vogue at the time of their introduction. Reclassified O3 in 1944 to clear the way for Thompson's O4 rebuilds. Withdrawals were between 1947 and 1952.
O2 class (Gresley), also GNR Class O2. The first Gresley design to use conjugated valve gear. Further orders placed by the LNER up to 1943. All passed to BR.

4-4-0

D1 class (Ivatt), also GNR Class D1.
D2 class (Ivatt), originally GNR Class D1.
D3 class (Ivatt), originally GNR Class D3. Some rebuilt from Class D4.
D4 class (Ivatt), originally GNR Class D2. Some rebuilt as Class D3.

An ex-GNR C1 4-4-2 Atlantic, No. 4421, with an A3 and a coaling tower in the background, on a misty day in 1936. (*HMRS ABJ 016*)

4-4-2

C1 class (Ivatt) – large-boiler version of GNR Class C1.
C2 class (Ivatt) 'Klondike' – small-boiler version of GNR Class C1.

4-4-2T

C12 class (Ivatt), originally GNR Class C2.

Hull & Barnsley Railway

0-6-0

J23 class (M. Stirling), originally H&BR Class B. Withdrawn over a lengthy period with the last in 1938.
J28 class (M. Stirling), originally H&BR Classes L, L1 and LS. Withdrawn between 1934 and 1938.
J80 class (M. Stirling), originally H&BR Class G2; just three built. Withdrawn in 1930 and 1931.

0-6-0T

J75 class (M. Stirling), originally H&BR Class G3; based on J80 but with smaller driving wheels. All withdrawn between 1937 and 1939 except one which passed to BR.

0-6-2T

N11 class, originally H&BR Class F1. Built by Kitson for the Lancashire Derbyshire & East Coast Railway, but the company was unable to pay and the locomotives were diverted to the H&BR, which used them as banking engines. Modified by the H&BR to meet its standard designs and then again by the LNER. All withdrawn between 1943 and 1946.
N12 class (M. Stirling), originally H&BR Class F2. Reboilered by the LNER. Withdrawn between 1936 and 1938.
N13 class (M. Stirling), originally H&BR Class F3. Fitted with domed boilers 1926–1934. All passed to BR.

0-8-0

Q10 class (M. Stirling), originally H&BR Class A. Withdrawn in 1931.

4-4-0

D24 class (M. Stirling), originally H&BR Class J. Withdrawn 1933–34.

Metropolitan Railway

0-6-4T

M2 class (Jones), originally Metropolitan Class G, passed to LNER in 1937 and modified to meet the composite loading gauge. Withdrawals started in 1943 due to non-standard design, but two survived to pass to BR.

4-4-4T

H2 class (Jones). Withdrawn 1942–1947.

2-6-4T

L2 class (Maunsell/Hally), originally Metropolitan Class K, based on Maunsell's Class N 2-6-0. Sold to LNER in 1937 on transfer of services north of Rickmansworth. Withdrawals started in 1943 due to non-standard boilers, but two passed to BR.

Mid-Suffolk Light Railway

0-6-0T

J64 class. All three fitted with jacks for re-railing as derailments were common, with one immediately scrapped by the LNRER and the other two numbered 8316 and 8317, but withdrawn in 1929 and 1930.

Midland & Great Northern Joint Railway

0-6-0

J40 and J41 class (Johnson), originally M&GNJR Class D, with J41 applied to locomotives rebuilt during the 1920s, not classified until 1942. Withdrawn in 1943 and 1944.
J93 class (Marriott), originally known simply as the M&GN 'Shunting' class, and classified by the LNER in 1942. Withdrawn between 1943 and 1949.

0-6-0ST

Fox Walker built two locomotives for the Great Yarmouth & Stalham Light Railway, which was taken over by the M&GNJR. One, No. 16 *Stalham*, passed to the LNER, but was never classified and was withdrawn in 1937.

4-4-0

M&GNJR Class 'A Rebuild', numbered 023–028 by LNER but not assigned a class number before withdrawal by 1941.
D52, D53 and D54S classes (W. Johnson), originally M&GNJR Class C; all withdrawn by 1945.

4-4-2T

C17 (Marriott),originally M&GNJR Class A. Officially described as rebuilds of 4-4-0Ts; numbered 09, 020 and 041 by the LNER. Withdrawn 1942–1944.

North British Railway

0-4-0 Petrol shunting locomotive

Y11 class four-wheel petrol shunting locomotive built by Motor Rail 'Somplex'. Initially classified Z6 but changed to Y11 in 1943. Numbered 8431 by the LNER in 1930, survived to be taken over by BR.

0-4-0

Y10 class (Wheatley), with two locomotives built for the NBR to handle short-distance goods traffic, with one passing to the LNER numbered 1011. Withdrawn late 1925.

0-4-0ST

Y9 class (Drummond), originally NBR Class G and nicknamed 'Pugs' by NBR railwaymen. Intended as dock shunters, many of the 38 built were used inland. Five were withdrawn in 1921–23, but the remainder survived to be passed to BR.

0-4-4T

G7 class (Holmes), originally NBR Class P. Withdrawn between 1926 and 1932.
G8 class (Drummond), originally NBR Class P. Withdrawn by the end of 1925.
G9 class (Reid), originally NBR Class M. Withdrawn 1936–40.

0-6-0

J31 class (Wheatley), originally NBR Class R. Withdrawals started in 1911, and continued until 1928 although two were kept for stationary use.
J32 class (Drummond), originally NBR Class C. Withdrawals started in 1921 and continued until 1925.
J33 class (Holmes), originally NBR Class D; a development of the J34 below, and rebuilt with new boilers between 1908 and 1913. Withdrawn between 1924 and 1938, although only two left after 1932.

J34 class (Drummond), originally NBR Class D. Received new boilers between 1892 and 1908; withdrawn between 1921 and 1928.
J35 class (Reid), originally NBR Class B, superheated between 1923 and 1942. Withdrawals started in 1946, but most passed to BR.
J36 class (Holmes), originally NBR Class C. All rebuilt between 1913 and 1923. Nicknamed 'Eighteen Inchers' after their cylinder sizes, while those used by the War Office abroad were given names, as shown in Appendix 4. Withdrawals started in 1931, but many survived into BR ownership. A popular choice to work snow ploughs.
J37 class (Reid), originally NBR Classes B and S, with the latter having a higher pressure boiler. All passed to BR.

0-6-0T

J82 class (Drummond), originally NBR Class R, influenced by Stroudley and virtually a more powerful 'Terrier'. New boilers fitted between 1908 and 1910. Withdrawn between 1922 and 1926. Named locomotives listed in Appendix 4.
J83 class (Holmes), originally NBR Class D. Rebuilt after passing to LNER. One withdrawn in 1947 but the remainder passed to BR.
J88 class (Reid), originally NBR Class F. Designed as dock shunters, with all passing to BR.

0-6-0ST

J81 class (Wheatley), originally NBR Class E. One passed to the LNER with most withdrawn in 1921.
J84 class (Wheatley), originally NBR Class E. Most withdrawn between 1915 and 1920, leaving three to pass to the LNER, which were withdrawn in 1924.
J85 class (Wheatley), originally NBR Class E. Withdrawn between 1919 and 1924, with just one passing to the LNER.
J86 class (Wheatley), originally NBR Class E, with just two built before production switched to the J81 type. Only one passed to the LNER, to be withdrawn in 1924.
All the above E class locomotives were built without cabs and fitted only with weatherboards, but some had makeshift cabs added later.

0-6-2T

N14 and N15 class (Reid), originally NBR Class A, with the original two NBR orders augmented by further construction after Grouping. Two converted to oil-firing during the 1926 strike, but reconverted back to coal after a few months. Withdrawals started in 1947, but most passed to BR.

2-4-0

E7 class (Wheatley), originally NBR Class P. Many rebuilt in 1915. All withdrawn by the end of 1927.

4-4-0

D25 class (Holmes), originally NBR Class N. Withdrawn by 1932 although some kept in store until 1935.
D26 class (Holmes), originally NBR Class K. Withdrawn by 1926.
D27 and D28 class (Drummond), originally NBR Class M 'Abbotsford'. Rebuilt 1902–04, with seven surviving Grouping, but withdrawn by late 1926.
D29 'Scott' class (Reid), originally NBR Class J, with superheating introduced by 1936.
D30 'Superheated Scott class (Reid)', originally NBR Class J.
D31 class (Holmes), originally NBR Class M.
D32 class (Reid), originally NBR Class K.
D33 class (Reid D33), originally NBR Class K.

D34 'Glen' class (Reid), originally NBR Class K. Numbered 2467 to 2498 in 1946.
D35 class (Holmes), originally NBR Class N. All withdrawn by the end of 1924.
D36 class (Holmes), originally NBR Class L.

4-4-0T
D50 class (Drummond), originally NBR Class P. Just three built.
D51 class (Drummond), originally NBR Class R, based on Class P, with 30 built, but all withdrawn by 1933.

4-4-2
C10 and C11 classes (Reid), originally NBR Classes I and H.

4-4-2T Atlantic Tank
Reid C15, originally NBR Class M.
Reid C16, originally NBR Class L.

North Eastern Railway

NB: Worsdell refers to Wilson Worsdell, with designs by his brother as T.W. Worsdell.

Electric locomotives
ES1 class Bo-Bo, built for the quayside at Newcastle with overhead electrification but with a third rail in tunnel. Survived to pass to BR.
EF1 and EB1 classes Bo-Bo, 1,500V dc overhead electrics, placed in storage in the late 1930s due to falling traffic, they returned to service after Nationalisation. Classification EF meant 'electric freight', but for a while they were classified as EB, 'electric banking', but never performed these duties.

The former NER electric locomotive No. 13 at Darlington in 1939. (*HMRS ACW 217*)

Petrol-electric autocars
Numbered 3170Y and 3171Y by the LNER Withdrawn 1931 and 1930 respectively.

Petrol rail motor bus

Numbered 130Y in the road fleet. Gutted by fire during refuelling November 1926.

0-4-0T

Y7 class (T.W. Worsdell), originally NER Class H dock shunters. Withdrawn 1929–32, but sold to industrial railways.
Y8 class (T.W. Worsdell), originally NER K. Built specifically for use at Hull docks. Three scrapped in 1936–37, but two passed to BR.

The Y7 0-4-0T was used mainly for shunting in the docks, and this one, No. 985, is at Hull Alexandra Dock. Coal is carried in one of the side tanks. Most of these useful little engines were sold to industrial users on being withdrawn by the LNER. (*HMRS AAB127*)

0-4-4T

G5 class (Worsdell), originally NER Class O, with most surviving past Nationalisation.
G6 class (Fletcher), originally known as NER 0-4-4T BTP (Bogie Tank Passenger). Withdrawn by 1929.

0-6-0

NER 1001 class (Bouch), originally built for the Stockton & Darlington Railway, the sole survivor at Grouping, No. 1275, was withdrawn in February 1923 before renumbering, and placed in preservation.
NER 398 class (Fletcher). Withdrawals started before Grouping but the LNER inherited 86, but did not allocate a class even though the last was not withdrawn until 1928.
J21 class (T.W. Worsdell), originally NER Class C, based on J15 designed for the GER. Built initially as simple engines but later versions were built as compound locomotives with higher pressure boilers, but W. Worsdell was requested to convert all locomotives back to the simple design to improve reliability. Withdrawals started in 1928, but many were still in service on Nationalisation.
J22 class (McDonnell), originally NER Class 59, all rebuilt by W. Worsdell, with withdrawal between 1924 and 1930.

J24 class (Worsdell), originally NER Class P, with superheating applied to a number, but eventually reverted to saturated steam. Withdrawn between 1933 and 1951.
J25 class (Worsdell), originally NER Class P1. Many loaned to the GWR during WWII having been kept in store after withdrawal in 1939. A substantial number entered BR ownership.
J26 class (Worsdell), originally NER Class P2, developed from the P1 with a larger boiler to increase the size of freight trains on the NER. All survived into BR ownership.
J27 class (Worsdell), originally NER Class P3, and developed from the P2. All survived into BR ownership.

0-6-0T

NER 44 class (Fletcher), rebuilt from saddle tanks between 1898 and 1902. Not given LNER classification or numbers and all withdrawn by the end of 1926.
J71 class (T.W. Worsdell), originally NER Class E, developed from the Class 44 locomotives. Withdrawals started in 1933, but stopped during the war so that two-thirds of the class passed to BR.
J72 class (Worsdell), originally NER Class E1, developed from the E1/J71 above with larger cylinders and smaller driving wheels. No. 2331 was fitted with a mechanical stoker in 1939 to allow one-man operation. All survived to pass to BR with more built in 1949–51.
J73 class (Worsdell), originally NER Class L. Developed as a more powerful alternative to the J71 class with just ten built. All survived to the mid-1950s.
Tennant J74, originally NER Class 8, designed by committee led by general manager. Withdrawn in 1930 and 1931.
J76 class (Fletcher), originally NER Class 124, developed from the 0-4-4T BPT (LNER G6 class). Built as well tanks before having side tanks fitted. Withdrawn between 1926 and 1929.
J77 class (Worsdell), originally NER Class 290. Withdrawals started in 1933, but most survived to pass to BR.
J79 class (Worsdell), originally NER Class H2. Just three built and when withdrawn during the late 1930s were sold to industrial users.

0-6-2T

N8 class (T.W. Worsdell N8), originally NER Class B, designed to haul mineral trains. Many fitted with superheaters between 1915 and 1927, but later the LNER reversed this programme. Withdrawals started in 1929, but were suspended during the war and a number passed to BR.
N9 class (Worsdell), originally NER Class N, basically a simplified N8, with almost all passing to BR.
N10 class (Worsdell), originally NER Class U, as a tank version of the J25 tender locomotive and with smaller wheels than the N9. All passed to BR.

0-8-0

Q5 class (Worsdell), originally NER Classes T and T1, based on Worsdell's B13 and B14 4-6-0 designs. T1s were used by the British Army in France during WWI, but all returned to the NER post-war. Withdrawn between 1946 and 1951.
Q6 class (Raven), originally NER Class T2. A larger boiler version of the Q5, but used to test different superheaters before standardising on the Schmidt, although the LNER later converted them to its Robinson standard superheater. All passed to BR.
Q7 class (Raven), originally NER Class T3, designed as a three-cylinder mineral locomotive, but extra power was not practical due to restrictions on the length of trains. Only five built initially, but LNER ordered ten more. All passed to BR.

2-2-4T

X1 class (Worsdell) *Aerolite*, originally built as a 2–2–2WT to haul the NER Mechanical Engineer's saloon coach. It was converted to a side tank in 1866 and numbered 66, while later it became a 4-2-2T, and in 1902 was converted to 2-2-4T. Withdrawn in 1933, it went into preservation at York the following year.
X2 class (Worsdell), formerly NER No. 957, built as a G6 class 0-4-4T, it was rebuilt in 1902 as a 2-2-4T to haul NER officers' saloons. Withdrawn in 1937 as the last single-driver to operate in the UK, apart from preserved locomotives.
X3 class (Worsdell), originally NER Class 190, consisting of two locomotives with the first built as a 2–2–2, and rebuilt as a 2-2-4T in 1881, and numbered 190. The second was built as a 4–2–0 and after three rebuilds emerged as a 2-2-4T in 1894. After Grouping it was numbered 1679. Both were withdrawn in the 1930s when it was no longer economically viable to provide inspection saloons for senior officers.

2-4-0

E5 class (Tennant), originally NER 1463 class, developed from the Fletcher 901 class and designed by a committee headed by the NER's general manager. All withdrawn by the end of 1929 with No. 1463 preserved at York.
NER 901 class (Fletcher). Not classified by LNER as last example withdrawn in 1925 and preserved at York.
Fletcher NER 1440 class. Not classified by LNER as last example withdrawn in 1925.

2-4-2T

F8 class (T.W. Worsdell), originally NER Class A. Withdrawn between 1928 and 1938.

4-4-0

NER 38 class (McDonnell), of which just one survived into LNER ownership and was withdrawn after 47 days.
D17 class (Worsdell), originally NER Classes M1 and Q. Mainly withdrawn by 1939 but a few survived to 1945.
D18 class (Worsdell), originally NER Class Q1, numbered 1869 and 1870, with both withdrawn in 1930.
D19 class (Worsdell), originally NER Class M but reclassified as 3CC in 1914 as an experimental compound engine.
D20 class (Worsdell), originally NER Class R. Many rebuilt after 1936.
D21 class (Worsdell), originally NER Class R1. Withdrawn 1942–46.
D22 class (T.W. Worsdell), originally NER Class F. Withdrawn by 1935.
D23 class (T.W. Worsdell), originally NER Class G. Built as 2-4-0 but rebuilt 1900–04. Withdrawn by 1935.

4-4-2

C6 class (Worsdell), originally NER Classes V and V/09.
Raven C7, originally NER Class Z.
Worsdell C8, originally NER Class 4CC, actually designed by Walter Smith as compound locomotives and numbered 730 and 731, scrapped 1930 and 1935.

4-4-4

Raven C9, variant of C7 above, with just two locomotives, 727 and 2171 fitted with boosters on replacement two-axle rear bogies, which were articulated with the tender, in 1931.

4-4-4T

Raven H1, rebuilt as 4-6-2T A8s between 1931 and 1936.

4-6-0

B13 class (Worsdell), originally NER Class S. First British-designed passenger 4-6-0. Withdrawn 1928–38.
B14 class (Worsdell), originally NER Class S1. Withdrawn 1929–31.
B15 class (Raven), originally NER Class S2. The first seven had saturated boilers, and the next 13 had superheating. Withdrawn 1944–47.
B16 class (Raven), originally NER Class S3. Many rebuilt 1944–47 as B16/3, with the last withdrawn in 1964.

4-6-2T

A6 class (Worsdell), originally built 1907–08 as NER Class W 4-6-0 tank locomotives. All ten were rebuilt between 1914 and 1917 with larger bunkers, requiring the addition of a trailing wheel to bear the weight.
A7 class (Worsdell), originally classified as NER Class Y but not built until Raven took over. Developed from NER Class T1 4-8-0T heavy shunters.

4-8-0T

T1 class (Worsdell), built by the NER and the LNER. All passed to BR.

Bibliography

Books

Allen, Cecil J., *Titled Trains of Great Britain*, Ian Allan, London, 1946–67

Beaumont, Robert, *The Railway King: A biography of George Hudson railway pioneer and fraudster*, Review, London, 2002

Bishop, D. and Davies, W.J.K., *Railways and War since 1917*, Blandford, London, 1974

Bonavia, M.R., *A History of the LNER*, three volumes, George Allen & Unwin, London, 1983

Crump, N., *By Rail to Victory: The story of the LNER in Wartime*, London & North Eastern Railway, London, 1947

Glover, J., *London's Underground*, Ian Allan, London, 1999

Gordon, D.I., *A Regional History of the Railways of Great Britain: Volume V1 – The Eastern Counties*, David & Charles, Newton Abbot

Gourvish, Terry, *British Railways 1948–73*, Cambridge University Press, 1987
———, *British Rail 1974–1997*, Oxford University Press, Oxford, 2002

Hamilton Ellis, C., *The Trains We Loved*, Allen & Unwin, London, 1947

Hands, Peter B., *The London & North Eastern A4, A3, A1 and A2 Pacific Locomotives*, Self-published, Solihull, 1980
———, *The London & North Eastern V2 2-6-2s*, Self-published, Solihull, 1980
———, *The LNER B1 4-6-0s*, Self-published, Solihull, 1981
———, *The LNER B16, B12, B2 and B17 4-6-0s*, Self-published, Solihull, 1981
———, *The LNER Tank Locomotives, N10, N15, N5, N1, N2, N7, A5, A8, T1 and Q1 Classes*, Self-published, Solihull, 1981
———, *The LNER 4-4-0s, D30, D34, D16, D11 and D48*, Self-published, Solihull, 1982
———, *The LNER 0-6-0s, J6, J11, J35, J37 and J19 Classes*, Self-published, Solihull, 1980
———, *The LNER Tank Locomotives, J67/J69, J68, J72 and J50 Classes*, Self-published, Solihull, 1984

Hoole, K., *A Regional History of the Railways of Great Britain: Volume V1 – The North East*, David & Charles, Newton Abbot

Jackson, Alan A., *London's Termini*, David & Charles, Newton Abbot, 1969

John, E., *Timetable for Victory: A brief and popular account of the railways and railway-owned dockyards of Great Britain and Ireland during the six years' war, 1939–1945*, The British Railways, London, 1946

Joy, David, *A Regional History of the Railways of Great Britain: Volume VIII – South and West Yorkshire*, David & Charles, Newton Abbot, 1975

Neele, George Potter, *Railway Reminiscences*, 1904

Nock, O.S., *Britain's Railways at War, 1939–1945*, Ian Allan, Shepperton, 1971

Peacock, A.J., *The Rise And Fall of the Railway King*, Sutton, Stroud, 1995.

Smullen, Ivor, *Taken For A Ride*; Herbert Jenkins, London 1968

Simmons, Jack, and Biddle, Gordon, *The Oxford Companion to British Railway History*, Oxford University Press, Oxford, 2000

Tavender, L., *HRMS Livery Register*, Historical Model Railway Society

Thomas, John, *A Regional History of the Railways of Great Britain: Volume V1 – Scotland*, David & Charles, Newton Abbot

White, H.P., *A Regional History of the Railways of Great Britain: Volume III – Greater London*, David & Charles, Newton Abbot

Wragg, David, *A Historical Dictionary of the Railways of the British Isles*, Wharncliffe, Barnsley, 2009
———, *Wartime on the Railways 1939–1945*, Sutton, 2006
———, *Signal Failure – Politics and Britain's Railways*, Sutton, 2004

Yeadon, W.B., *Yeadon's Register of LNER Locomotives*, up to 61 volumes and indices, Booklaw Publications, Nottingham, 2004 onwards

Websites

London & North Eastern Railway Encyclopaedia: *www.lner.info*

National Railway Museum, York: *www.nrm.org.uk*

Index

Page references in *italics* refer to illustrations.

Aberdeen, 4, 7–8, 15–16, 18, 19, 45–6, 49, 60–2, 70, 72–3, 82–4, 99–101, 105, 110, 112, 116, 123, 129–30, 132–3, 142, 168, 176, 194, 200, 206, 221
Aberdeen Railway, 15
'Aberdonian', 99–101
Accidents: Castle Cary, 166; Darlington, 165; Hull Paragon, 164–5; Penistone, 165; Potters Bar, 167; Welwyn Garden City, 165–6
Advertising, 63, 145–7, 151–2
Alexander & Sons, W., 163
Amsterdam, 8
Amsterdam, 158, 183
Antwerp, 102–3, 105, 132, 157–8, 182, 202
Antwerp, 157
Armstrong-Whitworth, 92–5, 211
Arnhem, 158
Articulated carriages/units, 7, 42, 66, 81, 94, 96, 101, 105, 110, 120–1, 138–42, *140–3*, *154*, 155, 207
Associated Humber Lines, 158
Atlantics, *33*, 69–71, 76, 80, 82, 84, *111*, 117–18, 220, *241*

Baedeker Raids, 199
Barry, C.E., 40
Bayes, Gilbert, 198
Berlin, 8
Berwick-on-Tweed, 18, 21, 70, 95, 110–12, 169–70
Beyer-Garratt, *77*, *145*, 216
'Big Four,' 7, 9, 11, 44, 62–3, 69, 124, 128, 151–2, 180, 193, 203, 211
Birkenhead, 31
Bishopsgate, 14, 31, 38–40
Blenheim, *86*
Boat trains, 101–103
Brackenhill Light Railway, 12, 23
Bradford, 17, 44, 112, 114, 119, 121–2, 138, 165, 167
British Empire Exhibition, 150
British Queen, *144*
British Railways, 7, 11, 42–3, 63, 72, 94, 128, 149, 204–6, 211, 222–3, 226, 236, 239
Broad Street, 17, 35, 38, 42, 196
Bruges, 157
Bus companies, 163

Caledonian Railway, 15–16, 18, 25, 48–9, 159
Caledonian & Dunbartonshire Railway, 24
Cambrian Railway, 12
Cambridge, 14, 17, 40–1, *41*, *53*, 54, 67, *103*, 104, *104*, 134, 139, *148*, *149*, 150, *172*, 198, 204, *237*
Cambridge Buffet Expresses, 104
Camping coaches, *134*, *135*, 139
Canadian Pacific Railway, 157
Capital formation, 61
Carter Paterson, 163
Central London Railway/Central Line, 41–2, 96, 98, 141
Channel Tunnel, 13, 19, 156
Cheshire Lines Committee, 12, 17, *30*, 31, 132
Churchill, Winston (later Sir), 96
City of Durham, *45*
City of Kingston-upon-Hull, *73*
City of London, *52*
Clacton, 14, 102, 105, 170
'Clacton Belle', 105
Clarence & Hartlepool Junction Railway, 12, 23
'Claud Hamilton' D15 Class, *62*, 71, 229, 236
Coal traffic, 7, 9, 12–15, 17–21, 23, 27–8, 30, 35–6, 39, 40, 42–4, 46, 49–50, 64, 70, 72, 76–80, 84, 87, 91–2, 98, 101, 111, 123–6, 129–30, 148, 156, 160–1, 164, 172, 188, 191–2, 194–5, 202–3, 206–7, 212, 235–6, 238, 244, 246
Coaling, 36, *48*, *70*, 80, 91, *172*, 173, *176*, *241*
Cock o' the North, 83, *100*, 101
Colne Valley & Halstead Light Railway, 12, 23, 227, 232
Common carrier obligation, 124–5
Crompton-Parkinson, 95
'Continentals', see Boat trains
'Coronation', 9, 66, 85, 105–6, 121, 155
Cramlington, 135
Cromer, 15, 27–9, 54

Dalmeny, *178*
Derwent Valley Light Railway, 31
Diesel traction, 7, 61, 67, 81, 87, 89–95, 98, 102, 148, 162, 206–7, 209, 211

Director-class, 71–3, 76, 112, 217
Dodman, Guard Arthur, 204
Dominion of Canada, 85
Doncaster, 14, 17, 21, 30, 45–6, 75, 78, 81, 83, *85*, *86*, 86–8, 92, 95, 98, 101, 114–15, 121–2, 123, 155, *169*, 188, 193–4
Drummond, Dugald, 18, 231, 243–5
Duddington, J, 86, 155
Dyce, 16, 46, 200

East & West Yorkshire Union Railway, 12, 23, 232
'East Anglian', 106–9
East Anglian Railway, 14
East Coast Joint Stock, 17
East Coast Main Line, 7, 17, 21, 48, 52, 59, 61, 63, 71, 92, 114, 168, *170*, 175, 192, 206–7
East Lincolnshire Railway, 12, 24,
East Midland Motor Services, 163
East Suffolk Railway, 14,
East Yorkshire Motor Services, 163
'Eastern Belle', 109
Eastern Counties Motor Services, 163
Eastern Counties Railway, 14, 25, 31, 38, 54–5
Eastern Group of Railways/ East Coast Group, 16, 45, 75, 109–10
Eastern National Motor Services, 163
Eastern Union Railway, 14
Edinburgh, 7–9, 17–19, 21, 24–5, 45–9, *47*, 59, 61–2, 70–3, 77, 79, 82–5, 90, 99–101, 105–6, 109–14, 117, 132–3, 135, 137, 143, 153–5, 161, 166–8, 170, 176, 187–8, 199, 204, 206, 208, 221
Edinburgh & Bathgate Railway, 12, 24
Edinburgh & Dalkeith Railway, 47
Edinburgh & Disrict Suburban Railway, 48
Edinburgh & Glasgow Railway, 24, 47
Edinburgh, Leith & Granton Railway, 47
Edward Thompson, 88
Electrification, 7, 9, 13, 15, 23, 27, 32, 37, 40–3, 48, 50, 52, 54–5, 59, 61, 64, 67–8, 72, 77, 79, 81, 87, 89–92, 94–6, 98, 140–3, 150, 183, 203, 205–7, 209, 211–12, 236, 238, 245
Ellerman Wilson Line, 158
English Electric, 95, 98, 102
Esbjerg, 158
Essex Ferry, 157
Euston Square Confederacy, 12, 17
Expressing Freight, 152

'Fair Deal' campaign, 150–1
Faringdon, Lord (Alexander Henderson), 13
Fay, Sir Sam, 13–14, 44, 65, 227, 235
Felixstowe, 14
Fenchurch Street, 25, 31, 59
Ferry services, 18–19, 50, 59, 156–60, 182, 188, 191
Fiennes, Gerald, 7
Fife, 18, 20, 26, 120, 123, 160–1, 191
Flushing, 158
Flying Fox, 153–4
Flying Scotsman: 66, 71, *74*, 84–5, 121, 135, 150, *190*, 194, *219*, 219–20
'Flying Scotsman': 9, 17, 74, 79–80, 83, 85, 99, *109*, 109–11, 114, 129, 133, 135, 138–9, 150, 154–5, 187, *219*
Fowler, 51
Forcett Railway, 12, 24
Fort William, 19, 100–1, 130
Forth & Clyde Junction Railway, 12, 24
Forth Bridge, 46–8, 63, 169, 178
Forward: The LNER Development Plan, 152

Garden City expresses, 104
Geddes, Eric .C. (later Sir, then Lord), 22, 65, 146
General Strike, 7, 9, 30, 42, 123, 134–5, 148, 164
George V, HM King, 13
Gibb, Geoffrey., 22
Gifford & Garvald Railway, 12, 24
Gimbert, Driver Benjamin, 198–9
Gladiateur, 153–4
Glasgow, 17–19, 24, 45, 48–50, 72–3, 77, 99–101, 110, 112–13, 117, 120, 132, 137, 155, 161, 166, 170, 186, 188, 206
Golden Fleece, 121
Golden Shuttle, 121
Gorton Works, Manchester, 13, 75, 233
Grand Parade, 166
Great Central Railway, GCR, 6, 7, 10–13, 17, 25–7, 30–3, 42–4, 45, 50, 52, 54, 60–1, 63–5, 68–73, 75–6, 81, 84, 90, 93, 98, 104, 112, 114, 116–18, 121, 123, 133–4, 145–6, 157–61, 169, 179, 188, 193, 196–8, 209, 213–18, 227–8, 233–5
Great Depression, 7, 64, 68, 78, 124, 159
Great Eastern Hotel, 40–1
Great Eastern Railway, 12, 14–15, 17, 25, 29, 31, 38–40, 54, 59, 63–9, 71–2, 77–8, 80, 101, 104, 109, 111, 113, 123, 134, 138, 157, 169–70, 178–9, 196, 229, 235–8
Great North of England Railway, 12
Great North of Scotland Railway, 12, 15–17, 46, 72–3, 75, 123, 156, 169, 209, 229, 238–9
Great Northern, 88, 220
Great Northern Railway, GNR, 9–17, 21, 24–32, 34–6, 38, 42–3, 46, 51, 54, 61, 63–72, 75–6, 78–80, 87–8, 90, 95, 104, 110, 114, 117–18, 121, 123, 126–7, 140–1, 145, 156–7, 168–9, 174–5, 178–9, 196, 209, 213–20, 229, 239–41
Great War/World War I, 7, 9, 11, 13, 132
Great Western Railway, GWR, 11, 13, 20, 32–3, 44, 63, 69, 78, 87, 99, 116, 128, 140, 143, 163, 180, 198, 247
Green Arrow, 84,129, 200, *224*;

Gresley, Sir Nigel, 7, 9, 17, 37, 42, 63–4, *66*, 66–7, 69–72, 74, 76–80, 83–4, 86–9, 92, 95, 98–9, 101–2, *109*, 133, 139–41, 150, 193, 216, 218–19, 221–2, 224–5, 229, 234, 239–41
Grimsby, 12–13, 17, 24, 42, 55, 90, 118, 158–61, 204;
Grouping, 9, 11–12, 19, 22–6, 29–33, 38, 42, 44, 46, 50–1, 54, 59–60, 63–77, 80, 95–6, 99, 105, 111, 114, 116–17, 119, 123–4, 130, 132, 136, 139, 143–5, 147–8, 157, 159–62, 164, 168–70, 174–5, 178, 180–1, 193, 206–7, 209, 219–20, 228, 232–3, 235–40, 243–9

Halifax, 17, 122
'Harrogate Pullman', *111*, 111–12
Harwich, 14–15, 33, 103, 157–60, *158*, *159*, 183, 188, 198, 203
Hawick, 18, 48
Haymarket (Edinburgh), 19, *45*, 47, 48
Hertford North, 96
Hexham, 18, 94
High pressure experiment, see 'Hush-hush'
'Highlandman', see 'Aberdonian'
Holden, James, 15, 21, 81, 229, 235–8
Holiday Handbook, 151
Hook of Holland, 15, 33, 101–3, 138, 157–8, 160, 182–3, 188, 202
Horncastle Railway, 12, 25
Hudson, George, 18, 24, 52, 59
Hudswell, 51
Hull, 18, 21–2, 45–6, 50–1, 59, 72, 75, 115–16, 122, 130, 132, 136, 142–3, 147–8, 158–61, 164–5, 172, 196, 246
Hull & Barnsley Railway, 12, 18, 21–2, 50, 72, 143, 160, 242
Hull & Netherlands Steamship Company, H&NSC, 158–9
Hull Paragon, 164–5
Humber Commercial Railway & Dock, 12, 25
Hunslet, 51
'Hush-hush' locomotive, 80, *109*, 218

Immingham, 13, 25, 77, 123, 136, 160
Ingemells, Driver John, 204
Inverness, 15, 99–101, 112
Inverurie, 15–16, 75, 239
Ivatt, Henry, 17, 35, 66, 69–70, 72, 77, 92, 117, 229, 239–41

Jackson, Passed Cleaner Geoffrey, 204
'Jazz Trains', 15, 42, 141
'Jellicoe Specials', 20

Karrier Cob, 128, 162
Keith, 15
Kilsyth & Bonnybridge Railway, 12, 25
King's Cross, 9, 17, *33*, 34–8, *37*, 45, 60–1, 64, 71–2, 77–80, 83–5, 92, 95, 99–101, 104–6, *109*, 109–15, 117–22, 129–30, 133, 135–6, 138–9, 141, *143*, 143–4, 150, 153–5, 166–8, 170, 180, 183, 187–90, 194, 196–9, 204, *240*
King's Lynn, 14–15, 27
Kingston-upon-Hull, see Hull
Kitson, 51, 93, 233–4, 242
Kitson-Still, *93*, 93, 148
Kittybrewster, 16

La Societe Belgo-Anglaise des Ferryboats, 157
Lanarkshire Group, 163
Lancashire & Yorkshire Railway, 12, 17, 27, 30, 46, 51–2, 66, 71
Lancashire Derbyshire & East Coast Railway, 13, 26, 233, 242
Lauder Light Railway, 12, 25
Leeds, 17, 20, 23–3, 38, 50–1, 59, 61, 92, 106, 111–13, 117, 121–2, 129, 132, 138–9, 166, 194
Leicester, 13, 28, 43–4, 112, 116, 118–19, 133
Lincoln, 14, 26, 114
Lincolnshire Road Car Company, 163
Linlithgow, *49*
Liverpool, 12, 17, 31, 113–14, 119, 129
Liverpool & Manchester Railway, 27, 51
Liverpool Street, 9, 14, 33, 38–42, 45, 55–6, 59, 61, 76–7, 80, 84, 86, 95–6, 101–6, 109, 111, 132, 135, 138, 140–1, 144, 170, 176, 180, *185*, 188, 195–6, 198, 203, 206
Livery, 13, 21, 96, 120, 149
LNER Silver Medal, 198–200, *199*, 204
LNER Magazine, 62, 80, 91, 94, 131, 136, 147–50, 155, 158, 180, 184, 188–9, 199, 202–5
Locomotives of the LNER, 151–2
London & Blackwall Railway, 12, 25, 31, 55, 172
London & North Western Railway, 12, 17, 20, 26–7, 31, 43, 51–2, 66, 71, 198, 234
London & York Railway, 17
London Tilbury & Southend Railway, 11, 25, 31–2, 163
London Transport/London Passenger Transport Board, 32, 44, 98, 141, 179, 180, 232
London: 4, 7–9, 11 *et al.*
London Midland & Scottish Railway, LMS, 11–12, 29–30, 52, 55, 60–5, 67, 69, 71, 74, 80, 83, 92, 94–6, 100, 112, 119, 123, 129, 131, 140, 147, 151, 155, 159–60, 163, 165, 169, 179–80, 184, 186–7, 192–4, 196, 198, 216
London Tilbury & Southend Railway, 11, 25, 31–2, 163
Lowestoft, 14, 29, 130, 156
Lyn & Fakenham Railway, 54

Mails, 17, *34*, 82, 99, 102, 158
Malines, 157
Mallard, 7, 66, 86, *153*, 155, *182*, 206, 221
Manchester, 13, 17, 27, 31, 33, 35, 43, 45, 51–2, 54–5, 97–8, 113–14, 119, 122, 129, 132, 136, 165, 172, 186–7, 197–8
Manchester Central, 31, 114, 122
Manchester, Sheffield & Lincolnshire Railway, 12, 17, 27, 31, 42, 50, 54, 158

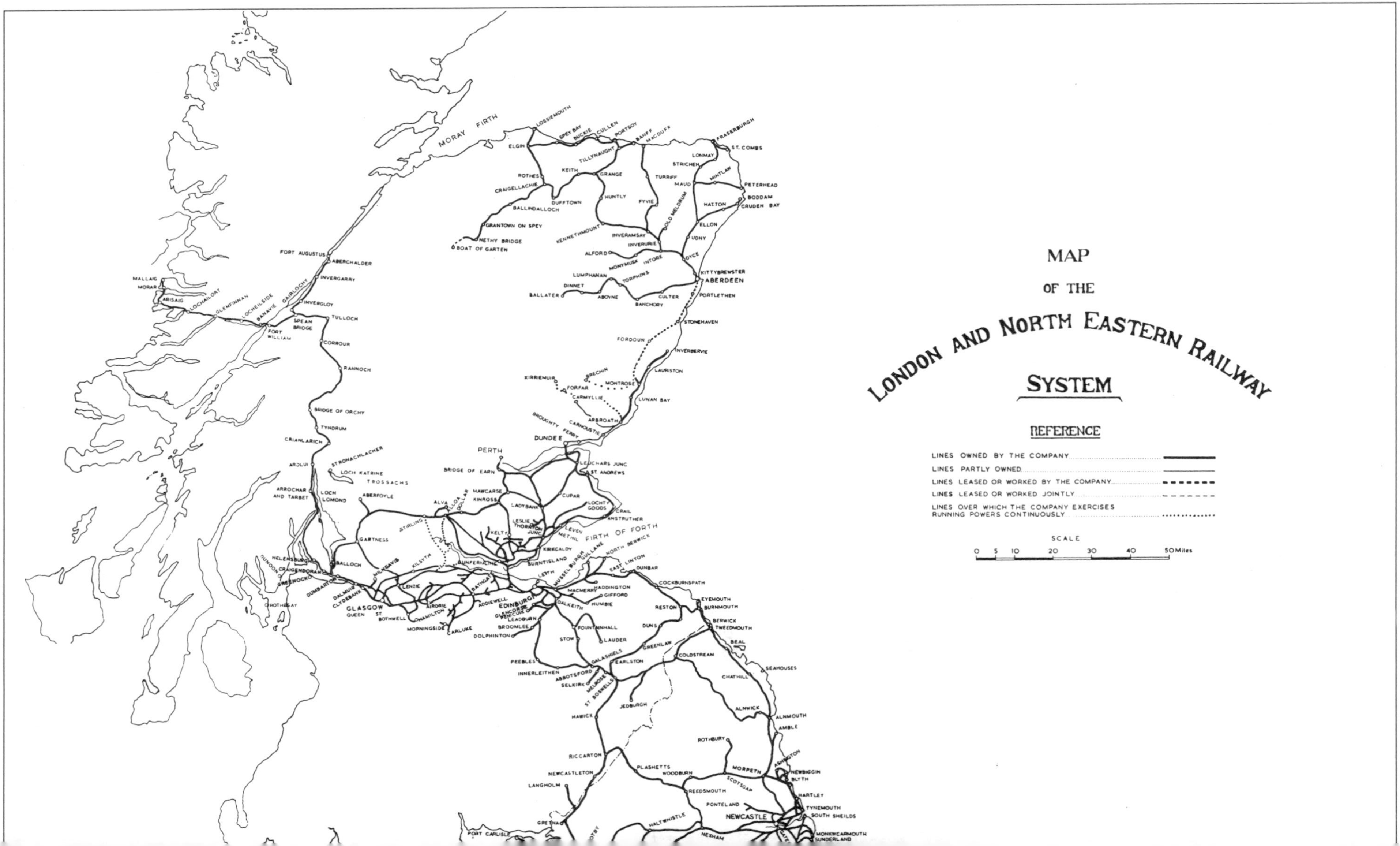
MAP
OF THE
LONDON AND NORTH EASTERN RAILWAY
SYSTEM
REFERENCE
LINES OWNED BY THE COMPANY
LINES PARTLY OWNED
LINES LEASED OR WORKED BY THE COMPANY
LINES LEASED OR WORKED JOINTLY
LINES OVER WHICH THE COMPANY EXERCISES RUNNING POWERS CONTINUOUSLY
SCALE
0 5 10 20 30 40 50 Miles
MORAY FIRTH
FIRTH OF FORTH
LOSSIEMOUTH
SPEY BAY
BUCKIE
CULLEN
PORTSOY
BANFF
MACDUFF
FRASERBURGH
ST. COMBS
ELGIN
TILLYNAUGHT
LONMAY
STRICHEN
MINTLAW
PETERHEAD
BODDAM
CRUDEN BAY
HATTON
ROTHES
KEITH
GRANGE
TURRIFF
MAUD
CRAIGELLACHIE
DUFFTOWN
HUNTLY
FYVIE
OLD MELDRUM
BALLINDALLOCH
ELLON
UDNY
GRANTOWN ON SPEY
KENNETHMONT
INVERAMSAY
INVERURIE
NETHY BRIDGE
BOAT OF GARTEN
ALFORD
MONYMUSK
INTORE
DYCE
KITTYBREWSTER
ABERDEEN
LUMPHANAN
TORPHINS
PORTLETHEN
DINNET
BALLATER
ABOYNE
CULTER
BANCHORY
STONEHAVEN
FORDOUN
INVERBERVIE
LAURISTON
KIRRIEMUIR
BRECHIN
MONTROSE
FORFAR
CARMYLLIE
LUNAN BAY
ARBROATH
BROUGHTY FERRY
CARNOUSTIE
DUNDEE
PERTH
LEUCHARS JUNC
ST ANDREWS
BRIDGE OF EARN
CUPAR
MAWCARSE
KINROSS
LADYBANK
LOCHTY GOODS
CRAIL
ANSTRUTHER
ALVA
ALLOA
DOLLAR
LESLIE
THORNTON JUNC
LEVEN
METHIL
KELTY
STIRLING
GARTNESS
KILSYTH
DUNFERMLINE
KIRKCALDY
BURNTISLAND
NORTH BERWICK
GULLANE
EAST LINTON
DUNBAR
LEITH
MUSSELBURGH
COCKBURNSPATH
MACMERRY
HADDINGTON
GIFFORD
HUMBIE
DALKEITH
EYEMOUTH
BURNMOUTH
RESTON
BERWICK
TWEEDMOUTH
EDINBURGH
ADDIEWELL
BATHGATE
GLENCORSE
PENICUIK
LEADBURN
BROOMLEE
DOLPHINTON
FOUNTAINHALL
LAUDER
DUNS
STOW
GREENLAW
COLDSTREAM
BEAL
PEEBLES
GALASHIELS
EARLSTON
INNERLEITHEN
ABBOTSFORD
SELKIRK
MELROSE
ST BOSWELLS
SEAHOUSES
CHATHILL
JEDBURGH
ALNWICK
ALNMOUTH
AMBLE
HAWICK
ROTHBURY
RICCARTON
PLASHETTS
WOODBURN
MORPETH
ASHINGTON
NEWBIGGIN
BLYTH
NEWCASTLETON
REEDSMOUTH
SCOTSGAP
HARTLEY
LANGHOLM
PONTELAND
TYNEMOUTH
SOUTH SHEILDS
NEWCASTLE
GRETNA
HALTWHISTLE
PORT CARLISLE
HEXHAM
MONKWEARMOUTH
SUNDERLAND
FORT AUGUSTUS
ABERCHALDER
INVERGARRY
MALLAIG
MORAR
ARISAIG
LOCHAILORT
GLENFINNAN
LOCHEILSIDE
BANAVIE
GAIRLOCHY
INVERGLOY
TULLOCH
SPEAN BRIDGE
FORT WILLIAM
CORROUR
RANNOCH
BRIDGE OF ORCHY
TYNDRUM
CRIANLARICH
STRONACHLACHER
ARDLUI
LOCH KATRINE
TROSSACHS
ARROCHAR AND TARBET
LOCH LOMOND
ABERFOYLE
HELENSBURGH
CRAIGENDORAN
DUNOON
GREENOCK
BALLOCH
MILNGAVIE
LENZIE
ROTHESAY
DUMBARTON
DALMUIR
CLYDEBANK
GLASGOW
QUEEN ST.
AIRDRIE
BOTHWELL
HAMILTON
MORNINGSIDE
CARLUKE

Reid, W.P., 70, 230–1, 243
Road haulage / collection & delivery, 62, 82, 124, 128–30, 148, 150, 162–3, 171, 182, 199
Robinson, John G., 13, 69–70, 72–3, 77, 88, 118, 227–8, 233–5, 247
Romford, 31, 40, 56
Rotterdam, 132, 157–8
Royal Train, 104
Rugby, 13, 24, 67, 114, 116

St George, 157
St Margaret's (Edinburgh), 19, 135
Scammell Mechanical Horse, 128, 162
Scandinavia, 158
'Scarborough Flyer', 117–18
Seaforth & Sefton Junction Railway, 12, 27
Seagull, 82
Sentinel, 8, 31, *77*, 77–8, 81, 94, 143, *144*, 212
Sheffield, 12, 17, 23, 27, 30–1, 33, 42–3, 45–6, 50, 54–5, 98, 112, 114, 116, 118–19, 121–2, 136, 158, 161, 188, 196, 198, 204
'Sheffield Pullman', 118
'Sheffield Special', 118–19
Shipping, 13, 15, 33, 51, 62, 101–3, 113, 132, 156–62, 182–2, 202
'Silver Jubilee, 9, 66, 85, 105–6, 115–16, 119–22, *120*, *154*, 155, 221
Silver Fox, 120, 194
Silver King, 120
Silver Link, 85, 120
Sir Nigel Gresley, 66
Sir Ralph Wedgwood, 221
Sleeping cars, 66, 82, 100–1, 112, 115, 138, 140, *141*, 187, 192
Slip coaches, 25, 118, 119, 134
Soham, 198–9
South Queensferry, 159
South Yorkshire Joint Line Committee, 30
Southend, 11, 14, 25, 31–2, 41, 55–6, 59, 74, 76, 91, 96, 141, 176, 206
Southern Railway, 8, 11, 23, 61, 71, 87, 91–2, 96, 124, 128, 138, 156–7, 170, 174, 177, 179–80, 182, 189, 193, 198, 206, 239
Spalding, 14
Speed record, 155
Spion Kop, 85
Spitalfields, 15;
Spitfire Fund, *190*, 194
Springbok, 87
Stamford & Essendine Railway, 12, 27
Stanier, Sir William, 83, 87, 193, 216
Stanley, PC Arthur, 204
Steam-diesel, see Kitson-Still
Stirling, Patrick, 17, 77, 150, 239
Stockton & Darlington Railway, SDR, 20–1, 23, 77, 90, 145–6, 150, 155, 246
Stratford (East London), 14–15, 31, 59, 67, 75, 78, 102, 132, 135, 141, *176*, 185, 200, 204
Streamlining, *52*, 84–6, 94, *154*, 218
Suffolk Ferry, 157
Sulzer, 95;
'Super Claud', 71
Swindon, 13, 116, 133

Taylor, Junior Porter Morven, 200
Tennant, Henry, 21–2
The White Knight, 177
Thompson, Edward, 67, 69, 84, 87–9, 215, 218, 220–5, 227, 233–34, 241
Thornton, Henry (later Sir), 15, 65, 67, 102, 111, 138
Train ferries, 157–159, 183
Train Ferry No.1, 157, *158*, 183
Train Ferry No.2, 157, 183
Train Ferry No.3, 157, 183
Trent Motor Traction, 163

United Automobile Services, 163

Victor Wild, 79
Vienna, 158, *160*, 183, *188*

War Office, 14, 31, 59, 66, 157–8, 179, 193, 210, 216, 234–4
Walker, Sir Herbert A., 23, 92, 206
Wath Yard, 13, 77, 98
Watkin, Sir Edward, 13, 42–3
Waverley, 19, 25, *47*, 47–9, 70, 79, 105, 109–13, 133, 137, 154–5, 166, 170, 188
Waverley, P.S., 159
Wedgwood, Sir Ralph, 9, 22, 62–3, 65, 67–8, 92, 148–50, 162, 185, 200
Welwyn Garden City, 96, 104, 135–6, 165–6, 168, 170, 175
'West Riding Limited', 9, 105, 121–2
West Riding Railway Committee, 12, 27
West Yorkshire Road Car Co, 163
Whitelaw, William, 9, *68*, 74, 154, 161, 220–1
Wilson's & North Eastern Railway Shipping Company, W&NERSC, 158–9
Wirral Railway, 31
Woodhead Tunnel, 12, 98
World War I, see Great War
World War II, 38; 42–4, 60, 65–7, 95, 98, 100–2, 106, 110, 112–14, 117–18, 121–2, 124, 128–9, 131–2, 138, 141, 158, 166, 169, 175–201
Worsdell, Thomas, 22, 70, 236, 238, 246–248

Yarmouth, 14–15, 27, 29, 39, 54, 103, 130, 212
York, 9, 17, 21, 23–5, 31, 51–2, 56, 59, 62, 64, 67, 71, 75, 90, 93, 95, 97, 100–1, 106, 110, 112–19, 122, 130, 133, 135, 142–5, 170, 188, 192–3, 196, 199–200, *201*, *202*, 204, 206, 209, 221, 248
York & North Midland Railway, 18, 20, 24, 50, 59
'Yorkshire Pullman', 121–3
Yorkshire Traction, 163
Yorkshire Woollen District, 163

Zeeland Shipping Company, 158

Manchester Ship Canal, 51–2
Manchester South Junction & Altrincham Railway, 27, 96, 169
Manning Wardle, 51, 223
Mansfield Railway, 12, 26
March, 14
Marylebone, 11, 13, 33, 42–45, 64, 71, 77, 84, 112, 118, 136, 150, 165, 169, 187, 196–8
'Master Cutler', 112
Mechanical stoker, see 'Nu-Way'
Metropolitan Railway/Line, 13, 32–3, 35–40, 42–4, 92, 95, 156, 176, 197, 214, 216, 218, 229, 232, 242
Mid-Suffolk Light Railway, 12, 26, 242:
Midland & Great Northern Joint Railway, 15, 17, 27–9, *28*, 54, 169, 232, 243
Midland Bus Services, 163
Midland Red, 163
Mikados, 76, *100*, 131, 221
Miller, John, 66–7
Midland Railway, 8, 12, 15, 17–18, 24, 30–2, 35, 42, 48–51, 54, 59, 63, 113, 169
Miners' Strike 1926, 7, 9, 30, 42, 50, 64, 68, 78, 123, 160

Nationalisation, 11, 23, 25–6, 31, 41–2, 54–5, 59, 63, 67–8, 72, 78, 88–9, 93, 95–6, 98, 101, 112–13, 117–18, 120–2, 124, 128, 141, 144, 149, 152, 158, 176, 180, 201–6, 211–12, 216, 221–3, 225–7, 233, 239, 245–6
Netherlands, 15, 98, 101–2, 157, 186, 195
New Works Programme, 85, 96, 98, 149–50
Newburgh & North Fife Railway, 12, 26
Newcastle Central, *51*, 51–2, 119, 153, 155, 169–70, 175
Newcastle-upon-Tyne, 18, 23–4, 45, *51*, 52–4, 71, 84–5, 90, 94–5, 105–6, 110–17, 119–23, 130, 132, 135, 138, 142, 147, 153, 155, 159–60, 166, 169–70, 175, 191, 206, 245
Newmarket, 14, 114
'Night Ferry', 8
'Night Scotsman', 112–13
Nightall, Fireman James, 198–9
Norfolk Railway, 14, 54–5
Norna, 51
'Norseman', 113
North Queensferry, 47, 159
North Western Road Car Co., 163
Northern General Motor Services, 163
Norwich & Brandon Railway, 54
North Berwick, 18, 48
North British Railway, NBR, 9, 11–12, 16–21, 24–5, 47–9, 52, 63, 65, 68–70, 72–6, 78, 81, 88, 90, 93, 123, 156, 159–61, 168–9, 170, 172, 178–9, 193, 209, 211–14, 216–18, 230–1, 240, 243–5
'North Briton', 113
'North Country Continental', 113–14
'North Eastern', 114–15
North Eastern Railway, NER, 12, 16–18, 20–5, 30, 50–1, 59–63, 65, 67, 69–70, 78, 90, 113, 146–8, 158, 168, 178–9, 245–9
North Lindsey Light Railway, 12, 26
'Northern Belle', 115
Norwich, 15, 27, 45, 52, 54, 106, 109, 114, 188
Nottingham, 13, 17, 28, 33, 42–3, 72, 77, 92, 112, 114, 116, 118–19, 121–2, 129, 132–3, 195
Nottingham & Grantham Railway, 12, 26
Nottingham & Grantham Railway, 12, 26
Nottingham Joint Station Committee, 12, 26
Nottingham Suburban Railway, 12, 26
Nottingham Victoria, *195*;
'Nu-Way', 87

Oakley, Henry, 17
Oil-firing of locomotives, 15, 77–8, 202, 206
Ortona, 163
Oslo, 113
Pacifics, 32, 37, *45*, *66*, 69–71, *73*, *74*, 75–80, 82–4, 86, 88–9, 100–1, 105, 113, 115–19, 121–2, 147, 153, 166, 174, *182*, 200, *219*, 220–1, 224, 232
Packet steamers, see shipping
Paris, 8
Parkeston Quay, 15, 101–3, 105, 109, 111, 113–14, 132, 157, 202
Papyrus, 84
Partick Central, *197*
Peebles, 48
Pennines, 7, 12, 50–1, 54, 62, 98, 123
Pennsylvania Railroad, 67, 71, 76
Peppercorn, Arthur, 87, 89, 98, 207, 215, 218, 222, 225
Perth, 100, 110, 112
Peterborough, 17, 27, 77, 101, 110–11, 115, 119, 129, 115, 158, *170*, 175, 187, 204
Phenomena, 81
Pickfords, 163
'Ports-to-Ports Express', 115–16
Prague, 158, 183
Princess Daffodil, 183
Princes Iris, 183
Private owner wagons, 125–8, 130, 196
Pullman, 32, *75*, 102–3, 105, 109, 111–12, 117–18, 121–2, 138–9, 187
Punctuality, 15, 18, 136, 148

'Queen of Scots', 117
Queen Street, Glasgow, 49–50, 110, 112, 117, 137, 166, 170, 188
Quicksilver, 85, *120*, 120

'Rail Air Plan', 201
Railcars, 13, 31, *81*, *93*, 93–4, 143
Railway Executive Committee, 68, 152, 178–9, 185, 187, 189, 191
Railway Gazette, 155;
Railway Passenger Duty, 96, 169
Railways Act 1921, 11, 128, 181
Raven, Vincent (later Sir), 20, 22–3, 45, 64, 70–1, 75–6, 90, 95, 206, 209, 220, 247–9